Constitutional Crises and Regionalism

ELGAR MONOGRAPHS IN CONSTITUTIONAL AND ADMINISTRATIVE LAW

**Series Editors:** Rosalind Dixon, *University of New South Wales, Australia,* Susan Rose-Ackerman, *Yale University* and Mark Tushnet, *Harvard University, USA*

Constitutions are a country's most important legal document, laying the foundation not just for politics, but for all other areas of law. They allocate power among different levels and branches of government, record and promote a society's shared values and protect the rights of citizens. Countries around the world are adopting written constitutions, though what defines a constitution is evolving to include a variety of sources beyond canonical texts, such as political conventions, statutes, judicial decisions and administrative law norms.

This cosmopolitan monograph series provides a forum for the best and most original scholarship in constitutional and administrative law, with each book offering an international, comparative or multi-jurisdictional approach to this complex and fascinating field of research.

For a full list of Edward Elgar published titles, including the titles in this series, visit our website at www.e-elgar.com.

# Constitutional Crises and Regionalism

Vito Breda

*Senior Lecturer in Law, School of Law and Justice, University of Southern Queensland, Australia*

ELGAR MONOGRAPHS IN CONSTITUTIONAL AND ADMINISTRATIVE LAW

Cheltenham, UK • Northampton, MA, USA

© Vito Breda 2023

All rights reserved. No part of this publication may be reproduced, stored in a retrieval system or transmitted in any form or by any means, electronic, mechanical or photocopying, recording, or otherwise without the prior permission of the publisher.

Published by
Edward Elgar Publishing Limited
The Lypiatts
15 Lansdown Road
Cheltenham
Glos GL50 2JA
UK

Edward Elgar Publishing, Inc.
William Pratt House
9 Dewey Court
Northampton
Massachusetts 01060
USA

A catalogue record for this book
is available from the British Library

Library of Congress Control Number: 2023939694

This book is available electronically in the **Elgar**online
Law subject collection
http://dx.doi.org/10.4337/9781839107108

Printed on elemental chlorine free (ECF)
recycled paper containing 30% Post-Consumer Waste

ISBN 978 1 83910 709 2 (cased)
ISBN 978 1 83910 710 8 (eBook)

Printed and bound in the USA

# Contents

| | | |
|---|---|---|
| *Acknowledgements* | | vi |
| Introduction to *Constitutional Crises and Regionalism* | | 1 |
| 1 | The UK and Northern Ireland: sectarianism and Brexit | 14 |
| 2 | Spain: Spanish legitimacy after the end of political violence in the Basque Country | 45 |
| 3 | Italy and Sicily: Mafia territorial sovereignty | 66 |
| 4 | North America: Quebec and Alaska | 88 |
| 5 | China and Hong Kong: an a-constitutional crisis | 115 |
| 6 | France: the end of New Caledonia's *sui generis* status | 147 |
| 7 | Australia and the Northern Territory: an unfortunate intervention | 171 |
| 8 | Papua New Guinea and Bougainville: civil war and a new sovereign state | 196 |
| Conclusion to *Constitutional Crises and Regionalism* | | 220 |
| *References* | | 230 |
| *Index* | | 264 |

# Acknowledgements

This book would not have been possible without the generous sponsorship of many universities who have hosted me during the global pandemic. The University of Brescia, the University of Deusto and the University of New Caledonia have supported my research during multiple research trips. I am particularly grateful to the Australian National University College of Law, the University of Lucerne, the University of Johannesburg and the organisers of the World Congress in Constitutional Law, which allowed me to present an early draft of this book.

I owe a debt of gratitude to Professor Antony Gray and Professor Matteo Frau for their support and friendship. I must express my gratitude to the University of Southern Queensland Research Office for allocating me the time to write this book. This has been a long project, and I am deeply grateful to my publisher, Edward Elgar, and its wonderful staff for their help, kindness and, above all else, their patience.

Parts of Chapter 6 appeared in an article entitled 'New Caledonia: The Archipelago That Does Not Want to Be Freed' in the Journal de Droit Comparé du Pacifique (Vol XXIV, 2019). I am indebted to Chief Editor Professor Toni Angelo, Professor Jennifer Corrin and the Journal de Droit Comparé du Pacifique's anonymous referees for their invaluable feedback. The author and the publisher would like to thank the University of Victoria in Wellington for the permission to reprint extracts from the article. As per usual, all errors are my own.

Finally, I would like to thank you Kathleen Hanssen and Erin Wolf O'Rourke for patiently and diligently reading my work. Without their help, this book would never have been completed.

Vito Breda<br>
August 2023

# Introduction to *Constitutional Crises and Regionalism*

Despite four decades of what Anthony David Smith called an 'ethnic revival', the wider constitutional implications of regionalism have just started to be analysed as a global social phenomenon.[1] Regional crises, without robust deliberative institutions, regularly degenerate into violence.[2] They often do so even when there are deliberative institutions.[3] This is frequently the case because these institutions are perceived as unrepresentative or because there is a foreign military intervention.[4] The recent Russia–Ukraine War is the latest event in a well-documented history of European wars in which a state has exploited ethnic claims on a neighbouring country to expand its borders.[5] This book discusses a sample of regional legitimation crises from Europe, North America, Oceania and East Asia. A crisis of legitimacy is often derived from diverging perceptions between regional and central identity groups. This monograph discusses cases from Northern Ireland, the Basque Country, Sicily, Alaska, Quebec, Hong Kong, New Caledonia, the Northern Territory in Australia and Bougainville.

Cynics might argue that constitutional institutions cannot create social cohesion out of thin air in deeply divided societies such as Northern Ireland, let alone stop a foreign invasion by yet another narcissistic sociopath at the helm of a fiefdom. There is an element of truth in that. However, in this book, I argue that a well-engineered system of regional governance can induce perceptions of the repressiveness of both central and regional institutions by channelling

---

[1] Brian CH Fong and Atsuko Ichijo (eds), *The Routledge Handbook of Comparative Territorial Autonomies* (Taylor & Francis Group 2022).

[2] Donald Horowitz, 'Some Realism about Constitutional Engineering' in Andreas Wimmer (ed), *Facing Ethnic Conflicts: Toward a New Realism* (Rowman & Littlefield 2004).

[3] Ron Levy and Graeme Orr, *The Law of Deliberative Democracy* (Routledge 2016).

[4] Francis Fukuyama, *Political Order and Political Decay: From the Industrial Revolution to the Globalisation of Democracy* (Profile Books 2014).

[5] ibid 4. Oksana Mikheieva, 'Motivations of Pro-Russian and Pro-Ukrainian Combatants in the Context of the Russian Military Intervention in the Donbas' in David R Marples (ed), *The War in Ukraine's Donbas* (Central European University Press 2022) 67.

alliances based on shared values into laws. Sometimes, these values are simply misnamed pragmatic monetary benefits, but in many instances, peace and collaboration are linked to the management of shared beliefs.[6] In this book, I explain that in multinational highly divided societies, a constitutional system might maintain a political system in a cycle of legitimation crises.

Public lawyers tend to focus more on the lexical construction of the rules and on the socio-political elements that lead to those rules being perceived as legitimate by a multinational constituency.[7] This is the case for good reason. The tendency to be lexically bound to the strictly formal aspects of the constitution is perhaps stronger in continental Europe. Constitutional law is, for instance, taught as a textual manifestation of normative principles.[8] One of the side effects of this pedagogic practice is the dissemination of the idea that a constitutional text can be ethnically 'neutral'. This is contrafactual. There is

---

[6] Horowitz (n 2).

[7] The literature on the effects of ideology in constitutional law is enormous. This is the list of studies that informed this book: David Marrani, *Dynamics in the French Constitution: Decoding French Republican Ideas* (Routledge 2013); Martin Loughlin, 'Reflection on the Idea of Public Law' in Emilios Christodoulidis and Stephen Tierney (eds), *Public Law and Politics: The Scope and Limits of Constitutionalism* (Ashgate 2008); Hèctor López Bofill, 'Hubris, Constitutionalism, and "the Indissoluble Unity of the Spanish Nation": The Repression of Catalan Secessionist Referenda in Spanish Constitutional Law' (2019) 17 International Journal of Constitutional Law 943; Arianna Giovannini and Davide Vampa, 'Towards a New Era of Regionalism in Italy? A Comparative Perspective on Autonomy Referendums' (2019) Territory, Politics, Governance 1.

[8] The correlation between semantic and constitutional law is explored in multiple outlets. This is another list of reading material that has been referred to in this book: Mark Elliott and Robert Thomas, *Public Law* (4th edn, Oxford University Press 2020); Luis López Guerra and others, *Derecho Constitucional Vol. I El ordenamiento constitucional Derechos y deberes de los ciudadanos* (8th edn, Editorial Tirant lo Blanch 2010); Gary Jacobsohn and Miguel Schor (eds), *Comparative Constitutional Theory* (Edward Elgar Publishing 2018); Augusto Barbera and Carlo Fusaro, *Corso di diritto pubblico. Nuova ediz.* (11th edn, Il Mulino 2020); P Carrozza, A Di Giovine and GF Ferrari, *Diritto costituzionale comparato* (4th edn, Laterza 2009); Guido Corso and Vincenzo Lopilato, *Il diritto amministrativo dopo le riforme costituzionali. Parte generale* (Giuffrè Editore 2006); Peter W Hogg, *Constitutional Law of Canada* (Carswell 2009); Anthony F Lang and Antje Wiener (eds), *Handbook on Global Constitutionalism* (Edward Elgar Publishing 2017); Marrani (n 7); Cheryl Saunders and Adrienne Stone (eds), *The Oxford Handbook of the Australian Constitution* (Oxford University Press 2018); George Williams, Sean Brennan and Andrew Lynch, *Blackshield and Williams Australian Constitutional Law and Theory* (7th edn, Federation Press 2018); Tom Ginsburg and Rosalind Dixon (eds), *Comparative Constitutional Law* (Paperback edition, Edward Elgar Publishing 2012); Rosalind Dixon and Tom Ginsburg (eds), *Comparative Constitutional Law in Asia* (Edward Elgar Publishing 2014).

no such thing as a semiotically or sociologically neutered constitutional text.[9] The lack of recognition of the inherent limits of constitutionalism is exploited with *gusto* by regionalist ethnic movements.

In the past three decades, comparative constitutional lawyers have witnessed the emergence of regionalism as a global phenomenon.[10] There are multifarious reasons that might explain this ethnic revival.[11] Sociologists such as Bauman associate this new trend with the desire to substitute collapsing ideologies, like socialism and liberalism, with local meaning providers.[12] Independently from the farrago of motivations that have led to the current situation, regional identities are becoming a driving factor of constitutional development in multinational societies.[13] This book explains the institutional limits, the possibilities and a few of the hard lessons learned during these developments.

*Constitutional Crises and Regionalism* explains the legal framework in which regional institutions operate and then focuses on the elements that are likely to affect present and future development in these regions. The methodology adopted in this book, like the one that preceded it, *Constitutional Law and Regionalism*, is called 'future studies'.[14] The methodology has been pioneered by the Constitution Unit at University College London.[15] The approach to the study of constitutional law considers the legal and pragmatic implications of constitutional norms as drivers of change. By comparison to textual analyses

---

[9] The role of the context is discussed as an element of a linguistic analysis by multiple authors: Jaakko Husa, *Interdisciplinary Comparative Law: Rubbing Shoulders with the Neighbours or Standing Alone in a Crowd* (Edward Elgar Publishing 2022) Introduction; 3; Stephen Levinson, 'Recursion in Pragmatics' (2013) 89 Language 149; Stephen Levinson, *Pragmatics* (Cambridge University Press 1983); Sol Azuelos-Atias, 'Semantically Cued Contextual Implicatures in Legal Texts' (2010) 42 Journal of Pragmatics 728.

[10] Liah Greenfeld and Zeying Wu (eds), *Research Handbook on Nationalism* (Edward Elgar Publishing 2020); Fong and Ichijo (n 1).

[11] Anthony Smith, *The Ethnic Revival* (1st edn, Cambridge University Press 2010); Zygmunt Bauman, *In Search of Politics* (Polity Press 1999); Liah Greenfeld (ed), *Advanced Introduction to Nationalism* (Edward Elgar Publishing 2016); Andreas Pickel (ed), *Handbook of Economic Nationalism* (Edward Elgar Publishing 2022).

[12] Jordan B Peterson, *Maps of Meaning: The Architecture of Belief* (1st edn, Routledge 2002).

[13] Fong and Ichijo (n 1); Giovannini and Vampa (n 7); Michael Keating, *The New Regionalism in Western Europe: Territorial Restructuring and Political Change* (Paperback ed repr, Edward Elgar Publishing 2003); Joseph Weiler, 'A Nation of Nations?' (2019) 17 International Journal of Constitutional Law 1301.

[14] Robert Hazell, *Constitutional Futures: A History of the Next Ten Years* (Oxford University Press 1999).

[15] Robert Agranoff and Mark Glover, 'Introduction: Forecasting Constitutional Futures' in Robert Hazell (ed), *Constitutional Futures Revisited: Britain's Constitution to 2020* (Palgrave Macmillan 2008).

of a constitutional system of governance, which might produce a classification of a legal system,[16] the future studies methodology provides an overview of the elements that are dynamically changing a constitutional system.

The Constitution Unit was, as far as I know, the first to adopt the future studies methodology in a study of constitutional system. Future studies provides, in a nutshell, a contextual methodology to study social events. As is often the case, innovation emerges because of necessity rather than farsightedness.[17] Contextual analyses are essential for a comparative legal evaluation but are often silently dismissed by constitutional lawyers.[18] However, the Constitution Unit operates as a multidisciplinary research centre that monitors the development of the UK constitutional system and its members often provide advice to the UK Parliament. In the period between 1998 and 2009, the UK constitutional system underwent a radical transformation. The role of courts, individual rights and its regional system of governance were modernised.[19] The pace of change made the role of analytical constitutional studies almost obsolete. Members of Parliament, public administrators and the public all wanted to know how those reforms would change their daily activities.

As far as I know, Rober Hazell's *Constitutional Futures: The History of the Next Ten Years* was the first large-scope publication that adopted the future studies methodology.[20] It has since provided one of the most insightful overviews of the UK constitutional system.[21] The collection of essays evaluated the

---

[16] Stephen Tierney, 'Federalism and Constitutional Theory' in Gary Jacobsohn and Miguel Schor (eds), *Comparative Constitutional Theory* (Edward Elgar Publishing 2018); Alex Warleigh-Lack and Luk Van Langenhove, 'Rethinking EU Studies: The Contribution of Comparative Regionalism' (2010) 32 Journal of European Integration 541.

[17] Agranoff and Glover (n 15).

[18] Husa (n 9).

[19] The reforms invested the UK constituent system between 1998 and 2009 included several areas. A general review is in: Vernon Bogdanor, *The New British Constitution* (Illustrated edition, Hart Publishing 2009). The key statutes that composed the complete overall of the UK system of territorial governance included: Scotland Act 1998 c 46; Government of Wales Act 1998 Ch 38 (Ch 38); The UK Government and The Government of Ireland, 'The Belfast Agreement: An Agreement Reached at the Multi-Party Talks on Northern Ireland 1998. Cm 3883 (the Belfast Agreement)' (20 May 1998); The Northern Ireland Act 1998 c 47. The reform of the judicial system is in: Constitutional Reform Act 2005 Ch 4; Human Rights Act 1998 c 42 1998.

[20] For instance: Robert Hazell, *Devolution and the Future of the Union* (The Constitution Unit 2015).

[21] Hazell, *Constitutional Futures* (n 14); ibid; Hazell, *Devolution and the Future of the Union* (n 20). For an anlaisys of the therotical structure of the UK Constitution system: Loughlin (n 7); Jens Meierhenrich and Martin Loughlin (eds), *The Cambridge Companion to the Rule of Law* (Cambridge University Press 2021); Bogdanor (n 19).

factors that might alter the UK constitutional system. It also includes a series of forecast scenarios which assess the combined effect of the UK reforms.[22]

The series of publications that followed *Constitutional Futures: The History of the Next Ten Years* proved that experts must have the ability to select the factors that will change the forthcoming developments in their area of study.[23] This might sound axiomatic. The idea of asking an expert for advice is often associated with the intention of knowing what might happen in the future.[24] Economic analyses of law, legal transplants and new technology regulations all require legal experts to evaluate future scenarios.[25] For instance, leading works on comparative methods, like Jaakko Husa's *Interdisciplinary Comparative Law*, make clear that legal transplants require an evaluation of future legal scenarios.[26] He asserted that making reasoned forecasts based on path dependency are the essential elements for the planning of legal transplants.[27] Similar claims are found in multiple studies.[28]

*Constitutional Crises and Regionalism* too adopts a contextual methodology. This book makes use of the assumption that modern liberal constitutions are dependent on the existence of a healthy partnership between institutions and political movements.[29] A political arena which is perceived as legitimate

---

[22] Hazell, *Constitutional Futures* (n 14); Robert Hazell, *Constitutional Futures Revisited: Britain's Constitution to 2020* (Palgrave Macmillan 2008); Rober Hazell and others, 'Answering the English Question' in Robert Hazell (ed), *Constitutional Futures Revisited: Britain's Constitution to 2020* (Palgrave Macmillan 2008).

[23] This selection of major research studies that forecast the effects of legal reforms: Hazell, *Constitutional Futures* (n 14); Hazell, *Constitutional Futures Revisited: Britain's Constitution to 2020* (n 22); Hazell, *Devolution and the Future of the Union* (n 20); Meg Russell and Daniel Gover, *Legislation at Westminster: Parliamentary Actors and Influence in the Making of British Law* (Oxford University Press 2017).

[24] Magali Sarfatti Larson, *The Rise of Professionalism: Monopolies of Competence and Sheltered Markets* (Routledge 2017). E Gary and Heiko A von der Gracht, 'The Future of Foresight Professionals: Results from a Global Delphi Study' (2015) 71 Futures 132, 139; Magali Sarfatti Larson, *The Rise of Professionalism: Monopolies of Competence and Sheltered Markets* (Routledge 2017).

[25] Maurice Adams, Jaakko Husa and Marieke Oderkerk (eds), *Comparative Law Methodology* (Edward Elgar Publishing 2017).

[26] Husa (n 9) 13–42, 114–48; James Mahoney, 'Path Dependence in Historical Sociology' (2000) 29 Theory and Society 535.

[27] Mahoney (n 26); William H Sewell, 'Historical Events as Transformations of Structures: Inventing Revolution at the Bastille' (1996) 25 Theory and Society 841.

[28] Mathias Siems, *Comparative Law* (Cambridge University Press 2022) ch 10; Mathias Siems, 'Malicious Legal Transplants' (2018) 38 Legal Studies 103; Vito Breda (ed), *Legal Transplants in East Asia and Oceania* (Cambridge University Press 2019).

[29] Michel Rosenfeld, *The Identity of the Constitutional Subject* (Routledge 2010); Bogdanor (n 19).

is dependent on balancing constitutional rules, recognition and representation.[30] None of these three elements are static.[31]

This book shows that in Northern Ireland, the Basque Country, Sicily, Alaska, Quebec, Hong Kong, New Caledonia, the Northern Territory in Australia and Bougainville, institutions have lost most of their perceived legitimacy.[32] The lack of credibility of these public institutions might be the result of recent events, such as in the case of Hong Kong,[33] or it might be due to a design fault in the constitution, as in the case of the Basque Country.[34] Independently from its starting point, large sections of the population in these regions perceive regional and central institutions as not representing their values.

This is worrying for constitutional theorists, who denounce the pernicious nature of nationalism, and for central governments, concerned with the pragmatic implications of ensuring that all citizens have access to the same rights and prerogatives.[35] These concerns are particularly strong in the regions considered in this book. In these regions, sub-state nationalist political parties and criminal organisations, such as the paramilitary organisations in Northern Ireland, derived much of their popularity by laying claim to inherent values, such as a shared language, ancestry and faith.[36] Individuals might be indoc-

---

[30] Jay E Gary and Heiko A von der Gracht, 'The Future of Foresight Professionals: Results from a Global Delphi Study' (2015) 71 Futures 132, 144.

[31] López Bofill (n 7).

[32] ibid; Nicholas Pengelley, 'The Hindmarsh Island Bridge Act: Must Laws Based on the Race Power be for the "Benefit" of Aborigines and Torres Strait Islanders?' (1998) 20 Sydney Law Review 144; Megan Davis, 'A Culture of Disrespect: Indigenous Peoples and Australian Public Institutions' (2006) 8 UTS Law Review 135.

[33] Samson Yuen and Sanho Chung, 'Explaining Localism in Post-Handover Hong Kong: An Eventful Approach' (2018) 2018 China Perspectives 19.

[34] Víctor Aparicio Rodríguez, 'The Basque Country', in *The Routledge Handbook of Comparative Territorial Autonomies* (Routledge 2022).

[35] Vernon Bogdanor, *Devolution in the United Kingdom* (Updated and reissued, Oxford University Press 2001); Jessica Arnett, *Between Empires and Frontiers: Alaska Native Sovereignty and U.S. Settler Imperialism* (ProQuest Dissertations Publishing 2018); Jon Altman and Susie Russell, 'Too Much "Dreaming": Evaluations of the Northern Territory National Emergency Response Intervention 2007–2012' (2012) Evidence Base: A Journal of Evidence Reviews in Key Policy Areas 1; Daron Acemoglu, Giuseppe De Feo and Giacomo Davide De Luca, 'Weak States: Causes and Consequences of the Sicilian Mafia' (2020) 87 The Review of Economic Studies 537.

[36] Anthony D Smith, 'The Origins of Nations' in John Hutchinson and Anthony D Smith (eds), *Nationalism* (Oxford University Press 1994); Jürgen Habermas, 'The European Nation State. Its Achievements and Its Limitations. On the Past and Future of Sovereignty and Citizenship' (1996) 9 Ratio Juris 125; Fukuyama (n 4).

trinated (or prevented from accessing education) and that has an effect on the stability of the legal system.[37]

This is not to say that regionalism is a negative element of modern democracy. Ancient democracy fostered homogenisation; modern democracy is instead fuelled by diversity.[38] Regional and national identities contribute to political debates and often create a sense of loyalty to their institutions.[39] It is this sense of loyalty to ideas such as 'nation, land, and faith', that helps to reduce internal conflicts over policies and values.[40] However, there are instances where these values diverge dramatically at the regional level.

Over the past century, whilst the international community has developed a diplomatic system and institutions aimed at reducing conflicts between national identities, most constitutional systems invested limited time and effort into the prevention and reduction of ethnic-based conflicts.[41] Horowitz, in his analysis of multi-ethnic constitutional systems, noted that elites often adopt a system of governance that ignores ethnic divisions: '[m]ost divided societies have crafted no institutions at all to attend their ethnic problems ... In fact some have crafted counterproductive provisions'.[42] One of the examples discussed in this book is the race clause of the Australian Constitution which gives the prerogative to the Federal Government to pass discriminatory statutes against Aboriginal people.[43] Article Two of the Spanish Constitution, which gives a normative priority to the Spanish nation over other nationalities, is another example of what Horowitz means when he refers to counterproductive provisions.[44]

In *Constitutional Law and Regionalism*, I argued that in the United Kingdom, Spain, Italy, the United States, Canada, Australia and New Zealand, regional identities are axiological elements of a multinational society. One of the consequences of multinationalism is that both central and regional insti-

---

[37] Allison McCulloch, 'Consociational Executives: Power-Sharing Governments Between Inclusion and Functionality' in Ferran Requejo and Marc Sanjaume-Calvet (eds), *Defensive Federalism* (Routledge 2022); Richard Lynn, 'In Italy, North–South Differences in IQ Predict Differences in Income, Education, Infant Mortality, Stature, and Literacy' (2010) 38 Intelligence 93.

[38] James Tully, 'The Unfreedom of the Moderns in Comparison to Their Ideals of Constitutional Democracy' (2002) 65 Modern Law Review 204; Jürgen Habermas, 'Democracy in Europe: Why the Development of the EU into a Transnational Democracy Is Necessary and How It Is Possible' (2015) 21 European Law Journal 546.

[39] Marrani (n 7).

[40] Horowitz (n 2).

[41] ibid.

[42] ibid 252.

[43] Commonwealth of Australia Constitution Act 1900 c.12 s 51 xxvi; Davis (n 32).

[44] Spanish Constitution 1978.

tutions are locked in a permanent negotiation process in which both parties seek to obtain recognition of their identities and, often, a fair distribution of resources. *Constitutional Crises and Regionalism* discusses instead whether there are constitutional limits to such negotiations.[45] Can constitutional principles be stretched by ethnocentric demands by either central or regional institutions to a point where the principle of equality is disembowelled of its intended meaning? This book explains that each constitution bears a distinctive and often self-referential system of assumptions that seeks to balance multiple and diverging drivers of change.

For instance, the traumatic memories of colonisation are still affecting perceptions of the legitimacy of policies for Territorian Aboriginal Peoples in Australia, Natives in Alaska, New Caledonian Kanaks and the Catholics in Northern Ireland.[46] The lingering suspicion of ethnic bias found in these examples reduces the ability of a constitutional system to channel political demands into negotiated solutions. For these communities, constitutional rules have a darker legacy. Whether that perception is currently only imagined is irrelevant to the process of the accommodation of regionalist demands.

The ability, or the lack of it, to amend or to provide a new interpretation for constitutional norms in a way that forms new agreements is particularly evident during crises where central and regional institutions have been involved in a regional conflict.[47] Northern Ireland (Chapter 1), the Basque Country (Chapter 2), New Caledonia (Chapter 6) and Bougainville (Chapter 8) are post-conflict societies in which the peace process was associated with a constitutional reform.[48]

In Sicily (Chapter 3), Alaska and Quebec (Chapter 4), Hong Kong (Chapter 5) and the Northern Territory (Chapter 7), communities have a distinctive historical claim regarding regional governance. The claim of regional gov-

---

[45] Vito Breda, *Constitutional Law and Regionalism: A Comparative Analysis of Regionalist Negotiations* (Edward Elgar Publishing 2018).

[46] Davis (n 32); Megan Mallonee, 'Selective Justice: A Crisis of Missing and Murdered Alaska Native Women Notes' (2021) 38 Alaska Law Review 93; Kay Goodall and others, 'Community Experiences of Sectarianism' <http://storre.stir.ac.uk/handle/1893/21622> accessed 14 July 2015; David Chappell, 'Decolonisation and Nation-Building in New Caledonia: Reflections on the 2014 Elections' (2015) 67 Political Science 56.

[47] Horowitz (n 2).

[48] Brendan O'Leary, 'Debating Consociational Politics: Normative and Explanatory Arguments' in Sidney John Roderick Noel (ed), *From Power Sharing to Democracy: Post-conflict Institutions in Ethnically Divided Societies* (McGill-Queen's University Press – MQUP 2005).

ernance might have emerged recently, as in the case of Hong Kong localism,[49] or it might be part of a pre-modern historical heritage, as is the case for the Australian Aboriginal Peoples.[50] Constitutional law in these instances sets the limits of constitutional negotiations over the recognition of regional cultural distinctiveness and the protection of rights.[51] In both post-conflict societies and in cultural communities seeking recognition, a constitution might act as a negative or as a positive driver of change.[52]

Constitutional law is a positive driver of change, among other factors in a crisis, when it allows a community to dissipate identity-fuelled tensions between regional and central institutions and to form agreements over shared values.[53] The series of constitutional reforms that followed the October Crisis in Quebec (Chapter 4) and the peace process in Bougainville (Chapter 8) are two examples in which constitutional law managed radical political stances. Constitutional law is instead a negative driver of change when it imposes ideological limits on the process of the recognition of identity claims.[54] Legalistic stances, like the idea that individuals can be discriminated against because of their race such as in the Australian Constitution (Chapter 7), or one that imposes a hierarchical order of nationalities, such as in the Spanish Constitution (Chapter 2), contribute to a perception that regional minorities are subjected to an external power and are not part of communal deliberative projects.

---

[49] Sebastian Veg, 'The Rise of "Localism" and Civic Identity in Post-Handover Hong Kong: Questioning the Chinese Nation-State' (2017) 230 The China Quarterly (London) 323.

[50] Altman and Russell (n 35).

[51] Stephen Tierney, *Constitutional Law and National Pluralism* (Oxford University Press 2004); Michael Keating, 'Stateless Nations or Regional States?', in *Quebec* (2nd edn, University of Toronto Press 2004).

[52] Hazell (n 20); Robert Hazell, 'Constitutional Reform in the United Kingdom: Past, Present and Future' in Caroline Morris, Jonathan Boston and Petra Butler (eds), *Reconstituting the Constitution* (Springer 2011).

[53] Tierney (n 16); Rosenfeld (n 29); Hèctor López Bofill, 'A Nation of Nations? A Reply to Joseph H. H. Weiler' (2019) 17 International Journal of Constitutional Law 1315; Georg Grote, *The South Tyrol Question, 1866–2010: From National Rage to Regional State* (Peter Lang 2012); Megan Davis, 'Political Timetables Trump Workable Timetables: Indigenous Constitutional Recognition and the Temptation of Symbolism over Substance' in Simon Young, Jeremy Patrick and Jennifer Nielsen (eds), *Constitutional Recognition of First Peoples in Australia: Theories and Comparative Perspectives* (Federation Press 2016).

[54] Claus Offe, '"Homogeneity" and Constitutional Democracy: Coping with Identity Conflicts through Group Rights' (1998) 6 Journal of Political Philosophy 113; Marrani (n 7); Hazell (n 20); Michael Keating, 'So Many Nations, so Few States: Territory and Nationalism in the Global Era' in James Tully and Alain Gagnon (eds), *Multinational Democracies* (Cambridge University Press 2001).

The book is divided into eight self-standing chapters that are grouped into three geographical areas: Europe, North America and Asia and Oceania. The European section includes an analysis of Northern Ireland, the Basque Country and Sicily. The first chapter discusses the devolution process in Northern Ireland. Northern Ireland is a post-conflict society that is experiencing the effects of a long-term cycle of legitimation crises. An inadequate institutional setting, sectarian politics and Brexit are the drivers of change that sustain a high level of mistrust in the regional and national institutions.[55]

Chapter 2 considers the case of the Basque Country in Spain. The disbandment of *Euskadi Ta Askatasuna* (ETA) was the latest event in a cycle of political violence that has lasted for over two centuries. However, the end of political violence has not coincided with the end of the crisis of legitimacy of the Spanish central institutions in the region. One of the reasons for the crisis is the couplable vagueness of the system of territorial governance set out in the Spanish Constitution.[56] The 1978 Constitution is one of the latest and most advanced West European constitutional projects. It includes multiple innovations that prepared the country for its entrance into the European Union. However, the Basque system of territorial governance is incomplete.[57]

The case of Sicily is discussed in Chapter 3. The crisis of legitimacy is related to the inability of public institutions to achieve *de facto* control over their territory.[58] Sicily is an autonomous region, and its status is constitutionally protected. Italian regionalism has a sophisticated process for the negotiation of regionalist demands.[59] However, almost all rural areas and several urban parts of Sicily are under the control of a cluster of mafia families.[60] These mafia families provide votes for political representatives who in turn act as intermediaries between mafia bosses and Italian central institutions.[61]

---

[55] McCulloch (n 37).
[56] Enric Espadaler Fossas, 'El principio dispositivo en el Estado autonómico' (2008) 71–72 Revista de Derecho Político 151.
[57] López Bofill (n 7).
[58] Diego Gambetta, *The Sicilian Mafia: The Business of Private Protection* (Harvard University Press 1996) 75.
[59] Salvatore Di Gregorio, *L'autonomia finanziaria della regione siciliana: il contenzioso con lo stato ed il ruolo della Corte costituzionale nell'attuazione della disciplina statutaria* (Jovene 2014).
[60] Direzione Nazionale Antimafia e Antiterrorismo Antimafia, 'Relazione Annuale Sulle Attività Svolte Dal Procuratore Nazionale Antimafia e Dalla Direzione Nazionale Antimafia Nonché Sulle Dinamiche e Strategie Della Criminalità Organizzata Di Tipo Mafioso Nel Periodo 1° Luglio 2018 – 31 Dicembre 2019' (Ministero dell'Interno 2020).
[61] Antonella Coco, 'Neopatrimonialism and Local Elite Attitudes: Similarities and Differences Across Italian Regions' (2015) 3 Territory, Politics, Governance 167.

The North American chapter discusses two very different regional crises. The first part of the chapter focuses on the historical events surrounding the October Crisis in Quebec. The second part instead examines the ongoing regional crisis in Alaska among Native Alaskan communities. The Canadian portion of this chapter examines a segment of Quebec history between the 1960s and 1970s during which Quebec nationalism directly promoted, or tolerated, political violence. Quebec and Northern Ireland are often compared as they are both consociative regional democracies.[62] Quebec benefits from stable, perhaps overly stable, regional institutions.[63] This part of the chapter describes a selection of the drivers of change that led to the current situation. It explains, for instance, that by 1960, the constitutional system that the Canadians inherited from the British Empire was legitimising an unrepresentative political system, which was perceived in Quebec as a form of cultural Imperialism. The October Crisis was one of the manifestations of such a perception.

The second regional crisis discussed in the North American chapter evaluates the regional crisis that affects Native Alaskan communities in Alaska. This section of the chapter focuses on the perception of the legitimacy of US central institutions among Alaskan communities. There is a direct link between the lack of delegation of powers by the central government to Native Alaskan institutions and violence against Alaska Native women.[64] The Native Alaskan institutions that are tasked to protect their members have limited jurisdiction over non-Natives.[65] The recent Violence Against Women Act Reauthorization Act of 2022 (VAWA), by allocating more powers to Native Alaskan institutions and established by the Alaska Native Claims Settlement Act 1971, is seeking to reduce the level of regional mistrust in central institutions.[66]

Chapter 5 opens the third geographical area considered in this book, Southeast Asia and Oceania. This part evaluates regional crises in Hong Kong

---

[62] Garth Stevenson, *Parallel Paths: The Development of Nationalism in Ireland and Quebec* (McGill-Queen's University Press 2006); Stefan Wolff, 'The Institutional Structure of Regional Consociations in Brussels, Northern Ireland, and South Tyrol' (2004) 10 Nationalism and Ethnic Politics 387.

[63] Stevenson (n 62); Wolff (n 62).

[64] The Department of Public Safety (Alaska), Division of Statewide Services, 'Felony Level Sex Offenses, Crime in Alaska Supplemental Report 2017' 4; Violence Policy Center, 'When Men Murder Women: An Analysis of 2017 Homicide Data' 5.

[65] Mallonee (n 46) 94; Alaska Native Women's Resource Center, 'Missing and Murdered Indigenous Women: An Action Plan for Alaska Native Communities'; Violence Against Women Act Reauthorization Act of 2022 (as a part of the Consolidated Appropriations Act, 2022 ) Pub.L. 117–103 2022.

[66] 'VAWA Special Domestic Violence Jurisdiction for Alaska Indian Tribes Is Essential | NIWRC' <www.niwrc.org/restoration-magazine/june-2020/vawa-special-domestic-violence-jurisdiction-alaska-indian-tribes> accessed 27 April 2022.

(Chapter 5), French New Caledonia (Chapter 6), the Australian Northern Territory (Chapter 7) and Bougainville (Chapter 8). These are again four distinct types of regional crises. Bougainville is, for instance, set to become a new sovereign state by 2027. Hong Kong is, at the end of the transitional period, destined to become absorbed into the Chinese administrative system.[67] Territorian Aboriginal People will instead probably continue their struggle for recognition in an institutionally racist environment.[68]

The case of Hong Kong localism discussed in Chapter 5 is another manifestation of the increasing role of regional identities in modern states. Questions over the meaning of the rule of law in the People's Republic of China's Standing Committee have been part of Hong Kong's legal debate for a while. However, the implications of what is perceived as legitimate in the Special Administrative Territory of Hong Kong (hereafter, the HKSAR) and what is expected from its institutions from the Chinese Communist Party (hereafter, the CCP) have triggered multiple mass protests.[69] In Beijing, rising Hong Kong localism is perceived as a direct challenge to the dominance of the Chinese state and the CCP. The CCP has shown a distinct lack of tolerance for regional identities, including the newly emerging Hong Kong national identity.[70] The interaction between the HKSAR and China is unique.[71] It is likely that Hong Kong will lose its special status within China. However, the case of Hong Kong shows that concepts such as the rule of law are contextual fabrications and that identity movements are still formed on the basis of the xenophobic intolerance of minute differences.[72]

Chapter 6 evaluates the lingering effect of New Caledonia's civil war. New Caledonia is a French overseas territory which is currently considered a *special collective*.[73] The constitutional status of the region is due to change soon, but at

---

[67] Albert H-y Chen, *The Changing Legal Orders in Hong Kong and Mainland China: Essays on 'One Country, Two Systems'* (City University of Hong Kong Press 2021); John Burton and Claire Levacher, 'The State That Cannot Absent Itself: New Caledonia as Opposed to Papua New Guinea and Australia' in Nicholas A Bainton and Emilia E Skrzypek (eds), *The Absent Presence of the State in Large-Scale Resource Extraction Projects* (ANU Press 2021).

[68] Davis (n 32).

[69] Veg (n 49); Hoi-Yu Ng, 'Hong Kong: Autonomy in Crisis' in Brian CH Fong and Atsuko Ichijo, *The Routledge Handbook of Comparative Territorial Autonomies* (1st edn, Routledge 2022).

[70] Yuen and Chung (n 33).

[71] Brian CH Fong, 'One Country, Two Nationalisms: Center-Periphery Relations between Mainland China and Hong Kong, 1997–2016' (2017) 43 Modern China 523.

[72] Yuen and Chung (n 33).

[73] French Constitution 1958 (as revised 23/07/2008) 1958 Article 73, 74. Loi constitutionnelle n° 2008-724 du 23 juillet 2008 de modernisation des institutions de la Ve République Article 9, 11, 39, 40, 39, 40.

the time of authoring this book, New Caledonia is a constitutionally recognised consociative regional democracy that is demographically divided along ethnic lines. The chapter discusses the distinctive role of French constitutionalism in one of the last French colonies. The region is entering into a new period of instability.[74] The plan of the French Government is to start negotiations in 2023 with the intention of changing the special status of the region. A series of referenda, which were part of a peace process that commenced over two decades previously, ended with a controversial plebiscite imposed by the French Government during the COVID-19 pandemic.[75]

A different example of a crisis of legitimacy that is connected to colonisation is discussed in Chapter 7, which reviews the Australian Northern Territory. The chapter focuses on the interaction between the Aboriginal Peoples and Torres Strait Islander communities that reside in the Northern Territory, and Australian federal institutions. Aboriginal Peoples make up a substantive part of the Territorian population, but they are not constitutionally recognised.[76] Ironically, the Australian Constitution allows the Australian Parliament to pass legislation that discriminates on the basis of race.[77] The two elements have a combined negative effect on the perception of the legitimacy of the Australian Constitution among territorial Aboriginal communities.

The last chapter of the book analyses the process of the constitutional recognition of Bougainville. The region is very likely to become an independent new nation by the end of this decade.[78] The analysis of the process that ended the civil war shows that direct deliberative institutions, such as civil assemblies, and gender might have a distinctive role to play in solving conflicts and developing a shared sense of ownership of a constitutional system.[79]

---

[74] Loi n° 99-209 organique du 19 mars 1999 relative à la Nouvelle-Calédonie (consolidée au 07 janvier 2019) 99–209.

[75] Sophie Boyron, *The Constitution of France: A Contextual Analysis* (Hart Publishing 2013) 23.

[76] Murray Goot and Tim Rowse, *Divided Nation?: Indigenous Affairs and the Imagined Public* (Melbourne Univ Publishing 2007); George Williams, 'Removing Racism from Australia's Constitutional DNA' (2012) 37 Alternative Law Journal 151. Australian Government, 'Indigenous Australians Data' (n 5); Altman and Russell (n 35).

[77] Davis (n 53); Davis (n 32).

[78] Steven Kolova, 'The Bougainville Independence Referendum Consultations Impasse' (2022) 37 Contemporary PNG Studies: DWU Research Journal 7.

[79] Anthony J Regan, 'Bougainville: Origins of the Conflict, and Debating the Future of Large-Scale Mining' in Colin Filer and Pierre-Yves Le Meur (eds), *Large-scale Mines and Local-level Politics: Between New Caledonia and Papua New Guinea* (ANU Press 2017).

# 1. The UK and Northern Ireland: sectarianism and Brexit

This chapter discusses the cycle of crises of governance in Northern Ireland. The British enclave in the Northeast corner of Ireland is entering its third decade of official peace.[1] However, in the past two decades, its devolved institutions have worked intermittently, the level of sectarian violence has increased and there is anxiety over the effects of post-Brexit negotiations.[2] Northern Ireland is sustained on the brink of ungovernability by multiple drivers of change, but in this section of the book, I will focus on the regional institutional setting,[3] the dynamics of sectarianism, which is coupled with political apathy,[4] and the effects of Brexit.[5] The chapter is divided into four sections, preceded by an introduction and followed by a conclusion. The first section provides a contextual analysis for the three sections which discuss the three drivers change selected for this chapter.

Northern Ireland is one of the devolved regions that constitute the United Kingdom of Great Britain and Northern Ireland (hereafter, the UK).[6] The UK

---

[1] *Fog in Belfast: A Hundred Years of Uneasiness, and No End in Sight* (Directed by Duncan Morrow, 2020).
[2] Daniel Wincott, Gregory Davies and Alan Wager, 'Crisis, What Crisis? Conceptualizing Crisis, UK Pluri-Constitutionalism and Brexit Politics' (2021) 55 Regional Studies 1528; Etain Tannam, 'Intergovernmental and Cross-Border Civil Service Cooperation: The Good Friday Agreement and Brexit' (2018) 17 Ethnopolitics 243.
[3] Mary C Murphy and Jonathan Evershed, 'Contesting Sovereignty and Borders: Northern Ireland, Devolution and the Union' (2021) 10(5) Territory, Politics, Governance 661.
[4] Duncan Morrow and Sir George Quigley Fund Committee, 'Sectarianism – A Review for the Sir George Quigley Foundation' (Ulster University 2019).
[5] European Union (Withdrawal Agreement) Act 2020 c.1 2020; Council Decision (EU) 2020/135 on the conclusion of the Agreement on the withdrawal of the United Kingdom of Great Britain and Northern Ireland from the European Union and the European Atomic Energy Community [2020] OJ L029/1; Agreement on the withdrawal of the United Kingdom of Great Britain and Northern Ireland from the European Union and the European Atomic Energy Community [2020] OJ L029/7 [2020] OJ L029/1 Article 187; Protocol on Ireland/Northern Ireland 2020] OJ L029/101.
[6] Vernon Bogdanor, *The New British Constitution* (Hart 2009).

Constitution is flexible,[7] uncodified[8] and multinational.[9] There is no explicit assertion of the division of political powers, as they are considered fused on the absolute legislative sovereignty of the 'King in Parliament'.[10] The Parliament holds all the political power of the state and can dissolve regional institutions at a moment's notice. This eventuality is highly improbable yet it is consequential for all devolved British regions.[11] Northern Ireland is, by comparison to the rest of the UK, a consociative regional democracy divided along sectarian and ethnic lines.[12] The ethnic and religious divisions are a legacy of the 1603 English invasion and the successive colonisation period.[13] The post-1606 influx of immigrants consisted predominantly of Presbyterians from Scotland, and English settlers, who were primarily Anglican. These immigrants formed a large Protestant enclave in the North of the island.[14] The events that followed were part of the staple diet of early British Imperial policies experienced around the globe:[15] dispossession, deportation and cultural and physical genocide.[16]

In 1920, the majority of Ireland manged to become independent. However, one of the side effects of the 1919–21 Irish independence movement was

---

[7] Andrew Le Sueur, Maurice Sunkin and Jo Eric Murkens, *Public Law: Text, Cases, and Materials* (Oxford University Press 2016) 52; Bogdanor (n 6) 12; 14.

[8] Le Sueur, Sunkin and Murkens (n 7) 17; Bogdanor (n 6) 10; Albert Venn Dicey, *Introduction to the Study of the Law of the Constitution* (London and New York, Macmillan and co, limited 1889).

[9] Le Sueur, Sunkin and Murkens (n 7) 161.

[10] Bogdanor (n 6) 13; Le Sueur, Sunkin and Murkens (n 7) 24.

[11] Bogdanor (n 6) 271; Alex Schwartz, 'Patriotism or Integrity? Constitutional Community in Divided Societies' (2011) 31 Oxford Journal of Legal Studies 503; Morrow (n 4).

[12] Morrow (n 4). Stefan Wolff, 'The Institutional Structure of Regional Consociations in Brussels, Northern Ireland, and South Tyrol' (2004) 10 Nationalism and Ethnic Politics 387; Garth Stevenson, *Parallel Paths: The Development of Nationalism in Ireland and Quebec* (McGill-Queen's University Press 2006); K Boyle and T Hadden, 'The Peace Process in Northern Ireland' (1995) 71 International Affairs 269; The UK Government and The Government of Ireland, 'The Belfast Agreement: An Agreement Reached at the Multi-Party Talks on Northern Ireland 1998. Cm 3883 (the Belfast Agreement)' (20 May 1998).

[13] Stevenson (n 12) 41.

[14] ibid.

[15] ibid. Geoffrey Plank, *Rebellion and Savagery: The Jacobite Rising of 1745 and the British Empire* (University of Pennsylvania Press 2015); RR Davies, 'Colonial Wales' (1974) Past & Present 3; Stevenson (n 12); Eric Hobsbawm, *Age of Empire: 1875–1914* (Hachette 2010). Bain Attwood, *Telling the Truth about Aboriginal History* (Allen & Unwin 2005).

[16] Stevenson (n 12) 41. Plank (n 15); Davies (n 15); Stevenson (n 12); Hobsbawm (n 15); Attwood (n 15).

the creation of a UK-controlled region in the Northeast of the island.[17] After the partition, the majority of the Northern Irish residents were Anglican or Presbyterian.[18] Scottish Presbyterians, even after the Act of Union 1707, continued to be discriminated against by British authorities, though less so than the Irish Catholics.[19]

The territorial decentralisation of legislative and administrative competences in Northern Ireland commenced in 1920.[20] Attempts were made previously to have a decentralised government for the whole of Ireland, but they were not successful.[21] The decentralisation system was never fully operational, and by the 1970s, the region was heading towards an open, yet undeclared, civil war.[22] 'Armed groups rooted in separated communities and territories dominated the political landscape, Belfast in particular, and Northern Ireland as a whole, became an international byword for religious war between Protestants and Catholics.'[23] The Belfast Agreement, or the Good Friday Agreement, as it is often called, set the basis for the current system of territorial governance and was a proxy for the amendment of the Irish Constitution.[24] I will return to this point later, but as part of a succinct analysis, the 1998 Belfast Agreement formally ended civil unrest and established the institutions of a consociative democracy.[25] The new system allocates the role of First Minister to the leader

---

[17] Stevenson (n 12) 39; Government of Ireland Act 1920 c 67 1920 67; 'Treaty between Great Britain and Ireland (Signed 6 December 1921) 626 LNTS 6, 9–19.'

[18] Stevenson (n 12) 39.

[19] ibid 42.

[20] Government of Ireland Act 1920 c 67; Murphy and Evershed (n 3) 4; Douglass Woodwell, 'The "Troubles" of Northern Ireland: Civil Conflict in an Economically Well-Developed State' in Paul Collier and Nicholas Sambanis (eds), *Understanding Civil War (Volume 2: Europe, Central Asia, & Other Regions): Evidence and Analysis* (The World Bank 2005).

[21] Eugenio F Biagini (ed), 'Home Rule as a "Crisis of Public Conscience"', in *British Democracy and Irish Nationalism 1876–1906* (Cambridge University Press 2007) 3; Alvin Jackson, *Home Rule: An Irish History, 1800–2000* (1st edn, Oxford University Press 2004); Government of Ireland Act 1920 c 67.

[22] Feargal Cochrane, *Northern Ireland: The Reluctant Peace* (Yale University Press 2013) 79; Morrow (n 4) 7; Woodwell (n 20); Hadden and Boyle (n 12).

[23] Morrow (n 4) 8.

[24] The UK Government and The Government of Ireland (n 12); The Northern Ireland Act 1998 c 47; Nineteenth Amendment of the Constitution Act 1998; Constitution of Ireland (Bunreacht na hÉireann) 1937 Articles: 2, 3.

[25] The Northern Ireland Act 1998 Ch. 47 (Ch 47), Stephen Tierney, 'Towards a Federal United Kingdom? Lessons from America' (2015) 6 Political Insight 16, 16; Robert Hazell, *Devolution and the Future of the Union* (The Constitution Unit 2015) 31; Murphy and Evershed (n 3) 8. Vernon Bogdanor, *Devolution in the United Kingdom* (Oxford University Press 1999); Bogdanor (n 6).

of the political party that collected the highest number of votes[26] and the role of the Deputy First Minister to the leader of the second largest political party.[27] I will explain later that such a mechanism of forced cooperation fosters instability.[28] The Belfast Agreement decreased, at least initially, politically motivated violence, but it did not improve the level of democratic accountability for the leaders of sectarian political factions,[29] who thrive by promoting cycles of legitimation crises.[30] Haljan uses the term constitutional disorder to describe a situation like that in Northern Ireland.[31] In these instances there is imbalance between rule of law and popular sovereignty.[32] The process in which this imbalance occurs is described with clarity by Mary Murphy and Jonathan Evershed.

> A cycle of crisis–talks–crisis has produced five further agreements since the Belfast/Good Friday Agreement was signed: St Andrews (2006), Hillsborough Castle (2010), Stormont House (2014), Fresh Start (2015) and New Decade, New Approach (2020), each of which has tweaked the devolution settlement in an attempt to put it on a more sustainable footing, with (self-evidently) somewhat mixed results.[33]

The effects of this devastating equilibrium hinder the economic and institutional development of the region.[34] It is also reasonably clear that the Belfast Agreement and its successive amendments did not establish a deliberative connection between communities and their constitutional system.[35]

For instance, Sinn Féin, one of the two political parties that claim to represent the Irish Nationalists, and which collected 29 per cent of the votes in the last election, refuses to accept the legitimacy of the UK Parliament and

---

[26] The Northern Ireland Act 1998 c 47 s 16A(4).
[27] ibid 16A(5).
[28] Cochrane (n 22); Wincott, Davies and Wager (n 2).
[29] Wincott, Davies and Wager (n 2).
[30] Morrow (n 4); ibid 4; Katy Hayward and Cathal McManus, 'Neither/Nor: The Rejection of Unionist and Nationalist Identities in Post-Agreement Northern Ireland' (2019) 43 Capital & Class 139, 140.
[31] David Haljan, *Constitutionalising Secession* (Hart Publishing 2014) 13.
[32] ibid.
[33] Murphy and Evershed (n 3) 5.
[34] Wincott, Davies and Wager (n 2); Robin Wilson and Rick Wilford, 'Northern Ireland: Polarisation or Normalisation?' in Robert Hazell (ed), *Constitutional Futures Revisited: Britain's Constitution to 2020* (Palgrave Macmillan 2008) 68.
[35] Henry Jarrett, 'Northern Ireland A Place Apart?' in Brian CH Fong and Atsuko Ichijo (eds), *The Routledge Handbook of Comparative Territorial Autonomies* (Taylor & Francis Group 2022).

of the role of the royal family in the UK Constitution.[36] Sinn Féin contests seats in each UK general election, but those elected are prevented by the party from sitting in the House of Commons.[37] A deeply rooted perception of the unrepresentativeness of UK institutions is also found in the Social Democratic and Labour Party (hereafter, the SDLP). The SDLP is the second largest Nationalist party in the region and its leadership allows elected representatives to go to London, but its elected MPs swear loyalty to the Crown under protest.[38] The internal dynamics of Unionist political parties are less extreme, but they are out of tune with the inclusive idea of British identity as it is normally promoted by the Conservative Party.[39]

In this chapter, I will explain that there are many elements that contribute to regional governance; however, I will focus on three drivers of change. The first negative driver of change is the institutional setting which was designed to foster cooperation between sectarian communities.[40] I will explain that despite signs of cross-sectarian collaboration, sectarianism still dominates regional politics in the region. For instance, *Together: Building a United Community* was supported, among others, by the Democratic Unionist Party (hereafter, the DUP) and Sinn Féin.[41] Yet, such initiatives have a limited soothing effect on sectarianism.[42] The second negative driver of change considered in the chapter is the identity-making formation of the two sectarian communities and of the Neither group.[43] Throughout the COVID-19 pandemic, sectarian tension was

---

[36] The Electoral Office of Northern Ireland – EONI, 'UK Parliamentary Election 2019 – Results'.

[37] Marie Coleman, 'Fighting an Election Only to Refuse a Seat: Sinn Féin and Westminster Abstention' (*The Conversation*); *McGuinness v United Kingdom* (Application no 39511/98; decision of 8 June 1999). Peter John McLoughlin, 'Northern Ireland's Government Is Back up and Running – Here's How It Happened and Why' (*The Conversation*) <https://theconversation.com/northern-irelands-government-is-back-up-and-running-heres-how-it-happened-and-why-129831> accessed 10 March 2020.

[38] Morrow (n 4) 45.

[39] Wincott, Davies and Wager (n 2) 1533; Michael Kenny and Jack Sheldon, 'When Planets Collide: The British Conservative Party and the Discordant Goals of Delivering Brexit and Preserving the Domestic Union, 2016–2019' (2021) 69 Political Studies 965, 975.

[40] Morrow (n 4); David Phinnemore, 'Brexit and Northern Ireland: The Latest Commitments Explained' (2020) The Conversation.

[41] Office of the First Minister and, *Report on the Inquiry Into Building a United Community: Fifteenth Report, Written Submissions (1–60)* (Stationery Office 2015).

[42] ibid 1.

[43] Morrow (n 4) 14.

on the rise and, with it, the level of sectarian violence.[44] The third driver of change is focused on the effect of Brexit on the region.[45] Brexit is a positive driver of change, because it increases the awareness of the uniqueness of Northern Ireland, which is, in all probability, the key element for the end to the current cycle of crises of governance.[46]

## UK DEVOLUTION IN NORTHERN IRELAND: A CONTEXTUAL BRIEF

Before discussing the three drivers of change that are, among other elements, altering the ongoing crisis of legitimacy in Northern Ireland, a series of analyses must be included as part of a contextual introduction. Northern Ireland has existed as a British enclave since 1921, and the Protestant and Catholic communities continued to live in relative peace until the late 1960s.[47] However, at the end of the 1960s, there were indications that things were beginning to fall apart.[48] In his autobiography titled *A Belfast Child*, John Chambers describes the public torturing of a Protestant woman in a Belfast street because she was believed to be romantically involved with a Catholic.[49] The woman was tied up to a telephone post at the side of the road, her hair was cut, red paint was poured on her body and she was left there in front of gathering crowds who

---

[44] Morrow (n 4); PSNI Statistics Branch, 'Police Recorded Security Situation Statistics' (Northern Ireland Statistics and Research Agency PSNI Statistics Branch 2017); Northern Ireland Statistics and Research Agency, 'Incidents and Crimes with a Hate Motivation Recorded by the Police in Northern Ireland Update to 30th September 2021'.

[45] Peter F Trumbore and Andrew P Owsiak, 'Brexit, the Border, and Political Conflict Narratives in Northern Ireland' (2019) 30 Irish Studies in International Affairs 195; Mary C Murphy, 'What Sinn Féin's Election Success Means for Irish Relations with the EU – and Brexit' (*The Conversation*) <http://theconversation.com/what-sinn-feins-election-success-means-for-irish-relations-with-the-eu-and-brexit-131507> accessed 10 March 2020; Matt Beech, 'Brexit and the Decentred State' (2022) 37(1) Public Policy and Administration 67.

[46] Wincott, Davies and Wager (n 2); Feargal Cochrane, 'How Northern Ireland's Government Went from Mutual Suspicion to Collapse' (*The Conversation*, 18 January 2017).

[47] Morrow (n 4) 7; Caroline Kennedy-Pipe, *The Origins of the Present Troubles in Northern Ireland* (Routledge 2014); Stacie Goddard, *Indivisible Territory and the Politics of Legitimacy: Jerusalem and Northern Ireland* (Cambridge University Press 2009); Stevenson (n 12) ch 2.

[48] Stevenson (n 12) 281–88; 295. John Coakley, 'Adjusting to Partition: From Irredentism to "Consent" in Twentieth-Century Ireland' (2017) 25 Irish Studies Review 193, 194.

[49] John Chambers, *A Belfast Child: My True Story of Life and Death in the Troubles* (John Blake 2020) ch 2.

enthusiastically shouted insults and spat on her.[50] At the time of this event, Chambers was one of the many children who stood there looking at this brutalised woman. She was left bound to a post as a living warning for those who might be thinking of similar conduct.[51] This form of punishment is still currently used in Northern Ireland.[52]

It is difficult to think of a better manifestation of a process of identity formation based on the intolerance of minor differences than a case in which someone is publicly humiliated for loving another individual.[53] Chambers' personal experience also revealed a change in the dynamics of the identity-formation process that occurred in Northern Ireland between the 1960s and 1970s. He is one of three children from a mixed Catholic–Protestant marriage, which was possible, yet not easy before 1970.[54] However, during the civil war that developed in the years that followed, mixed green-and-orange marriages, as they are called, became a rare occurrence indeed.

The 1998 devolution process in Northern Ireland was intended to reduce the effects of sectarianism, like that described by Chambers, and this decentralisation process is distinguishable from the devolution in Scotland and Wales.[55] In 1998, the Scotland Act and the Government of Wales Act established a regional democracy in Scotland and Wales, respectively.[56] England is directly controlled by the UK Parliament.[57] Each of the devolved regions (Northern Ireland, Wales and Scotland) benefits from a bespoke decentralisation system which grants a distinctive level of administrative or legislative

---

[50] ibid.

[51] ibid.

[52] 'Gang of up to 50 Capture, Bind, Beat and Cover in Paint Fugitive Sex Offenders in Northern Ireland' *belfasttelegraph* <www.belfasttelegraph.co.uk/news/northern-ireland/gang-of-up-to-50-capture-bind-beat-and-cover-in-paint-fugitive-sex-offenders-in-northern-ireland-36857060.html> accessed 1 October 2022.

[53] Sigmund Freud, *Civilization and Its Discontents* (Prabhat Prakashan 2015) V; Michael Ignatieff, *The Warrior's Honor: Ethnic War and the Modern Conscience* (Vintage 1999); Sigmund Freud, *Group Psychology and the Analysis of the Ego* (Lulu.com 2018) 30–31.

[54] Chambers (n 49) ch 1.

[55] Scotland Act 1998 c 46; Government of Wales Act 1998 Ch 38 (Ch 38); Tierney (n 25); Alan Trench, 'Scotland and Wales: The Evolution of Devolution' in Robert Hazell (ed), *Constitutional Futures Revisited: Britain's Constitution to 2020* (Palgrave Macmillan 2008).

[56] Scotland Act 1998 c 46 (n 55); Government of Wales Act 1998 Ch 38; Tierney (n 25); Trench (n 55).

[57] Ailsa Henderson and others, 'England, Englishness and Brexit' (2016) 87 The Political Quarterly 187.

autonomy.[58] However, the decentralisation process in Wales and Scotland was promoted by the New Labour Government and was intended, among other elements, to reduce the impetus of the regional Nationalist parties in both regions.[59] Nationalist parties, like the Scottish National Party and Plaid Cymru in Wales, were poaching voters from the working class, the traditional reservoir of votes for the Labour movement in regional Britain.[60] Furthermore, the newly elected-to-power Labour Party, which was called, at the time, the New Labour Party, was aware that its turns at the helm of the UK Government were traditionally short-lived, and that one of the reasons that made their election more difficult was the allegation of governmental inexperience.[61] The regional governments would ensure that its new emerging Labour talents would get the experience needed to run the country.[62] It is reasonable to suggest that political realism, rather than a normative recognition of its multinational nature, was the driving force behind the Northern Irish devolution process.[63] This is unrelated to our discussion, but the New Labour plan of using regional institutions as 'political nurseries' worked only in Wales.[64]

The reasons for Northern Irish devolution were different from the motivations for Scottish and Welsh devolution. In 1998, the New Labour Party had no significant political presence in Northern Ireland.[65] Instead, the Belfast Agreement, like the Dayton Accords for Bosnia, was one of the manifestations of a peace process that was internationally promoted by the Republic of Ireland, the UK Government, the Council of Europe and US diplomacy.[66] The agreement established the institutions of a consociative regional democracy

---

[58] Ian Loveland, Constitutional Law, *Administrative Law, and Human Rights: A Critical Introduction* (Oxford University Press 2018) pt III.

[59] Vito Breda, *Constitutional Law and Regionalism: A Comparative Analysis of Regionalist Negotiations* (Edward Elgar Publishing 2018) 29; 'Labour Party Manifesto, General Election 1997 [Archive]'.

[60] Richard Wyn Jones and Roger Scully, *Wales Says Yes: Devolution and the 2011 Welsh Referendum* (University of Wales Press 2012); Trench (n 55); Donald Horowitz, 'Some Realism about Constitutional Engineering' in Andreas Wimmer (ed), *Facing Ethnic Conflicts: Toward a New Realism* (Rowman & Littlefield 2004) 249.

[61] Trench (n 55) 32.

[62] Breda (n 59) 33.

[63] Horowitz (n 60); Bogdanor (n 6); Wyn Jones and Scully (n 60); Stevenson (n 12).

[64] Breda (n 59) 33.

[65] Robert Hazell and Mark Sandford, 'English Question or Union Question? Neither Has Easy Answers' (2015) 86 Political Quarterly 16; P Leyland, 'The Multifaceted Constitutional Dynamics of U.K. Devolution' (2011) 9 International Journal of Constitutional Law 251, 261.

[66] Stevenson (n 12) 330; Morrow (n 4) 27; Andrew Gilbert and Jasmin Mujanović, 'Dayton at Twenty: Towards New Politics in Bosnia-Herzegovina' (2015) 15 Southeast European and Black Sea Studies 605; Soeren Keil and Anastasiia Kudlenko, 'Bosnia

that was supposed to reduce the level of sectarian violence.[67] As mentioned earlier, the negotiations between the UK institutions and the representatives of the different political parties took the form of a peace process that aimed at reducing, and ideally ending, open hostilities between religious communities.[68] It is not within the aims of this chapter to provide a comprehensive analysis of the process surrounding the Belfast Agreement, yet there are a few aspects that have an effect on the qualification of the current drivers of change. First, neither the representatives of the Catholic minority nor the Protestant majority were content with the idea of sharing political power.[69] Catholics had to relinquish their demand for unification, by force if necessary, with the Republic of Ireland.[70] The commitment to dispose of weapons was perceived as tantamount to an admission of defeat.[71] The DUP was, at the time of the Belfast Agreement, the largest political party with the informal support of the British Army, and it had little incentive to share a regional government with Sinn Féin.[72]

The agreement brought a reluctant peace. Amanda Hall uses the term 'negative peace' to critique the Belfast Agreement institutions.

> 'Negative peace' refers to the condition of peace in which violence is managed or reduced, but the conflict has yet to be transformed ... This allows for the continuance of past structures and fails to address the root causes of conflict – facts that, this article argues, make 'peace' in Northern Ireland more illusory than realised today.[73]

Indeed, after two decades of decreasing terrorism, the level of paramilitary violence in the region is now rising.[74] For instance, in 2017, the police recorded 66 casualties and 29 bombing incidents linked to paramilitary activities.[75] In

---

and Herzegovina 20 Years after Dayton: Complexity Born of Paradoxes' (2015) 22 International Peacekeeping 471.

[67] Cochrane (n 22) 295. The Belfast Agreement included a commitment to amend Article 2 and 3 of the Irish Constitution in way that recognised the possibility of unification only by a democratic means but at the same time asserted an EU porosity of the UK/Irish border. Nineteenth Amendment of the Constitution Act 1998; Murphy and Evershed (n 3) 14.

[68] Hadden and Boyle (n 12).

[69] Wilson and Wilford (n 34); Morrow (n 4) 4; Stevenson (n 12) ch 8; Tannam (n 2); Goddard (n 47).

[70] Stevenson (n 12) 331.

[71] Wilson and Wilford (n 34) 57; Cochrane (n 22); Adrian Guelke, 'Northern Ireland's Flags Crisis and the Enduring Legacy of the Settler-Native Divide' (2014) 20 Nationalism and Ethnic Politics 133, 163; Office of the First Minister and (n 41) 98.

[72] Wilson and Wilford (n 34) 56; Stevenson (n 12) 320; Morrow (n 4).

[73] Amanda Hall, 'Incomplete Peace and Social Stagnation: Shortcomings of the Good Friday Agreement' (2018) 4 Open Library of Humanities.

[74] PSNI Statistics Branch (n 44) 2.

[75] ibid.

the previous year, there were 58 casualties and 66 bombing incidents.[76] The practice of kneecapping, a form of torture usually involving a gunshot wound to the knee, is still commonly used as an agreed form of punishment, and explosive related offences have recently increased.[77] The number of arrests have instead decreased, indicating that sectarian paramilitary operations are protected by the community.[78]

The economic situation in the region is also being affected by sectarian tensions.[79] For instance, the Gross Domestic Product (hereafter, GDP) per capita gives an indication of the performance of the region. The GDP per capita of Northern Ireland is €24,000 against the €74,000 of the neighbouring Republic of Ireland and the €41,000 of the UK.[80] This makes the region dependent on a stream of economic aid that is substantially mismanaged.

> Redistribution of the dividends of economic development (such as they have been) have tended to be subject to an ethno-sectarian carve-up: a quid pro quo politics of the 'pork-barrel' whereby resources are divided up between the DUP and Sinn Féin at the centre and then conveyed back to their respective 'communities' through patronage networks.[81]

The effects on the economic development of parasitic neo-patrimonialist networks is well studied and does not need to be reproduced here.[82] It is sufficient to say that in Northern Ireland, institutional corruption supports sectarianism by providing resources to incompetent affiliates whose ineptitude hinders the economic performance of their communities.[83] The reduction in economic performance makes Northern Irish institutions more dependent on aid, which is then mismanaged by sectarian leaders.[84]

---

[76] ibid.
[77] Northern Ireland Statistics and Research Agency (n 44) 4.
[78] ibid.
[79] Wilson and Wilford (n 34) 63.
[80] Northern Ireland Assembly, Department for Public Leadership and Social Enterprise, 'Briefing Note: The Consequences for the Northern Ireland Economy from a United Kingdom Exit from the European Union'.
[81] Murphy and Evershed (n 3) 7.
[82] Richard A Posner, 'Creating a Legal Framework for Economic Development' (1998) 13 The World Bank Research Observer 1.
[83] Atsuko Ichijo, 'What Are Territorial Autonomies and Why the Handbook?' in Brian CH Fong and Atsuko Ichijo (eds), *The Routledge Handbook of Comparative Territorial Autonomies* (Routledge 2022) 3; Daniel C Bach, 'Patrimonialism and Neopatrimonialism: Comparative Trajectories and Readings' (2011) 49 Commonwealth & Comparative Politics 275.
[84] Cochrane (n 46).

This is a broad analysis of a large set of elements; however, I think there is enough material in the previous pages to indicate that the Northern Irish devolved institutions are grappling with an extraordinarily corrosive set of elements.[85] The region is still affected by the aftermath of civil war and the economic situation is degrading.[86] Brexit, which will be discussed in the penultimate part of this chapter, has increased the tensions in an already precarious system of governance.[87] The remainder of the chapter discusses a reasoned selection of drivers of change that control, among many other factors, the cycle of regional legitimacy crises. These drivers of change are the system of governance established by the Belfast Agreement,[88] the identity formation of sectarian groups[89] and the effects of Brexit.[90]

## NEGATIVE DRIVER OF CHANGE: INSTITUTIONAL SETTINGS

In the previous section, I explained that Northern Irish devolution is part of a social engineering project that is aimed at reducing the level of violence in the region, and perhaps developing the conditions for human flourishing.[91] It is reasonable to argue that neither of those two aims will be fully achieved in the near future.[92] Murphy and Evershed provide a succinct analysis of the key factors of the lingering instability.

> Far from addressing the root cause of Northern Ireland's Troubles, that is, the fundamental conflict between divergent Nationalist and Unionist constitutional interpretations and aspirations, the Belfast/Good Friday Agreement has instead reinscribed this conflict as an organising logic of governance in Northern Ireland.[93]

Norms, and in particular constitutional norms, are important because they set the limits around what a politically acceptable debate is. They also set the conditions under which political conduct, such filibustering or condoning extrem-

---

[85] Morrow (n 4).
[86] Cochrane (n 22).
[87] Trumbore and Owsiak (n 45); Tannam (n 2); Cathy Gormley-Heenan and Arthur Aughey, 'Northern Ireland and Brexit: Three Effects on "the Border in the Mind"' (2017) 19 The British Journal of Politics and International Relations 497.
[88] Schedule II, 1 The Northern Ireland Act 1998 c 47.
[89] Morrow (n 4); Kennedy-Pipe (n 47).
[90] Trumbore and Owsiak (n 45); Wincott, Davies and Wager (n 2); Tannam (n 2).
[91] Stevenson (n 12) 330; Wilson and Wilford (n 34).
[92] Trumbore and Owsiak (n 45).
[93] Murphy and Evershed (n 3) 7. The second part of the text is an extract from John Nagle, 'Between Conflict and Peace: An Analysis of the Complex Consequences of the Good Friday Agreement' (2018) 71 Parliamentary Affairs 395, 405.

ism, is punished. There are multiple sets of arrangements that define Northern Irish devolution and are currently part of the UK constitutional assets.[94] In this section, I will focus on the constitutional setting in which devolved institutions operate. It will be explained that, as it is currently structured, there are few institutional incentives for political parties to cooperate.[95]

The current attempt to establish a functional regional democracy began with the Northern Ireland Act 1998.[96] The normative underpinning of the text might be open to diverging interpretations.[97] The central state, that is the crown in the UK Parliament,[98] holds the so-called sovereign prerogatives.[99] They are international relations,[100] taxes and social security payments,[101] national security,[102] currencies[103] and immigration.[104] The remaining legislative competences are devolved, but there are areas in which central and regional institutions are required to legislate together.[105] These are termed 'reserved matters'.[106] The Assembly cannot legislate in reserved matters without the assent of London.[107] The list of reserved matters includes the prevention of terrorist activities,[108] prisons,[109] financial services[110] and the regulation of public processions.[111]

At a general level, the list of exclusive and concurring competences for the Northern Irish institutions is within the gamut of variation of any comparative

---

[94] Wincott, Davies and Wager (n 2); Tannam (n 2); Beech (n 45); McLoughlin (n 40); Jarrett (n 35) 233.
[95] Jarrett (n 35) 233; James Tilley and Geoffrey Evans, 'Political Generations in Northern Ireland' (2011) 50 European Journal of Political Research 583.
[96] The Northern Ireland Act 1998 c 47; Stevenson (n 12).
[97] Stephen Tierney, '"We the People": Constituent Power and Constitutionalism in Plurinational States' in Martin Loughlin and Neil Walker (eds), *The Paradox of Constitutionalism: Constituent Power and Constitutional Form* (Oxford University Press 2007).
[98] Schedule II, 1 The Northern Ireland Act 1998 c 47.
[99] Schedule II, 2 ibid.
[100] This excluded the shared activities with the Republic of Ireland and the implementation of human rights principles. Schedule II , 3 (a–c) ibid.
[101] Schedule II, 9–11 ibid.
[102] Schedule II, 4–5, 18–19 ibid.
[103] Schedule II, 14 ibid.
[104] Schedule II, 8 ibid.
[105] ibid 4.
[106] ibid.
[107] ibid.
[108] Schedule III, 9 (ii) The Northern Ireland Act 1998 c 47.
[109] Schedule II, 9 (1) (h) ibid.
[110] Schedule III, 7, 23. ibid.
[111] Schedule III, 9. ibid.

analysis, similar to that found in other UK decentralised regions.[112] However, the system of governance is, as mentioned earlier, distinctive.[113] The election adopts a proportional system and allocations of the seats within the Northern Irish Executive are based on the electoral performance of whatever party contests the election.[114] The First Minister is chosen by the political party that collects the highest number of votes.[115] The Deputy First Minister is, however, chosen by the second largest party.[116] This is part of Strand One of the Belfast Agreement and it has delivered the conditions for the coexistence between the sectarian communities.[117] The other two strands deal with cooperation between Irish, Northern Irish and British institutions.[118]

Included in Strand One are a series of measures that are intended to protect minorities. For instance, cross-policy vetoes and the requirement for qualified majorities in the Assembly are inserted to ensure the protection of culturally diverse communities.[119] The aim is to reduce the possibility that a majority might take control of the Assembly and enforce discriminatory policies.[120] Recall that the tyranny of the majority is a distinctive concern in consociative democracies because of its historically devastating effect on minorities.[121]

---

[112] Jarrett (n 35); Wales Act 2017 Ch. 4; Marine (Scotland) Act 2010 2010 (Asp 5); Hazell and Sandford (n 65); Michael Keating, 'So Many Nations, so Few States: Territory and Nationalism in the Global Era' in James Tully and Alain Gagnon (eds), *Multinational Democracies* (CUP 2001).

[113] Jarrett (n 35) 232.

[114] Stevenson (n 12) 331.

[115] The Northern Ireland (St Andrews Agreement) Act 2006 c 53 s 4.

[116] ibid 5.

[117] The Northern Ireland Act 1998 c 47 pts 1–4; Wincott, Davies and Wager (n 2); Jarrett (n 35) 236; Murphy and Evershed (n 3) 7; John Barry, 'From Power Sharing to Power Being Shared Out' (Green European Journal); Morrow (n 4); Northern Ireland Statistics and Research Agency (n 44); PSNI Statistics Branch (n 44).

[118] The Northern Ireland Act 1998 c 47 pt V; Murphy and Evershed (n 3) 3; Tannam (n 2).

[119] Hadden and Boyle (n 12).

[120] ibid.

[121] Wolff (n 12); Stevenson (n 12); Zoran Oklopcic, 'Constitutional (Re)Vision: Sovereign Peoples, New Constituent Powers, and the Formation of Constitutional Orders in the Balkans' (2012) 19 Constellations 81; David Chappell, 'The Kanak Awakening of 1969–1976: Radicalizing Anti-Colonialism in New Caledonia' (2003) Journal de la société des océanistes 187; Jens Woelk, 'South Tyrol is (not) Italy: A Special Case in a (De)federalizing System' (2013) 369 L'Europe en Formation 126; Jessica Leslie Arnett, 'Unsettled Rights in Territorial Alaska: Native Land, Sovereignty, and Citizenship from the Indian Reorganization Act to Termination' (2017) 48 Western Historical Quarterly 233; Wincott, Davies and Wager (n 2); Attwood (n 15).

The Northern Ireland power-sharing mechanism is intended to encourage consensus,[122] but overlooks the internal dynamics of ethnic and religious groups.[123] For instance, the St Andrews Agreement allows 30 members of the Assembly to demand cross-community support for any matter discussed in the Assembly.[124] This prerogative, given that it comes without political or economic repercussions for the community that adopts it, promotes a polarisation of political stances.[125] In a non-consociative system, it is expected that a party acting against the common good will be punished, to put it simply, by the electorate in the next election.[126] The electoral performance of sectarian parties in a consociative democracy is instead linked to ideological stances[127] and to the ability to marginalise individuals with moderate religious views.[128]

Wilson and Wilford describe the historical effects of sectarian politics in the party politics of the DUP and Sinn Féin.

> The DUP is primarily a vehicle for the maintenance of such a Protestant ethnic power as can be held in circumstances more strained than before the abolition of the unionist *ancient régime,* while the SF [*Sinn Féin*] is an ethno-nationalist organisation run on Leninist command principles, far removed from the original secular goals of Irish republicanism.[129]

In other words, there is little incentive for sectarian parties to be moderate political movements. Both parties support sectarian policies that trigger retaliation.[130] This retaliation gives way to a narrative of victimisation, which in turn perpetuates mistrust towards the 'Other' group and violence.[131]

Devolved institutions in consociative democracies are normally established to end the cycle of retaliation by incentivising collaboration and penalising

---

[122] Esman Milton, 'Ethnic Pluralism; Strategies for Conflict Management' in Andreas Wimmer (ed), *Facing Ethnic Conflicts: Toward a New Realism* (Rowman & Littlefield 2004) 206.

[123] Nukhet Ahu Sandal, 'Religious Actors as Epistemic Communities in Conflict Transformation: The Cases of South Africa and Northern Ireland' (2011) 37 Review of International Studies 929, 943.

[124] The Northern Ireland Act 1998 c 47 s 42 (1).

[125] My emphasis: Wilson and Wilford (n 34).

[126] Wolff (n 12).

[127] Ahu Sandal (n 123) 943.

[128] Milton (n 122) 206; Hayward and McManus (n 30).

[129] Wilson and Wilford (n 34) 57.

[130] John D Brewer and Bernadette C Hayes, 'Victims as Moral Beacons: Victims and Perpetrators in Northern Ireland' (2011) 6 Contemporary Social Science 73, 76.

[131] ibid.

extreme stances.[132] The 1998 Northern Irish devolution process has instead established a permanent cycle of crises in which tensions between sectarian groups and violence are accepted by both sectarian communities.[133] The situation is described as a 'bumpy ride' or as a 'catastrophic equilibrium'.[134] In this institutional setting, manipulating loyalties at the expense of moderation is one of the many accepted consequences for a reduction in violence.[135] Sectarian leaders have a vested interest in keeping the level of animosity just below that of an all-out civil war.[136] Unrest might stop the financial support from external parties, such as the EU, and it might turn public opinion against the leadership of sectarian groups. However, the leadership of both sectarian communities cannot relinquish the power to strike both the 'Other' group and internal dissenters without losing control of the allocation of the resources that are used to keep their affiliates loyal.[137] A balanced amount of violence instead ensures the dependence of residents on paramilitary organisations and guarantees a flux of money from Brussels and London.

In other words, the 1998 Northern Irish institutional setting does not effectively incentivise democratic deliberation.[138] It is inducive instead of a 'catastrophic equilibrium'.[139] Northern Irish institutions oscillate from political stagnation to violent protest,[140] and it is relatively clear that such fluctuations

---

[132] Wolff (n 12); Emma Lantschner, 'History of the South Tyrol Conflict and Its Settlement' in Jens Woelk, Francesco Palermo and Joseph Marko (eds), *Tolerance Through Law: Self Governance and Group Rights in South Tyrol* (Brill 2007); Verena Wisthaler, Josef Prackwieser and Marc Röggla, 'South Tyrol' in Brian CH Fong and Atsuko Ichijo, *The Routledge Handbook of Comparative Territorial Autonomies* (Routledge 2022).

[133] Murphy and Evershed (n 3) 6.

[134] Wilson and Wilford (n 34). Wincott, Davies and Wager (n 2) 1534.

[135] John Kleinig, *On Loyalty and Loyalties: The Contours of a Problematic Virtue* (Oxford University Press 2014).

[136] Northern Ireland Statistics and Research Agency (n 44).

[137] Kleinig (n 135). The latest agreement named Windsor Framework: A New Way Forward between the UK, Ireland, and the EU Commission will not substantially change the power dynamics of sectarian politics. European Commission and UK Government, 'Joint Declaration of the Union and the United Kingdom in the Joint Committee Established by the Agreement on the Withdrawal of the United Kingdom of Great Britain and Northern Ireland from the European Union and the European Atomic Energy Community of 24 March 2023 on Article 13(3a) of the Windsor Framework (See Joint Declaration No 1/2023)' PUB/2023/435 [2023] OJ L102/90.

[138] Horowitz (n 60).

[139] Economists use the term 'diffeomorphic transformation' to explain the events that move a system to from a complex yet flowing situation (e.g. a balanced market) to a crisis (e.g. collapsing offer and demand). Yves Balasko, 'Economic Equilibrium and Catastrophe Theory: An Introduction' (1978) 46 Econometrica 557.

[140] ibid.

are directly linked to a dysfunctional institutional setting.[141] The system is due to be reformed, but at the time of writing this chapter, the new proposal to change intergovernmental relations does not engage the cycle of sectarian interactions (and their effects) in the region.[142]

It is obvious for all involved that managing identity-based tensions in consociative democracies is the key priority for a system of territorial governance.[143] Ignoring identity demands – by assuming that social differences do not exist (*à la Française*) or by proposing permanent solutions that ignore the internal dynamics of the identity-making process – makes conflict almost unavoidable.[144] It is not the aim of this book to offer quixotic solutions, but consociative democracies tend to find their way out of diffeomorphic transformation cycles when there is a culture that supports a reduction in ethnic discrimination, and that provides economic incentives to collaborate at the individual level. This reduction of violence requires institutions that promote professional working relationships between public officials.[145] The South Tyrol consociative model, for instance, is based on a multi-layered system of governance in which every policy has to be agreed at both regional and local levels.[146] The culture of finding compromises within South Tyrol institutions increases the speed at which public services are allocated to individuals and businesses. The positive effects of having more shared resources in turn reduces the level of mistrust

---

[141] Wincott, Davies and Wager (n 2); Trumbore and Owsiak (n 45); Nicola McEwen and others, 'Intergovernmental Relations in the UK: Time for a Radical Overhaul?' (2020) 91 The Political Quarterly 632, 633.

[142] UK Government Cabinet Office and UK Government Department for Levelling Up, Housing and Communities, 'Review of Intergovernmental Relations' (2022).

[143] Wolff (n 12); Stevenson (n 12).

[144] Francisco J Llera, José M Mata and Cynthia L Irvin, 'ETA: From Secret Army to Social Movement – the Post-Franco Schism of the Basque Nationalist Movement' (1993) 5 Terrorism and Political Violence 106; Stevenson (n 12); Emma Lantschner, 'History of the South Tyrol Conflict and Its Settlement' in Jens Woelk, Francesco Palermo and Joseph Marko (eds), *Tolerance Through Law: Self Governance and Group Rights in South Tyrol* (Brill 2007); Allison McCulloch, 'Consociational Executives: Power-Sharing Governments Between Inclusion and Functionality' in Ferran Requejo and Marc Sanjaume-Calvet (eds), *Defensive Federalism* (Routledge 2022); Jarrett (n 35).

[145] Horowitz (n 60); Jens Woelk, Francesco Palermo and Joseph Marko, *Tolerance through Law* (Martinus Nijhoff Publishers 2008); Wolff (n 12).

[146] Georg Grote, *The South Tyrol Question, 1866–2010: From National Rage to Regional State* (Peter Lang 2012); Lantschner (n 132); Wisthaler, Prackwieser and Röggla (n 132) 290.

between ethnic groups.[147] It is fair to suggest that Strand One of the Northern Ireland devolution process has not managed to trigger this virtuous loop.[148]

Strand Two of the Belfast Agreement provides for international collaboration between Northern Ireland and Irish institutions, which could promote the collaboration between identity groups.[149] This is also known as the North–South axis of institutional collaboration.[150] Strand Three relates to the agreement between Irish and British institutions. This is the East–West axis of cooperation.[151] It is outside the scope of this chapter to discuss in detail the functioning of the institutions that are linked to Strands Two and Three. I will simply say that institutions that have been created by Strands Two and Three are functioning within the limits of their purview.[152] However, their limited role fosters rather than reduces the cycle of crises of legitimacy in the region.[153]

For instance, the North/South Ministerial Council (hereafter, the NSMC) was established as a part of Strand Two of the Belfast Agreement.[154] Agriculture, education, environment, health and transport, and the Special EU Programmes Body (called the SEUPB) are covered by Strand Two. Tourism was not inserted in the list but it was *de facto* incorporated into the NSMC competences and it is one of the areas where North and South cooperation has been most effective.[155] The NSMC has been successful in implementing the SEUPB's policies.[156] The SEUPB was founded by the European Commission and it allocates money for initiatives that promote social integration between regional communities.[157] The aptly named PEACE III (Operational Programme United Kingdom–Ireland) was specifically designed to help the post-1998 pacifica-

---

[147] Wolff (n 12).

[148] Murphy and Evershed (n 3) 5; UK Government (n 142); McEwen and others (n 141).

[149] The Northern Ireland Act 1998 c 47 pt 5; Murphy and Evershed (n 3) 4; Tannam (n 2) 248–50.

[150] The Northern Ireland Act 1998 c 47 pt 5; Murphy and Evershed (n 3) 4; Tannam (n 2) 248–50.

[151] The Northern Ireland Act 1998 c 47 s 54; Murphy and Evershed (n 3) 4.

[152] Murphy and Evershed (n 3) 4.

[153] Tannam (n 2).

[154] The Northern Ireland Act 1998 c 47 s 54; Murphy and Evershed (n 3) 4.

[155] Tannam (n 2) 249.

[156] Northern Ireland Assembly, Department for Public Leadership and Social Enterprise (n 80).

[157] 'Operational Programme "United Kingdom – Ireland" – (PEACE III) – Regional Policy – European Commission'; European Union – European Regional Development Fund, 'A Review of PEACE III and Considerations for PEACE IV'; Northern Ireland Assembly, Department for Public Leadership and Social Enterprise (n 80) 9; Tannam (n 2) 251.

tion of Northern Ireland, and it has been extended, despite Brexit, to 2023.[158] However, the NSMC had a limited effect on increasing the level of cooperation between the leaders of the sectarian communities.[159]

It is logical to suggest that Northern Irish institutions are dependent on external aid from the UK, Ireland and the EU,[160] but such support prevents sectarian political leaders from developing their own mediation strategies.[161] In other words, the flux of aid to Northern Ireland is an attempt to solve a problem where the solution is part of the problem.[162] The negative effects of external aid on economically depressed areas has been studied in multiple contexts and does not need to be reproduced here.[163] It is the case in Northern Ireland, as is the case in other post-conflict societies, that the taking over of regional governance by a third party is welcomed by those who depend on those resources, yet it reduces the accountability of regional institutions.[164]

In short, devolution has not created adequate conditions for any form of responsible government. Quite the contrary. The Assembly is not perceived as a deliberative arena that fosters political agreements. It is, instead, a place where extreme and uncompromising political stances are manifested. Regional administrations, with a few exceptions, are instead perceived by sectarian leaders as resources that are open to colonisation. The system of rules that supports these institutions does not discourage, or does not discourage enough, either ideological stances or corruption. It is from this perspective that Northern Irish devolution is considered a negative driver of change.

## NEGATIVE DRIVER OF CHANGE: SECTARIANISM IN A CONSOCIATIVE DEMOCRACY

In the previous section, it was argued that the two-tier system of territorial governance adopted in Northern Ireland is conducive to the devastating polit-

---

[158] 'Operational Programme "United Kingdom – Ireland" – (PEACE III) – Regional Policy – European Commission' (n 157); European Union – European Regional Development Fund (n 157); Northern Ireland Assembly, Department for Public Leadership and Social Enterprise (n 80).

[159] Tannam (n 2) 254.

[160] Northern Ireland Assembly, Department for Public Leadership and Social Enterprise (n 80); Thomas D Grant, 'Aid as an Instrument for Peace: a Civil Society Perspective' (2015) 109 The American Journal of International Law 68; Posner (n 82).

[161] Tannam (n 2) 254.

[162] Lant Pritchett and Michael Woolcock, 'Solutions When the Solution Is the Problem: Arraying the Disarray in Development' (Center for Global Development 2002) 10.

[163] Grant (n 160); Posner (n 82); Pritchett and Woolcock (n 162).

[164] Pritchett and Woolcock (n 162).

ical equilibrium.[165] In this section, I discuss the identity-formation process of sectarian communities.[166] I will argue that religious groups and the Neithers, who abstain from the sectarian dichotomy, have adopted an identity-making process that normalises and benefits from having inoperative institutions.[167] Sectarianism, like any other ideology, acts a complex meaning provider.[168] Despite rhetoric references to past events, the current identity-making process in Northern Ireland emerged in the two communities as a result of recent historical occurrences.[169] In the 1960s, mostly British university-educated Catholics formed a new Nationalist elite that promoted a violent insurrection.[170] The move from ideology to action was an expected one. In 1970, the region was affected by a series of violent events. The legacy of the violent struggle of the 1970s still defines current internal policies. At the same time, Protestant elites developed a British identity that was unique to Northern Ireland and that was, and still is, intolerant of minute differences.[171] The majority of residents consider themselves part of the Neither group and have refused to engage in regional politics.

Both Nationalist and Protestant identities are made up of complex and dynamic socio-political elements.[172] As mentioned earlier, both Catholics and Protestants might make identity-based historical claims that go back to the fifteenth century and beyond, but there is a general agreement that modern perceptions of sectarianism were changed by a series of events that occurred

---

[165] Wincott, Davies and Wager (n 2); Wilson and Wilford (n 34).

[166] Stevenson (n 12); Wolff (n 12); Margaret O'Callaghan, 'Genealogies of Partition; History, History-Writing and "the Troubles" in Ireland' (2006) 9 Critical Review of International Social and Political Philosophy 619; Marysia Zalewski and John Barry, *Intervening in Northern Ireland: Critically Re-Thinking Representations of the Conflict* (Routledge 2014); Kennedy-Pipe (n 47); Wincott, Davies and Wager (n 2).

[167] Hayward and McManus (n 30); O'Callaghan (n 166); 'The Monitor' (The Constitution Unit, University College London 2022) 14.

[168] Z Bauman, 'Identity: Then, Now, What For?' in M Kempny and others (eds), *Structuring of Identities in 20th Century Europe: East/West Convergence and Divergence; Identity in Transformation Postmodernity, Postcommunism, and Globalization*; Jordan B Peterson, *Maps of Meaning: The Architecture of Belief* (Routledge 2002).

[169] Stevenson (n 12); Zalewski and Barry (n 166); Goddard (n 47); Kennedy-Pipe (n 47).

[170] Stevenson (n 12) 285.

[171] Conservative and Unionist Party, 'The Conservative and Unionist Party Manifesto 2019' <www.conservatives.com/our-plan> accessed 1 January 2022; Stevenson (n 12) 285.

[172] Morrow (n 4).

in the 1960s.[173] One of the key transformative moments was the establishment of the 1967 Northern Ireland Civil Rights Association.[174] In April 1969, as a result of a mid-term UK election, a Nationalist candidate and a Northern Ireland Civil Rights Association activist, Bernadette Devlin, defeated the Ulster Unionist Party candidate in the Mid-Ulster parliamentary constituency.[175] In the weeks that followed, the Ulster Volunteer Force laid down a paramilitary campaign of intimidation that included several terrorist bomb attacks.[176] It was one of the many 'sliding-door moments' for the history of both religious communities. On 12 August in the same year, the Nationalists retaliated.[177] On 14 August, the British Army was sent in to provide a buffer between the two communities, but after a period of adjustment, the Army, albeit unofficially, took sides with the Unionists. In 1971, the first British Army soldier was killed by the Irish Republican Army (IRA).[178] In January 1972, in a single incident, 14 unarmed civilians participating in an unauthorised Northern Ireland Civil Rights Association march were gunned down by the 1st Battalion of the British Parachute Regiment.[179] The reputation of the British Army in Northern Ireland, and perhaps abroad, has never recovered.[180] 'The British Army continued to operate in a major back-up role, but almost exclusively in republican areas, and therefore highlighted the partisan nature of British arbitration.'[181] The massacre was popularised with the name 'Bloody Sunday'.[182] Two months after Bloody Sunday, the UK Government established direct rule (again) in the region.[183]

In the period that followed the Bloody Sunday incident, there were several attempts to deviate from the cycle of violence and retaliation, but the intolerance of minor differences had taken root.[184] Large political parties in Northern Ireland were opposed to violence.[185] For instance, throughout the 1970s, the

---

[173] The series of incidents that marked the start of the civil war are too many to be reproduced here. For a general historical overview see: Brendan O'Leary and John McGarry, *The Politics of Antagonism: Understanding Northern Ireland* (Bloomsbury Publishing 1996) ch 4.
[174] Stevenson (n 12) 286.
[175] ibid.
[176] ibid 295.
[177] ibid.
[178] ibid 290; Nagle (n 93).
[179] O'Leary and McGarry (n 173) 196; Stevenson (n 12) ch 8.
[180] Stevenson (n 12) 291.
[181] O'Leary and McGarry (n 173) 204.
[182] Stevenson (n 12) 291.
[183] ibid; Nagle (n 93) 203; Steve Bruce, *God Save Ulster: The Religion and Politics of Paisleyism* (Clarendon Press 1986) 101.
[184] Stevenson (n 12) 257, 288, 351.
[185] ibid 328; Tannam (n 2) 246.

SDLP was the largest of the Northern Irish Nationalist groups. One of the distinctive stances of the party was its unequivocal support for unification by peaceful means.[186] However, the leaders of paramilitary groups, which took on the role of representatives of the sectarian communities, were acting as an unofficial government by providing services, symbols, martyrs and jobs.[187] Each new terrorist attack against a community reinforced the need for a stronger defence by the relevant paramilitary organisation, which in turn was able to inflict more damage.[188] One of the legacies of the 1970s arms race is the current militarisation of the identity-making process in both sectarian communities manifested during the marching season.[189]

In the middle of the ongoing civil war, singular events, like Bloody Sunday, also changed the attitude of the international community.[190] For instance, in 1995, Bill Clinton, who claimed Irish ancestry, was a proxy for the US brokerage with the Council of Europe for the Belfast Agreement.[191] The 9/11 attacks instead increased the speed of IRA arsenal decommissioning.[192] However, the level of politically motivated regional violence is still extraordinary. For instance, in the period between 2020 and 2021, during a time in which the region experienced multiple COVID-19-related lockdowns, Northern Ireland's police reported 40 casualties of paramilitary-style assaults (excluding fatalities), 16 casualties of paramilitary-style shootings and 17 cases of illegal firearms confiscation.[193] In addition to the 'normal' sectarian criminal activities, there were 132 arrests without a warrant under Section 41 of the Antiterrorism Act 2000.[194] This level of organised criminal activity for a population of under two million is exceptional. To put these numbers into a European perspective, Slovenia, another post-conflict society with a population of over two million,[195] reports, for the same period considered here, two cases of terrorism-related

---

[186] The Irish and the UK Governments, instead wanted this costly and embarrassing problem to end. Stevenson (n 12) 328; Tannam (n 2) 246.

[187] Tom Nairn, *The Break-up of Britain: Crisis and Neonationalism* (2nd expanded edn, NLB and Verso Editions 1981); Anthony D Smith, *The Ethnic Revival* (CUP 1981).

[188] William H Sewell, 'Historical Events as Transformations of Structures: Inventing Revolution at the Bastille' (1996) 25 Theory and Society 841.

[189] McLoughlin (n 40).

[190] Stevenson (n 12) 291.

[191] ibid 330.

[192] ibid; Morrow (n 4) 7; Brewer and Hayes (n 130).

[193] Terrorism Act 2000 (as revised) c 11; Northern Ireland Statistics and Research Agency, 'Police Recorded Security Situation Statistics 1 December 2020 to 30 November 2021' (PSNI Statistics Branch 2021) 4.

[194] Terrorism Act 2000 (as revised) c 11; Northern Ireland Statistics and Research Agency (n 193) 4.

[195] Jarrett (n 35) 230.

crime.[196] The criminological data from Mafia-controlled Palermo, discussed in Chapter 3 of this book, during the same period, with its 1.2 million inhabitants, included only one mafia homicide.[197] In short, Northern Ireland is, by way of comparison to any other area of Western Europe (which includes territories that are controlled by gangs of criminals like Sicily), bewildering.[198]

It is also extraordinary that such a high level of violence is perceived as normal.[199] The high level of sectarian violence in relation to the identity formation among Northern Irish residents is, most probably, indicative of the capillary control of the territory by paramilitary organisations.[200] There are signs, for instance, that local institutions are 'captured' by local gangs and that individuals do not report corruption.[201] It is accepted that the leaders of both communities reward their affiliates by allocating jobs and contracts in the public sector on the basis of their loyalty.[202] For instance, in 2019 the Northern Ireland Assembly reconvened for a short period after a three-year hiatus that was triggered by the resignation of the Deputy First Minister.[203] The resignation was connected to the refusal of the First Minister to take political responsibility for a financial scandal.[204] Peter McLoughlin succinctly describes this recent political development:

> What really forced the deal between Sinn Féin and the DUP, however, was intervention from the British and Irish governments ... This approach triggered claims of blackmail, and exasperation by others that it took 'outsiders' to force Northern Ireland's squabbling parties to face up to their responsibilities.[205]

Indeed, both the British and the Irish governments facilitated the partial re-activation of the Northern Irish devolved institutions.[206] The agreement, like the one that preceded it, are partly about 'private dealings' between factions,

---

[196] The Republic of Slovenia, Statistical Office, 'SiStat Database' <https://pxweb.stat.si/sistat/en> accessed 27 December 2021.

[197] ISTAT Istituto Nazionale di Statistica, 'Delitti Denunciati Dalle Forze Di Polizia All'autorità Giudiziaria'.

[198] 'Eurostat – Data Explorer' <https://appsso.eurostat.ec.europa.eu/nui/submitViewTableAction.do> accessed 27 December 2021.

[199] Morrow (n 4).

[200] ibid.

[201] Northern Ireland Statistics and Research Agency (n 193); PSNI Statistics Branch (n 44); Morrow (n 4) 30.

[202] Tilley and Evans (n 95) 76; Wilson and Wilford (n 34) 68.

[203] David Phinnemore, 'Brexit and Northern Ireland: The Latest Commitments Explained' The Conversation (1 November 2019).

[204] Cochrane (n 46).

[205] McLoughlin (n 40).

[206] PSNI Statistics Branch (n 44).

which allows the patrimonial system to thrive within each community and the devastating equilibrium to persist as the only shared political strategy available.[207] Barry describes the process that sustains the equilibrium in a cogent narrative:

> Northern Ireland looks like its heading towards a One party Janus faced system, where each ethnic champion publicly appeals to its sectarian base for electoral power by blaming the 'Other' for all the Assembly's faults while privately collaborating with the very same 'Other' to ensure they remain the dominant power in the political process.[208]

In short, there is limited political accountability and a high level of corruption.[209]

While sectarianism divides communities along geographical lines, it also fosters the ever-growing group of individuals who are rejecting the duality of the Nationalist/Unionist narratives.[210] The old sectarian politics of fawning and granting concessions might be under pressure from the new generation who have grown tired of it.[211] The new emerging group of non-aligned individuals is predominantly composed of female, highly qualified professionals, with mixed Catholic–Protestant school backgrounds.[212] The Neither group is by far the largest of the political groups in Northern Ireland.[213] Both identity-based political parties did not perform well in the latest election.[214] However, the most significant contribution to the debate over the future of the region by the Neither group is 'silence'. Silence (the avoidance of direct engagement in political debates) creates a platform whereby the Neither group indirectly supports the status quo.[215] This is, given the high level of violence, understandable, yet the apathy of the Neither group allows identity-based narratives to run amok in the corridors of power of Northern Irish institutions.[216] These institutions

---

[207] Barry (n 117).

[208] ibid.

[209] Gero Erdmann and Ulf Engel, 'Neopatrimonialism Reconsidered: Critical Review and Elaboration of an Elusive Concept' (2007) 45 Commonwealth & Comparative Politics 95; Barry (n 117). A general analysis of the effect neopatrimonialism in deliberative democracy is in: Bach (n 83); Shmuel Noah Eisenstadt, *Traditional Patrimonialism and Modern Neopatrimonialism* (SAGE Publications Ltd 1973); Erdmann and Engel.

[210] Hayward and McManus (n 30); Murphy and Evershed (n 3) 14.

[211] Tilley and Evans (n 95).

[212] Hayward and McManus (n 30) 142.

[213] ibid 143.

[214] Cochrane (n 46); McLoughlin (n 40).

[215] Murphy and Evershed (n 3) 14.

[216] Hayward and McManus (n 30) 153; Murphy and Evershed (n 3) 14. Wilson and Wilford (n 34) 59.

are, in turn, correctly perceived by the Neither group as lacking democratic legitimacy. The lack of representativeness is then considered a reason for not engaging with politics, making the policy of apathy self-sustaining.[217]

In short, the nihilism of the Neithers is combined with the blatant sectarian interest in maintaining the region at the edge of ungovernability. It is from this perspective that the identity-making process of both sectarian communities and the Neithers should be considered a negative driver of change.

## POSITIVE DRIVER OF CHANGE: BREXIT

In this part of the chapter, I will argue that Brexit is a positive driver of change. To be clear, the effects of Brexit are not positive in the sense that they are good for the region. The Assembly is, for instance, still largely not fully functional as a government institution due to, among other reasons, the dispute over the Protocol negotiations.[218] I consider Brexit an irritant that might change the socio-economic and democratic development of Northern Ireland.[219] There is, in particular, the possibility that such an irritant might tilt the region, which is currently governed as a neo-patrimonial system, out of its current catastrophic equilibrium.[220]

On 23 June 2016, the majority of UK voters indicated that they would prefer to leave the EU.[221] The result of the referendum set a process in motion to exit the EU.[222] After a series of events which included a historical qualification of the role of the UK Government within the UK Parliament and a multistage international negotiation, the UK left the EU.[223]

The negative economic and social effects of Brexit on Northern Ireland are, by way of comparison to other parts of the UK, extensive.[224] The EU directly subsidises the post-1998 peace process,[225] and given that Northern Ireland is

---

[217] Murphy and Evershed (n 3) 14.
[218] 'The Monitor' (n 167) 15.
[219] Wincott, Davies and Wager (n 2).
[220] ibid.
[221] Tannam (n 2) 253.
[222] Robert Schütze, 'Subsidiarity After Lisbon: Reinforcing the Safeguards of Federalism?' (2009) 68 The Cambridge Law Journal 525.
[223] Tannam (n 2) 258.
[224] Northern Ireland Assembly, Department for Public Leadership and Social Enterprise (n 80). Murphy and Evershed (n 3) 2; Wincott, Davies and Wager (n 2); Gormley-Heenan and Aughey (n 87); Trumbore and Owsiak (n 45).
[225] 'Operational Programme "United Kingdom – Ireland" – (PEACE III) – Regional Policy – European Commission' (n 157); European Union – European Regional Development Fund (n 157); Northern Ireland Assembly, Department for Public Leadership and Social Enterprise (n 80).

one of most economically depressed area in Europe, the region receives structural financial support from Europe.[226] The region also shares its entire land border with an EU Member State: Ireland. The Republic is Northern Ireland's largest economic partner and one of the fastest growing economies in the EU.[227] Put it simply, Northern Ireland's future is axiomatically entangled with the EU.

The 2020 Protocol on Ireland/Northern Ireland was intended to reduce the negative effects of Brexit on Northern Ireland.[228] The Protocol, also known as the 'Front-stop', took over the previous agreement which was an annex of the Withdrawal Agreement and was commonly referred to as the 'backstop'.[229] However, UK Government, while negotiating with the EU, was not coherently engaged by Northern Irish institutions.[230] Murphy and Evershed argued, for instance, that Northern Irish institutions' endemic dysfunction was the reason for such poor engagement with a crucial regional policy. 'Vulnerable to suspension, collapse and stalemate on select policy issues, Northern Ireland's devolved system was unable to engage effectively with the wider UK Brexit conversation.'[231] Gregory Davies and others go even deeper:[232] they argue that Northern Irish interests were only discussed informally with Unionists, thus making both Protocols unrepresentative.[233] Given the dependant relationship between the Conservatives and Unionists, the result was that the Conservative Government was the sole negotiator for the two Protocols.[234]

Davies' conclusion is echoed by Murphy and Evershed, who focused on the effect of such deals on the Union. '[Brexit] has the potential to portend the end of Northern Ireland's devolved political settlement, as part of a wider possible

---

[226] 'A dedicated North-South body – the Special European Union Programmes Body – implemented the EU Programme for Peace and Reconciliation in Northern Ireland, allocating 2.3 billion euros of funding.' Gormley-Heenan and Aughey (n 87) 449; Northern Ireland Assembly, Department for Public Leadership and Social Enterprise (n 80).

[227] Northern Ireland Assembly, Department for Public Leadership and Social Enterprise (n 80).

[228] European Union (Withdrawal Agreement) Act 2020 c.1.

[229] ibid; Council Decision (EU) 2020/135 on the conclusion of the Agreement on the withdrawal of the United Kingdom of Great Britain and Northern Ireland from the European Union and the European Atomic Energy Community [2020] OJ L029/1; Agreement on the withdrawal of the United Kingdom of Great Britain and Northern Ireland from the European Union and the European Atomic Energy Community [2020] OJ L029/7 [2020] OJ L029/1 Article 187; Protocol on Ireland/Northern Ireland 2020] OJ L029/101.

[230] Murphy and Evershed (n 3) 13.

[231] ibid 9; 13.

[232] Wincott, Davies and Wager (n 2).

[233] ibid 1533; Kenny and Sheldon (n 39) 975.

[234] Wincott, Davies and Wager (n 2) 1533; Kenny and Sheldon (n 39) 975.

disintegration of the UK.'[235] The assertion that the UK system of territorial governance might collapse is not under review in this chapter.[236] There are indications instead that the UK Government is aware of the critiques levelled against the current system, and policies might be adopted in the near future that engage these shortcomings directly.[237] At the time of writing this chapter, however, it is reasonable to suggest that the debacle surrounding the Protocol's negotiations increased the perception of the uniqueness of Northern Ireland within the UK system of governance.[238]

Recall that since the UK joined the EU community in 1972, Northern Ireland and the Republic have been economically and, at least partially, legally unified.[239] The 1998 Belfast Agreement has left the institutional interaction between Northern Ireland and the Republic virtually untouched.[240] 'The Front-stop Protocol has left most of the economic relationship between Northern Ireland and the Republic unaffected by Brexit but has substantially reduced the ability of the British diplomacy to influence EU policies as a third-party state.'[241] The lack of political representation in Brussels has multiple implications for Northern Ireland. Katy Hayward and others describe the effects of EU policies in Northern Ireland after the Protocol in a clear narrative.

> Legislation that will continue to directly affect Northern Ireland (vis-à-vis the rest of the UK as well as the EU) will be decided at the UK–EU level through both the implementation of the Protocol and the future relationship. In a real way, Northern Ireland is at risk of being subject to legislation coming from both Brussels and

---

[235] My Emphasis Murphy and Evershed (n 3) 15.

[236] Alan Trench, 'Tying the UK Together?' in Robert Hazell (ed), *Constitutional Futures Revisited: Britain's Constitution to 2020* (Palgrave Macmillan 2008); McEwen and others (n 141); UK Government (n 142).

[237] Trench (n 236); McEwen and others (n 141); UK Government (n 142).

[238] Morrow (n 4) 20; Wincott, Davies and Wager (n 2) 1533.

[239] Although the border between Northern Ireland and the Republic of Ireland was retained, it was transformed and virtually disappeared as a physical barrier. Cross-border relationships and cooperation were buttressed by all-island institutions, and all-Ireland markets were encouraged. Murphy and Evershed (n 3) 2.

[240] European Union (Withdrawal Agreement) Act 2020 c.1; Council Decision (EU) 2020/135 on the conclusion of the Agreement on the withdrawal of the United Kingdom of Great Britain and Northern Ireland from the European Union and the European Atomic Energy Community [2020] OJ L029/1; Agreement on the withdrawal of the United Kingdom of Great Britain and Northern Ireland from the European Union and the European Atomic Energy Community [2020] OJ L029/7 [2020] OJ L029/1 Article 187; Protocol on Ireland/Northern Ireland 2020] OJ L029/101.

[241] Katy Hayward, David Phinnemore and Milena Komarova, 'Anticipating and Meeting New Multilevel Governance Challenges in Northern Ireland after Brexit' (The UK in a Changing Europe – Queen's University Belfast 2020).

London without having full sight or scrutiny of it, let alone a chance to shape/annul those decisions.[242]

The effect of a substantive democratic gap between the EU and Northern Ireland is compounding an already precarious political situation.[243] Recall that regional democracy in Northern Ireland is faltering,[244] identity-based policies hijack the deliberative process and violent protests are perceived as a legitimate political device to pursue political gains.[245] The process by which the Front-stop Protocol is democratically reviewed by the Assembly does little to add to its perception of democratic illegitimacy. The agreement is for the Assembly to review it every four years and, in cases of cross-community support, every eight years.[246]

The Front-stop Protocol is a permanent source of irritation for the Unionists.[247] Recall that sectarianism is an ideological meaning provider.[248] The establishment of border controls between the UK and Northern Ireland, after the reassurance that such an eventuality would not take place, left a bitter taste in the mouths of Unionists.[249] Many of the Unionists voted in favour of Brexit because of their ideological beliefs and not because of their private interests.[250] At the time of the referendum, Northern Ireland was, and still is, an economically depressed region that relies heavily on European money.[251] For instance, between 2007 and 2014, the EU contributed €240 million via PEACE III and the SEUPB.[252] The PEACE III scheme was followed by the PEACE PLUS

---

[242] ibid.
[243] Marija Bartl, 'The Way We Do Europe: Subsidiarity and the Substantive Democratic Deficit' (2015) 21 European Law Journal 23.
[244] 'The Monitor' (n 167) 14.
[245] Morrow (n 4); Wincott, Davies and Wager (n 2); Gormley-Heenan and Aughey (n 87); McLoughlin (n 40).
[246] Murphy and Evershed (n 3) 11. European Commission and UK Government (n 137). UK Government, Irish Government and EU Commission, 'HM Government, Financing Agreement between the United Kingdom of Great Britain and Northern Ireland, Ireland and the European Commission on the PEACE PLUS Programme 2021–2027, CP 823' (as revised March 2023) 823.
[247] European Union (Withdrawal Agreement) Act 2020 c.1.
[248] Wincott, Davies and Wager (n 2) 1534.
[249] Morrow (n 4) 21.
[250] ibid 17; Gormley-Heenan and Aughey (n 87); Tannam (n 2) 253.
[251] Northern Ireland Assembly, Department for Public Leadership and Social Enterprise (n 80).
[252] Gormley-Heenan and Aughey (n 87) 499; Northern Ireland Assembly, Department for Public Leadership and Social Enterprise (n 80) 13.

scheme which will lapse in 2027.[253] The disturbing implications of this eventuality were lost in the pre-referendum debate. Murphy and Evershed again deliver the analysis of the Brexit campaign in Northern Ireland in a succinct narrative:

> Where Nationalists were wholeheartedly opposed to a UK exit from the EU, Unionists tended, by a factor of 2:1, to favour it ... Northern Ireland's 56% vote in favour of remaining in the EU did not facilitate any coalescing of Unionist and Nationalist positions. Instead, it precipitated the sharpening and hardening of ethno-national dividing lines ... Unionists of all shades moved to support the Leave position, while Nationalist opposition to Brexit crystallized around calls for 'Special Status' for Northern Ireland. As with other issues in Northern Ireland politics, Brexit quickly became starkly 'Orange' versus 'Green'.[254]

There are indications that large numbers of DUP supporters did not comply with the party line and voted in favour of remaining in the EU.[255] However, most Unionists, as deduced from voting statistics, voted to leave the EU.[256] It is no surprise that this is hindering the economic development of a community which is already lagging behind other UK and European regions.

> In other words, [the Protocol] has stoked dissatisfaction with the functionality of devolved governance, re-enlivened the debate about the constitutional future of the island of Ireland, and imbued the question of Irish unity with an urgency it has not had since the height of the Troubles.[257]

In short, Brexit has brought instability to a dysfunctional system of governance.

It is not the aim of this book to suggest future scenarios, yet, in relation to Brexit, it is safe to say that it has destabilising economic, social and political effects on Northern Ireland.[258] The current border arrangements, as well as the ones that might emerge in the near future, will reduce the economic development of the region and indirectly increase the pressure on dysfunctional regional institutions to re-focus on economic development.[259] The question of

---

[253] Clare Rice, 'A Road to Nowhere? The UK's Approach to Implementing the NI Protocol' (*UK in a Changing Europe*, 23 May 2020).
[254] Murphy and Evershed (n 3) 9; Rice (n 253).
[255] Morrow (n 4) 20.
[256] ibid 18.
[257] [My Emphasis] Murphy and Evershed (n 3) 13.
[258] Gormley-Heenan and Aughey (n 87); Tannam (n 2); 'Can Northern Ireland Survive Brexit? – POLITICO'; Giovanni Di Lieto, 'What's the Deal (or No-Deal) with Brexit? Here's Everything Explained' (*The Conversation*); Northern Ireland Assembly, Department for Public Leadership and Social Enterprise (n 80).
[259] Northern Ireland Assembly, Department for Public Leadership and Social Enterprise (n 80).

whether the economic pressure will reduce or increase the fight over resources or stimulate cross-community negotiation is not for this chapter to discuss. It is reasonable to suggest, instead, that Brexit is incrementally changing the conditions that allowed the establishment of the devastating equilibrium system and, for this reason, it has been classified as a positive driver of change for the regional system of governance.

## CONCLUSION

Northern Ireland is still without a functioning government.[260] This has been the case for years. This chapter discussed three drivers of change that, among a plurality of factors, sustain a cycle of legitimation crises in Northern Ireland. The region is experiencing the effects of the 'bumpy ride' scenario forecasted two decades ago by the multidisciplinary experts at the Constitution Unit.[261] Wincott and others use a more poignant term: 'devastating equilibrium'. Both terms, however, describe the same dysfunctional political system in which Northern Irish dysfunctional institutions.[262] The first driver of change considered in the chapter discussed the details of the 1998 process of devolution.[263] I explained that regional and central institutions established by the 1998 devolution facilitated a 'stable' cycle of crises and promoted civic unrest.[264]

The second driver of change discussed in the chapter was the identity-formation process of the Protestants, the Catholics and the Neither group.[265] Sectarianism, as a group, is a recent phenomenon.[266] The current formation of the ideals of the Unionists and Nationalists developed in the 1960s.[267] The identity of the Neither group, which is a demographically larger political community in the region, has recently been consolidated.[268] All three groups might claim a long history but they are a legacy of the recent civil war.[269] The search for identity in Northern Ireland is part of an endless circle in which individuals retreat into an identity group to find stability in a unsafe world.[270] In an ideal homogenous state, a national identity is the default community where

---

[260] 'The Monitor' (n 167) 14.
[261] Wilson and Wilford (n 34) 64.
[262] Wincott, Davies and Wager (n 2).
[263] ibid; Gormley-Heenan and Aughey (n 87).
[264] Morrow (n 4).
[265] Stevenson (n 12) 285.
[266] Bauman (n 168).
[267] Peterson (n 168).
[268] Stevenson (n 12); Zalewski and Barry (n 166); Goddard (n 47); Kennedy-Pipe (n 47).
[269] Stevenson (n 12) ch 8; Morrow (n 4); Gormley-Heenan and Aughey (n 87).
[270] Zygmunt Bauman, *In Search of Politics* (Polity Press 1999).

individuals find meaning, and there is a direct connection between loyalty to a group and instability.[271] In the case of Northern Ireland, leaders of sectarian communities have taken over the role of safety and meaning providers.[272] The existence of these meaning providers is dependent on a lingering fear which the leadership cultivates by provoking the 'Other' group.[273] These provocations trigger reactions which aliment more fear, making the identity-formation process self-sustaining.[274] The Neither group embraces political apathy.[275] This group is statistically composed of female professionals who have grown tired of paramilitary parades, violence and political squabbling.[276] The lack of personal investment in the regional politics of the Neither group sustains the cycle of crises.[277]

The third driver of change considered in this chapter focused on the effects of Brexit in Northern Ireland.[278] The 'Front-stop' Protocol has spared Northern Ireland from some of the effects of Brexit.[279] There are rational reasons for making a special case for Northern Ireland. For instance, the current peace process is dependent, among other factors, on direct economic support from the EU.[280] The regional economy is depressed, and it relies heavily on trade with Ireland, which is one of the richest EU members.[281] In short, every resident in the region benefits directly or indirectly from an open border with Ireland.[282] The 'Front-stop' is, however, contested by part of Northern Ireland's popula-

---

[271] ibid.
[272] Morrow (n 4).
[273] O'Leary and McGarry (n 173); Wincott, Davies and Wager (n 2).
[274] Wilson and Wilford (n 34); Wincott, Davies and Wager (n 2); Cochrane (n 22).
[275] Hayward and McManus (n 30).
[276] ibid 142.
[277] Hayward and McManus (n 30).
[278] Gormley-Heenan and Aughey (n 87); Tannam (n 2); Kenny and Sheldon (n 39).
[279] European Union (Withdrawal Agreement) Act 2020 c.1; Council Decision (EU) 2020/135 on the conclusion of the Agreement on the withdrawal of the United Kingdom of Great Britain and Northern Ireland from the European Union and the European Atomic Energy Community [2020] OJ L029/1; Agreement on the withdrawal of the United Kingdom of Great Britain and Northern Ireland from the European Union and the European Atomic Energy Community [2020] OJ L029/7 [2020] OJ L029/1 Article 187; Protocol on Ireland/Northern Ireland 2020] OJ L029/101.
[280] 'A dedicated North-South body – the Special European Union Programmes Body – implemented the EU Programme for Peace and Reconciliation in Northern Ireland, allocating 2.3 billion euros of funding.' Gormley-Heenan and Aughey (n 87) 449; Northern Ireland Assembly, Department for Public Leadership and Social Enterprise (n 80).
[281] Northern Ireland Assembly, Department for Public Leadership and Social Enterprise (n 80).
[282] ibid.

tion because it has a symbolic effect on the regional identity-making process.[283] The riots and the negotiations related to the Brexit saga in Northern Ireland are a manifestation of the devastating equilibrium system discussed earlier in this chapter. I explained that Brexit has increased the awareness among all Northern Irish residents that Northern Ireland is unique.[284] Such an awareness pre-existed Brexit, yet the 'Front-stop' is a constant reminder that neither the UK nor Ireland perceive the rescuing of the region as part of their identity process.[285]

In conclusion, the three drivers of change discussed here are a small selection of a range of factors that are affecting the cycle of crises of governance in Northern Ireland. The devastating equilibrium, which is the favoured system of governance, is fostering patrimonialism within the sectarian groups and apathy in the Neither group.[286] The institutions established by the Belfast Agreement are inducive of a predictable yet devastating equilibrium.[287] Given that internally, identity politics are helped by the instability of the current institutional setting, there is little interest in any future institutional reform.[288]

---

[283] Wincott, Davies and Wager (n 2) 1533; Kenny and Sheldon (n 39) 975.
[284] Northern Ireland Assembly, Department for Public Leadership and Social Enterprise (n 80).
[285] ibid.
[286] Wilson and Wilford (n 34).
[287] Guelke (n 71); Wincott, Davies and Wager (n 2).
[288] Murphy and Evershed (n 3) 9, 20.; Rice (n 253).

## 2. Spain: Spanish legitimacy after the end of political violence in the Basque Country

### INTRODUCTION

This chapter discusses the constitutional drivers of change that led to the cessation of political violence in the Autonomous Community of the Basque Country (hereafter, the Basque Country).[1] In 2011, whilst comparative lawyers were still discussing whether the Spanish Constitutional Court was right to deny the status of a nation to the Catalans,[2] a paramilitary organisation in the Basque Country called Basque Euskadi Ta Askatasuna (hereafter, ETA) announced a permanent ceasefire.[3] The ETA announcement officially ended the last overt violent struggle for independence in Western Europe.[4]

It might appear that the end of the crisis of governability partially overlapped with the start of another.[5] In the decade that followed the normalisation of Basque politics, Catalonia experienced one of the deepest crises

---

[1] Spanish Parliament, Ley Orgánica 3/1979, de 18 de Diciembre, de Estatuto de Autonomía Para El País Vasco (1979) <http://e-spacio.uned.es/fez/eserv/bibliuned:BFD-1980-5-3060/PDF>; Spanish Parliament, Ley 7/2014, de 21 de Abril, Por La Que Se Modifica La Ley 12/2002, de 23 de Mayo, Por La Que Se Aprueba El Concierto Económico Con La Comunidad Autónoma Del País Vasco (2014).

[2] Constitutional Court Decision n31 28/06/2010 172 (Suplemento 11409) BOE 1 (Constitutional Court).

[3] Euskadi Ta Askatasuna, 'Declaración de ETA (8.1.2011)'; Luis R Aizpeolea, 'ETA pone fin a 43 años de terror' *El País* (Madrid, 20 October 2011).

[4] Julen Zabalo and Iker Iraola, 'Current Discourses and Attitudes in Favour of the Independence of the Basque Country' (2022) 32 Regional & Federal Studies 73; Xabier Itçaina, 'Catholic Mediation in the Basque Peace Process: Questioning the Transnational Dimension' (2020) 11 Religions 216.

[5] Alejandro Quiroga and Fernando Molina, 'National Deadlock. Hot Nationalism, Dual Identities and Catalan Independence (2008–2019)' (2020) 4 Genealogy 15, 9. For an economic implications of dual crisis of the Spanish system of governance see: David Gardner, 'Why Basques and Catalans See Independence Differently' *Financial Times* (12 July 2019).

of legitimacy for a West European region.[6] The Government of Catalonia, following the result of a consultive referendum over secession from Spain, declared independence.[7] The referendum was declared unconstitutional by the Constitutional Court, and the members of Catalonia Executive who declared independence were arrested or had to escape overseas.[8] During the interval of time that preceded the disbandment of the Catalonian Parliament, the Spanish Government wantonly and strategically precluded any deliberative activities that could have solved the crisis.[9]

The Catalonia crisis will not be discussed in this chapter,[10] but the failed attempt at unilateral secession and its violent repression provide an indication of a lingering tension between central and regional institutions in Spain. The chapter will focus instead on the crisis of legitimacy of the Basque Country. In particular, the chapter will analyse two drivers of change. The first is the effect of an imprecise constitutional system of territorial governance.[11] The second driver of change is the legacy of a lengthy period of political violence as an element that defines Basque nationalism.[12] Both drivers of change have negative effects on the perception of the legitimacy of the Spanish institutions in the Basque Country.

Before the analysis of the two drivers of change are discussed in detail, a series of issues have to be engaged as part of a preliminary debate. First, the Basque nation includes a community of circa three million people residing in

---

[6] Marta Soler Alemany, 'Catalonia from Autonomy to Self-Determination' in Brian Fong and Atsuko Ichijo (eds), *The Routledge Handbook of Comparative Territorial Autonomies* (Routledge 2022); Quiroga and Molina (n 5); Paul Williams and others, 'The Legitimacy of Catalonia's Exercise of Its Right to Decide: A Report by a Commission of International Experts' (Global Studies Institute University of Geneva – Departament d'Afers i Relacions Institucionals i Exteriors i Transparència 2017); Joseph Weiler, 'A Nation of Nations?' (2019) 17 International Journal of Constitutional Law 1301; Hèctor López Bofill, 'A Nation of Nations? A Reply to Joseph H. H. Weiler' (2019) 17 International Journal of Constitutional Law 1315; Hèctor López Bofill, 'Hubris, Constitutionalism, and "the Indissoluble Unity of the Spanish Nation": A Rejoinder to Antonio Bar' (2019) 17 International Journal of Constitutional Law 984.

[7] Soler Alemany (n 6); Williams and others (n 6); Constitutional Court (Spain), *Recurso: 1638–2017* (2017).

[8] Williams and others (n 6); Court (Spain) (n 7).

[9] Williams and others (n 6); Zabalo and Iraola (n 4) 77.

[10] For a recent update see: Soler Alemany (n 6).

[11] Enric Espadaler Fossas, 'El principio dispositivo en el Estado autonómico' (2008) 71–72 Revista de Derecho Político 151.

[12] Rogelio Alonso, 'Why Do Terrorists Stop? Analyzing Why ETA Members Abandon or Continue with Terrorism' (2011) 34 Studies in Conflict & Terrorism 696; Anthony Spencer and Stephen Croucher, 'Basque nationalism and the Spiral of Silence: An Analysis of Public Perceptions of ETA in Spain and France' (2008) 70 International Communication Gazette 137.

the North Eastern part of the Pyrenees.[13] The ethnic group is divided into six provinces.[14] Three of these provinces are in Spain and three are in the French Republic (hereafter, France).[15] This chapter will consider only the Spanish provinces.[16] The Southern Basque Country also includes the autonomous region of Navarra with its capital Pamplona, made famous by Hemingway's *The Sun Also Rises*.[17] Basque nationalism demands the unification of all the Basque provinces, but in this book, I will focus on the Autonomous Basque Country.[18] The economic capital of the Autonomous Basque Country is Bilbao, which is also the largest city, but the political capital is the city of Vitoria-Gasteiz.[19]

Second, throughout modern history, the Basques have developed a distinctive ability to resist the effect of historical cycles that are part of the Spanish nation-building process.[20] The social features that are associated with the Basque nation are a historical claim of fiscal autonomy which is linked to a regional administration based on royal charters (*fueros*),[21] a unique non-Indo-European language[22] and a tendency to favour conservative Catholic stances.[23] Whether Basque particularism was the result of a tendency for self-governance or whether self-governance was the result of a shared culture is a chicken and egg question.[24] It is, however, important to note that a combination of the two processes (a level of autonomy and a claim of uniqueness) are currently entangled.[25]

---

[13] Soler Alemany (n 6) 133; Ludger Mees, 'Ethnogenesis in the Pyrenees: The Contentious Making of a National Identity in the Basque Country (1643–2017)' (2018) 48 European History Quarterly 462, 463.

[14] Mees (n 13) 463, 469.

[15] Manuel Castells and Gurutz Jauregui, 'Political Autonomy and Conflict Resolution: The Basque Case' in Kumar Rupesinghe and VA Tishkov (eds), *Ethnicity and Power in the Contemporary World* (United Nations University Press 1996) 210.

[16] Spencer and Croucher (n 12) 137.

[17] Ernest Hemingway, *The Sun Also Rises* (Hemingway Library edition, Scribner Book Company 2016).

[18] Alonso (n 12) 697; Castells and Jauregui (n 15) 218.

[19] Víctor Aparicio Rodríguez, 'The Basque Country', in *The Routledge Handbook of Comparative Territorial Autonomies* (Routledge 2022) 134.

[20] Mees (n 13) 463; Soler Alemany (n 6) 133.

[21] Soler Alemany (n 6) 137; Mees (n 13) 465.

[22] Zabalo and Iraola (n 4) 75; Mees (n 13) 465; Soler Alemany (n 6) 137.

[23] Mees (n 13) 463; Sebastian Balfour and Alejandro Quiroga, *The Reinvention of Spain: Nation and Identity since Democracy* (Oxford University Press 2007) 128; Soler Alemany (n 6) 133.

[24] Julen Zabalo Bilbao and Onintza Odriozola Irizar, 'The Importance of Historical Context: A New Discourse on the Nation in Basque Nationalism?' (2017) 23 Nationalism & Ethnic Politics 134, 148.

[25] Balfour and Quiroga (n 23) 128; Alonso (n 12) 697.

Third, the 2011 ETA permanent ceasefire was coupled to a process of demilitarisation supervised by an International Verification Committee.[26] It was not the first time that ETA had gone through an existential crisis.[27] Between 1981 and 1983, a high number of ETA members left the movement. They did so for many reasons. It is reasonable to suggest that a few of its members were persuaded that the Spanish dominion over the Basques had ended.[28] The ETA-named *político-militar* also disbanded.[29] However, it was substituted by the ETA *militar*, which simply renamed itself as 'ETA'. At this time, the Herri Batasuna political party acted as the principal ETA's political intermediary.[30] During the 1980s, a large group of former ETA members (that is, over 300) took advantage of the reinsertion into civil life programme offered by the Spanish Government, but the ETA leadership labelled the defectors as traitors and several were killed.[31] The key difference between the 2018 crisis and the 1981 crisis is that in 2018, ETA had lost its credibility as a secessionist movement.[32] In 2018, in a document sent to El País, ETA declared its disbandment: 'With communication we want to inform you of the decision that Euskadi Ta Askatasuna has just taken. ETA has decided to end its historical cycle and its function, putting an end to its journey. Therefore, ETA has completely dissolved all its structures and has terminated its political activities.'[33] However, I will explain about the ETA victimhood narrative, which is one of the many elements of the Basque identity-formation process that is still lingering and that has a negative effect on the political interaction between central and regional institutions.[34]

---

[26] Itçaina (n 4) 15; Soler Alemany (n 6) 134; Euskadi Ta Askatasuna (n 3).
[27] Aizpeolea (n 3).
[28] Alonso (n 12) 699.
[29] Soler Alemany (n 6) 134.
[30] Alonso (n 12) 699.
[31] ibid 702.
[32] Alonso (n 12); Spencer and Croucher (n 12).
[33] 'Por medio de esta comunicación os queremos dar a conocer la decisión que Euskadi Ta Askatasuna acaba de tomar. ETA ha decido dar por terminados su ciclo histórico y su función, dando fin a su recorrido. Por tanto, ETA ha disuelto completamente todas sus estructuras y ha dado por terminada su iniciativa política' (author translation); Euskadi Ta Askatasuna, 'La carta en la que ETA anuncia su disolución'.
[34] Alonso (n 12); Spencer and Croucher (n 12); Mees (n 13).

## NEGATIVE DRIVER OF CHANGE: AN IMPRECISE CONSTITUTION

The text of the Spanish Constitution is the result of mediation between civic society and the military junta.[35] It was not an ideal setting for a deliberative activity, and one among the many unresolved issues was related to the recognition of regional entities such as the Basque Country.[36]

The level of indeterminism intrinsic in a rule and debate over its implications is an old jurisprudential chestnut which has been well covered by legal theorists like HLA Hart, Neil MacCormick and, more recently, by legal semiotic and natural language analysts.[37] The clusters of debate do not need to be reproduced here, but it is important to say that extreme relativistic stances and those who advocate for true objective interpretation are both unplausible.[38] Legal textual interpretations consciously or unconsciously follow relatively narrow interpretative rules that linguists, like Stephen Levinson, associate with a branch of semiotics called 'pragmatism'.[39] Skoczeń explains, for instance, that legal interpretation, in the majority of instances, is much narrower than that deduced by critical legal philosophers.[40] There is no need to dig too deep into the analysis. Suffice to say that in each legal system, a cluster of cognitive interpretative practices are adopted in reading constitutional norms.[41] A precise use of words is therefore critical because it narrows (but does not exclude) the spectrum of interpretations that judges accept as a reasonable interpretative activity.[42]

---

[35] Soler Alemany (n 6) 134.

[36] Spanish Constitution 1978.

[37] HLA Hart, *The Concept of Law* (Penelope A Bulloch and Joseph Raz eds, 3rd edn, Oxford University Press 2012); Neil MacCormick, *Legal Reasoning and Legal Theory* (Clarendon Press 1994); Izabela Skoczeń, 'Minimal Semantics and Legal Interpretation' (2016) 29 International Journal for the Semiotics of Law – Revue internationale de Sémiotique juridique 615; Sol Azuelos-Atias, 'Semantically Cued Contextual Implicatures in Legal Texts' (2010) 42 Journal of Pragmatics 728.

[38] Hart (n 37) 121.

[39] Stephen Levinson, *Pragmatics* (Cambridge University Press 1983); Skoczeń (n 37); Marek Zirk-Sadowski, 'Interpretation of Law and Judges Communities' (2012) 25 International Journal for the Semiotics of Law – Revue internationale de Sémiotique juridique 473.

[40] James Boyle, 'The Politics of Reason: Critical Legal Theory and Local Social Thought' (1985) 133 University of Pennsylvania Law Review 685.

[41] Pierre Legrand, 'Against a European Civil Code' (1997) 60 The Modern Law Review 44.

[42] Azuelos-Atias (n 37).

Rules do indeed project a penumbra of uncertainty.[43] Constitutional rules, in comparison to the administrative rules that prevent vehicles from entering into a park, are more general. It is so for good reasons.[44] Rules have to be adapted to fit new emerging needs. However, there are areas of public law, like territorial governance, where the fluctuation of jurisprudential interpretations of the constitutional text might tear a political system apart.[45]

The Spanish Constitution is, for historical reasons, extraordinarily imprecise.[46] To begin with, the system of governance and the regions that are beneficiaries of decentralised powers are not clearly named.[47] Belfour and Quiroga describe the process that formed the 1978 Constitution in a succinct narrative:

> the 1978 Constitution was a feat of semantic engineering and political consensus, facilitating the perception that alternative narratives of Spanish nationalism and regional nationalisms could coexist. ... Yet each party involved in the negotiation of the Constitution sought to assert opposed concepts of nation, identity, and state within the perceived limits of the democratic settlement, all of which were diluted.[48]

The lack of precision in defining national identities was, according to the two authors, intentional.[49] The term 'Spanish nation', for instance, is defined in the text as an overarching shared identity that did not exist in 1978 (nor does it now).[50] The national identities, instead, that were historically part of multinational Spain, were decanted into a new sociological genus: the nationalities.[51] Neither of the two categories, that is, the Spanish nation and the nationalities, contributed to the formation of a multinational constitution for Spain.[52]

The Constitution makes a reference, for instance, to the Spanish nation in Section 2 (1) and to the nationalities in the second paragraph of the same

---

[43] Hart (n 37) 120–23.
[44] Michel Rosenfeld, *The Identity of the Constitutional Subject* (Routledge 2010).
[45] Fernando Molina and Alejandro Quiroga, 'Mixed Feelings: Identities and Nationalisations in Catalonia and the Basque Country (1980–2015)' (2019) 21 National Identities 93; López Bofill, 'Hubris, Constitutionalism, and "The Indissoluble Unity of the Spanish Nation"' (n 6).
[46] Hèctor López Bofill, 'Hubris, Constitutionalism, and "the Indissoluble Unity of the Spanish Nation": The Repression of Catalan Secessionist Referenda in Spanish Constitutional Law' (2019) 17 International Journal of Constitutional Law 943.
[47] Soler Alemany (n 6) 133.
[48] Balfour and Quiroga (n 23) 46.
[49] ibid 51. The system of territorial governance currently includes 17 autonomous regions, three historical nationalities (the Basque Country, Galicia and Catalonia), and two autonomous cities in Morocco.
[50] Spanish Parliament Cortes Generales, *Spanish Constitution* (1978) Article 2.
[51] Balfour and Quiroga (n 23) 51; Molina and Quiroga (n 45).
[52] Balfour and Quiroga (n 23) 59.

article.[53] The Basque Country and Navarra are the only sub-state entities that are mentioned in the Transitional Provisions, but not in a way that directly indicates a level of self-government or recognition.[54] Article 151 granted them a fast-track process for the recognition of administrative and legislative competences that was intended exclusively for the historical nationalities, but there is no mention of which nationality might be qualified as an historical nationality.[55] Instead, Article 5 of the Transitional Provisions qualified the *órgano foral* as the deliberative and executive name for the new autonomous regions.[56] However, the most consequential of the Transitional Provisions for the Basque Country was the repeal of the Act of October 25 (1839), which at the time disbanded the *foral* systems.[57] The result of the 'repeal of the repeal' was to reinstate the *órgano foral*. The pre-modern deliberative institutions had the prerogative to collect the bulk of the inland revenues in the Basque Region. That mediaeval prerogative was revived by the repel of the repeal: '[t]o the extent that it may still retain some validity, the Act of October 25, 1839, shall be definitively repealed in so far as it applies to the provinces of Alava, Guipúzcoa and Vizcaya'.[58] As a recognition of one of the most extensive manifestations of fiscal federalism in Europe, it is difficult to imagine a more oblique acknowledgement.[59]

Sebastian Balfour and Alejandro Quiroga summarise the general themes that emerged from the 1978 Constitution as a contradictory mediation between diverging ideological stances: '[t]he territorial model envisaged by the Constitution is thus based on an underlying contradiction rather than complementarity between regional and state-wide governance'.[60] The lack of clarity had multiple repercussions in the national administrative structure, but it had the most overt implications on those regions like the Basque Country that did not 'buy into' the idea of the unity of the Spanish nation.

> The moderate nationalist Basque parliamentary group also attempted to amend 'unity' to 'union', probably in order to attribute a voluntary and multinational character to the constitutional definition of Spain ... Since all parties (except the nationalists in the Basque Country and Catalonia) accepted the notion of Spain as a nation, such demands were consciously rhetorical.[61]

---

[53] Generales (n 50).
[54] Balfour and Quiroga (n 23) 59.
[55] Generales (n 50).
[56] ibid.
[57] Soler Alemany (n 6) 134.
[58] Generales (n 50).
[59] Balfour and Quiroga (n 23) 58.
[60] ibid 60.
[61] ibid 127.

In other words, the newly enacted 1978 Constitution was tasked to do to many things and ended up doing all of them precariously.[62]

The Constitution signalled the end of tyranny, created the conditions for Spain to join the European Economic Community and established a new form of social democracy.[63] Yet there was no process of reconciliation, no reference to crimes against humanity or demands for forgiveness for the atrocities committed by the lapsed regime.[64]

> The new Constitution and the rule of law in the new democracy were thus based on a wilful amnesia. Any reference to the democratic legality against which sections of the army rose in 1936 and the repression the Franco regime exercised for almost forty years was barred from the text as part of the supposed price of democracy.[65]

That was a bad deal for many of the victims, but it was a particularly bitter blow for the Basques. Many Basques violently opposed the regime and, by comparison to other Spanish sub-state nationalities, suffered disproportionally during Franco's dictatorship. I will return to this point in the next part of this chapter, but the Basques still perceive the 1978 Constitution as a betrayal of the memory of their martyrs.[66] In this section, it is important to note that the 1978 Constitution only obliquely recognised a distinctive role for historical nationalities.

That lack of clarity had immediate pragmatic consequences. Article 151, for instance, granted a fast-track process of recognition to the unnamed historical nationalities like Galicia, Catalunya and the Basque Country.[67] The lack of a specific list of historical nationalities was construed by a left-wing party in Andalusia as a reason to demand the inclusion of Andalusia in the regions that benefited from the fast-track recognition system set in Article 151.[68] In 2006, Valencia self-proclaimed itself as an additional historical nationality in its new 2006 Statute of Autonomy.[69] Again, the Spanish Parliament approved the statute.[70]

---

[62] ibid 64.
[63] Alonso (n 12) 700.
[64] ibid.
[65] Balfour and Quiroga (n 23) 43.
[66] Quiroga and Molina (n 5) 9; Spencer and Croucher (n 12).
[67] Spanish Constitution; Balfour and Quiroga (n 23) 53.
[68] Ley Orgánica 6/1981, de 30 de diciembre, de Estatuto de Autonomía para Andalucía 1982 517; Balfour and Quiroga (n 23) 60.
[69] Balfour and Quiroga (n 23) 106; Ley Orgánica 1/2006, de 10 de abril, de Reforma de la Ley Orgánica 5/1982, de 1 de julio, de Estatuto de Autonomía de la Comunidad Valenciana 2006 13934 Articles: 1(1), 4 (5), 63.
[70] Ley Orgánica 1/2006, de 10 de abril, de Reforma de la Ley Orgánica 5/1982, de 1 de julio, de Estatuto de Autonomía de la Comunidad Valenciana.

The ambiguity of the Constitution extends to the list of legislative competences that are reserved for the central state (Article 149) and for the regions (Article 148).[71] A region can, for instance, organise cultural events which might promote the regional language.[72] Article 149 instead includes a list of sovereignty powers, such as the monetary policy and defence.[73] However, the list of central state competences has been interpreted as a 'closed list', whereas the list of regional heads of power was considered open.[74] Given that there was no indication of which region should be the beneficiary of these legislative powers, and there were no limits on the competences (outside of those set in Article 149), most of the regions opted to collect all unnamed legislative prerogatives.[75] This process is considered one of the manifestations of the dispositive principle.[76] The application of the dispositive principle was, and still is, a proxy for claiming new and more extensive clusters of regional legislative prerogatives.[77]

It is clear that the drafters did not intend to create such a mindboggling system of governance: '[i]t is this contradiction that has given rise to a dynamic of competitive federalism and comparative grievance that has taken everyone by surprise. The autonomies have been demanding the devolution of ever more competencies from the central state'.[78] Hundreds of these demands reached the Constitutional Court, creating, as far as I know, one of the most

---

[71] Spanish Constitution; Alberto Garrido and M Ramon Llamas (eds), *Water Policy in Spain* (1st edn, CRC Press 2009).
[72] Generales (n 50) Article 148; Parliament, Ley Orgánica 3/1979, de 18 de Diciembre, de Estatuto de Autonomía Para El País Vasco (n 1).
[73] Generales (n 50) ss 149, 11, 4.
[74] Espadaler Fossas (n 11).
[75] Balfour and Quiroga (n 23) 61; Carles Viver, 'Spain's Constitution and Statutes of Autonomy: Explaining the Evolution of Political Decentralization' in Michael Burgess and G Alan Tarr (eds), *Constitutional Dynamics in Federal Systems: Sub-national Perspectives* (MQUP 2012); Ley Orgánica 7/1982 30 de julio, de Armonización del Proceso Autonómico (LOAPA) 198; Decision 76/1983, de 5 de agosto (BOE núm 197, de 18 de agosto de 1983); Ley 12/1983, de 14 de octubre, del Proceso Autonómico. 1985 1.
[76] Balfour and Quiroga (n 23) 61; Viver (n 75); Ley Orgánica 7/1982 30 de julio, de Armonización del Proceso Autonómico (LOAPA) 198; Decision 76/1983, de 5 de agosto (BOE núm. 197, de 18 de agosto de 1983) (n 75); Ley 12/1983, de 14 de octubre, del Proceso Autonómico. 1.
[77] Enric Espadaler Fossas, 'El Control de Constitucionalitat Dels Estatuts d'autonomia' (2011) Revista catalana de dret públic 21.
[78] Balfour and Quiroga (n 23) 60.

prolonged and heaviest jurisprudential loads related to regional border disputes in a Western-style democracy.[79]

The dispute between regions and central institutions often defined new powers which were punctually claimed by regional institutions by reference to the dispositive principle.[80] However, the extraordinary flexibility of the dispositive principle is limited by the assumption that Spain is composed only of the Spanish nation and inferior nationalities, which harmoniously convive within the same political system.[81] However, historic nationalities do not perceive themselves as inferior.[82]

The 1981 harmonisation processes increased both the animosity against the central state by historic nations, such as the Basques, and legal conflicts between ordinary regions.[83] The harmonisation was perceived as another 'slap in the face' by the historical nations.[84] This is, once more, particularly the case in the Basque Region, which has, exactly for historical reasons, never accepted the idea of convivence as an inferior nationality within the Spanish identity[85] and where symbols of Spanish nationalism are ostracised by private individuals and political institutions.[86] The insistence on using the concept of the 'Spanish nation' as an hegemonic ideology for all citizens by the Constitutional Court and by central institutions contributes to a sense of alienation in the Basque population. It also add to a perception of the unrepresentativeness of central institutions in the autonomous region.[87] This has a negative effect on the future development of the institutional relations between central and Basque regional institutions, and it is one of the negative drivers of change that distinguishes the interaction between Bilbao and Madrid.[88]

---

[79] Francesc Morata and Lucia Popartan, 'Spain' in Michael J Baun and Dan Marek (eds), *EU Cohesion Policy after Enlargement* (Palgrave Macmillan 2008) 73.

[80] Espadaler Fossas (n 11) 152.

[81] López Bofill, 'Hubris, Constitutionalism, and "the Indissoluble Unity of the Spanish Nation"' (n 46); Balfour and Quiroga (n 23) 56; Espadaler Fossas (n 11).

[82] Balfour and Quiroga (n 23) 60.

[83] ibid 61. Ley Orgánica 7/1982 30 de julio, de Armonización del Proceso Autonómico (LOAPA).

[84] Molina and Quiroga (n 45) 95; Balfour and Quiroga (n 23) 61.

[85] Molina and Quiroga (n 45) 105.

[86] ibid 94; Spencer and Croucher (n 12); Ekain Rojo-Labaien, 'Football and the Representation of Basque Identity in the Contemporary Age' (2017) 18 Soccer & Society 63, 72.

[87] Zabalo and Iraola (n 4) 90.

[88] The administrative capital of the region is Victoria.

## NEGATIVE DRIVER OF CHANGE: ETA'S SYMBOLIC LEGACY

The Spanish Constitution is a manifestation of one of the most advanced European grand constitutional projects.[89] However, the system of governance that is included in the text is hindered by incongruences. The rules are ambiguous, and the dispositive principle has been a proxy for an overcomplicated system of territorial governance that is precariously limited by, among other elements, a contrafactual idea which gives the Spanish identity normative priority over regional national identities.[90] In this part of the chapter, I will discuss the legacy of ETA violence. I will explain that several decades of political violence had the effect of reshaping the Basque national identity in a way that has hindered the development of institutions that represent a multinational society.[91]

The current effect of ETA activities in the Basque identity-building process is explained eloquently by Molina and Quirota: 'ETA's violence retained its "pedagogic" function in terms of excluding Spanish national symbols and hampering public identification with Spain on a daily basis. Notwithstanding ETA's declaration of a permanent ceasefire in October 2011, violence continued to cast a long shadow over Basque society.'[92] The idea that political violence has a pedagogical function might indicate a positive legacy that most studies,[93] including this one, find uneasy to accept.[94] However, it is a part of the elemental ideological structure of nationalism to make reference to violence and martyrdom.[95] The complex relation between the ideology of Basque

---

[89] Morata and Popartan (n 79); Aparicio Rodríguez (n 19); Espadaler Fossas (n 77).
[90] Espadaler Fossas (n 11); Generales (n 50) Article 2; Balfour and Quiroga (n 23) 106.
[91] Zabalo and Iraola (n 4) 90; Michael Keating, 'So Many Nations, so Few States: Territory and Nationalism in the Global Era' in James Tully and Alain Gagnon (eds), *Multinational Democracies* (Cambridge University Press 2001).
[92] Molina and Quiroga (n 45) 94.
[93] Claus Offe, *Varieties of Transition: The East European and East German Experience* (MIT Press 1997); Jürgen Habermas, 'The European Nation State. Its Achievements and Its Limitations. On the Past and Future of Sovereignty and Citizenship' (1996) 9 Ratio Juris 125; Karlo Basta, 'The State between Minority and Majority Nationalism: Decentralization, Symbolic Recognition, and Secessionist Crises in Spain and Canada' (2018) 48 Publius: The Journal of Federalism 51.
[94] Alonso (n 12) 704; Spencer and Croucher (n 12).
[95] Fernando Reinares, 'Nationalist Separatism and Terrorism in Comparative Perspective' in Tore Bjorge (ed), *Root Causes of Terrorism: Myths, Reality and Ways Forward* (Routledge 2005). 128; Habermas (n 93).

nationalism and political violence is described by Mees in an unsettling narrative:

> The worship of ETA and its priests, i.e. the activists in the underground, the prisoners and the fallen soldiers, was regularly celebrated in public meetings and ritual practices, which in some sense might be described as Sironneau's 'sacred ceremonies'. They were reproduced by a great number of initiatives and organizations that made up the broad network of radical pro-ETA nationalism. Including the complete subordination of the individual to the (national) faith.[96]

The images of ETA martyrs displayed in little stalls at local festivals might not have the grandeur of the London Cenotaph or the Roman Altar of the Fatherland, but the functional effect of remembering those who died for the homeland is a common element of nationalist natives the world over. It might be easy to pick holes in the deductive reasoning derived from an ideology like nationalism.[97] However, monuments to won battles, mausoleums dedicated to unknown soldiers and flags are part of multiple aspects of most modern societies in which citizens are expected to acknowledge and sanctify the violent exegesis of their national identity.[98] Historically, Basque nationalism had similar expectations from its supporters.[99]

After the end of the dictatorship, ETA relinquished its racist narrative but maintained a strong connection with a reactionary form of Catholicism.[100] The idolatry of martyrdom is a powerful and easy-to-deliver narrative that is charged with emotional meaning. The pictures of martyrs were often displayed at local festivals in stalls which collected financial support for the independent movement.[101]

> Under the influence of the writings of Fanon, Mao, Che Guevara and others and with the success of third-world national liberation movements as its reference, ETA adopted the revolutionary-war model of colonized countries and tailored it

---

[96] Mees (n 13) 476.
[97] Claus Offe, '"Homogeneity" and Constitutional Democracy: Coping with Identity Conflicts through Group Rights' (1998) 6 Journal of Political Philosophy 113, 120; Elie Kedourie, *Nationalism* (Hutchinson 1960) 18; Jurgen Habermas, *Between Facts and Norms: Contributions to a Discourse Theory of Law and Democracy* (William Rehg ed, reprint edn, The MIT Press 1998) 111–115; Lior Erez, 'Patriotism, Nationalism, and the Motivational Critique of Cosmopolitanism', in *Handbook of Patriotism* (Springer 2018); Mees (n 13) 475.
[98] Ernest Renan, *What Is a Nation?* (Presses-Pocket 1882).
[99] Zabalo Bilbao and Odriozola Irizar (n 24) 138; Mees (n 13) 475.
[100] Zabalo Bilbao and Odriozola Irizar (n 24) 140.
[101] Paddy Woodworth, *Dirty War, Clean Hands: ETA, the GAL and Spanish Democracy* (Cork University Press 2001).

to Basque reality in order to respond to what it called the dual contradiction of the Basque revolution: national liberation and social liberation.[102]

ETA was both a revolutionary and reactionary political movement, and the Northeast region of the Basque Country provided an ideal topography for a violent secessionist organisation. The Northeast region of the Basque Country includes hundreds of villages situated relatively close to the French border in the mountainous region of the Northern Pyrenees.[103] The support for ETA also spread to Bilbao, where Spanish immigration triggered the usual xenophobic rhetoric generated by economic diasporas in advanced economies.[104]

Overall, the level of popular support for ETA is difficult to quantify. It is plausible that many Basque nationalists had an ambivalent stance in relation to the armed struggle.[105] It is not easy to discern whether this support involved genuine sympathy towards the extreme manifestations of nationalism or a cynical attempt to corral electoral support from the fringes of democracy which might have gone somewhere else. It is reasonably clear that the majority of the Basque population supported, and still support, a moderate and democratic idea of national identity as represented by the Basque nationalist Party (hereafter, the PNV).[106]

What was distinctive of the Basque Country, by comparison to other Spanish autonomous regions, was how violence was perceived.[107] This was the case, among other reasons, because in a distinctive social context that supported Basque ethnic nationalism, there was little space for Smiths' polycentric national identity. A polycentric national identity presupposes a mutual interaction between peers, negotiating diversity and respect for human rights.[108] Instead, the popular support for ETA relied on a combination of narratives of Spanish betrayal and victimhood which were not deeply questioned until the events of 11 September 2001.[109]

> After the end of the Francoist dictatorship, ETA became a totalitarian organization because it refused to accept the basic norms of liberal democracy by establishing centralized control (by the military leadership) over all its followers, rejecting and even physically eliminating all opposing political and cultural dissidences, aiming

---

[102] Zabalo Bilbao and Odriozola Irizar (n 24) 141.
[103] Mees (n 13) 472.
[104] Zabalo Bilbao and Odriozola Irizar (n 24) 142.
[105] Zabalo and Iraola (n 4) 90; Spencer and Croucher (n 12).
[106] Basque Government, 'Archivo de resultados electorales. Presentación'.
[107] Zabalo and Iraola (n 4).
[108] Alonso (n 12) 705; Zabalo Bilbao and Odriozola Irizar (n 24) 136; Anthony D Smith, *Nationalism: Theory, Ideology, History* (Polity Press; Blackwell 2001) 17.
[109] Alonso (n 12) 705; Molina and Quiroga (n 45) 128.

to achieve political goals at any cost and legitimizing the use of violence against all the enemies of the nation.[110]

Al Qaeda's attacks against the United States changed the attitude towards political violence in Spain and in neighbouring France.[111] France had, for several decades, tolerated the presence of ETA members who used the bordering regions with Spain as a safe haven for its supporters and for storing its military arsenal.[112]

The 9/11 attack was a watershed moment in the history of Basque political violence.[113] In the year that followed the attack on the Twin Towers, the support for political violence decreased, yet ETA continued to organise multiple attacks against Spanish tourist infrastructure, such as museums and airports.[114] The aim of these attacks was to damage the Spanish economy and to reduce collateral casualties.[115] The bombs strikes on buildings, however, still produced innocent victims, which further damaged ETA's reputation.[116] In his evaluation of ETA's final years, Reinares explains that ETA became a self-serving organisation, looking for internal rather than external legitimacy.[117]

> It is commonly assumed that terrorist organizations or armed groups systematically practising acts of terrorism tend to follow a logic of self-maintenance ... Terrorism ceases to be a means to achieve nationalist ends and becomes an end in itself, both a way of life and a lifestyle for the terrorists.[118]

Part of the Basque population became aware of ETA's internal struggle and quite rightly perceived the last wave of terrorist activities as self-serving.[119] That was an additional nail in the coffin of ETA as a secessionist movement. Furthermore, the French authorities started to collaborate with Spanish police,

---

[110] Mees (n 13) 476.

[111] 'Eta: Basque Separatists Begin Weapons Handover' *BBC News* (8 April 2017) <www.bbc.com/news/world-europe-39536136> accessed 28 May 2022.

[112] Woodworth (n 101) 192; 'Eta: Basque Separatists Begin Weapons Handover' (n 111).

[113] Alonso (n 12); Spencer and Croucher (n 12); William H Sewell, 'Historical Events as Transformations of Structures: Inventing Revolution at the Bastille' (1996) 25 Theory and Society 841.

[114] Alonso (n 12) 704; Caroline Guibet Lafaye and Pierre Brochard, 'Methodological Approach to the Evolution of a Terrorist Organisation: ETA, 1959–2018' (2021) Quality & Quantity 18.

[115] Lafaye and Brochard (n 114) 18.

[116] Reinares (n 95) 128.

[117] ibid.

[118] ibid.

[119] ibid.

and ETA members, who tried to find refuge in France, were arrested.[120] In Spain, Ley Organica 6/2002, which demanded that all political parties had to denounce the use of violence, also forced the hands of Basque nationalist parties whose elected members could not take office without a clear statement that rejected political violence.[121] All these elements had a cumulative effect, and by 2011, ETA was *de facto* disabled as a paramilitary political organisation.[122]

After 2011, Basque nationalism had to grapple with a strategic dilemma. Basque nationalist aspirations of autonomy were blocked in Madrid by both socialist and conservative political parties which refused *a priori* to engage in a constructive democratic dialogue with secessionist parties.[123] This uncompromising refusal was one of the reasons for the crisis in Catalonia.[124] Central institutions were aware that by refusing to engage with Basques, they would make any attempt to increase their autonomy be perceived as undemocratic by the majority of the population outside of the Basque Country.[125] The effects of such a policy within the Basque Country was quite different. Alonso provides a description of the effect of the new wave of support for secession: 'It is true that the majority of Basque society and nationalist sectors condemn the methods [that is, terrorism activities] to achieving those aims, but ... delegitimization lends strength to the belief that such violent methods are not only necessary but useful.'[126] Ley Organica 6/2002 indeed deprives the [PNV] of the control, for first time since its opening, of the Basque Parliament.[127] Even the Spanish Government realised that such a stance was counterproductive. The effects of the policy were rolled back.[128]

The cessation of violent activities, the disbandment of ETA and the clear commitment by all Basque political parties to reject violence as a means to obtain political aims led to the end of the terrorist recognition process.[129] In the Basque Country, the cessation of paramilitary operations coincided with an increased awareness of the role of the Basque constitutional identity and

---

[120] Alonso (n 12) 704.
[121] Ley Orgánica 6/2002, de 27 de junio, de Partidos Políticos 2002.
[122] Alonso (n 12); Euskadi Ta Askatasuna (n 3).
[123] Zabalo Bilbao and Odriozola Irizar (n 24) 148.
[124] López Bofill, 'Hubris, Constitutionalism, and "the Indissoluble Unity of the Spanish Nation"' (n 46).
[125] Spencer and Croucher (n 12) 148.
[126] Alonso (n 12) 711.
[127] Ley Orgánica 6/2002, de 27 de junio, de Partidos Políticos.
[128] Molina and Quiroga (n 45) 102.
[129] Reinares (n 95) 128; 'Wounds Persist in Spain, Ten Years after ETA Lays down Arms' (*France 24*, 20 October 2021).

the comparative irrelevance within the Basque Country of the Spanish constitutional identity.[130]

This is a new phase for the development of the Basque identity and its interaction with Spanish nationalism. In assessing the indicators of nationalism, the Spanish population is considered one of the least nationalist in Europe.[131] Furthermore, there are hints that Spanish nationalism is reducing.[132] This trend is in tune with the internationalist intentions of the drafter of the 1978 Constitution. As mentioned in the introduction of the 1978 Constitution, it had, among many functions, the aim of transforming Spanish society into a European social democracy.[133]

However, one the conditions imposed by the previous regime was the relinquishment of claims based on past atrocities.[134] The narrative promoted by the military junta was that many of the events of the past (including mass murders of innocents and violations of basic human rights) were unfortunate consequences of the historical context.[135] There were certainly victims, yet the perpetrators were acting in good faith (whatever that means).[136] The re-examination of the past would likely not benefit the victims of those 'diligent' public servants. The new Constitution provided the base for developing a new society that respected human rights and it allowed Spain to join the European Union as a liberal nation.[137] As in the case of the mythical Prometheus who had his liver torn apart by birds by day just to regrow it by night, the idea of creating a new Spain was cursed in the Basque Country from its exegesis. There were too many victims, and there were no culprits. A large section of the Basque population was left with a sense of vulnerability linked to transgenerational trauma, and in general, there was too much violence to forget.[138]

Indeed, the Constitution did not reduce the perception that Franco's atrocities had been left unrepaired.[139] In the region, the injustice perpetrated by the fascist regime against the Basque civilians depicted in Picasso's *Guernica* was perceived as a constant reminder of the duplicity of the Spanish nation.[140] At the political level, ETA supporters, for instance, completely rejected the

---

[130] Balfour and Quiroga (n 23) 59; Zabalo and Iraola (n 4) 90.
[131] Florian Bieber, 'Is Nationalism on the Rise? Assessing Global Trends' (2018) 17 Ethnopolitics 519, 526; Balfour and Quiroga (n 23) 16.
[132] Bieber (n 131) 16.
[133] Balfour and Quiroga (n 23) 60.
[134] ibid 44.
[135] ibid 47.
[136] ibid.
[137] Alonso (n 12) 700.
[138] Zabalo Bilbao and Odriozola Irizar (n 24) 139.
[139] ibid.
[140] ibid.

legitimacy of the 1978 Constitution.[141] The majority of the Basque population instead adopted a less dogmatic stance. The bulk of the population and the political parties that represented it accepted the legitimacy of democratic institutions that were linked to the Constitution, but refused to endorse the idea that, as a whole, the Constitution represented their nation, and crucially, that Basques were a nationality that was inferior to the Spanish nation.[142] The drafters and the members of the ruling military junta were concerned that Spain might disintegrate.[143] The responses to the potential danger posed by secessionist movements were multifarious. The reinstalment of the monarchy in the 1978 Constitution, the idea of unity and the superiority of the Spanish nation,[144] and the adoption of a rigid amendment system were two of the constitutional arrangements that aspired to preserve the union of Spain.[145] It did so, but as explained throughout this chapter, that came at a cost.

The text indeed confirmed the perception by many Basques that the Spanish could not be trusted and this had lingering effects on social attitudes.[146] Multisector sociological analyses of the Basque attitude towards symbols of Spanish identity, which ranged from children wearing red garments in school[147] to support for international Spanish athletes,[148] indicate a substantial gap between the Basque mental attitude towards their identity and the Spanish national identity.[149] There is, for instance, a small number of individuals who claim to carry a dual national identity. That is a key indicator of an ethnic form of nationalism which entrenched social dichotomies.[150] Recall that modern nationalism, whilst sharing the ideological underpinnings of ethnocentric nationalism, presupposed the recognition of other national groups as peers.[151] Whether that is a direct connection to a constituent idea that put Spanish identity ahead of the Basque nationality is not for this chapter to discuss.[152] The

---

[141] Francisco J Llera, José M Mata and Cynthia L Irvin, 'ETA: From Secret Army to Social Movement – the Post-Franco Schism of the Basque Nationalist Movement' (1993) 5 Terrorism and Political Violence 106.

[142] Balfour and Quiroga (n 23) 43; Zabalo and Iraola (n 4).

[143] Zabalo Bilbao and Odriozola Irizar (n 24).

[144] Generales (n 50) Article 2.

[145] Espadaler Fossas (n 11); Balfour and Quiroga (n 23) 56; Generales (n 50) pt X; Zabalo and Iraola (n 4).

[146] Zabalo and Iraola (n 4); Rojo-Labaien (n 86) 72.

[147] Begoña Echeverria, 'Schooling, Language, and Ethnic Identity in the Basque Autonomous Community' (2003) 34 Anthropology & Education Quarterly 351, 359.

[148] Rojo-Labaien (n 86).

[149] Zabalo and Iraola (n 4); Rojo-Labaien (n 86) 72.

[150] Echeverria (n 147) 359.

[151] Smith (n 108).

[152] Echeverria (n 147) 359.

constitutional stance that divides national identities and puts them in a pecking order has, however, direct negative implications for the role of the Constitution as a social engineering projects.[153] It does have a negative effect, because the lack of recognition of an equal standing between the various national communities has the effect of humiliating members who find themselves, without a choice, as the bearers of an identity that is constitutionally classified as inferior.[154]

It could be argued that resentment and a sense of betrayal that followed each of the Spanish regionalist reforms was substituted by a form of disdained indifference.[155] In recent years, the Spanish economic crisis tilted Basque society towards a more pragmatic stance.[156] In particular, the debate that surrounded demands for more autonomy was substituted by a discussion over day-to-day issues, such as rising unemployment, the lack of investment and, more recently, the response to the COVID-19 pandemic.[157] One of the indicators of the change in attitude was the electoral performance of the Batzume Party that was considered the political voice of ETA. During this period, most of its supporters, it can be deduced from voting patterns, moved over to the more moderate PNV.[158]

As mentioned earlier, by 2008, ETA's political support fizzled out, and with it, its ability to conduct a sustain terrorist campaign.[159] Police forces in both France and Spain had become more effective at tracking down and imprisoning ETA collaborators.[160] In the period that followed the 9/11 attack, ETA's leadership might have realised that its capability to show military strength was dwindling and its aspiration to be the catalyst for a Basque Country secessionist insurrection was quixotic.[161] However, the decreased effectiveness of ETA's paramilitary apparatus did not coincide with increased support for the Spanish constitutional system in the Basque Country.[162]

---

[153] Balfour and Quiroga (n 23) 46.
[154] Constitutional Court Decision n.31 28/06/2010 (n 2).
[155] Zabalo and Iraola (n 4).
[156] Spencer and Croucher (n 12) 139.
[157] Zabalo and Iraola (n 4).
[158] Alonso (n 12) 705; Francisco José Llera, Rafael Leonisio and Sergio Pérez Castaños, 'The Influence of the Elites' Discourse in Political Attitudes: Evidence from the Basque Country' (2017) 19 National Identities 367, 369.
[159] Spencer and Croucher (n 12) 148.
[160] Alonso (n 12) 704.
[161] Spencer and Croucher (n 12) 148; Rogelio Alonso, 'Pathways Out of Terrorism in Northern Ireland and the Basque Country: The Misrepresentation of the Irish Model' (2004) 16 Terrorism and Political Violence 695.
[162] Spencer and Croucher (n 12); Alonso (n 12).

In 2003, the Basque Parliament initiated the process to reform the 1981 Statute of Autonomy, demanding the status of a free association with Spain.[163] The proposal, which is commonly known as the Ibarretxe Plan, was taken from the name of the one-time leader of the Basque coalition government, Juan José Ibarretxe, who proposed it.[164] The new Statute of Autonomy envisaged a complex reform of the relationship between Basque and central institutions.[165] One of the supporting reasons for promoting the new statute was the possibility that ETA might be ending its military campaign.[166]

The Ibarretxe Plan was ambitious to the point of being quixotic. For instance, the idea that the Basque Country would become a free associated region with Spain did not make sense under international law. Free association countries are uncommon in international public law.[167] This assumes a relationship between two states that are considered, internationally, as sovereign entities, but that have decided to have a special relationship with another sovereign state.[168] However, the Basque Country is a region within an internationally recognised sovereign state.

It is safe to say that the key aspiration of Ibarretxe for the Plan was not to create a microstate. The Plan intended, instead, to adjust the balance of meso-governance between Spanish central and regional institutions.[169] A close reading of the proposal shows, for instance, that its key aspiration was to adjust central/regional financial arrangements and to give the opportunity for Basque institutions to attend EU meetings. Similar prerogatives are allocated to the Scottish Government as a part of the 1998 Devolution and they did not require a change in the international status of Scotland.[170] Furthermore, the technical fiscal elements of the Plan which focused on finance were later approved without much fanfare later in 2014 by representatives of both the Basque and

---

[163] Balfour and Quiroga (n 23) 63; Llera, Leonisio and Pérez Castaños (n 158) 370.
[164] ibid; ibid.
[165] Balfour and Quiroga (n 23) 65.
[166] ibid 64.
[167] Vito Breda, *Constitutional Law and Regionalism: A Comparative Analysis of Regionalist Negotiations* (Edward Elgar Publishing 2018) 158.
[168] ibid.
[169] Michael Keating and Zoe Bray, 'Renegotiating Sovereignty: Basque Nationalism and the Rise and Fall of the Ibarretxe Plan' (2006) 5 Ethnopolitics 347.
[170] Scottish Ministers, the Welsh Ministers and the Northern Ireland Executive Committee, 'Devolution: Memorandum of Understanding and Supplementary Agreements'; Scotland Act 1998 c 46.

Spanish Governments.[171] This was another case in which nationalist ideological narratives obfuscated the real implications of the Plan.[172]

The lack of engagement in the technical elements of state–regional relationships is, however, a common element of regionalist negotiations that are driven by extreme nationalist narratives.[173] The interactions between regionalist and central states are generally part of a dynamic multifactorial partnership which invests in both institutions and political parties. The diverging agendas that are pursued by different actors foster a constant justling for power and resources, which is considered one of the engines of modern democracy.[174] Yet, the results of these processes are often manifested in minute administrative adjustments that are not inserted into mainstream media.[175]

Despite its legal oddity, the request of a free association between Spain and the Basque Country confirms the diverging dynamics of the Spanish and Basque constitutional identities. The idea of solidarity between nationalities and the unity of Spain in the 1978 Constitution not only have limited traction within Basque institutions, but are also a constant reminder of the unfairness of the present constitutional assumptions among the Basque population. The document was designed to be a 'Spanish' Constitution and not a constitution for a multinational Spain. The persistent divergence might no longer support the idea of violent insurrection, yet it maintains the perception of the illegitimacy of the Spanish institutions in the autonomous region. In short, it is, in the debate over the development of a multinational connotational identity, a negative driver of change.

## CONCLUSION

Even before the recent Catalonia unilateral independence saga, the Spanish Constitution fascinated constitutional comparative lawyers.[176] The Spanish Constitution is considered as one of the latest 'grand' European constitutional

---

[171] Parliament, Ley 7/2014, de 21 de Abril, Por La Que Se Modifica La Ley 12/2002, de 23 de Mayo, Por La Que Se Aprueba El Concierto Económico Con La Comunidad Autónoma Del País Vasco (n 1).

[172] Keating and Bray (n 169).

[173] Keating (n 91).

[174] Llera, Leonisio and Pérez Castaños (n 158) 373.

[175] Balfour and Quiroga (n 23) 64; Alonso (n 12) 699; Spencer and Croucher (n 12) 139.

[176] Balfour and Quiroga (n 23); Luis Andrés Cucarella Galiana, 'Constitutional Justice in Spain: Appeals to the Spanish Constitutional Court' (2013) 5 Revista de Estudos Constitucionais, Hermenêutica e Teoria do Direito 2; Helen Graham, *War and Its Shadow: Spain's Civil War in Europe's Long Twentieth Century* (Sussex Academic Press 2012).

moments.[177] The process ferried Spain, which is one of the oldest European nation states, from a fascist dictatorship into a liberal democracy and, eventually, into the European Union.[178] However, recent events in Catalonia have brought critical international scrutiny to bear on the Spanish system of territorial governance.[179]

In the Basque Country, the 1978 Constitution was, and still is, perceived as an incomplete endeavour.[180] I discussed two drivers of change, from among the many sociological factors, which explain the Basque dissatisfaction with the current system of governance. The first element is an imprecise and highly inefficient system of territorial governance which frustrates all involved, but particularly Basque nationalists and, even though it was not discussed in this chapter, the Catalans. The second negative driver of change considered in this chapter was the legacy of ETA. I argued that the conditions that supported decades of armed struggle are no longer present. However, the implications of a diverging perception of constitutional legitimacy still defines the present and near-future process surrounding the recognition of the Basque identity.

In other words, Basque political violence has ended but the crisis that underpinned it is still lingering on. What is distinctive of the Basque constitutional crisis is a tendency, by a large part of the population, to reject some of the normative values supporting the 1978 Constitution. The rejection is generally associated with the symbolic elements and the teleological assumptions of the Spanish Constitution.[181] There are indications idea that the monarchy, flags, language and the European Union could be a unifying element for a multinational democracy is rejected at all levels of Basque society.[182] There is an overall lingering sense of normative detachment between the central and regional institutions.[183] It is not the aim of this book to forecast scenarios, yet the lack of engagement with the issues related to the multinational nature of Spanish society (in which both Spanish and Basque identities are constructed as equal partners) is an unstable platform for the development of a constitutional system, and the cycle of crises is likely to continue to alter the interactions between central and regional institutions.

---

[177] López Bofill, 'Hubris, Constitutionalism, and "the Indissoluble Unity of the Spanish Nation"' (n 46).
[178] Balfour and Quiroga (n 23).
[179] López Bofill, 'Hubris, Constitutionalism, and "the Indissoluble Unity of the Spanish Nation"' (n 46).
[180] Keating and Bray (n 169).
[181] Ludger Mees, 'Nationalist Politics at the Crossroads: The Basque Nationalist Party and the Challenge of Sovereignty (1998–2014)' (2015) 21 Nationalism & Ethnic Politics 44.
[182] ibid.
[183] Spencer and Croucher (n 12); Zabalo and Iraola (n 4) 90.

# 3. Italy and Sicily: Mafia territorial sovereignty

## INTRODUCTION

The chapter discusses two from among the many factors that maintain Sicily in a state of perpetual constitutional disorder.[1] The first driver of change is the effect of the neo-patrimonialism of Italian public institutions.[2] The second driver of change that is considered is the territorial system of governance by Mafia syndicates.[3] These criminal syndicates have no ideological aspirations nor any overt intention of separating from the Italian State. Mafia families have instead, like hemiparasitic plants, an interest in maintaining the flood of resources from the Central State to Sicily, which provides jobs for their affiliates and remunerative public contracts.[4]

The Italian Republic, hereafter Italy, has an asymmetric system of territorial governance derived from the French territorial model.[5] The country is divided into 15 regular regions and five special autonomous regions.[6] The legislative, administrative and fiscal competences of the central and regional institutions are guaranteed by constitutional law.[7] In one of the longest articles to be found in any constitution, the Italian Constitution lists out the exclusive and concurrent competences of central institutions.[8] The residual competences are

---

[1] David Haljan, *Constitutionalising Secession* (Hart Publishing 2014) 12.

[2] Gianluca Fiorentini and Sam Peltzman, *The Economics of Organised Crime* (Cambridge University Press 1997).

[3] Diego Gambetta, *The Sicilian Mafia: The Business of Private Protection* (Harvard University Press 1996); Daron Acemoglu, Giuseppe De Feo and Giacomo Davide De Luca, 'Weak States: Causes and Consequences of the Sicilian Mafia' (2020) 87 The Review of Economic Studies 537.

[4] Gambetta (n 3); Acemoglu, De Feo and De Luca (n 3).

[5] Mario Einaudi, 'The Constitution of the Italian Republic' (1948) 42 The American Political Science Review 661.

[6] Constitution of the Italian Republic 1948 Articles 114–33.

[7] ibid; Constitutional Law n.1 31.1963; Constitutional Law n. 2 26.02.1948; Constitutional Law n. 3 26.02.1948; Constitutional Law n. 4 26.02.1948; Constitutional Law n. 5 26.02.1948.

[8] Constitution of the Italian Republic Article 117, 2–3.

allocated to the regions.[9] Most of the Central State's exclusive and concurring heads of powers can be transferred, using an ordinary statute, to any region.[10] The process in which such delegation might occur is not set and, in the past few years, those regions that demanded more competences incorporated a regional consultative referendum to support their claims.[11]

The autonomous regions, like regular regions, are fiscally self-governing.[12] They can collect revenues, and the Central State should ensure that they have the ability to deliver services for which they have been granted legislative and administrative competences.[13] They can also seek loans on the financial market, but such liabilities cannot be guaranteed by central institutions.[14] One of the most distinctive features of the Italian system of territorial governance is the prerogative given to the regions to withhold a large chunk of their regional fiscal revenues.[15] This has served the residents in the North of Italy well, but has limited benefits for the regions in the South.[16] Regional institutions in Sicily, for instance, are heavily dependent on the relocation of fiscal revenues from Rome.[17]

The autonomous region of Sicily, with its population of five million residents, includes the main island and a series of minor archipelagos in the South Mediterranean Sea.[18] There are multiple elements that make Sicily distinctive within the Italian population, but in relation to the aim of this chapter, one factor has multidimensional implications.[19] The per capita income for the region is one of the lowest in Italy, where 26 per cent of the population live below the poverty line.[20] Poverty has multiple repercussions on other sociolog-

---

[9] ibid Article 117, 4.
[10] ibid Article 117, 6.
[11] 'Italian Regions of Lombardy and Veneto Vote for More Autonomy – The New York Times' <www.nytimes.com/2017/10/22/world/europe/lombardy-veneto-referendums.html> accessed 23 September 2020.
[12] Constitution of the Italian Republic Article 119, 1; Law n. 5 21.05.2009.
[13] Constitution of the Italian Republic Article 119, 3; Constitutional Law n.3 18.10.2001 Article 5.
[14] Constitution of the Italian Republic Article 119, 5.
[15] Luca Antonini, *Federalismo all'italiana* (Marsilio 2013).
[16] ibid.
[17] Salvatore Di Gregorio, *L'autonomia finanziaria della regione siciliana: il contenzioso con lo stato ed il ruolo della Corte costituzionale nell'attuazione della disciplina statutaria* (Jovene 2014).
[18] ISTAT Istituto Nazionale di Statistica, 'Resident Population' 2020.
[19] Richard Lynn, 'In Italy, North–South Differences in IQ Predict Differences in Income, Education, Infant Mortality, Stature, and Literacy' (2010) 38 Intelligence 93, 98.
[20] ISTAT Istituto Nazionale di Statistica, 'Dati Statistici per Il Territorio: Regione Sicilia'.

ical factors, such as the level of criminality and education.[21] Fifty-one per cent of Sicilian adults under 25 are unemployed.[22] According to the Organisation for Economic Co-operation and Development (hereafter, OECD), 90 per cent of the population of South Italy and Sicily cannot carry out basic cognitive tasks.[23] Whilst it is true that the Italian population is performing comparatively poorly among the 38 OECD members (over 70 per cent of the Italian population cannot efficiently process text nor do simple maths),[24] the weak results in Sicily are at odds with the level of regional spending per capita on education, which is roughly uniform across Italy.[25] This point is delicate, and so I must be precise. It is the low quality of education provided by institutions affected by endemic corruption that is the main cause of this comparatively poor performance in the area of education.[26] The low level of individual wealth is also probably directly connected to the resilience of organised crime syndicates.[27] The elevated level of unemployment is linked to an above-the-national-average level of irregular temporary jobs (e.g., fruit picking) that is directly or indirectly connected to Mafia families.[28] A low-skilled work force which seeks employment in a poorly performing economy tends to aspire to finding jobs in the public sector.[29] The Mafia is the most likely proxy to help an aspiring

---

[21] Ben Palmer, 'The Bell Curve Review: IQ Best Indicates Poverty' 22, 2. Sicilians perform relatively poorly in IQ tests. The average score is 89 which is considered in a low average standard variation group. Lynn (n 19) 97.

[22] 'Disoccupazione giovanile record: la Sicilia in coda alla classifica europea' (*la Repubblica*, 30 April 2019) <https://palermo.repubblica.it/cronaca/2019/04/30/news/disoccupazione_giovanile_record_la_sicilia_in_coda_alla_classifica_europea-225142583/> accessed 26 May 2020.

[23] The World Bank Group and The European Commission, 'Doing Business in the European Union 2020: Greece, Ireland and Italy'.

[24] OECD, *Skills Matter: Further Results from the Survey of Adult Skills* (OECD 2016) 28.

[25] Santino Piazza, 'Autonomia Scolastica e Regionalismo Differenziato. Un Confronto Tra i Rendimenti Del Sistema Scolastico in Alcune Autonomie Speciali e Regioni a Statuto Ordinario' (Rubbettino Editore 2018) 190.

[26] ibid.

[27] Theodoros Rakopoulos, 'Façade Egalitarianism? Mafia and Cooperative in Sicily' (2017) 40 Political and Legal Anthropology Review 104.

[28] Theodoros Rakopoulos, *From Clans to Co-Ops: Confiscated Mafia Land in Sicily* (Berghahn 2018); David Cantor and Kenneth C Land, 'Unemployment and Crime Rate Fluctuations: A Comment on Greenberg' (2001) 17 Journal of Quantitative Criminology 329, 330.

[29] European Commission, Directorate-General for Justice, Freedom and Security., 'Competitiveness in Low-Income and Low-Growth Regions – The Lagging Regions Report'.

uneducated and unqualified individuals to find a job in the public sector.[30] That job comes in exchange for a lifetime of loyalty.[31] Sicily has one of the highest number of regional public servants per head of population in Italy, but given the low skill level of its workers and the high cost of transactions, which are directly or indirectly controlled by Mafia syndicates, Sicily is unable to provide the services that are available in the rest of Italy.[32] Security, for historical reasons, is one of the areas in which the public sector performs particularly badly and it is therefore natural for individuals and businesses to rely on Mafia cartels for protection.[33] It is a utilitarian choice that altered the role of public institutions in the region.

As an example of what Haljan defines as a case of constitutional disorder, that is, a radical imbalance between the rule of law and popular sovereignty, it is difficult to find a clearer example than Sicily.[34] In practice, the region is poor, has a large number of unskilled unemployed individuals and security is provided by Mafia syndicates.[35] As for the rest of the cases considered in this book, there are multiple factors that make public institutions unable to govern the island. However, I will focus only on two negative drivers of change. The first driver of change is the role of a corrupt and – as a result – inefficient system of governance.[36] The second driver of change instead describes the functioning of the Mafia as the guarantor of legal and illegal commercial operations in the region.[37]

## THE MAFIA AND ITS HISTORY IN SICILY

Before the two drivers of change are analysed in detail, a series of discussions need to be engaged as part of a preliminary debate. Firstly, Mafia syndicates are a manifestation of a historically complex phenomenon, yet there is enough

---

[30] John Dickie, *Cosa Nostra: A History of the Sicilian Mafia* (Hodder & Stoughton 2009).
[31] ibid.
[32] Antonini (n 15); Fabio Pammolli, '01-2017 – La spesa sanitaria delle Regioni in Italia - Saniregio2017' (*Fondazione Cerm*) <https://fondazionecerm.it/2017/05/18/01-2017-la-spesa-sanitaria-delle-regioni-italia-saniregio2017/> accessed 5 October 2020; *La Finanza Territoriale 2018* (Rubbettino Editore 2018) 65, 76, 138, 180; Emanuele Felice, *Perché Il Sud è Rimasto Indietro* (Il Mulino 2013).
[33] Gambetta (n 3).
[34] Haljan (n 1) 13.
[35] Gambetta (n 3) 75.
[36] Fiorentini (n 2).
[37] Gambetta (n 3); Acemoglu, De Feo and De Luca (n 3).

research to suggest that the Mafia established itself as the *de facto* system of governance in Sicily in parallel with the formation of the Italian State.[38]

Multiple Mafia syndicates have, over the years, fostered a sense of communal loyalty among their sympathisers that overlaps a regional identity and is concurrent with a sense of belonging to an Italian national identity.[39] The modern Mafia, according to Diego Gambetta, developed after the abolition of a Sicilian feudal system in which land barons collected rent with the help of private enforcers.[40] By 1861, with the violent annexation of the island by the Kingdom of Piedmont, multiple organised groups of violent thugs moved from the countryside to the urban areas. They provided private security to local businesses.[41] Often, the protection was paid in kind.[42] For instance, a wholesale merchant paid for security with products, transporters offered free deliveries and so on.[43] The access to reduced-cost products and services facilitated the establishment of Mafia-controlled businesses, which helped with the process of money laundering.[44]

The administrative system established in Sicily by the Kingdom of Piedmont did not change substantially when the Savoy family called its new conquered lands the Kingdom of Italy. The 1948 Republican Constitution brought with it the aforementioned regional autonomy.[45] The comprehensive control of regional businesses, like the wholesale fish market in Palermo, was established in the period after World War II.[46] Currently, entire sectors of production (such as industrial agricultural processing, the wholesale fishing industry,

---

[38] Italian Parliament, Commisione Parlamentare di Inchiesta Sule fenomeno della mafia, 'Report by the Procuratore Nazionale Antimafia'.

[39] Letizia Paoli, 'Mafia Brotherhoods: Organized Crime, Italian Style' (2008); Luis Nardin and others, 'Simulating Protection Rackets: A Case Study of the Sicilian Mafia' (2016) 30 Autonomous Agents and Multi-Agent Systems 1117; John Hutchinson and Anthony D Smith, 'Introduction' in John Hutchinson and Anthony D Smith (eds), *Nationalism* (Oxford University Press 1994); Ernest Gellner, *Nationalism* (Phoenix 1998).

[40] Gambetta (n 3) 81; Theodoros Rakopoulos, 'The Limits of "Bad Kinship": Sicilian Anti-Mafia Families', *From Clans to Co-ops*, vol 4 (Berghahn Books 2018); Paoli, 'Mafia Brotherhoods' (n 39); Antonio La Spina, 'The Fight against the Italian Mafia' in Letizia Paoli (ed), *The Oxford Handbook of Organized crime* (Oxford University Press 2014).

[41] Gambetta (n 3) 87; Letizia Paoli, 'The Italian Mafia' in Letizia Paoli (ed), *The Oxford Handbook of Organized Crime* (Oxford University Press 2014) 123.

[42] Gambetta (n 3).

[43] ibid.

[44] ibid 88.

[45] Constitutional Law n. 2 26.02.1948.

[46] Salvatore Lupo, 'The Allies and the Mafia' (1997) 2 Journal of Modern Italian Studies 21.

transport and heavy carpentry), which expanded during the nineteenth- and twentieth-century industrialisation of Italy, are still under the direct control of Mafia families.[47] The development of significant infrastructure during the 1950s brought about the need to coordinate the activity of multiple crime groups. The 'Mafia Commission', which is sometimes referred to as the *Cupola* (dome), acted as the liaison institution between criminal cartels.[48] Over the past three decades, multiple police investigations indicate that lucrative public contracts for road maintenance, telecommunications and transport have been piloted by Mafia families that often form *ad hoc* regional cartels. The coordination of these activities is planned during Commission meetings.[49]

I will return to this point when I discuss the role of the Mafia as a sociological driver of change, but it is important to note that the *Cupola* is chaired by a secretary, also known as the boss of bosses.[50] In addition to its steering and coordinating role, in cases of internal conflict, the *Cupola* acts as a mediator.[51] It can also sanction violent punishments against whoever is acting against the interests of Mafia syndicates.[52] From the 1960s onwards, the Commission ensured that all public contracts in Sicily were collected and divided between Mafia families.[53] The so-called sack of Palermo occurred in this period.[54]

The sack of Palermo was a pivotal moment in the history of the Sicilian Mafia because it exponentially increased the flow of cash from the Mafia's illegal and legal activities. For a number of reasons, large sections of Palermo's heritage were levelled out to make space for high-rises. In the 1960s and 1970s, a series of statutes were passed by the Italian Parliament to increase the safety of buildings in the event of earthquakes that periodically occur in Italy.[55] The stringent measures, instead of generating a culture of safe building practices, were a proxy for an illegal market of complicit building surveyors who received regular payments from Mafia families.[56] In Palermo, the 'cement boom' also increased the competition between Mafia cartels over the control of rich urban areas.[57] The first Mafia war was an internal affair and most of its victims were Mafia affiliates.[58] Starting roughly in 1970, the second Mafia war

---

[47] Gambetta (n 3) 88, 94.
[48] ibid 110.
[49] Lupo (n 46) 31.
[50] Gambetta (n 3) 113, 229.
[51] ibid 114.
[52] ibid.
[53] Dickie (n 30) 276–78.
[54] ibid 282.
[55] Law n.1684 25.11.1962; Law n.1086 5.11.1971; Law n. 64 2.2.1974.
[56] Dickie (n 30) 286.
[57] ibid 303.
[58] ibid.

targeted high-ranking police officers who could not be corrupted,[59] and for the first time, politicians, who rebelled or more generally displeased their Mafia kingpins.[60] One of the offshoots of the second war was the Corleonesi family establishing its dominance.[61] In 1992, the chief prosecutor of Palermo and his bodyguards were murdered using an improvised explosive device (IED).[62] After that attack, IEDs became the weapon of choice to kill heavily protected senior police officers, State functionaries and judges.[63]

The two Mafia wars also signalled the existence of incorruptible public functionaries and politicians.[64] These individuals were brave, at the limit of the quixotic. It was in this period that Parliament passed Law n.646.[65] The Private Bill, from which the statute originated, was supported by an opposition MP for the Sicilian Communist Party called Pio La Torre and a Catholic Party MP called Virginio Rognoni.[66] The enactment of Law n.646 was intended to end the control of Mafia syndicates over Sicily.[67] First, Law n.646, for the first time, inserted the crime of Mafia association in the Italian Criminal Code.[68] Article 1 provides for three or more individuals who have acted as part of an informal organisation to obtain economic advantages, commit crimes and silence witnesses perhaps being sentenced to up to nine years in prison.[69] The law also gives the prerogative to criminal investigators to incriminate individuals who have committed different crimes in different locations in a single judicial proceeding.[70] Second, the statute allows magistrates and police forces to change the way in which they had been conducting investigations.[71] Magistrates and police could now share information, which often revealed

---

[59] ibid 383.
[60] ibid 333, 382.; Gambetta (n 3) 256.
[61] Dickie (n 30) 370–74.
[62] ibid 384.
[63] William Pizzi and Luca Marafioti, 'New Italian Code of Criminal Procedure: The Difficulties of Building an Adversarial Trial System on a Civil Law Foundation' (1992) 17 The Yale Journal of International Law 1.
[64] Dickie (n 30) 376.
[65] Law n. 646 25.09.1982.
[66] Dickie (n 30) 382.
[67] ibid.
[68] Vito Breda, *Constitutional Law and Regionalism: A Comparative Analysis of Regionalist Negotiations* (Edward Elgar Publishing 2018); Luca Antonini, *Federalismo all'italiana: Dietro le quinte della grande incompiuta. Quello che ogni cittadino dovrebbe sapere* (Marsilio Editori 2013); Giancarlo Pola, *Principles and Practices of Fiscal Autonomy: Experiences, Debates and Prospects* (Routledge 2016).
[69] Law n. 646 25.09.1982 Article 1.
[70] Dickie (n 30) 389–90.
[71] ibid 15.

criminal conspiracies.[72] Third, the law relocated suspected Mafia bosses away from their territory, making them less protected and less able to control their syndicates.[73] Fourth, the law allowed investigators to seize the assets of Mafia associates and their spouses.[74]

It is clear that Law n.646 hindered the core business of the Sicilian Mafia. Despite numerous myths attached to the idea of men of honour, the core business model of the Mafia is based on exchanging protection for resources.[75] The resources, which can be money or goods, are necessary to pay Mafia associates who might easily rebel against their insolvent boss. It is important to remember that Mafia associates are almost exclusively men, often unskilled and uneducated labourers whose entire livelihood is dependent on the economic success of their criminal syndicate.[76] The possibility that their boss might not have the resources to pay his affiliates either because he is incompetent or because he is unlucky has the same destabilising effect.[77]

The response to Law n.646 from the *Cupola* was clear. La Torre was killed a few months before the enactment of Law n.646. To the present day, judges (and their families) who are too effective at implementing Law n.646 require special protection, reducing their mobility, and making them less effective.[78] Independently from the number of individuals who have lost their lives in the fight against Mafia syndicates, the La Torre–Rognoni Statute opened up a new season on the Italian State–Mafia relationship that defines the current system of governance of the island. In 1993, the restrictive incarceration measures that were implemented to reduce terrorist activities in Italy were extended to Mafia bosses.[79] In particular, suspected Mafia criminals were held in island prisons and restrictions were extended to their guards. Recall that the process of the allocation of jobs, even in the prison service, can be easily manipulated by Mafia bosses.[80] So it is not only the Mafia affiliates who are imprisoned who have be isolated; the guards who monitor them must also be put under special supervision.[81] It is difficult to make causal links in the analysis of any complex social interaction, but after the enactment of Law n.636, there was an unprecedented number of Mafia affiliates who defected and agreed to speak

---

[72] ibid.
[73] Law n. 646 25.09.1982 Article 10.
[74] ibid Article 14. 5.
[75] Gambetta (n 3).
[76] ibid 101.
[77] ibid 33–77.
[78] Dickie (n 30) 376.
[79] ibid 411.
[80] Decision n. 4032 Tribunal of Palermo 17/7/2013 717.
[81] ibid.

out against their bosses.[82] One of the effects of the new powers given to the prosecution was the unprecedented arrest of the then-secretary of the *Cupola*.[83]

The isolation of Mafia affiliates is, however, an administratively expensive and invasive process that has been deemed by the European Court of Human Rights to be partly incompatible with Article 3 of the European Convention on Human Rights.[84] In the 1990s, a new police group called the Divisione Investigativa Anti-Mafia (hereafter, DIA) under the control of a specially appointed judge was established with the sole purpose of investigating Mafia-related crimes.[85] The DIA includes individuals from multiple law enforcement agencies comprising fiscal controllers, and crucially, a special group of prison guards. These prison guards are tasked with reducing the ability of Mafia bosses to manage their syndicates after they have been imprisoned.[86] These changes reduced the ability of Mafia bosses to coordinate attacks against State officials but did not significantly reduce the Mafia syndicates' control of the territory.[87]

## A NEGATIVE DRIVER OF CHANGE: THE ITALIAN PUBLIC SECTOR AND NEO-PATRIMONIALISM

The Mafia is a social phenomenon that has deep roots in the history of Sicily. In the previous part of the chapter, I explained that Mafia syndicates maintain capillary control of several areas of Sicily.[88] I also clarified that a Mafia syndicate is a commercial corporation whose profit is linked to a projection of power over those individuals who reside in its controlled area. Its commercial operations are not normally challenged by public institutions.[89] The Mafia relationship with the State is, instead, analogous to the one existing between

---

[82] Dickie (n 30) 408.
[83] ibid.
[84] *Bernardo Provenzano v Italy* (Application no 55080/13).
[85] Dickie (n 30) 399.
[86] ibid.
[87] Gambetta (n 3); Dickie (n 30); Pizzi and Marafioti (n 63); Direzione Investigativa Antimafia, 'Semester Report 2019 Semester II'; Direzione Investigativa Antimafia, 'Semester Report 2019 Semester I'; Letizia Paoli (ed), *The Oxford Handbook of Organized Crime* (Oxford University Press 2014); Paoli, 'The Italian Mafia' (n 41).
[88] Direzione Investigativa Antimafia, 'Semester Report 2019 Semester II' (n 87); Direzione Investigativa Antimafia, 'Semester Report 2019 Semester I' (n 87); Italian Parliament, Commisione Parlamentare di Inchiesta Sule fenomeno della mafia, 'Report by the Procuratore Nazionale Antimafia', Italian Parliament, Commisione Parlamentare di Inchiesta Sule fenomeno della mafia (n 38).
[89] Gambetta (n 3) 251; John D'Attona, 'Explaining Italian Tax Compliance. A Historical Analysis' in Sven Steinmo (ed), *The Leap of Faith: The Fiscal Foundations of Successful Government in Europe and America* (1st edn, Oxford

a plant and its hemiparasite.[90] In this section, I will explain that the Italian neo-patrimonialistic system contributes, among other factors, to the Mafia syndicates' control over Sicily.

As mentioned earlier, there is no nexus of causality between the dysfunctional structure of neo-patrimonialist public institutions and the Mafia. There is, however, a connection between the corruption of public institutions and criminal activities.[91] Many states in Europe and around the world do have neo-patrimonialist administrative systems. However, there are only a few, such as the Italian system, in which patrimonialism has fostered a network of organised crime syndicates with capillary control over their territory.[92] The Mafia's monopoly over the market of violence is, it is reasonable to suggest, facilitated, rather than caused, by the inefficacy of the Italian public sector.[93]

Kelsen provides one of the clearest analyses of the relationship between compliance and legal normativity:

> But it cannot be denied that a legal order is considered to be valid only if the human behavior to which this order refers is, by and large, in conformity with the order. If this conformity ... is termed effectiveness, then effectiveness is a condition of the validity of the law.[94]

In Sicily, the term *effectiveness* is almost exclusively associated with Mafia operations. The corrupt practices that facilitated these Mafia operations are

---

University Press 2018); John D'Attoma, 'What Explains the North–South Divide in Italian Tax Compliance? An Experimental Analysis' (2019) 54 Acta Politica 104.

[90] Angeli and others (n 29).

[91] D'Attoma (n 89).

[92] European Commission, Directorate-General for Justice, Freedom and Security. and Center for the Study of Democracy, *Examining the Links between Organised Crime and Corruption* (CSD 2011); Charles M Fombad and Nico Steytler (eds), *Corruption and Constitutionalism in Africa* (Oxford University Press 2020); Peter Van der Hoek, 'Enlarging the European Union: Taxation and Corruption in the New Member States' in Robert McGee (ed), *Taxation and Public Finance in Transition and Developing Economies* (Springer US 2008); Philip Gounev and Tihomir Bezlov, 'Examining the Links between Organised Crime and Corruption' (2010) 13 Trends in Organized Crime 326; Massimo Sargiacomo and others, 'Accounting and the Fight against Corruption in Italian Government Procurement: A Longitudinal Critical Analysis (1992–2014)' (2015) 28 Critical Perspectives on Accounting 89; Gambetta (n 3) 251; Andreas Buehn and Friedrich Schneider, 'Size and Development of Tax Evasion in 38 OECD Countries: What Do We (Not) Know?' (2016) 3 Journal of Economics and Political Economy 1.

[93] European Commission, Directorate-General for Justice, Freedom and Security. and Center for the Study of Democracy (n 92) 62; Gambetta (n 3) 22.

[94] Hans Kelsen, 'Law, State and Justice in the Pure Theory of Law' (1947) 57 Yale Law Journal 377, 378. See also Haljan (n 1) 2.

often blatant. Corrupt politicians collect bribes and votes in exchange for public procurement contracts and jobs that are allocated to Mafia affiliates.[95] This exchange is described as the 'golden triangle', where the Mafia corrupts politicians and where public servants are the cornerstones of a system designed to feast on public resources.[96] For instance, in the period between 1970 and 1992, between 40 and 70 per cent of elected national politicians from the Sicilian Catholic Democratic Party were directly associated with a Mafia family.[97] The institutions, such as the judiciary and the police, which are constitutionally bound to reduce the effects of corruption, are often limited in their activities by statutes approved by a parliament that is partly composed of corrupt politicians. It is also the case that public servants, who are personally associated with a clientele network that provided them with underserving positions, are unqualified and incompetent.[98] Consequently, personal incapacity is coupled with institutional limitations which, in turn, allow Mafia families to take over the role of public service providers.[99]

Public functionaries who are appointed thanks to their connection with a Mafia group report to the person who provides them with their underserving job.[100] The awareness of the dominance of the Mafia over regional and State competition for jobs is common knowledge,[101] and so is the awareness that such individuals might be incompetent and might respond directly to a local boss instead of to their supervisor.[102] The lack of a substantive connection between civil servants and the institution that pays them affects all public

---

[95] European Commission, Directorate-General for Justice, Freedom and Security. and Center for the Study of Democracy (n 92) 37; Dickie (n 30) 275, 285–91; Gambetta (n 3) 286; 'Voto Di Scambio in Sicilia, 96 Indagati. C'è Anche l'ex Governatore Cuffaro – La Repubblica' <https://palermo.repubblica.it/cronaca/2019/03/14/news/voto_di_scambio_in_sicilia_96_indagati_c_e_anche_cuffaro-221577560/> accessed 2 October 2020.

[96] European Commission, Directorate-General for Justice, Freedom and Security. and Center for the Study of Democracy (n 92) 39. ibid 37; Dickie (n 30) 275, 285–91; Gambetta (n 3) 286.

[97] Dickie (n 30) 285–88; Gambetta (n 3).

[98] D'Attona (n 89).

[99] ibid.

[100] Antonella Coco, 'Neopatrimonialism and Local Elite Attitudes. Similarities and Differences Across Italian Regions' (2015) 3 Territory, Politics, Governance 167, 168.

[101] European Commission, Directorate-General for Justice, Freedom and Security. and Center for the Study of Democracy (n 92) 37; Dickie (n 30) 275, 285–91; Gambetta (n 3) 286; Rakopoulos, 'Façade Egalitarianism?' (n 27).

[102] Gambetta (n 3) 257; Coco (n 100) 169.

policies. However, the most damaging effect of this lack of accountability is in the area of public safety.[103]

The Weberian requirements for an ideal bureaucrat are well known.[104] A public servant is expected, among other requirements, to have received a formal qualification, act independently within the assigned role, be competent and to separate her personal interests from her administrative duties.[105] The fulfilment of these requirements is directly linked to a perception of the legitimacy of all administrative activities and, even if less rigorously applied, to the political leadership of elected officials. It is safe to say that none of those principles are applied in Sicily.

At the time of writing this book, 278 out of 391 Sicilian city councils have been put into administration by central institutions because they are unable to manage their budgets.[106] The incompetence of the administrators, appointed by the Mafia via rigged public competitions, is probably sufficient for the Mafia to prosper. Recall that 90 per cent of the population cannot process mildly complex cognitive activities and many must rely on patronage to get a job in a market flooded with unskilled labourers.[107] Note that these administrators are often in a situation of permanent debt to their respective kingpins,[108] and their discretionary administrative power, in relation to whatever task they might be asked to do, is at the disposal of their 'Mafia handlers'.[109]

In addition to massive financial incompetence, there are currently 202 Italian city councils that have been deemed to be controlled by Mafia syndicates.[110] Over 130 of these councils are based in Sicily and the nearby region of Calabria.[111] A staggering number of Italian residents – that is, 2.4 million – officially live in a community in which their political representatives have been selected by the Mafia. Furthermore, the most recent DIA report on Mafia activities indicates that the majority of urban areas in Sicily and almost all

---

[103] Max Weber, *Economy and Society: A New Translation* (Harvard University Press 2019).

[104] ibid 348.

[105] ibid.

[106] Francesco Tarantino, 'Sicilia, commissari in 278 Comuni che non hanno approvato il bilancio: c'è anche Palermo' *Giornale di Sicilia* <https://gds.it/articoli/politica/2022/08/10/sicilia-commissari-in-278-comuni-che-non-hanno-approvato-il-bilancio-f410930a-eeb7-4a68-919f-33ce1510f8c0/> accessed 15 August 2022.

[107] The World Bank Group and The European Commission (n 23).

[108] Coco (n 100) 170.

[109] ibid.

[110] 'Salgono a 201 i comuni attualmente sciolti in Italia' (*Openpolis*, 23 March 2020).

[111] ibid.

rural areas are controlled by one of the 1,000 Mafia families.[112] There are indications that despite the effects of Law n. 636, the situation is not improving. For instance, in 2006, 83 city councils in Southern Italy were controlled by an organised crime syndicate.[113] The current number of suspended city councils has increased to 130.[114]

I could continue to reproduce the depressing flow of data but, in relation to the aim of this section, it is sufficient to say that most Italians perceive their public institutions as corrupt.[115] The process is described by Antonella Coco with crystal clarity:

> [T]he primacy of [informal] vertical over horizontal ties and the variety of personalisation processes (related to power concentration, leadership forms and to the nature of power and relations throughout society) result in certain practices which become systemic and accepted, such as political and patronage-based appointments, clientelism, nepotism, corruption, draining public resources and undermining the capacity of bureaucracy to implement policies and undertake routine tasks.[116]

Italy is, it is clear from Coco's narrative, a low-trust society where justice is associated with power rather than reason.[117]

Furthermore, the dysfunctional clientele system of the Italian public sector fosters a perception that the Mafia's efficiency is to be preferred as a market regulator.[118] Gambetta noted, for instance, that over 50 per cent of the Sicilian population reported that the Mafia was beneficial to their village.[119] The egalitarian structure of Mafia families also compares favourably with the hierarchy and incompetence of Italian public institutions.[120] One long-term study monitoring the perceptions of the employees of an agricultural cooperative in Sicily indicated that they considered the Mafia's process for the allocation of resources to be in tune with egalitarian principles.[121]

The Italian public sector mimics efficiency without delivering it. The institutional structure of the Italian tax office is one of the best examples of this simulated efficacy. In Italy, inland revenues are collected and monitored

---

[112] Direzione Investigativa Antimafia, 'Semester Report 2019 Semester II' (n 87).
[113] 'Salgono a 201 i comuni attualmente sciolti in Italia' (n 110).
[114] ibid.
[115] D'Attona (n 89).
[116] Coco (n 100) 169.
[117] Gambetta (n 3) 42.
[118] ibid 53; European Commission, Directorate-General for Justice, Freedom and Security and Center for the Study of Democracy (n 92).
[119] Gambetta (n 3) 65, 68, 79.
[120] Paoli, *The Oxford Handbook of Organized Crime* (n 87) 128.
[121] Rakopoulos, 'Façade Egalitarianism?' (n 27) 107.

by a military organisation called the Guardia di Finanza (hereafter, GdF).[122] It is an international oddity among the 38 OECD countries.[123] A task that is normally carried out by civil servants, that is, collecting taxes, is carried out in Italy with the help of 60,000 soldiers.[124] However, Italy, according to multiple estimates, suffers from one of the highest tax-evasion rates in Europe and has the world's largest undeclared economy.[125] There are multifarious methodologies to estimate a country's level of fiscal evasion,[126] however, indicators such as international capital transfers suggest that in the period between 1999 and 2010, 8 per cent of Italy's gross domestic product was derived from an untaxed shadow economy.[127] In the same period, only five countries in the world managed to do worse: Bulgaria, Malta, Mexico, Romania and Turkey.[128]

As with other sociological analyses that focus on complex phenomena, the inability of public institutions like the GdF to deliver on their institutional commitments cannot be explained via simple deductive reasoning.[129] The deregulation of the Italian financial sector, for instance, and the decriminalisation of financial reporting in 2002 might partly explain the inefficiency of Italian tax collectors.[130] John D'Attona, in his analyses of the Italian attitude towards paying taxes, explains it in a few words: 'There is ample evidence in the literature suggesting that individuals are more likely to pay taxes if they believe that their government is honest and efficient … It is no wonder that tax evasion is so rampant in Italy.'[131] Thus, people perceive public functionaries as corrupt and inefficient, and that includes the soldiers serving among the ranks of the GdF.

---

[122] D'Attona (n 89).

[123] Buehn and Schneider (n 92); Giampaolo Arachi and Alessandro Santoro, 'Tax Enforcement for SMEs: Lessons from the Italian Experience' (2007) 5 eJournal of Tax Research 225; D'Attona (n 89).

[124] Buehn and Schneider (n 92); Arachi and Santoro (n 123); D'Attona (n 89).

[125] Josef Hien, 'Tax Evasion in Italy. A God given Right' in Sven Steinmo (ed), *The Leap of Faith: The Fiscal Foundations of Successful Government in Europe and America* (1st edn, Oxford University Press 2018).

[126] ibid; Arachi and Santoro (n 123); D'Attona (n 89).

[127] Buehn and Schneider (n 92) 8.

[128] ibid.

[129] ibid.

[130] July 13th and others, 'Italy's Latest Legislation on Accounting Fraud Highlights the Country's Difficulty in Pursuing Real Economic and Political Reform' (*EUROPP*, 13 July 2015) <https://blogs.lse.ac.uk/europpblog/2015/07/13/italys-latest-legislation-on-accounting-fraud-highlights-the-countrys-difficulty-in-pursuing-real-economic-and-political-reform/> accessed 6 September 2020; Hien (n 125); Arachi and Santoro (n 123); D'Attona (n 89).

[131] D'Attona (n 89) 108.

These perceptions are often substantiated.[132] In a recent scandal, for instance, a large-scale conspiracy network tried to insert its incompetent affiliates into the military ranks of the GdF.[133] The criminal network of civil servants who tried, but in this case failed, to allocate middle-management jobs and infiltrate military tax collectors involved over 50 civil servants.[134] The list of suspected individuals involved in rigging the national competition included an apparently eclectic group. The list of conspirators included military personnel, police officers, firefighters and civil servants with offices a thousand kilometres from each other.[135]

It is reasonable to suggest that the endemic corruption of the GdF is just one of among many examples of a dysfunctional public sector covered by a veneer of hollow institutional aspirations. From medical professionals to tax collectors via commissioned officers, underserving individuals are slotted into jobs where they are expected to perform poorly.[136] The *Lancet*, one of the leading scientific medical journals, reported on Italian health workers as follows:

> Inadequate working conditions, little stability, growth, or potential for career progression, low salaries, the commixture of politics and the healthcare system, and fake recruitment committees (the notorious Concorsi Truccati) hit the headlines regularly ... The rest of the world is moving fast, and Italy is reaching a point of no return.[137]

In Sicily, there are several implications that arise from having Italian public institutions populated by underserving individuals.[138]

---

[132] Coco (n 100) 170.

[133] ibid.

[134] 'Concorsi nelle Forze dell'ordine truccati, 8 misure cautelari' (*Agi*) <www.agi.it/cronaca/news/2020-06-12/concorsi-forze-ordine-truccati-8877278/> accessed 6 September 2020.

[135] ibid.

[136] Stefano Nespor, 'La Fabbrica Dei Nullafacenti' (2007) il Mulino; Redazione Scuola, 'Augusto Fantozzi e i 7 Arrestati: Ecco Chi Sono i Docenti Dello Scandalo Concorsi Truccati' (*Corriere della Sera*, 25 September 2017) <www.corriere.it/scuola/universita/cards/corruzione-universita-ecco-chi-sono-docenti-arrestati-dove-insegnano/ex-ministro-fantozzi_principale.shtml> accessed 20 December 2017; 'Esami Truccati al Concorso Della Guardia Di Finanza: Arrestati Due Marescialli Accusati Di Corruzione' (*Identità Insorgenti*, 3 May 2017) <www.identitainsorgenti.com/guardia-di-finanza/> accessed 6 September 2020.

[137] Luca La Colla, 'Health Worker Gap in Italy: The Untold Truth' (2019) 394 The Lancet 561, 562.

[138] Gambetta (n 3) 101.

For instance, Sicilian businesses compete in an open European market for goods, services and workers.[139] The inability to deliver prompt justice fosters a reduction in private investments[140] and increases in regional labour costs that are directly associated with productivity.[141] Given the high level of attrition that regional businesses are suffering because they are competing in unfavourable markets, credit institutions have increased interest rates to compensate for the augmented risk, which perpetuates a negative economic development loop.[142]

There are a few indications that the judiciary has also been affected by the patrimonial system.[143] Recently, the apex of the administrative justice system has been shaken by corruption scandals.[144] Antonino Calderone, one of the rural Mafia bosses in Sicily, reported in one his depositions to the Parliamentary Anti-Mafia Commission that an investigative judge halved the term of Calderone's restraining order in exchange for a 'gift'.[145] Subsequently, the judge befriended Calderone and asked the Mafia boss if he could alter the route for the construction of a highway that would have cut the judge's estate into two parts. The highway route, Calderone reported, was promptly altered to meet the magistrate's wishes.[146] It is also worth mentioning that the deposition by the Mafia boss, due to the extraordinary short-term nature of the statute of limitations in the Italian criminal system, had no administrative or criminal effect on the corrupt judge.[147] The fact that a judge was found to have colluded with a Mafia boss and yet continued to work might appear extravagant. However, recall that Italians expect their public servants to be both incompetent and corrupt.[148]

As is the case for the other chapters in this book, the aim here is not to forecast the institutional developments of Italian bureaucracy.[149] The aim of

---

[139] Consolidated versions of the Treaty on European Union and the Treaty on the Functioning of the European Union (TFEU) [2016] OJ C202/1. Title IV.

[140] European Commission, Directorate-General for Justice, Freedom and Security (n 29) 13.

[141] ibid 15.

[142] ibid 19.

[143] 'La banda dei giudici corrotti: l'inchiesta che sta sconvolgendo la magistratura' (*l'Espresso*, 19 February 2019) <http://espresso.repubblica.it/plus/articoli/2019/02/18/news/giudici-corrotti-1.331753> accessed 28 September 2020.

[144] ibid.

[145] Commisione Parlamentare di Inchiesta Sule fenomeno della mafia, 'Audizione Del Collaboratore Della Giustizia Antonino Calderone – Presidenza Del Presidente Luciano Violante' 77.

[146] ibid.

[147] Gambetta (n 3) 180.

[148] D'Attona (n 89) 108.

[149] Robert Hazell, *Constitutional Futures Revisited: Britain's Constitution to 2020* (Palgrave Macmillan 2008).

the chapter is instead to assess a selection of drivers of change that might influence the development of an effective system of territorial governance in Sicily.[150] The neo-patrimonialist nature of Italian regional and national institutions is, in this analysis, a negative driver of change. Incompetent civil and military employees have a personal stake in maintaining a system that provides them with bribes and gifts. The Mafia syndicates instead have an interest in supporting the inefficiency of regional and local public administrations by inserting their loyal affiliates into the ranks of Italian institutions.[151] The two interests produce a vicious loop of inefficiency and corruption that is exploited by Mafia syndicates.

## A NEGATIVE DRIVER OF CHANGE: THE MAFIA SYSTEM OF TERRITORIAL GOVERNANCE

In the previous section, I discussed the effects of patrimonialism on the Italian public institutions.[152] In this section, I will consider the influence of the Mafia system of territorial governance in Sicily as a negative driver of change.

Sicily is in a circular institutional crisis where constitutional rights and freedoms cannot be enforced because a criminal organisation has the monopoly over the market of violence.[153] At a general level, Mafia families are, by way of comparison to public institutions, effective at protecting all types of private transactions.[154] The territorial control of commercial transactions, both legal and illegal, is linked to the economic success of Mafia syndicates across the island. An elevated level of accountability is expected from all those involved in Mafia syndicates.[155] A Mafia mediator, for example, working in a section of a wholesale fish market, is expected to prevent violations of trade agreements in his supervised areas.[156] The fee for this service does not normally exceed 10 per cent of the value of the transaction. The mutual obligation, once that fee is collected, is systematically and consistently enforced.[157] A seller who does not

---

[150] Coco (n 100); European Commission, Directorate-General for Justice, Freedom and Security and Center for the Study of Democracy (n 92).

[151] Coco (n 100) 170. European Commission, Directorate-General for Justice, Freedom and Security and Center for the Study of Democracy (n 92) 37; Dickie (n 30) 275, 285–91; Gambetta (n 3) 286.

[152] Daniel C Bach, 'Patrimonialism and Neopatrimonialism: Comparative Trajectories and Readings' (2011) 49 Commonwealth & Comparative Politics 275.

[153] Paoli, *The Oxford Handbook of Organized Crime* (n 87) 130.

[154] Gambetta (n 3) 100.

[155] ibid 159; European Commission, Directorate-General for Justice, Freedom and Security (n 29) 20.

[156] ibid.

[157] ibid.

deliver the expected goods might be publicly punished.[158] A delay in a payment by the buyer might also result in a public beating.[159] Repeat offenders are dealt with by a hitman.[160] It is difficult to assess the relationship between a crime and an economic activity, but Gambetta's analysis of the operation of the fruit market in Palermo recorded eighteen murders over a period of two years.[161] The violent enforcement is expected by traders and by the Mafia associates working in that sector.[162] Incompetence or dishonesty, in all the ranks of a Mafia family, is also swiftly dealt with.[163] According to police reports, in Sicily, there are over 300 economic sectors completely controlled by cartels which ensure the enforcement of over 100,000 transactions per year.[164]

There are over 1,000 Mafia families with over 5,000 suspected mafiosi who operate within strictly enforced and well-known geographical areas.[165] The DIA's six-month reports insert updated and detailed maps of the territories controlled by Mafia families.[166] Most of these families operate as local service providers, but the 'market of violence' also has a vertical dimension.[167] As mentioned earlier, since the 1950s, the *Cupola* has worked as a facilitator for operations that require the coordination of multiple families.[168] The *Cupola* has its internal set of rules.[169] A representative of a Mafia family at a Commission meeting cannot also be the boss of that particular cartel.[170] The *Cupola* does not function as a government cabinet;[171] instead, it conducts itself as a politically

---

[158] Gambetta (n 3) 210.
[159] ibid.
[160] ibid 206.
[161] ibid 210.
[162] ibid 206.
[163] Tribunal of Palermo, 'Witness Transcript of Tommaso Buscetta to Judge G. Falcone' 4; Direzione Investigativa Antimafia, 'Semester Report 2019 Semester II' (n 87) 123.
[164] Gambetta (n 3) 201.
[165] Italian Parliament, Commisione Parlamentare di Inchiesta Sule fenomeno della mafia (n 88); Direzione Investigativa Antimafia, 'Semester Report 2019 Semester II' (n 87); Direzione Investigativa Antimafia, 'Semester Report 2019 Semester I' (n 87).
[166] Italian Parliament, Commisione Parlamentare di Inchiesta Sule fenomeno della mafia (n 88); Direzione Investigativa Antimafia, 'Semester Report 2019 Semester II' (n 87); Direzione Investigativa Antimafia, 'Semester Report 2019 Semester I' (n 87).
[167] Dickie (n 30) 3.
[168] 'La banda dei giudici corrotti: l'inchiesta che sta sconvolgendo la magistratura' (n 143) 16.
[169] Tribunal of Palermo (n 163).
[170] Dickie (n 30) 302.
[171] ibid.

representative institution that coordinates policies and reduces the potential tensions between cartels.[172]

A Mafia cartel also has an internal territorial hierarchical structure.[173] An individual is responsible for a provincial area, called a *mandamento*, which might include several Mafia families.[174] A single family is also institutionally divided. Each Mafia boss has at least one advisor.[175] The foot soldiers, like the mediator in the Palermo wholesale market, might act as mediators or as enforcers.[176] Local intermediaries also ensure a low level of criminality on the streets by controlling petty crime.[177] Unruly teenagers as young as twelve might be killed for committing trivial crimes in areas controlled by the Mafia.[178]

The police reports indicate that the Mafia's territorial control is also becoming more sociologically entrenched.[179] Electronic communications have facilitated the coordination of activities between criminal families in all commercial areas.[180] A recent police operation, for instance, revealed that Mafia cartels used e-communications to coordinate the market takeover of energy service providers, which have recently been liberalised, in Sicily.[181]

The Mafia has absolute and capillary control of all criminal transactions.[182] Even minute individual challenges to the monopoly in the area of criminal activity, such as pickpocketing, are dealt with via extreme brutality.[183] Operations that require some level of organisation, such as drug trafficking, illegal gambling and insurance scams are all controlled by Mafia cartels.[184] Criminal activities and their profits are managed in strictly defined areas[185] and the territorial boundaries seldom move.[186] As mentioned previously, the

---

[172] ibid; Tribunal of Palermo (n 163) 4.
[173] Paoli, *The Oxford Handbook of Organized Crime* (n 87) 128.
[174] Tribunal of Palermo (n 163) 4; Direzione Investigativa Antimafia, 'Semester Report 2019 Semester II' (n 87) 123.
[175] Tribunal of Palermo (n 163) 14.
[176] Dickie (n 30) 32.
[177] Direzione Investigativa Antimafia, 'Semester Report 2019 Semester II' (n 87) 123.
[178] Gambetta (n 3) 174.
[179] Direzione Investigativa Antimafia, 'Semester Report 2019 Semester II' (n 87) 115.
[180] ibid 114.
[181] ibid 117.
[182] ibid 122; Jerry Ratcliffe, 'Predictive Modeling Combining Short and Long-Term Crime Risk Potential: Final Report' 131.
[183] Gambetta (n 3) 174.
[184] Direzione Investigativa Antimafia, 'Semester Report 2019 Semester II' (n 87) 132.
[185] ibid 156.
[186] ibid 139.

economic success of each clan member is dependent on the ability to collect money from the fiefdom.[187]

Situations occur in which a criminal activity cannot be easily coordinated by a single local syndicate. For instance, the rigging of a public contract might be in the interest of multiple families, such as with the building of a motorway[188] or the election of national political candidates.[189] The level of coordination that Mafia families display in these criminal activities is particularly concerning because they show sophistication and foresight.

Going back to the example of the Mafia boss who altered the route of a highway to please a friendly judge,[190] the public contract was allocated to a company who won a national competition that was, in all probability, rigged. We might assume with a degree of certainty that the route of such a motorway was agreed during the engineering planning stage by all the Mafia families affected by such an endeavour. The route change requested by the judge, logic suggests, would have required an alteration in planning permission in one of the most inefficient regulatory systems in Europe,[191] and it might have added substantive costs.[192] Most probably, a single Mafia family could not have carried out all these tasks by itself nor might it have benefited from that in the long term. Magistrates are regularly transferred, and once this corrupt magistrate was moved out of the family-controlled territory, all this effort might have been for nothing. However, a group of Mafia families communally perceive the affiliation of a career judge as a worthy investment, because in the long term, the benefits he might provide to a large criminal conglomerate will outstrip the cost of this transaction.

The Mafia Commission's key asset is efficiency. It does not have, by way of comparison to public institutions, a rigid hierarchical structure. The loosely connected family syndicates adopt the principle of subsidiarity.[193] This might be the case when rigging construction bids, funnelling votes to national political representatives or orchestrating terrorist campaigns.[194] In the area of illegal activities, such as drug smuggling, the Mafia has an absolute monopoly. In the legitimate economy, the Mafia's bosses might have to compete with services

---

[187] Gambetta (n 3).
[188] Direzione Investigativa Antimafia, 'Semester Report 2019 Semester II' (n 87) 143, 154; Paoli, 'The Italian Mafia' (n 41).
[189] Gambetta (n 3).
[190] Commisione Parlamentare di Inchiesta Sule fenomeno della mafia (n 145) 77.
[191] The World Bank Group and The European Commission (n 23).
[192] Direzione Investigativa Antimafia, 'Semester Report 2019 Semester II' (n 87); Dickie (n 30).
[193] Paoli, 'The Italian Mafia' (n 41).
[194] Coco (n 100); Paoli, 'The Italian Mafia' (n 41); La Spina (n 40).

provided by State institutions, but these are rare instances. Overall, business and State institutions are directly or indirectly controlled by Mafia families that have a vested interest in avoiding any alterations to the system of governance in Sicily.

## CONCLUSION

In this chapter, I discussed the autonomous region of Sicily as another extreme case of a crisis of regional governance. Mafia families operate as the *de facto* government of the island in all areas that might produce some economic benefits. By comparison to other cases discussed in this book, there are no ongoing demands for secession nor any politically motivated violence.[195] The autonomous administration of the island is already both institutionally and pragmatically outside of the control of Italy. And it has been for a considerable time.

The chapter discussed two negative drivers of change that contribute to maintaining Sicily's out-of-control from public institutions. I explained that Italian public institutions are neo-patrimonialist.[196] Constitutionally and administratively, Italian public institutions might adopt strict principles of efficiency normally associated with modern Weberian states,[197] yet in practice, they operate as a multiple network of clienteles where kingpins predatorially collect public resources and re-distribute them among their clientele.[198]

The patronage system makes public officials easy prey for Mafia syndicates.[199] The self-referential cycles of corruption in the public sector affect all areas, but the long-term implications are particularly evident in the area of education.[200] The OECD's comparative analysis of its members shows that 90 per cent of the population in Sicily cannot efficiently carry out mildly complex cognitive tasks.[201] A functionally illiterate population in a developed country is conducive to a high level of unemployment, which in turn provides a reservoir of unskilled workers for the Mafia's illegal activities.[202]

---

[195] Widuto Agnieszka and European Parliamentary Research Service, 'Regional Inequalities in the EU'; Gambetta (n 3); Banca d 'Italia, 'Economie Regionali L'economia Delle Regioni Italiane Dinamiche Recenti e Aspetti Strutturali'; Acemoglu, De Feo and De Luca (n 3).

[196] Bach (n 152); Dickie (n 30); Felice (n 32); Acemoglu, De Feo and De Luca (n 3); Shmuel Noah Eisenstadt, *Traditional Patrimonialism and Modern Neopatrimonialism* (SAGE Publications Ltd 1973).

[197] Constitution of the Italian Republic art 1.

[198] Direzione Investigativa Antimafia, 'Semester Report 2019 Semester II' (n 87).

[199] Paoli, 'The Italian Mafia' (n 41).

[200] OECD (n 24) 28.

[201] ibid.

[202] Rakopoulos, *From Clans to Co-Ops* (n 28); Cantor and Land (n 28) 330.

Furthermore, studies on the interaction between corruption and criminal organisations suggest that an attempt to separate Mafia syndicates from the civil sector in Italy is part of a conceptual fabrication.[203] At the time of authoring this book, over 2 million Italians are living in local constituencies that are deemed to be under the complete control of Mafia families.[204] Administrators appointed by the Central Italian Government to take over these local institutions are seldom supported by residents. Given the ineffectiveness of national and regional public officials, Mafia syndicates and their cronies are often perceived as a better alternative to an inefficient State apparatus.[205]

Mafia bosses are, by comparison to Italian civil servants, efficient and accountable administrators.[206] The internal dynamics of a single Mafia group ensures a level of democratic accountability for its associates. The competition with other families instead fosters efficiency.[207] Economic accountability at the local level is also expected at the regional level. The regional coordination of crime activities, when needed, might fall into the hands of a commission of local representatives.[208] These collaborations reduce the levels of border conflict and coordinate resources for common projects such as the election of national politicians. In short, Sicily is experiencing the effects of a cycle of ungovernability in which Mafia syndicates are effective corporations that have taken on the role of a territorial government and contribute to the inefficiency of the public sector.

---

[203] European Commission, Directorate-General for Justice, Freedom and Security and Center for the Study of Democracy (n 92).

[204] ibid.

[205] European Commission, Directorate-General for Justice, Freedom and Security (n 29).

[206] Gambetta (n 3) 19.

[207] Veronica Ronchi, 'The Hybrid State Destatization and Neopatrimonialism' (Fondazione Eni Enrico Mattei 2020).

[208] Gambetta (n 3) 111.

# 4. North America: Quebec and Alaska

This chapter discusses two examples of differing historical crises. The first example describes the period in which Quebec nationalism collapsed into political violence.[1] This period lasted from 1968 until 1974 and included 63 terrorist attacks.[2] The second example discusses the effects of the ongoing genocide of Alaskan Native women and its effect on the perception of the legitimacy of US central institutions.[3] The two crises are different in nature but have been inserted into a single chapter as they are located in Northern America.[4]

The drivers of change that induced Québécois to relinquish their weapons and Alaskan tribes to build (or not to build) trust in public institutions cannot be compared.[5] As shown in the previous chapters of this book, a gamut of historical elements allow a constitutional system to spiral into a crisis and for others to foster the accommodation of identity claims within recognised institutions.[6] One assumption of the Constitutional Futures methodology is

---

[1] Garth Stevenson, *Parallel Paths: The Development of Nationalism in Ireland and Quebec* (McGill-Queen's University Press 2006) ch 8; William Tetley, *The October Crisis, 1970 an Insider's View* (McGill-Queen's University Press 2007); Dominique Clément, 'The October Crisis of 1970: Human Rights Abuses Under the War Measures Act' (2008) 42 Journal of Canadian Studies 160; 'The October Crisis of 1970' (1975) 33 The Advocate (Vancouver) 218.

[2] Raphael Cohen-Almagor, 'The Terrorists' Best Ally: The Quebec Media Coverage of the FLQ Crisis in October 1970' (2000) 25 Canadian Journal of Communication 254.

[3] Sandhya Ganapathy, 'Alaskan Neo-Liberalism Conservation, Development, and Native Land Rights' (2011) 55 Social Analysis 113; Martha Hirschfield, 'The Alaska Native Claims Settlement Act: Tribal Sovereignty and the Corporate Form' (1992) 101 The Yale Law Journal 1331; William Robinson, 'The Benefits of a Benefit Corporation Statute for Alaska Native Corporations' (2016) 33 Alaska L Rev 329.

[4] Robinson (n 3).

[5] Stevenson (n 1) 341.

[6] Anthony Spencer and Stephen Croucher, 'Basque Nationalism and the Spiral of Silence: An Analysis of Public Perceptions of ETA in Spain and France' (2008) 70 International Communication Gazette 137; Duncan Morrow, *Sectarianism – A Review* (Ulster University 2019); M Rafiqul Islam, 'Secession Crisis in Papua New Guinea: The Proclaimed Republic of Bougainville in International Law' (1991) 13 University of Hawaii Law Review 453; Alan Berman, 'Future Kanak Independence in New Caledonia: Reality or Illusion?' (1998) 34 Stanford Journal of International Law 287; Theodoros Rakopoulos, 'Façade Egalitarianism? Mafia and Cooperative

that drivers of change cannot be compared because they are often structurally different and are inserted into a unique timeline.[7] In other words, even when a driver of change appears to be similar to another, the context in which each driver acts creates diverging legal and sociological effects.

For instance, the Alaska Native Claims Settlement Act 1971[8] and the Aboriginal Land Rights (Northern Territory) Act 1976[9] are both land-management statutes triggered by a land claim, but the respective political aims were different. The Alaska Native Claims Settlement Act 1971 sought to reduce widespread poverty among the original inhabitants by inserting tribal lands into the mainstream US economy. The Aboriginal Land Rights (Northern Territory) Act 1976 instead wanted to compensate, among other aims, for previous predatory colonial policies.[10] The aim of this chapter is not to suggest that these types of comparisons are not possible or beneficial.[11] The argument purported here is instead that constitutional narratives set the boundaries of political debates and there is much to gain by inserting constitutional narratives into their distinctive socio-political scenarios.[12]

## THE OCTOBER CRISIS IN QUEBEC: THE RISE AND FALL OF THE SUPPORT FOR POLITICAL VIOLENCE

In this section, I will discuss the Quebec crisis. In particular, I will consider the period that started, with a margin of approximation, in the middle of the 1960s and lasted into the second half of the 1970s.[13] The start of the crisis coincided

---

in Sicily' (2017) 40 Political and Legal Anthropology Review 104; P Coaldrake, 'Reflections on the Repositioning of the Government's Approach to Higher Education, or I'm Dreaming of a White Paper' 22, Part 1 Journal of Higher Education Policy and Management 9.

[7] Robert Agranoff and Mark Glover, 'Introduction: Forecasting Constitutional Futures' in Robert Hazell (ed), *Constitutional Futures Revisited: Britain's Constitution to 2020* (Palgrave Macmillan 2008) 6.

[8] ANCSA, 43 U.S.C.

[9] Aboriginal Land Rights (Northern Territory) Act 1976; Aboriginal Land Rights (Northern Territory) Regulations 2007.

[10] Hirschfield (n 3) 1351; Pat Turner and Nicole Watson, 'The Trojan Horse' in Jon C Altman and Melinda Hinkson (eds), *Coercive Reconciliation: Stabilise, Normalise, Exit Aboriginal Australia* (Arena Publications Association 2007).

[11] Maurice Adams, Jaakko Husa and Marieke Oderkerk (eds), *Comparative Law Methodology* (Edward Elgar Publishing 2017).

[12] Jaakko Husa, *Interdisciplinary Comparative Law: Rubbing Shoulders with the Neighbours or Standing Alone in a Crowd* (Edward Elgar Publishing 2022) 148.

[13] Tetley (n 1) xxxii; Stevenson (n 1) ch 8; Clément (n 1); Cohen-Almagor (n 2). See Haljan, for analysis of the current implication of Quebec secession gambit. David Haljan, *Constitutionalising Secession* (Hart Publishing 2013) ch 9.

with an increasing level of self-awareness regarding Quebec identity.[14] During this period of social instability, the *Front de la Libération du Québec* (hereafter the FLQ) conducted a series of violent attacks which culminated in the kidnapping and murder of a Quebec cabinet minister.[15] The events that led to the murder, among others, of the Minister of Commerce are also known as the 1970 October Crisis.[16] I will explain that, among a series of factors, two drivers of change laid the groundwork for the crisis and for its subsequent dissipation. The first driver of change considered in this section is a constitutional system that, at the time, did not provide sufficient conditions for fostering the newly flourishing Québécois identity.[17] The second driver of change discussed in this section was an increasing awareness of Québécois identity among French speakers brought about by a cultural movement called the Quiet Revolution.[18]

Before I move on to the analysis, a series of qualifications must be inserted as part of the preliminary debate. First, I will use the term *French-speaking Canadians* to indicate a linguistic minority. The term was, at least until 1965, used to describe French-speaking Quebec inhabitants. From around 1965, the term *Québécois* was normally associated with Canadian French speakers who supported Quebec French identity. Geneviève Zubrzycki noted, for instance, a shift in the language: 'French-speaking people in Quebec were beginning to refer to themselves as "Québécois", a term that had hardly ever been used before the 1960s.'[19] She argued that this shift in meaning was part of a sociological transformation of symbolism associated with Quebec national identity.[20]

Second, the Canadian constitutional system is currently considered to be one of the best examples of a multinational political system.[21] The theoret-

---

[14] Michael D Behiels, *Prelude to Quebec's Quiet Revolution: Liberalism versus Neo-Nationalism, 1945–1960* (McGill-Queen's University Press – MQUP 1985).

[15] Stevenson (n 1) 270.

[16] Tetley (n 1) 33.

[17] ibid 1; Stevenson (n 1) ch 8.

[18] Cohen-Almagor (n 2).

[19] Geneviève Zubrzycki, 'Aesthetic Revolt and the Remaking of National Identity in Québec, 1960–1969' (2013) 42 Theory and Society 423, 423; Stevenson (n 1) 272.

[20] Zubrzycki (n 19).

[21] Alain-G Gagnon and Xavier Dionne, 'Historiographies et Fédéralisme Au Canada' (2009) Revista d'estudis autonòmics i federals 10, 11; Michael Keating, 'Rethinking Sovereignty: Independence-Lite, Devolution-Max and National Accommodation' (2012) 16 Revista d'Estudis Autonòmics i Federals 9, 9.

ical works of James Tully,[22] Alain Gagnon[23] and Will Kymlicka[24] prepared the basis for a systematic theory of regional governance around the globe.[25] Instead, the *Reference Re Secession of Quebec* by the Canadian Supreme Court established what are considered the globally accepted constitutional pillars of the interaction between regions and central institutions.[26] A national majority cannot trump a regional majority,[27] and negotiations between representatives of regional and central institutions have to be conducted in good faith.[28] These principles have since been inserted overtly or implicitly in multiple constitutional systems.[29] However, Quebec nationalists who supported the use of political violence in the 1960s were operating in a very different constitutional setting.[30]

---

[22] Alain-G Gagnon and James Tully (eds), *Multinational Democracies* (Cambridge University Press 2001).

[23] There is a plethora of studies on the Canadian multinational model. For a theoretical view which shows a connection between the process of recognition of Canadian original inhabitants and the development of multinational political system, see Gagnon and Tully ibid.

[24] Will Kymlicka, 'Multinational Federalism in Canada; Rethinking the Partnership' in Roger Gibbins and Guy Laforest (eds), *Beyond the Impasse: Towards Reconciliation* (McGill-Queen's University Press 1998).

[25] Michael Keating, 'So Many Nations, so Few States: Territory and Nationalism in the Global Era' in James Tully and Alain-G Gagnon (eds), *Multinational Democracies* (CUP 2001).

[26] *Reference Re Secession of Quebec* [1998] 2 SCR 217, [1998] 217, 263, 266–7.

[27] ibid 267.

[28] ibid; Stephen Tierney, 'Popular Constitutional Amendment: Referendums and Constitutional Change in Canada and the United Kingdom' (2015) 41 Queen's Law Journal 41, 48. The contagious effect of the decision is also evident in international law: Article 9 Declaration on the Rights of Indigenous Peoples (GA Res 61/295, UN Doc A/RES/47/1 (2007)). Donald Horowitz, 'Some Realism about Constitutional Engineering' in Andreas Wimmer (ed), *Facing Ethnic Conflicts: Toward a New Realism* (Rowman & Littlefield 2004).

[29] Arianna Giovannini and Davide Vampa, 'Towards a New Era of Regionalism in Italy? A Comparative Perspective on Autonomy Referendums' (2019) Territory, Politics, Governance 1, 581; Sujit Choudhry, 'Secession and Post-Sovereign Constitution-Making After 1989: Catalonia, Kosovo, and Quebec' (2019) 17 International Journal of Constitutional Law 461, 468; Hèctor López Bofill, 'Hubris, Constitutionalism, and "The Indissoluble Unity of the Spanish Nation": The Repression of Catalan Secessionist Referenda in Spanish Constitutional Law' (2019) 17 International Journal of Constitutional Law 943, 456.

[30] Alain Gagnon, 'Empowerment through Different Means Nationalism and Federalism in the Canadian Context' in Alain-G Gagson and José María Sauca (eds), *Negotiating Diversity: Identity, Pluralism, and Democracy* (PIE Peter Lang 2014) 42; Stevenson (n 1) 352.

Third, the 1763 Treaty of Paris transferred modern-day Quebec to the British Empire.[31] Article IV (2) of the Treaty of Paris included, as one of the conditions to peace, that the British Crown would respect the right of Catholics and the prerogatives of the Catholic Church.[32] The Quebec Act that enacted the treaty ensured a level of tolerance between the Anglican Church and the 'Church of Rome' but did not mention language or national identity.[33] The lack of acknowledgement of an identity group was, given the time of the enactment, normal. Smith explained that until the nineteenth century, national identities were not associated with political systems.[34] Historically, the social existence of multiple national identities was not related to the legitimacy of European Imperial institutions.[35] The combination of independent territorial institutions within the British Imperial Crown and the separation of the two adjacent communities divided along linguistic, religious and legal traditions fostered the development of two economically interdependent groups.[36] Conflicts over resources were to be expected, and the 1838 and 1848 Quebec rebellions were, within the limit of historical deduction, against the Imperial Crown rather than against the English-speaking community.[37]

The modern Canadian constitutional system began with the British North America Act 1867, commonly called the Constitution Act 1867.[38] The act unified three colonies into a single dominion under the name of Canada. The second phase of Canadian history coincided with the patriation and the

---

[31] King of Great Britain and King of France, 'The Definitive Treaty of Peace and Friendship between His Britannick Majesty, the Most Christian King, and the King of Spain (The Treaty of Paris)'; Stevenson (n 1) 31.

[32] King of Great Britain and King of France (n 31); Stevenson (n 1) 31.

[33] The Quebec Act 1774 14 Geo. III c. 83 s IV–VI, XV.

[34] Anthony D Smith, *Nationalism: Theory, Ideology, History* (Polity Press; Blackwell 2001) 123. There is consensus that the European model of the nation state that spread all over the world emerged after 1800. A general analysis of the connection between industrialisation and nationalism is in: Ernest Gellner, *Nationalism* (Phoenix 1998). There is also a general consensus among historians that European nation state as a model of political association developed over a long period of time. Eric Hobsbawm, *Age Of Empire: 1875–1914* (Hachette; 2010) ch 6. This analysis does not apply to China where the process of nation building commenced much earlier. Francis Fukuyama, *The Origins of Political Order: From Prehuman Times to the French Revolution* (Profile Books 2012) 134. Benedict Anderson, *Imagined Communities: Reflections on the Origin and Spread of Nationalism* (Verso 1983).

[35] Eric Hobsbawm, *Nations and Nationalism since 1780: Programme, Myth, Reality* (Cambridge University Press 1992).

[36] Stevenson (n 1) 51.

[37] ibid.

[38] The Constitution Act, 1867, 30 & 31 Vict, c 3 (renamed from the British North America Act 1867 by the Constitution Act 1982 s.53 (2); Gagnon and Dionne (n 21) 12.

enactment of the Constitution Act 1982 by the British Parliament.[39] The Constitution Act 1982 (UK) is considered as the pivotal moment in Canadian constitutional history in which the former colony finally cut its ties to its former Imperial master. The Canadian Constitution Act 1982 is in Schedule B of the Constitution Act 1982 (UK).[40] In this chapter, it will simply be referred to as the Constitution Act 1982.[41]

## A NEGATIVE DRIVER OF CHANGE: THE LEGACY OF CONSTITUTIONAL UNRECOGNITION

In the period that preceded the Constitution Act 1982, there was an element of uncertainty related to where Canadian sovereignty might end and where British Imperial legislative sovereignty might commence.[42] The Constitution Act 1982 relegated the role of British constitutional law to an unbounding interpretive narrative.[43] The Constitution Act 1982 includes the recognition of the Aboriginal Peoples of Canada[44] *but does not recognise Quebec national identity*.[45] It focused instead on the prerogative of linguistic communities without clarifying the role of Quebec national identity.[46] The 1995 pre-legislative consultative referendum over secession promoted by the Quebec Government was won by a small margin by the supporters of the Federation.[47] The legitimacy of the referendum was engaged, as mentioned earlier, in *Reference Re Secession*

---

[39] Stephen Tierney, 'Popular Constitutional Amendment: Referendums and Constitutional Change in Canada and the United Kingdom' (2015) 41 Queen's Law Journal 41.
[40] Canadian Charter of Rights and Freedoms, s 7, Part I of the Constitution Act, 1982, being Schedule B to the Canada Act 1982 (UK), 1982, c11.
[41] The Constitution Act 1982.
[42] Tierney (n 39) 70.
[43] Peter W Hogg, *Constitutional Law of Canada* (Carswell 2009) 7.
[44] The Constitution Act 1982 ss 25, 35.1; James Tully, 'Introduction' in Alain-G Gagnon and James Tully (eds), *Multinational Democracies* (Cambridge University Press 2001) 6, 14; James Tully, *Strange Multiplicity: Constitutionalism in an Age of Diversity* (Cambridge University Press 1995) 15–16, 57, 63.
[45] 'Dans l'ordre constitutionnel de 1982, la nation canadienne reconnait les peuples autochtones, les minorités anglo-québécoise et franco-canadiennes du ROC15, de même que la diversité issue de l'immigration16, mais le peuple québécois ne figure pas dans cet ordre constitutionnel'. ('Within the 1982 constitutional system, the Canadian nation recognises the original inhabitants, the French and English minorities of the ROC15 and the cultural diversity of immigration but the people of Quebec are not recognized within this constitutional system') (author translation). Michel Seymour, 'La Nation Québécoise Peut-Elle Se Donner La Constitution de Son Choix?' (2015) Revue québécoise de droit international 246.
[46] The Constitution Act 1982 ss 16–23.
[47] Prime Minister of Quebec, Draft Bill on the Sovereignty of Quebec 1995.

*of Quebec*, at the Canadian Supreme Court.[48] The decision had multiple readings and is considered a landmark in the study of regionalist movements.[49]

However, the period considered in this part of the chapter focuses on a selection of drivers of change that affected Quebec nationalism between the middle of the 1960s and the end of the 1970s.[50] It is in this segment of Quebec history that the flourishing economic French-speaking elites developed a new sense of identity that was frustrated by a lack of institutional recognition.[51] Before 1970, over 70 per cent of executive jobs within Quebec corporations consisted of English speakers.[52] The French speakers represented over 80 per cent of the regional population but owned only 50 per cent of businesses and 15 per cent of the added value sector.[53] After 1970, the adoption of statutory measures, such as the Official Languages Act of 1969, indirectly helped the employment of French-speaking civil servants.[54]

The new economically driven self-awareness of the Quebec national community was not, simply put, mirrored in the Constitution. The constitutional system that channelled the crisis and informed its institution relied on the text in the Constitution Act 1867.[55] The act was, by the 1970s, in need of reform, but the relative stability of the Quebec Government kept any such reform off of the agenda. Two sections had direct implications for the October Crisis. Section 51 of the Constitution Act 1867 provided for a series of protected constituencies with an English-speaking majority that had a relatively small population.[56] The protected constituencies had distorted elections since the enactment of the Constitution Act 1867. In the 1970 election however, the new up and coming Parti Québécois obtained 24 per cent of the votes but managed

---

[48] *Reference Re Secession of Quebec* [1998] 2 SCR 217 (n 26).
[49] Giacomo Delledonne and Giuseppe Martinico (eds), *The Canadian Contribution to a Comparative Law of Secession: Legacies of the Quebec Secession Reference* (Springer International Publishing 2019).
[50] Stevenson (n 1) 256–78.
[51] The Constitution Act, 1867, 30 & 31 Vict, c 3 (renamed from the British North America Act 1867 by the Constitution Act 1982 s 53 (2).
[52] Cohen-Almagor (n 2) 259.
[53] Gagnon (n 30) 42; Stevenson (n 1) 263.
[54] Official Languages Act (1969) 1970, R.S.C, Ch. 0-2.
[55] The Constitution Act, 1867, 30 & 31 Vict, c 3 (renamed from the British North America Act 1867 by the Constitution Act 1982 s 53 (2).
[56] ibid.

to elect only seven representatives in the National Assembly of Quebec (out of 107 available).[57]

> [O]n the 6th December 1970, within eight months of his election, Bourassa introduced Bill 65, An Act respecting Electoral Districts, which abolished thirteen constituencies protected under section [51] of the British North America Act of 1867 … There were actually eighteen such constituencies by 1970, and, though they had few voters, their boundaries could not be enlarged without constitutional change. They had distorted Quebec elections for fifty years but no premier had dared to face the problem.[58]

The gap between the number of votes and those elected to office increased the frustration felt by all nationalists in the electoral system but it was received particularly badly by the FLQ members.[59] In its manifesto, which was publicly broadcast during the October 1970 Crisis, the FLQ voiced its lack of trust in a system in which the number of MPs did not align with the number of casted votes.

The second aspect of the Constitution Act 1867 that affected the October Crisis was the possibility of passing special laws during periods of instability.[60] These were the so-called War Measures.[61] Section 91 of the Constitution Act 1867 includes a list of Federal competences, but allows, in the case of an 'apprehended insurrection', for laws to be passed for the peace and order of Canada.

> It shall be lawful for the Queen, by and with the Advice and Consent of the Senate and House of Commons, to make Laws for the Peace, Order, and good Government of Canada, in relation to all Matters not coming within the Classes of Subjects by this Act assigned exclusively to the Legislatures of the Provinces.[62]

The statutory measures that transferred this power to the Government were enacted in 1914 and the act was aptly called 'The War Measures Act 1914'.[63] However, Sections 3 and 6 allow the Governor in Council to pass statutes in

---

[57] 'Results and Statistics' (*Élections Québec*), Tetley (n 1) 9.

[58] William Tetley, *October Crisis, 1970: An Insider's View* (McGill-Queen's University Press 2014) 8.

[59] Tetley (n 1) 13; Front de la Libération du Québec, 'FLQ Manifesto 1970' 1, Footnotes: 4–5; 3 Footnote: 11.

[60] The War Measures Act 5 1914 c 2 1914; War Measures Act, R.S.C. 1970, c W.-2; Clément (n 1); Peter Rosenthal, 'The New Emergencies Act: Four Times the War Measures Act' (1991) 20 Manitoba Law Journal 563.

[61] The War Measures Act 5 1914 c 2; War Measures Act, R.S.C. 1970, c W.-2; Clément (n 1); Rosenthal (n 60).

[62] British North America Act 1867 (C3).

[63] The War Measures Act 5 1914 c 2; War Measures Act, R.S.C. 1970, c W.-2.

times of peace when there is a risk of an 'apprehended insurrection'.[64] There was little that suggested a probable Canadian insurrection in 1914 and, even less so, during the October 1970 Crisis.[65] I will return to this point when I discuss the identity-formation process that sustained the October Crisis, but Tetley argues that the War Measures – and therefore Section 91 of the Constitution Act 1867 – were the key factor that brought the October Crisis to an end. Following the enactment of the War Measures Act, the Canadian Army was sent to Montreal to provide auxiliary support to the police.[66] The key point, in relation to the perception of legitimacy of Federal institutions in Quebec is that: two months after the invocation of the War Measures Act 1970, polls indicated that a large part of the Canadian population within and outside Quebec supported the Government decision to use emergency powers.[67] However, the new emergency measures were perceived as a breach of negotiations by the FLQ, and as retaliation, the kidnapped Quebec Minister of Commerce was strangled to death by his captors.[68]

## POSITIVE DRIVER OF CHANGE: THE QUIET REVOLUTION

The Constitution Act 1867 was one of the many drivers of the 1970 Crisis. In this part of the chapter, I will discuss the Quiet Revolution, which was the cultural movement in the FLQ that emerged as the leading paramilitary group in the region.[69] The series of sociological events that were part of the Quiet Revolution indicate a radical change in popular perceptions.[70] As mentioned earlier, the cultural revolution was directly connected to economic changes.

> In Quebec ..., the decade of the 1950s was one of rapid economic and demographic growth. The province's population increased by 30 per cent during the decade, while that of Montreal (including its suburbs) increased by more than 50 per cent in the same period. With rapid industrial growth, largely driven by foreign direct investment, added to very low inflation and virtually full employment, Quebec entered the age of mass consumption.[71]

---

[64] Cohen-Almagor (n 2).
[65] Clément (n 1).
[66] Stevenson (n 1) 274; Tetley (n 58) 62.
[67] Canadian Museum of History, 'Gallup Poll 1970: Justification for Invoking the WarMeasures Act' Tetley (n 58) 104.
[68] Tetley (n 58) 141.
[69] Tetley (n 1) xxxi.
[70] Stevenson (n 1) 258.
[71] ibid.

An item which made its way onto the must-have list of the 1950s newly wealthier Québécois family was the TV set.[72] The privatisation of TV frequencies in the 1960s allowed French-only speaking TV stations to broadcast programmes that were locally produced.[73]

The new medium had a transformative effect in all of Canada, but it was particularly so among the French-speaking minority. Until the 1950s, Radio Canada was the leading promoter of the Québécois identity.[74] Paul Rutherford describes Radio Quebec as the 'soul' of French Canada.[75] However, by the end of the 1960s, over 90 per cent of Quebec households had a TV set[76] that was tuned to a privately owned TV station which broadcasted locally produced programmes in French.[77] It was a miracle medium, as Rutherford points out, and it made studios in Montreal the centre of French-speaking Quebec's cultural life.[78] The uniqueness of French identity in Canada was also enhanced by the tendency of English-speaking Canadians to follow US broadcasters.[79] A significant part of the Canadian population lives in close proximity to the US border and, in 1960, once they were given the possibility of watching US-broadcasted television, they often preferred it over Canadian television because they were given access to US sporting events.[80] The transformation of Radio Quebec 'as the soul of French Canada' into a revolutionary tool was gradual, but by the October Crisis, it was clear that TV broadcasters had a substantial role in defining Canadian multinationalism.[81]

The TV set increased the cultural gap between English- and French-speaking Canadians.[82] It also changed the French-speaking attitude internally. The most significant aspect was the tilting of their identity towards more liberal political stances and a reduced appeal among young individuals for conservative policies and the Catholic Church. It was within the fringes of the Quiet Revolution that the new leftist narratives found specific targets in the form of public institutions, such as the Royal family, and corporations, such as the Canadian

---

[72] Kathryn-Jane Hazel, 'The Media and Nationalism in Quebec: A Complex Relationship' (2001) 2 Journalism Studies 93, 97; Paul Rutherford, *When Television Was Young: Primetime Canada 1952–1967* (University of Toronto Press 1990) 5.
[73] Hazel (n 72) 97.
[74] Stevenson (n 1) 259.
[75] Rutherford (n 72) 5.
[76] Hazel (n 72) 97.
[77] ibid.
[78] Stevenson (n 1) 258.
[79] Rutherford (n 72) 106.
[80] ibid 242.
[81] ibid 20; Cohen-Almagor (n 2); Rutherford (n 72) 433, 494.
[82] Rutherford (n 72) 20; Cohen-Almagor (n 2); Rutherford (n 72) 433, 494.

National Railways or Air Canada.[83] This tendency to transform ideological narratives in a search for scapegoats that had to be physically eliminated was one of the elements that appeared in the FLQ's manifestos.[84]

Television transformed the 'soul' of French Canada, and new radical left narratives that appeared in newspapers and magazines like *Le Devoir* started to infiltrate Quebec's intelligentsia.[85] This new group of intellectuals who were labelled as the *citélibrists* included a young lawyer who was moonlighting as a journalist, Pierre Elliott Trudeau.[86] The *citélibrists'* moniker was derived from the magazine *Cité Libre*.[87] The magazine was often used as a platform in which Trudeau and many others pointed out the conservative nature of Quebec politics and, in particular, of its connection with the Catholic Church.[88] In 1967, Trudeau had the chance to transform those ideas into policy by commencing a process of liberalising the Canadian legal system in the area of family law, abortion and homosexuality.[89]

Trudeau's natural ability to perform in front of the TV camera helped him to gather support for his policies in the Canadian Parliament.[90] However, opposition to the decriminalisation of homosexuality, divorce and other policies was particularly strong in Quebec.[91] Stevenson describes the complex interaction between conservative politics and the Church using a clear narrative: 'Quebec before 1960 was conservative, backward, and subservient to clerical authority.'[92] The Church controlled a large network of private schools and hospitals. Before Medicare was introduced, the Catholic Church was the largest private medical care organisation in Quebec, making the Catholic Church the largest Quebec employer.[93] The Catholic Church in Quebec was operating covertly as a State within the State. The Union National, which controlled the National Assembly of Quebec (which at the time was called the Legislative Assembly of Quebec), had strong ties with the Catholic Church and was perceived by the *citélibrists* as being corrupt: 'It is against that backdrop that education, health, and welfare were slowly but solidly confessionalized, turning the Church in French Canada into a "crypto-state" until the creation of the provincial welfare

---

[83] Stevenson (n 1) 269.
[84] Front de la Libération du Québec (n 59); Stevenson (n 1) 270.
[85] Stevenson (n 1) 261.
[86] ibid 260.
[87] ibid 261; Rutherford (n 72) 172.
[88] The Criminal Law Amendment Act S.C. 1968–69, c 38 38; Stevenson (n 1) 261.
[89] Rutherford (n 72) 430.
[90] ibid 431.
[91] (n 1) 218.
[92] ibid.
[93] ibid 261.

state in the 1960s.'[94] The perception of a corrupt and backward Québécois identity changed during the Quiet Revolution.

From 1965 onwards, Québécois were either indifferent to the Church or were anticlerical.[95] The large majority of the new professional middle class who spoke French adopted a form of aloof laicity in which the separation of State and Church[96] never reached the level of militancy developed in France after 1870.[97] The lack of enthusiasm for secularism as the unofficial meaning provider for post-1965 Québécois identity[98] did not reduce the support for independence.[99] In the late 1960s, the *Maîtres chez nous* slogan, translated as Masters in Our Own House, appeared in political rallies and in the French-speaking media.[100] French President De Gaulle's emphatic support for the French community was manifested in his visit as the President of the French Republic to Montreal.[101] In one of his public engagements, he ended his speech with '*Vive le Québec! Vive le Québec libre!*') ('Long live Quebec! Long live a free Quebec!').[102] The 15,000 people attending the speech responded by chanting '*Maître chez nous*' ('Masters in our own home') in what appears from the archive videos to be a hotbed of nationalist fervour.[103]

However, there are indications that the declaration was not part of French diplomatic policy but rather a manifestation of De Gaulle's personal belief.[104] The official stance of France on regionalist movements is discussed at length in the New Caledonia chapter. Independently from France's diplomatic stance, the statement by the French President is considered a watershed moment in the Quiet Revolution.[105] In 1970, the French Government committed itself to sending financial support to Quebec's regional government.[106] The offer was

---

[94] ibid 260.
[95] ibid 276; Front de la Libération du Québec (n 59) 8.
[96] Geneviève Zubrzycki, *Beheading the Saint: Nationalism, Religion, and Secularism in Quebec* (University of Chicago Press 2016); David Marrani, *Dynamics in the French Constitution: Decoding French Republican Ideas* (Routledge 2013).
[97] Zubrzycki (n 96) 463; Marrani (n 96); Vito Breda, 'Balancing Secularism with Religious Freedom: In Lautsi v Italy the European Court of Human Rights Evolved' in Angus JL Menuge (ed), *Legitimizing Human Rights* (Ashgate 2013).
[98] Zubrzycki (n 96) 463; Marrani (n 96); Breda (n 97).
[99] ibid; ibid; ibid.
[100] French Republic, FranceArchives Archives, 'Visite Officielle Du Général de Gaulle à Montréal, Exposition Universelle de Montréal'; Stevenson (n 1) 273.
[101] French Republic, FranceArchives Archives (n 100).
[102] ibid.
[103] *Discours de Montréal 'Vive le Québec libre' Panorama – 28.07.1967* (Directed by Jean Lanzi, Office national de radiodiffusion télévision française 1967).
[104] French Republic, FranceArchives Archives (n 100).
[105] Stevenson (n 1) 263.
[106] ibid 273.

refused, but that reinforced the idea that the Québécois struggle for greater autonomy and secession was viewed as legitimate by parts of the international community.[107]

The noble reasons for the actions of the FLQ might have received international validation by De Gaulle, but the ordinary crimes committed by the group were part and parcel of the logistics of running a paramilitary organisation.[108] The FLQ's criminal activities were well organised in a secret schedule of programmed robberies and bomb attacks.[109] The FLQ's ideology might have been borrowed from Marxist narratives that were popular among the Quiet Revolution supporters, but it embraced Leninist strategies.[110] Media broadcasters had a significant role in focusing public attention on the ideology of the FLQ and less on its methods.[111] The combination of social instability and indirect media support which appeared smitten by the Che Guevara look-alike FLQ leader made it very difficult to assess the effective size of the FLQ and its operational abilities.[112] However, there is no evidence that support for the violence had a large membership base.[113] Quite the contrary. The most optimistic estimate was that it had fewer than 400 members.[114]

The 1960s and 1970s were years of turmoil. There were strikes, and at the beginning of October 1970, in short succession, the FLQ kidnapped a British diplomat and a member of the Quebec Government.[115] The media coverage of the kidnapping was initially tilted in favour of the FLQ.[116] On 15 October negotiations came to an impasse and the Canadian Government considered the situation in Quebec to be so destabilised that an insurrection was imminent.[117] The First Minister invoked the powers set in the War Measures Act.[118] As mentioned in the analysis of the indirect effect of the enactment of the War Measures Act, the FLQ killed the Quebec Minister of Commerce, Pierre La Porte.[119]

---

[107] ibid.
[108] Cohen-Almagor (n 2) 4.
[109] Tetley (n 58) 21.
[110] ibid 19.
[111] Cohen-Almagor (n 2).
[112] Tetley (n 58) 30.
[113] ibid; 'HC (CAN) 16 October 1970, Vol I, 124'.
[114] Tetley (n 1) 30.
[115] Tetley (n 58) 40.
[116] Cohen-Almagor (n 2).
[117] Tetley (n 58); Cohen-Almagor (n 2) 254; Hazel (n 72).
[118] The War Measures Act 5 1914 c 2; War Measures Act, R.S.C. 1970, c W.-2; British North America Act 1867 s 91.
[119] Cohen-Almagor (n 2) 264.

The murder of an innocent individual made the support for the FLQ vanish overnight.[120] The Quiet Revolution returned to being a liberal anticonservative movement that progressively and democratically changed Quebec society.[121] Put simply, Quebec nationalism continued to develop as a liberal and democratic movement. In 1973, the Parti Québécois gained 6 per cent (but lost a seat), and in 1976, it won the majority in the National Assembly of Quebec.[122] The 1980 referendum and the 1982 constitutional reform did not result in the recognition of the sovereignty of Quebec or its acknowledgement as a distinctive nation, but confirmed a distinctive commitment to procedural liberal democracy that cares for human rights.[123] The distinctive commitment to procedural liberal democracy was, and probably still is, the legacy of the Quiet Revolution as a positive driver of change in the crisis which occurred between the 1960s and 1980s.

## AFTER THINGS FELL APART: AN ANALYSIS OF QUEBEC'S 'PAST–FUTURE' SCENARIOS

In October 1970, things did fall apart in Quebec. This section provides an indication of the role that the drivers of change played in altering the Canadian Constitution as a result of the October Crisis.[124] Wilson and Wilford, in describing the ongoing cyclical crisis in Northern Ireland, used the term 'steady as she goes' to define a scenario in which political parties endorse democratic values and where territorial socio-economic issues are resolved by the daily activity of central and regional governments.[125] The 'steady-as-she-goes' scenario did not materialise in Northern Ireland. It is, within a margin of approximation, what has emerged from the 1970 Crisis in Quebec.

The perceived lack of legitimacy of the 1867 Constitution fostered a period of political violence and a military response by the Canadian Government.[126] The October Crisis was one, among many elements, that distinguished the sociological transformation of Quebec identity.[127] The crisis culminated in a series of violent events in October 1970.[128] The 'tit for tat' between terrorists

---

[120] ibid.
[121] Stevenson (n 1) 274; Cohen-Almagor (n 2); Hazel (n 72).
[122] 'Results and Statistics' (n 57).
[123] Gagnon (n 30).
[124] Stevenson (n 1) ch 7.
[125] Robin Wilson and Rick Wilford, 'Northern Ireland: Polarisation or Normalisation?' in Robert Hazell (ed), *Constitutional Futures Revisited: Britain's Constitution to 2020* (Palgrave Macmillan 2008) 64.
[126] Tetley (n 58); Cohen-Almagor (n 2); 'The October Crisis of 1970' (n 1).
[127] Behiels (n 14).
[128] Stevenson (n 1) 274.

and institutions had the effect of producing a dramatic change in public opinion.[129] A few aspects of the crisis regarding the legitimisation of the Canadian constitutional system still linger today.[130] For instance, in 2006, the House of Commons approved a motion put forward by the First Minister that recognised that the Québécois form 'a nation within a united Canada'.[131]

However, the constitutional role of Quebec within the Canadian Federation is stable.[132] As mentioned earlier, the 'steady-as-she-goes' scenario considered by Wilson and Wilford never materialised in Northern Ireland.[133] The region is still in the 'bumpy ride scenario' in which institutions move backwards and forwards between periods of sectarian violence and mediated agreements.[134] In Quebec, the period of violence channelled nationalist aspirations into developing a cultural distinctness.[135] The 'steady-as-she-goes' scenario that emerged after the Constitutional Act 1982 altered the role of the courts.[136] Boundary disputes, even over radical prerogatives, such as the possibility of having a referendum over secession, are discussed by judges without triggering civic unrest.[137]

## THE UNITED STATES: THE ALASKA CRISIS AND A GENOCIDE WITH COGNITION

The previous section of this chapter discussed a period of Quebec history where a legitimacy crisis led to a period of political violence.[138] Despite the similarities with Northern Ireland, the period of instability did not spiral out of control and into civil war.[139] This part of the chapter discusses instead the epidemic of violence against Alaskan Native women, which has led to the role of central institutions among Native Villages being questioned.[140] The recent

---

[129] Cohen-Almagor (n 2); Stevenson (n 1) 274.
[130] Alain Gagnon, 'Québec-Canada's Constitutional Dossier' in Alain-G Gagnon (ed), *Quebec: State and Society, Third Edition* (University of Toronto Press 2004) 139–40.
[131] 'HC (Can) 27 November 2006 Vol 141, 39'.
[132] Wilson and Wilford (n 125).
[133] ibid.
[134] ibid 57.
[135] Stevenson (n 1) 274.
[136] Tierney (n 39).
[137] Delledonne and Martinico (n 49); López Bofill (n 29); Germa Bel, *Disdain, Distrust and Dissolution: The Surge of Support for Independence in Catalonia* (Sussex Academic Press 2015).
[138] Clément (n 1).
[139] Stevenson (n 1); Spencer and Croucher (n 6).
[140] Megan Mallonee, 'Selective Justice: A Crisis of Missing and Murdered Alaska Native Women Notes' (2021) 38 Alaska Law Review 93, 94; Alaska Native Women's

enactment of the Violence Against Women Act Reauthorization Act of 2022 (VAWA 2022) engages the issue directly by decentralising criminal policies.[141] The new VAWA 2022 is the latest coordinated response to a crime epidemic that has disproportionally affected a historically discriminated regional community where policies are formed by consulting with Native Indian and Alaskan representatives.[142]

There is an emotive charge surrounding the violence against Alaskan Native women.[143] The final Canadian report by the National Inquiry into Missing and Murdered Indigenous Women and Girls describes the increasing number of homicides as a 'genocide' with cognition.[144] The latest report from the Alaska State Department of Public Safety indicates that: 'Alaskan Native females were reported to have the highest victimization rate of any gender or racial group, comprising 42% of all reported victims.'[145] However, Alaskan Native females make up only 7 per cent of Alaskan residents.[146] There are indications that these homicides replicate a process of violent racial domination.[147]

The genocide of Alaskan Native women is a regional crisis.[148] Two hundred and twenty-nine of the 566 recognised Indian tribes and Alaskan Native

---

Resource Center, 'Missing and Murdered Indigenous Women: An Action Plan for Alaska Native Communities'; Violence Against Women Act Reauthorization Act of 2022 (as a part of the Consolidated Appropriations Act, 2022 ) Pub.L. 117–103) 2022; Jamie Bartosch, 'Why Are So Many Indigenous Women in Alaska Coming Up Missing and Murdered?' (A&E) <www.aetv.com/real-crime/missing-murdered-indigenous-women-native-alaska-other-states> accessed 25 April 2022.

[141] Violence Against Women Act Reauthorization Act of 2022 (as a part of the Consolidated Appropriations Act, 2022 ) Pub.L. 117–103).

[142] Mallonee (n 140) 95.

[143] National Indigenous Women's Resource Center, 'Rising for Justice for MMIW | NIWRC'.

[144] National Inquiry into Missing and Murdered Indigenous Women and Girls (Canada), 'Executive Summary of the Final Report: Reclaiming Power and Place: The Final Report of the National Inquiry into Missing and Murdered Indigenous Women and Girls 2019' 2. For an example of latest consultation see: US Department of Justice, Tribal Consultations & Advisory Groups, 'Consultation on Public Safety and Missing or Murdered Indigenous Persons' (16 March 2022) <www.justice.gov/tribal/tribal-consultations-advisory-groups> accessed 7 May 2022.

[145] The Department of Public Safety (Alaska), Division of Statewide Services, 'Felony Level Sex Offenses, Crime in Alaska Supplemental Report 2017' 4.

[146] US Census Bureau, 'American Indian Alaska Native Population Growth' (*Census.gov*).

[147] Violence Policy Center, 'When Men Murder Women: An Analysis of 2017 Homicide Data' 52.

[148] US Department of Justice, Office on Violence Against Women, 'Annual Report Proceedings, Government-to-Government Violence Against Women Tribal Consultation' 11.

Villages are in Alaska.[149] According to the 2020 Census, 15 per cent of the Alaskan population identified as First Nations individuals, which is one of the highest in the US States.[150] In areas such as the Bethel census region in northeast Alaska, 86 per cent of residents consider themselves Alaskan Natives.[151] As discussed in the chapter that analysed the Intervention in the Northern Territory, it is expected that Alaskan Natives will look with suspicion at all policies arising from central institutions.[152]

I will describe two drivers of change, among many, that are altering the trajectory of the current crisis. The first driver of change is the legal framework in which Native American and Alaskan institutions operate. The second is the distinctive identity-formation process of the Alaskan Native communities. Before the two drivers of change are discussed, two qualifications are needed. First, I will use the term *Alaskan Natives* and their communities to describe a kaleidoscope of nations with distinctive traditions. Alaskan Natives might call themselves, for instance, Inuit, Yupiit or Dine' he.[153] They are ethnically classified as belonging to a group named as American Indians, Eskimos and Aleuts.[154] I will use the term *Indian tribes* to describe the communities of the original inhabitants of the United States, excluding Alaska. These are reductive terms which include a kaleidoscope of nations with a distinctive claim to sovereignty.[155] Second, this part of the chapter is not intended to provide a comprehensive analysis of the relationship between the legal status of Alaskan Native tribes and their members in the US legal system.[156] The aim is instead to provide a constitutional analysis in a regional context.

---

[149] Mallonee (n 140) 95.

[150] 'Alaska – 2020 Census Bureau Profile'.

[151] ibid.

[152] Alan Taylor, *American Colonies: The Settling of North America (The Penguin History of the United States, Volume 1)* (Penguin 2002); Mallonee (n 140); Wayne Edwards, *Sovereignty and Land Rights of Indigenous Peoples in the United States* (Palgrave Macmillan US 2020) 21.

[153] David S Case and David A Voluck, *Alaska Natives and American Laws: Third Edition* (University of Alaska Press 2012) 1.

[154] ibid 1, Note 1.

[155] *Alaska Chapter, Associated General Contractors of America v Pierce*, 694 F2d 1162 (9th Cir 1982).

[156] Case and Voluck (n 153).

# A POSITIVE DRIVER OF CHANGE: INDIAN JURISPRUDENCE AND THE ALASKAN NATIVE CORPORATIONS

The VAWA 2022 is the latest attempt by Congress to grapple with the genocide of Alaskan Native women.[157] In this section, I will explain the constitutional setting which allows a confusing jurisdictional system to linger on and the effects of the latest VAWA 2022.[158]

Alaskan Natives became part of the United States after the enactment of the US Constitution and they are not mentioned in it.[159] There is, in Article 1, a well-known reference to Indian tribes: 'The Congress shall have Power ... to regulate Commerce ... with the Indian Tribes.'[160] There is ongoing demand for the increasing recognition of Alaskan Native sovereignty, but that is not currently associated with a demand to amend the US Constitution.[161] Until 1934, there were doubts about the status of Alaskan Natives. It was generally assumed that Alaskan Native land was to be treated as any estate owned by non-Natives.[162] The Indian Reorganization Act 1934, however, confirmed the existence of an Indian sovereignty which was, already, implicitly recognised by common law.[163] The Indian Reorganization Act 1934 recognised

---

[157] US Department of Justice, Office on Violence Against Women (n 148) 11.

[158] Department of Justice, Annual Government-to-Government and Violence Against Women Tribal Consultation, '2021 Update on the Status of Tribal Consultation Recommendations'; US Department of Justice, Tribal Consultations & Advisory Groups, 'Tribal Consultation Reports'. Violence Against Women Act Reauthorization Act of 2022 Pub.L. 117–103 2022.

[159] US Congress and Majesty the Emperor of all the Russias, 'Treaty Concerning the Cession of the Russian Possessions in North America by His Majesty the Emperor of All the Russias to the United States of America (20 March 1867) (Ratified 28 May 1867) Treaty of Cession 15 Stat. 539'.

[160] US Const. Art. 1 § 8 cl.3.

[161] Hope M Babcock, 'A Civic-Republican Vision of Domestic Dependent Nations in the Twenty-First Century: Tribal Sovereignty Re-Envisioned, Reinvigorated, and Re-Empowered' (2005) 2005 Utah Law Review 443, 551.

[162] Case and Voluck (n 153) 25.

[163] *Johnson v M'Intosh* 21 US 543 (1823) *Cherokee Nation v Georgia* 30 US 1 (1831); *Worcester v State of Georgia* (1831) 31 US 515. Caprice L Roberts, 'A Desert Grows between Us – The Sovereignty Paradox at the Intersection of Tribal and Federal Courts The Washington and Lee Law Alumni Association Student Notes' (2008) 65 Washington and Lee Law Review 347, 349; Frank Pommersheim, *Braid of Feathers: American Indian Law and Contemporary Tribal Life* (University of California Press 1997) 7; Frank Pommersheim, 'At the Crossroads: A New and Unfortunate Paradigm of Tribal Sovereignty' (2010) 55 South Dakota Law Review 48, 50; *Cherokee Nation v Georgia* 30 US 1 (1831); *Worcester v State of Georgia* (1831) 31 US 515; *Johnson v M'Intosh* 21 US 543 (1823).

Alaskan Natives as having the status of American Indians, which allowed them to access all the benefits provided by the Bureau of Indian Affairs.[164] 'Notwithstanding any other provision of this Act (1) each Indian tribe shall retain inherent sovereign power to adopt governing documents.'[165] The tribal sovereignty, as constructed by the US constitutional system, is extremely regulated. Both Hirschfield and Thomson question whether the use of the term *Indian sovereignty* is fitting in terms of its common usage.[166] Instead, Pommersheim's evaluation of recent Indian cases suggests the existence of a 'new paradigm' of Indian sovereignty.[167]

In addition to recognising Indian sovereignty, the Indian Reorganization Act 1934 explicitly indicated that Indian law applied to Native Alaskans and Eskimos.[168] This was a watershed moment for Alaskan Natives. Congress's decision to include Alaskan Natives was most probably based on the consideration that the White population still considered them savages and, like the Indians, they needed paternalistic oversight.[169] The authority for this was derived from the common law assumption that reflects the idea that the original Indigenous peoples were dependent upon the US Government.[170] This line of authority was developed between 1823 and 1831 in three well-known cases: *Johnson v M'Intosh*, *Cherokee Nation v Georgia* and *Worcester v State of Georgia*.[171] *Johnson v M'Intosh* established the 'doctrine of discovery', which allocates the original land title for much of the land owned by Indian tribes to the first-discovering European power.[172] *Cherokee Nation v Georgia* established the idea that Indian tribes are dependent nations: 'It may well be doubted whether those tribes which reside within the acknowledged

---

[164] Frank Pommersheim, *Braid of Feathers: American Indian Law and Contemporary Tribal Life* (University of California Press 1997); Frank Pommersheim, 'At the Crossroads: A New and Unfortunate Paradigm of Tribal Sovereignty' (2010) 55 South Dakota Law Review 48.

[165] Indian Reorganization Act 1934 Pub.L. 73–383 2022 s 16 (h) 1; Babcock (n 161) 495.

[166] Benjamin W Thompson, 'The De Facto Termination of Alaska Native Sovereignty: An Anomaly in an Era of Self-Determination' (1999) 24 American Indian Law Review 421, 454; Martha Hirschfield, 'The Alaska Native Claims Settlement Act: Tribal Sovereignty and the Corporate Form' (1992) 101 The Yale Law Journal 1331; Frank Pommersheim, *Braid of Feathers: American Indian Law and Contemporary Tribal Life* (University of California Press 1997).

[167] Pommersheim, 'At the Crossroads' (n 163) 54.

[168] Indian Reorganization Act 1934 Pub.L. 73–383 s 19.

[169] Case and Voluck (n 153) 21.

[170] *Cherokee Nation v Georgia* (n 163) 2.

[171] Case and Voluck (n 153) 2; *Johnson v M'Intosh* (n 163); *Cherokee Nation v Georgia* (n 163); *Worcester v State of Georgia* (n 163).

[172] *Johnson v M'Intosh* (n 163) 543, 573.

boundaries of the United States can, with strict accuracy, be denominated foreign nations. They may more correctly, perhaps, be denominated domestic *dependent nations*.'[173] The idea that Indian tribes, and later Alaskan Native communities, have an innate inability to have full control over their destiny still has multiple implications.[174]

There were substantial differences between the legal treatment of Indian tribes and the Alaskan Natives. At the time of the enactment of the Indian Reorganization Act 1934,[175] there was very limited recognition of the relationship between Alaskan Native Villages and their land.[176] The establishment of Alaskan Native reserves that followed from the Indian Reorganization Act 1934 was fraught with difficulties and had limited appeal for Alaskan Natives.[177] In 1974, their connection with the land was officially engaged by Congress through the Alaska Native Claims Settlement Act.[178] The discovery of oilfields and the necessity to construct 800km pipelines in a territory that was claimed by Alaskan Natives made the settlement a Federal priority.[179] The Alaska Native Claims Settlement Act extinguished the previous Alaskan Native land claim and provided monetary support to Alaskan Natives.[180] The act did not reduce the application of Indian law to Alaskan Natives nor the stream of benefits that were derived from considering Alaskan Villages as equated to Indian tribes.[181]

The Alaska Native Corporations were established by the Alaska Native Claims Settlement Act 1971.[182] The act was a proxy for establishing Alaska

---

[173] Emphasis added. *Cherokee Nation v Georgia* (n 163) 3.

[174] Case and Voluck (n 153) 37; Pommersheim, *Braid of Feathers* (n 166) 7; Howard Zinn, *A People's History of the United States* (Reissue edition, Harper 2017) ch 1.

[175] Case and Voluck (n 153) 23.

[176] ibid 30.

[177] 1 March 1985, *The Theory of Communicative Action, Volume 1: Reason and the Rationalization of Society* (Beacon Press 1985) 30.

[178] Hirschfield (n 166).

[179] Case and Voluck (n 153) 33; Christian G Vazquez, 'A Business Entity by Any Other Name: Corporation: Community and Kinship' (2016) 33 Alaska L Rev 353, 358. Alaska Native Claims Settlement Act, [1971] 43 U.S.C. (2012). Alaska Native Claims Settlement Act 1974 (Public Law n. 92-203) is currently codified as 43 U.S.C. §§ 1601–1629h.

[180] Alaska Native Claims Settlement Act, [1971] 43 U.S.C. (2012) s 4; Vazquez (n 179) 357.

[181] Donald Warne and Linda Bane Frizzell, 'American Indian Health Policy: Historical Trends and Contemporary Issues' (2014) 104 American Journal of Public Health S263; Case and Voluck (n 153) 30, Chapter 7.

[182] Alaska Native Claims Settlement Act, [1971] 43 U.S.C. (2012); Vazquez (n 179) 354.

Regional Native Corporations and the Alaska Native Village Corporations. There are over 200 Village Corporations and the traditional institutions within these Villages have a jurisdictional power over Alaskan Natives who live in, or nearby, these Villages.[183] Native Corporation Villages are *sui generis* economic entities that provide care for their shareholders and, at the same time, are considered a manifestation of Native self-government.[184] 'Native non-profit corporations became service delivery vehicles primarily for the Bureau of Indian Affairs and Indian Health Service programmes in rural Alaska under provisions of the Indian Self-Determination Act.'[185] The newly established corporations, like the money that was transferred in exchange for settlement, were intended to lift Alaskan Natives out of poverty and to establish a form of administrative self-reliance.[186] At the start, the managing of corporations by communities with no corporate experience was difficult, and by the middle of the 1990s, many of them were on the edge of bankruptcy.[187] A reform of the Native fiscal system has altered the situation and Alaska Native Corporations are among the wealthiest in the State.[188] The large majority of their income, that is over 70 per cent, is derived from business carried out outside Alaska.[189]

The financial performance of Alaska Native Corporations is coupled with a demand to increase the power of traditional institutions within the over 200 Alaska Native Villages.[190] For instance, after 2000, the Alaskan Native tribunal was granted the prerogative to enact protection orders.[191] After, 2013, Alaskan Native jurisdictions could investigate crimes committed by Alaskan Natives. In relation to serious crimes like sexual assault, kidnapping and murder, almost all Native Villages are dependent on State Troopers located several hours away from the Villages.[192] However, the strict formalism that distinguishes criminal

---

[183] *Oliphant v Suquamish Indian Tribe* (1978) 435 US 191, 2008; Hunter Cox, 'ICRA Habeas Corpus Relief: A New Habeas Jurisprudence for the Post-Oliphant World?' (2017) 5 597, 598.
[184] Vazquez (n 179) 360.
[185] Case and Voluck (n 153) 178.
[186] ibid 37.
[187] Vazquez (n 179) 362; Hirschfield (n 166).
[188] Vazquez (n 179) 364.
[189] Thompson (n 166) 454; Case and Voluck (n 153) 183;198.
[190] Case and Voluck (n 153) 380, 396, 399; Hirschfield (n 166) 1336.
[191] Alaska Legal Services Corporation, 'Tribal Court Jurisdiction in Alaska' 23.
[192] Mallonee (n 140).

law procedures was perceived as ill-suited to Native Village jurisdictional activity.[193]

> Historically, community consensus was used in Alaska to address offending behavior. The community and councils openly discussed the offender's behavior, and reached a consensus that resulted in the offender being invited to appear before one of the traditional councils in the community, such as a clan gathering, a tribal council, Elders Council or other group with community significance and respect. Traditional councils focused on healing the offender and identifying a path back into society.[194]

The exclusion of non-Indians by Indian police in regard to investigations for crimes committed on Indian land is derived from *Oliphant v Suquamish Indian*.[195]

VAWA 2013 allowed 229 Native Alaska Villages to join the pilot scheme that granted them investigative power over non-Native offenders.[196] VAWA 2022 sought to increase this number.[197] The new system was recommended in a report that followed the 2021 Tribal Consultation.[198] In addition, to extend the jurisdictional prerogatives of Alaskan Native policing powers, in VAWA 2022, a clear obligation was inserted into the act to share information between Alaskan Native agencies, State agencies and Federal agencies specifically regarding crime prevention.[199] Indian police agencies already had the possibil-

---

[193] Alaska Legal Services Corporation (n 191) 27.
[194] ibid 28.
[195] *Oliphant v Suquamish Indian Tribe* (n 183) 2008; Cox (n 183) 598.
[196] Violence Against Women Act Reauthorization Act of 2022 (as a part of the Consolidated Appropriations Act, 2022) Pub.L. 117–103) 25 USCA § 1304:SEC. 813.
[197] Violence Against Women Act Reauthorization Act of 2022 Pub.L. 117–10325 USCA § 1304; SEC. 813. The exemption from Indian jurisdiction was set in *Oliphant v Suquamish* and then in *Wheeler*. *Oliphant v Suquamish Indian Tribe* (n 183); *United States v Wheeler* 435 US 313 (1978); Alaska Legal Services Corporation (n 191) 10.
[198] Department of Justice, Annual Government-to-Government and Violence Against Women Tribal Consultation (n 158) 4:
> Tribal leaders recommended that federal agencies support legislation restoring tribal criminal jurisdiction over non-Indian perpetrators of domestic violence, sexual assault, dating violence, stalking, and sex trafficking … Finally, for those tribes already implementing special domestic violence criminal jurisdiction (SDVCJ) under VAWA 2013, tribal leaders recommended increased funding and resources to support the costs of implementation, including detention and healthcare costs for non-Indian inmates sentenced by tribal courts.

[199] Violence Against Women Act Reauthorization Act of 2022 Pub.L. 117–103 s Sec 813 (d) 9. This was one the recommendations of the: US Department of Justice, Office on Violence Against Women (n 148) 4. US Department of Justice/Department of the Interior, 'Report to the President: Activities and Accomplishments of the First Year of Operation Lady Justice' 19. This is a qualification of 2020 Sec 6 of Savanna's

ity to access criminal databases such as the National Crime Information Centre and the National Missing and Unidentified Persons Database.[200] However, in Alaska, a missing person's data is inserted into the Alaskan Department of Public Safety's Missing Persons Clearing House, which might not be accessible to other police agencies within America.[201] The latest incarnation of VAWA crucially compels all the agencies involved in a missing person's case to coordinate the sharing of information.[202]

I can continue to provide examples, but there are enough indications that US central institutions are aware of the distinctive problems faced by Native Alaskan Villages in regard to violence against women. The US constitutional setting has the potential to protect Indian tribes and to allow for the development of new Alaskan Native institutions which, in the long term, might increase the perception of the legitimacy of central and regional institutions. It is, from this perspective that it might be considered a positive driver of change.

## A NEGATIVE DRIVER OF CHANGE: THE LEGACY OF COLONISATION

In the previous section, I explained how the current structure of Alaskan Native law operates. In this part of the chapter, I will discuss the violence against Native women as one of the legacies of colonisation.[203] Violence against Native women is perceived as a deeply rooted legacy of a history of colonial patriarchal exploitation that has a negative effect on the perception of the legitimacy of central policies.[204]

---

Act 2020. To update the online data entry format for federal databases relevant to cases of missing and murdered indigenous women (Savanna's Act) Pub.L 116–165 2020. The moniker of the Act was derived from the name of a murder victim called Savanna LaFontaine-Greywind. The police agencies that investigated the disappearance of LaFontaine-Greywind were found to act without coordination.

[200] US Department of Justice/Department of the Interior (n 199) 58.
[201] ibid.
[202] Violence Against Women Act Reauthorization Act of 2022 Pub.L. 117–103 s Sec 813 (d) 9.
[203] Teresa Evans-Campbell, 'Historical Trauma in American Indian/Native Alaska Communities: A Multilevel Framework for Exploring Impacts on Individuals, Families, and Communities' (2008) 23 Journal of Interpersonal Violence 316, 331; Lisa Wexler, 'Looking across Three Generations of Alaska Natives to Explore How Culture Fosters Indigenous Resilience' (2014) 51 Transcultural Psychiatry 73, 73; Eduardo Duran and Bonnie Duran, *Native American Postcolonial Psychology* (SUNY Press 1995) 93.
[204] Wexler (n 203) 73; Duran and Duran (n 203) 93.

The legacy of colonisation is explained in multiple outlets,[205] but Liz Hill delivered one of the clearest narratives on the subject.[206]

> Native American cultures, languages, lands and lives were all systematically and forcibly taken through colonization. Our ancestors endured genocide and assimilation for more than five centuries. Today, there is ample evidence that genocide still occurs through the inhumane conditions on reservations, the jurisdictional issues that prevent the prosecution of non-Native perpetrators on tribal lands and ignoring the Missing and Murdered Indigenous Women (MMIW) crisis.[207]

As mentioned earlier, Alaskan Native women are several times more likely to be victims of a homicide.[208] In over two-thirds of cases, the perpetrator is a White man.[209] This is a criminalistic anomaly and one of the factors, among many, that contributes to the high level of cross-ethnic violence, which is, in no uncertain terms, related to the lingering effects of colonisation.

As for any sociological phenomenon, there are multiple reasons for deviance.[210] One of the proven assumptions, based on the availability of accurate records, is that the majority of violent crimes are 'not interracial'. For instance, over 90 per cent of murders in which the victim is an Afro-American are committed by Afro-Americans in the United States.[211] White Americans are also 81 per cent more likely to be killed by White Americans.[212] In the case of violence against Alaskan Native women, however, there is an extraordinary divergence that might have a very unsettling explanation. In two-thirds of cases regarding the homicide of Alaskan Native women, the perpetrator is a non-Alaskan native.[213] This is a remarkable deviation from normality. Note that interracial violence against Alaskan Native women produces normal results. That is, over 90 per cent of violent crimes are committed by individuals who are part of

---

[205] Gilpin Lyndsey, 'Native American Women Still Have the Highest Rates of Rape and Assault' (7 June 2016) <www.hcn.org/articles/tribal-affairs-why-native-american-women-still-have-the-highest-rates-of-rape-and-assault> accessed 25 April 2022; Mallonee (n 140); Winter Allison, 'Native American Women Are Missing and Murdered. Will the Federal Government Act?' *The Colorado Independent* (18 February 2020); Tami Truett Jerue, 'A Tribal Perspective on the Crisis of Alaska Native Women and MMIW | NIWRC' <www.niwrc.org/restoration-magazine/june-2019/tribal-perspective-crisis-alaska-native-women-and-mmiw> accessed 27 April 2022.
[206] Lyndsey (n 205); Mallonee (n 140); Allison (n 205); Truett Jerue (n 205).
[207] Hill Liz, 'Domestic Violence, Sexual Violence and MMIW' *Alaska Native News* (3 May 2021).
[208] Mallonee (n 140) 95.
[209] ibid.
[210] Edwards (n 152) 22.
[211] Violence Policy Center (n 147) 5.
[212] ibid.
[213] ibid.

the same ethnic group.[214] Only the data for homicides delivers an unexpected result. There are, in short, strong indications that Alaskan Native women are hunted down, raped, and killed by non-Alaskan native men.[215]

Researchers like Mallonee as well as Native Alaskan activist groups, make a direct connection between the genocide of women and colonisation: 'Colonization eroded this status and dehumanized Indigenous women, destroying original protections within their nations. The current spectrum of violence against Indigenous women is intertwined with systemic barriers embedded within the US federal government.'[216] It is the perception that US Federal institutions are unpardonably hindering the role of the Alaskan Native institutions.[217] Similar narratives are replicated by the Canadian National Inquiry Report on the Genocide of Canadian Indigenous Communities.

> The National Inquiry's findings expose contemporary policies that are clearly linked to the colonial era and ongoing colonial violence, demonstrating a 'manifest pattern' attributable to present-day Canadian state conduct with Indigenous communities. This conduct includes both proactive measures ... as well as omissions by the Canadian government to ensure safety, equality, and access to essential services which have had direct, life-threatening consequences on Indigenous communities ... in particular on women, girls, and 2SLGBTQQIA people.[218]

The perceived lack of care for Alaskan Native women commenced with the Russian exploration of the northwest of the continent.[219] Alan Taylor describes the modus operandi of Russian fur trading companies: 'At gunpoint, the victors held the native women and children for ransom, while releasing the Aleut men to fill a large quota of furs ... In the interim, the Russians [non-Alaskan Native] exploited women as sex slaves.'[220] This practice normalised the objectification of Alaskan Native females.[221] The Treaty of Cessation from Russia to the United States did not change these cultural practices.[222]

---

[214] André Rosay, 'Violence Against American Indian and Alaska Native Women and Men' (2016) NIJ Journal 38; Liz (n 207).

[215] National Indigenous Women's Resource Center (n 143).

[216] ibid.

[217] Taylor (n 152).

[218] 'The National Inquiry's Consolidated Literature Review of Reports Relating to Violence Against Indigenous Women, Girls, and 2SLGBTQQIA People' 46.

[219] 'Russia started exploring Alaska around 1741, eventually establishing colonies in what it called Russian Alaska. Russia's approach to Alaska was the typical colonial enterprise of plunder.' Edwards (n 152) 21.

[220] Emphasis added. Taylor (n 152).

[221] Mallonee (n 140) 110.

[222] US Congress and Majesty the Emperor of all the Russias (n 159) Article III.

Alaskan Natives were still considered uncivilised and as not bearing individual rights.[223] One of the legacies of the Russian sexual exploitation of Alaskan Native women was the perceived promiscuity of Alaskan Native females.[224] Outside folkloristic narratives, most probably written by non-Alaskan Native men for other non-Alaskan Native men, the idea that Alaskan Native females were or are promiscuous is unproven.[225] There are instead indications that historically, Alaskan Native females are under a strong cultural pressure to be monogamous.[226] Poverty and heightened levels of alcohol are, instead, the most significant indicators of female sexual patterns across Alaskan Native Villages.[227] The loss of relevance of customary tribal authorities, which was one of the direct effects of colonisation, also increased levels of sexual violence.[228] Mallonee describes the process of the colonial inculcation of the role of Native women in Alaskan society with an emotional narrative: 'Western gender hierarchies were beaten into the children. Thus, violence against Indigenous women was a function of the successful colonization of the United States.'[229] It is reasonable to argue that the sexual promiscuousness of Native Alaskan women is a colonial myth that was forced onto women, and the possibility of exploiting women was one of the narratives that attracted men into the 'exploration' of Alaska.[230] The current wave of violence against Alaskan Native women is the latest manifestation of such imperialistic propaganda.

It is unfortunate that a lack of effective policing in rural communities allows for a level of inter-ethnic violence. The ineffectiveness of institutional interventions is considered by Alaskan Natives and Canadian First Nations as one of the legacies of colonialism.[231] Most rural Alaskan Native Villages had no permanent police authorities.[232] A few of the remote Villages had an individual who, in addition to acting as a local crime-prevention person, also acted as

---

[223] ibid Article III.
[224] Arthur E Hippler, 'Patterns of Sexual Behavior: The Athabascans of Interior Alaska' (1974) 2 Ethos 47.
[225] ibid.
[226] ibid 64.
[227] ibid 60.
[228] ibid.
[229] Mallonee (n 140) 110.
[230] Emphasis added. Taylor (n 152). A general review of sexual exploitation of Natives is in: Andrea Smith, 'Not an Indian Tradition: The Sexual Colonization of Native Peoples' (2003) 18 Hypatia 70.
[231] National Inquiry into Missing and Murdered Indigenous Women and Girls (Canada) (n 144); US Department of Justice, Tribal Consultations & Advisory Groups (n 144).
[232] Violence Against Women Act Reauthorization Act of 2022 (as a part of the Consolidated Appropriations Act, 2022) Pub.L. 117–103 25 USCA § 1304:SEC. 813.

a fire officer and first emergency medical responder.[233] However, in the very isolated communities, a police presence consists of a yearly visit from a State Trooper. Even in a case of reported violence, it is not uncommon for the victim not to be seen by a police officer for days. Therefore, the victim is forced to exist alongside her alleged attacker.[234] It is too early to see the effects of VAWA 2022. However, it is relatively clear that official oversights and delays will continue to support the social perception that non-Native State institutions consider Alaskan Native women as expendable. These types of perceptions are not easily eradicated, even after such crimes decrease.

Section 813 of the Violence Against Women Act Reauthorization Act of 2022 is one of the latest manifestations of policies aimed at decreasing the level of violence against Alaskan Native women.[235] In this succinct analysis of the Alaskan Native women's crisis, I explained that the current constitutional setting is a positive driver of change because it is likely to reduce the lingering suspicion that US institutions are still acting as a colonial power. The enactment of VAWA 2022 shows that the US Federal Government and Alaskan Native institutions are delivering policies that are based on peer-to-peer consultations. The second driver of change considered in this part of the chapter considered the role of colonial stereotypes and crimes against women.[236] The Russian and US colonisation of Alaska had a negative effect on the Native population, but it had a distinctively adverse impact on women. The colonial sexual objectification of Alaskan Native women, imposed with force, was one of the strategies adopted to attract men to an unhospitable land.[237] The myth of promiscuous Native women still attracts sexual predators in rural Alaska and Canada. The consequences of widespread sexual violence are particularly disrupting in remote communities, where Native institutions are generally not trusted with the power to investigate and prosecute White suspects.[238] The lack of trust in Native Alaskan institutions is perceived by women as a continuation of lingering colonial policies. VAWA 2022 might change that perception in the future, but currently, Alaskan Natives remain suspicious of both Federal and State institutions. It is for these reasons that cultural mistrust on non-Native Alaskan institutions will continue to be a negative driver of change in the current Alaskan regional crisis.

---

[233] Mallonee (n 140).
[234] ibid 93.
[235] Violence Against Women Act Reauthorization Act of 2022 (as a part of the Consolidated Appropriations Act, 2022) Pub.L. 117–103 25 USCA § 1304:SEC. 813.
[236] Taylor (n 152); Mallonee (n 140); Smith (n 230).
[237] Mallonee (n 140); Taylor (n 152).
[238] Mallonee (n 140).

# 5. China and Hong Kong: an a-constitutional crisis

Hong Kong has seen a reduction in recent civic unrest due to the strict rules to prevent the spread of COVID-19 related virus. However, in the years prior to the pandemic, Hong Kong experienced the effects of a series of prolonged mass protests against perceived illegitimate interference by the Chinese Communist Party in Hong Kong's legal system.[1] For those outside Hong Kong, the reforms that triggered these mass protests might be perceived as mild technical changes;[2] however, in the Special Administrative Territory, a large part of Hong Kong's population sees these changes as violations of a historically enshrined regional autonomy.[3] This chapter will discuss two, among many, of the drivers of change that have influenced the cycle of crises surrounding the legitimacy of central institutions in Hong Kong. The first driver of change is the difference in ideological roles that constitutional law has in China and in Hong Kong. For the Chinese Communist Party, the Chinese Constitution is one of the institutional devices that helps in the promotion of its socialist agenda,[4] whereas in Hong Kong, constitutionalism and the rule of law are foundational elements of Hong Kong identity.[5] The second driver of the crises

---

[1] Hoi-Yu Ng, 'Hong Kong: Autonomy in Crisis' in Brian CH Fong and Atsuko Ichijo, *The Routledge Handbook of Comparative Territorial Autonomies* (1st edn, Routledge 2022); Daniel TL Shek, 'Protests in Hong Kong (2019–2020): A Perspective Based on Quality of Life and Well-Being' (2020) Applied Research in Quality of Life 1; Milan Ismangil and Maggy Lee, 'Protests in Hong Kong during the Covid-19 Pandemic' (2021) 17 Crime, Media, Culture: An International Journal 17; Ngok Ma and Edmund W Cheng (eds), *The Umbrella Movement: Civil Resistance and Contentious Space in Hong Kong* (Amsterdam University Press 2020).

[2] Ng (n 1) 193.

[3] Brian CH Fong, 'One Country, Two Nationalisms: Center-Periphery Relations between Mainland China and Hong Kong, 1997–2016' (2017) 43 Modern China 523.

[4] Yuk-man Cheung, 'Neo-Authoritarianism: A New Type of Chinese' in Liah Greenfeld and Zeying Wu (eds), *Research Handbook on Nationalism* (Edward Elgar Publishing 2020) 1340.

[5] Jaakko Husa, '"Accurately, Completely, and Solemnly": One Country, Two Systems and an Uneven Constitutional Equilibrium' (2017) 5 The Chinese Journal of Comparative Law 231; Jaakko Husa, 'Constitutional Biography of Hong Kong and Ambiguities of One Country, Two Systems Policy' (2021) 9 The Chinese Journal of Comparative Law 268; Albert Chen Hung-yee, *The Changing Legal Orders in Hong*

is the emergence of a regional identity under the term *localism*.[6] Hong Kong localism is a different moniker for a nationalist movement that sits uneasily with communist hegemonic policies.[7]

Hong Kong is a Special Administrative Region (hereafter, SAR or HKSAR) that is part of the People's Republic of China (hereafter, China). Since 2004, Hong Kong has experienced the effects of mass demonstrations and civil unrest against its own autonomous institutions and against Chinese state policies.[8] China is a socialist unitary state that has transplanted much of its constitutional system from the former Union of Soviet Socialist Republics (hereafter, USSR).[9] The fourth and current Constitution of China was adopted in 1982.[10] The adoption of socialism is enshrined in Article 1 of the Constitution, and any form of opposition that is perceived as disruptive to socialism is forbidden.[11] China adopts a regional system of governance which divides the country into 31 provinces, five regions with limited autonomy, four cities that are directly controlled by the central government and two SARs.[12] One of these SARs is Hong Kong and the other is Macao.[13] The Hong Kong Basic Law preserve a capitalist system and (hereafter Basic law) allocated a series of competences to regional institutions.[14] The Basic Law allows regional institutions to collect and manage taxes without an obligation to transfer any of those revenues to

---

*Kong and Mainland China: Essays on 'One Country, Two Systems'* (City University of Hong Kong Press 2021).

[6] Samson Yuen and Sanho Chung, 'Explaining Localism in Post-Handover Hong Kong: An Eventful Approach' (2018) 2018 China Perspectives 19; Sebastian Veg, 'The Rise of "Localism" and Civic Identity in Post-Handover Hong Kong: Questioning the Chinese Nation-State' (2017) 230 The China Quarterly (London) 323; Ma and Cheng (n 1); Ng (n 1) 195.

[7] Ng (n 1) 195.

[8] Ma and Cheng (n 1); Veg (n 6); Yuen and Chung (n 6); Tommy Leung Yiu-man, 'Mapping the Matrix of Nationalisms in Hong Kong: On the Six Generations of Hongkonger Identities from the 1920s to 2020 and Their Generational Conflicts' in Liah Greenfeld and Zeying Wu (eds), *Research Handbook on Nationalism* (Edward Elgar Publishing 2020); Cheung (n 4).

[9] Husa, '"Accurately, Completely, and Solemnly"' (n 5) 234; Husa, 'Constitutional Biography of Hong Kong and Ambiguities of One Country, Two Systems Policy' (n 5) 274–77; Chang Wang, Nathan Madson and Al Maleson, *Inside China's Legal System* (Elsevier Science & Technology 2013) 2. For a compressive and articulated view of the role of Hong Kong within the Chinese constitutional system: Chen (n 5).

[10] Constitution of the People's Republic of China (as amended) 1982.

[11] ibid Article 1.

[12] ibid Articles III, IV.

[13] ibid.

[14] Basic Law of the Hong Kong Special Administrative Region of the People's Republic of China OCW CD 825 (HK) 1997 art 14 (public order), 110 (finance), 118 (economy), 136–7 (education), 138 (health), 140 (culture).

China.[15] Furthermore, Hong Kong courts are independent and are bound by previous decisions on the basis of the doctrine of precedent.[16] In contrast with Hong Kong and like the former USSR, the Chinese state follows a Marxism–Leninism ideology that hinges on the hegemonic authority of the one-party system.[17]

The Chinese Constitution is, by comparison to a liberal system, not perceived as a foundational element of the state, and the hierarchy of values that dominate state polices are directly derived from the doctrinal stance of the Communist Party of China (hereafter, CCP), which is perceived as the voice of the people.[18] The preservation of the CCP, the promotion of the commonwealth of the Chinese people, and the Constitution are instead fused together.[19]

There is a plethora of critiques on the internal incoherence and the negative implications of having a legal system that is subordinated to an ideological stance that does not put the individual at the centre of its system of values; however, this aspect is outside of the aims of this book.[20] The constitutional priority of the doctrinal position held by the CCP has multiple implications for the relationship between central and Hong Kong institutions. Some of these stances, such as the rejection of the rule of law as interpreted by judges, have been the catalyst for a series of governability crises in Hong Kong.[21]

In this chapter, I will focus on two drivers of change that have influenced the current interaction between central and regional institutions in Hong Kong. These two elements are the diverging assumption of what constitutionalism should be in China and Hong Kong, and the formation of sub-state ethnocentric nationalism in Hong Kong. This selection, as mentioned throughout this book, is not intended to infer deterministic connections between a social and legal narrative.[22]

---

[15] ibid 62, 73, 106, 108.
[16] ibid 8, 18–19.
[17] Constitution (Fundamental law) of the Union of Soviet Socialist Republics 1936 ch IV, V.; Henn-Juri Uibopuu, 'Soviet Federalism under the New Soviet Constitution' (1979) 5 Review of Socialist Law 171; Constitution of the People's Republic of China (as amended).
[18] General Office of the State Council of the People's Republic of China, 'The Socialist System of Laws with Chinese Characteristics'; Constitution of the People's Republic of China (as amended) Article 1.
[19] Constitution of the People's Republic of China (as amended) Article 3; Hio Tong Wong and Shih-Diing Liu, 'Cultural Activism during the Hong Kong Umbrella Movement' (2018) 13 Journal of Creative Communications 157; Veg (n 6);
[20] Wang, Madson and Maleson (n 9) XXVI, 133.
[21] Hio Tong Wong and Shih-Diing Liu (n 19).
[22] Robert Hazell, *Constitutional Futures: A History of the next Ten Years* (Oxford University Press 1999) 20; Robert Agranoff and Mark Glover, 'Introduction:

## CHINA AND HONG KONG: A COMPLEX HISTORICAL CONTEXT

China is the most populated country in the world, and it is one of the most complex regional states considered in this book. Before the two drivers of change are considered, a series of contextual analyses are needed. The Chinese unitary system of territorial governance is inspired by the pre-reform French prefectures that was initially adopted by the Japanese constitutional system and then by many Southeast Asian states.[23] The role of European influence, Tsung-Fu Chen explains, via Japan, extends to the adoption of the civil code.[24] The adaptation of the French and German legal traditions into the Japanese feudal system and later into the Chinese Imperial system was not a mechanical operation in either nation.[25] The legal principles were adapted in both legal systems to meet specific social needs.[26] The adoption of legal principles is part of large-scale transplants, and a level of non-compliance is expected. However, the influence of Confucianism on the Chinese population has fostered an extraordinary level of conformity.[27] This level of compliance is, it is reasonable to assume, due to the homogeneity of its population. Demographically, China is a multinational state, yet over 90 per cent of the population is considered part of the Han ethnic group.[28] The cultural inertia that a population of over a billion individuals has on the rest of the country is difficult to compare with any other country considered in this book.[29]

China includes sizeable minorities, and the country's ethnic population is, within a margin of approximation of any large demographic description, divided obliquely from Northeast to Southwest.[30] The Han ethnic majority (that is 91 per cent of the Chinese population) dominates the Southeast triangle.[31] North of the Northeast to Southwest imaginary line includes several

---

Forecasting Constitutional Futures' in Robert Hazell (ed), *Constitutional futures revisited: Britain's constitution to 2020* (Palgrave Macmillan 2008).

[23] Tsung-Fu Chen, 'Transplant of Civil Code in Japan, Taiwan, and China: With the Focus of Legal Evolution' (2011) 6 National Taiwan University Law Review 44.

[24] ibid; Yiu-man (n 8) 299.

[25] Yiu-man (n 8) 298.

[26] Chen (n 23) 416–22.

[27] Wang, Madson and Maleson (n 9) 27, 32; Husa, 'Constitutional Biography of Hong Kong and Ambiguities of One Country, Two Systems Policy' (n 5) 276.

[28] William A Joseph, 'Studying Chinese Politics' (2014) Politics in China 36, 7.

[29] ibid; Ric Neo and Chen Xiang, 'State Rhetoric, Nationalism and Public Opinion in China' (2022) 98 International Affairs 1327.

[30] Joseph (n 28) 7.

[31] ibid.

ethnic minorities and is considered Outer China.[32] Currently, the Chinese State Council recognises 56 ethnic minorities that account for 124 million individuals.[33]

The territorial system of governance divides the Chinese state into 31 provinces, four cities that are centrally administered, five autonomous regions with limited control over state-sponsored culture (Guangxi, Inner Mongolia, Ningxia, Tibet and Xinjiang) and two SARs.[34]

The Chinese prefecture system inspired by the French Model fitted well into the so-called 'Chongfanpinan administrative reform' that reorganised Imperial China from 1731 to 1911.[35] There are multiple present-day effects arising from the Chongfanpinan administrative reform. During this period, the Imperial administration adopted Weberian administrative principles, such as institutional accountability, transparency and efficacy, which are commonly associated with present-day European states.[36] In relation to identity building, one of the effects of the Chongfanpinan reform was to increase the spread of a national language, which was an effective template for the development of the modern image of a Chinese national identity.[37] The Chongfanpinan administrative reform also divided the Chinese territorial system of governance into territorial units.[38] The general aim of the sub-division was, and still is, to improve the efficacy of public action and tax collection.[39] It was not, and this is crucial for our discussion, intended to recognise regional or local communities.

---

[32] Francis Fukuyama, *The Origins of Political Order: From Prehuman Times to the French Revolution* (Profile Books 2012) 130; Benedict Anderson, *Imagined Communities: Reflections on the Origin and Spread of Nationalism* (Verso 1983) 41.

[33] National Bureau of Statistics, 'Main Data of the Seventh National Population Census 2020'.

[34] Joseph (n 28) 5; National Bureau of Statistics (n 33).

[35] Han Wang, Andrés Rodríguez-Pose and Neil Lee, 'The Long Shadow of History in China: Regional Governance Reform and Chinese Territorial Inequality' (2021) 134 Applied Geography 135.

[36] Fukuyama (n 32) 128; Max Weber, Guenther Roth and Claus Wittich, *Economy and Society: An Outline of Interpretive Sociology* (University of California Press 1978) 120; HG Creel, 'The Beginnings of Bureaucracy in China: The Origin of the Hsien' (1964) 23 The Journal of Asian Studies 155.

[37] Anderson (n 32) 41.

[38] Wang, Rodríguez-Pose and Lee (n 35) 134.

[39] Larry N Gerston, *American Federalism: A Concise Introduction* (ME Sharpe 2007); Carolyn Moore, Wade Jacoby and Arthur B Gunlicks, 'German Federalism in Transition?' (2008) 17 German Politics 393; Ronald L Watts, 'Daniel J. Elazar: Comparative Federalism and Post-Statism' (2000) 30 Publius 155.

In China, there are periodical national, regional and local elections,[40] yet the provinces are under the complete administrative and legislative control of central institutions.[41] All Chinese citizens have the right to be elected and to vote;[42] however, the selection of candidates follows a single-party rule which opens the public sector up to webs of patronage.[43] The key governing institutions, such as the Politburo and the Standing Committee, are theoretically elected, but the selection process for suitable candidates is heavily influenced by informal consultations.[44] Access to the Chinese civil sector is, at least in theory, separated from the party structure, and it occurs via national competitions.[45] It is considered highly selective and generally meritocratic.[46] Yet, the selective process for public servants only reduces the level of entanglement between the hierarchy within the CCP-sponsored patronage system and the civil sector. Joseph describes the relationship between civil servants and the CCP in a clear narrative.

> The head of the party organisation – the party secretary – at any level of administration is the real 'boss' in local political and policy matters. For example, the city of Shanghai has both a party secretary and a mayor, but the party secretary is the one with the greater authority, although the mayor is also a high-ranking party member.[47]

It is reasonably clear that the CCP holds the 'real' administrative and legislative power at any level of the Chinese state. The moniker 'functional emperor' is, for instance, used to indicate that the CCP has taken over the role of the previous Imperial dynasties.[48]

## Hong Kong

In 1999, Hong Kong was handed back to China by the UK Government.[49] The handover was part of an international negotiation between China and the United Kingdom which culminated in the 1984 Joint Declaration on

---

[40] William A Joseph, *Politics in China: An Introduction* (Second edition, Oxford University Press 2014) 196.
[41] Wang, Madson and Maleson (n 9) 222; Joseph (n 40) 5; Constitution of the People's Republic of China (as amended) ch III (5), IV.
[42] Constitution of the People's Republic of China (as amended) Article 34.
[43] Joseph (n 40) 133, 196.
[44] ibid.
[45] ibid.
[46] ibid.
[47] ibid 193.
[48] Yiu-man (n 8) 299.
[49] Joseph (n 40) 453; Ng (n 1) 193.

the Question of Hong Kong, which is also referenced as the Sino–British Declaration.[50] In concomitance, we had the promulgation of the Basic Law of the Hong Kong Special Administrative Region of the People's Republic of China (hereinafter, Basic Law).[51] The Basic Law established the 'one country two systems' relationship between HK SAR and China.[52] Article 1, for instance, asserts the sovereignty of China , Articles 8 and 18 preserves the 'common law system' and article 19 protect the judiciary from external interferences.[53] The HKSAR covers an area of 1086 km$^2$ with less than 400 km$^2$ being land.[54] Over 90 per cent of the inhabitants are Chinese Han,[55] yet in the latest surveys, the majority of the population (which is made up of 7.4 million people) considers itself Hongkongese and of mixed origin.[56] A long-term survey shows that such a high level of self-identification with the Hong Kong identity is a new phenomenon that is primarily associated with those born after the handover to China.[57]

The origin of the colony is, however, perceived as a part of a dark phase of Chinese history.[58] I will discuss the details of this point in the section of this chapter that describes the Chinese identity-making process, but the formation of the HKSAR was indicative of a humiliating moment in Chinese history

---

[50] 'Joint Declaration on the Question of Hong Kong (Adopted 19 December 1984 , Entered into Force 12 June 1985) 1399 UNTS 33 1985'; Ng (n 1) 193–4; Frank Welsh, *A History of Hong Kong* (HarperCollins 1993) 513.

[51] Constitution of the Special Administrative Region of Hong Kong.

[52] Ng (n 1) 193; Husa, 'Constitutional Biography of Hong Kong and Ambiguities of One Country, Two Systems Policy' (n 5) 270; Chen (n 5); Fong (n 3).

[53] Constitution of the Special Administrative Region of Hong Kong.

[54] Central Intelligence Agency, 'The World Factbook – Hong Kong' (2005); Ng (n 1) 193.

[55] Central Intelligence Agency, 'The World Factbook – Hong Kong' (n 54).

[56] Centre for Communication and Public Opinion Survey, 'The Identity and National Identification of Hong Kong People Survey Results'; Public Opinions Programme, 'National Issues. People's Ethnic Identity' <www.hkupop.hku.hk/english/header.html> accessed 12 November 2021.

[57] The city, which was little more than a fishing village was inhabited by the Hakka people, received the free port status in 1841. The Hakka are anthropologically a Chinese Han subgroup which probably migrated from the North of China. The Hakka people were recognised by the British administration as the original inhabitants of the regions. Fu-Lai Tony Yu and Diana S Kwan, 'Social Construction of National Reality: Chinese Consciousness versus Hong Kong Consciousness' (2017) 3 Contemporary Chinese Political Economy and Strategic Relations 657, 669.

[58] Kerry Brown, *Contemporary China* (Macmillan International Higher Education 2019) 49; Ng (n 1) 196; Yiu-man (n 8) 296. The Government SAR, 'Basic Education Curriculum Guide – Building on Strengths (2002): Four Key Tasks – Achieving Learning to Learn – 3A Moral and Civic Education'.

in which the state could not defend its borders.[59] Opium arrived from India and silver from other parts of the British Empire.[60] The Chinese Government attempted to stop the trade but the British Empires reacted violently. After the second Opium War in 1860, the British colony was expanded.[61] External enemies and civil unrest are often related. In the nineteenth and twentieth centuries, political instability in China culminated in the 1911 Revolution that fostered the flow of immigration towards Hong Kong.[62] The instability continued during the Civil War period and the Cultural Revolution of the mid-1960s.[63] The effects of wars and civic instability were dramatic and long term. Large sections of the Chinese population experienced famines well into the twentieth century.[64]

The instability of the motherland fostered multiple waves of Chinese emigration. Since its establishment as a British colony, Hong Kong has increased in population due to an intake of refugees from China who could not or would not go back.[65] The stability of the CCP's control over mainland China and its poor pre-1990s' economic performance reduced the appetite for returning home for many of the mainland Chinese immigrants.[66] In contrast with the widespread poverty of China, between 1950 and 1980, Hong Kong experienced the effect of several decades of economic growth.[67] The opportunities provided by a rapidly expanding economy convinced many of its newcomers not only not to go back to the Chinese mainland but also not to emigrate elsewhere.[68]

In the same period, the population increased several fold and with it came a distinctive form of civic attachment to the 'Lion on the Rock'.[69] The Lion on the Rock was one of the newly created Hong Kong national images that represented both the economic strength of the colony and the emerging

---

[59] Brown, *Contemporary China* (n 58) 49; Yiu-man (n 8) 296. The Government SAR (n 58).

[60] Joseph (n 40) 44, 406; Chris Feige and JeffreyA Miron, 'The Opium Wars, Opium Legalization and Opium Consumption in China' (2008) 15 Applied Economics Letters 911, 912; Cheung (n 4) 318.

[61] Joseph (n 40) 44, 406; Yiu-man (n 8) 296.

[62] Ng (n 1) 192, 194.

[63] Joseph (n 40) 69, 81.

[64] ibid 168; Cheung (n 4) 320.

[65] Joseph (n 40) 69, 81.

[66] ibid 168; Cheung (n 4) 320.

[67] Christopher Howe, 'Growth, Public Policy and Hong Kong's Economic Relationship with China' (1983) The China Quarterly 512.

[68] Yu and Kwan (n 57) 672; Ng (n 1) 193.

[69] Yu and Kwan (n 57) 672.

core values of a community.[70] The making of Hong Kong's uniqueness can be said to be due to three main factors: the Lion Rock spirit, the rise of the popularity of Hong Kong's pop culture and entertainment industries, and the birth of Hong Kong's core values.[71] The mixture of cultural and sociological elements are distinctive of romantic nationalism that was, according to Smith and Kedourie, fostered by the creation of several European states, including Belgium, Germany and Italy.[72] The popular narrative of the Lion on the Rock facing the Chinese Dragon, which is the representation of China, re-emerged in the narratives of the current localist movement.

> The myth originated from a popular Cantonese song, 'Beneath the Lion Rock', which was the theme tune of a television series aired in the 1970s depicting the life stories of many lower-class people in Hong Kong. The 'Lion Rock Myth' has several major tones. Explicitly, Hong Kong is a community of immigrants who came together and overcame obstacles and sacrifices.[73]

The newly fabricated identity had, until recently, developed alongside and not in opposition to other traditional Chinese values, such as Confucianism, Taoism and Buddhism.[74]

The negotiation process that led to the handover of Hong Kong to China concerned many of its residents.[75] It was clear from the start of the negotiations that Hong Kong could not become a sovereign nation.[76] From the outset, the special conditions – that is, the wars of aggression to protect the sale of drugs in which the United Kingdom obtained control of Hong Kong – limited the outcomes of the negotiation.[77] Hong Kong was, from a British perspective, a colony and, as part of the process of decolonisation, there was both internal and external pressure to reduce the effect on past Imperial policies.[78] Recall

---

[70] Yiu-man (n 8) 300.
[71] Yu and Kwan (n 57) 672.
[72] Anthony D Smith, *Theories of Nationalism* (Duckworth 1971); Elie Kedourie, *Nationalism* (Hutchinson 1960).
[73] Benny Yiu-ting Tai, 'Stages of Hong Kong's Democratic Movement' (2019) 4 Asian Journal of Comparative Politics 352, 354.
[74] Wang, Madson and Maleson (n 9) 28; Ng (n 1) 195.
[75] Sze Yuen Chung, *Hong Kong's Journey to Reunification : Memoirs of Sze-Yuen Chung* (Chinese University Press 2001) 151; Roger Buckley, *Hong Kong: The Road to 1997* (Cambridge University Press 1997) 95–130.
[76] United Nations General Assembly, 'UNGA Res 2908 (1972) GAOR 27th Session Supp 29, 08'.
[77] Buckley and Roger (n 75) XV.
[78] ibid 130; Ng (n 1) 193.

that wars of aggression are against international law and, in general, imperialism tends to be detrimental to the populations subjugated by a foreign power.[79]

Hong Kong might have been one of the few exceptions.[80] While it was not a self-governing democratic entity, the enclave benefitted from a prosperous economy, an effective legal system and respect for the rule of law.[81] However, from the perspective of international law, Hong Kong was a part of the sovereign territory of China that was held by the United Kingdom as a result of two wars of aggression and a series of unfair treaties.[82] This was one of the reasons that led the General Assembly to pass Resolution 2908, in which it accepted the recommendation from the United Nations Special Committee on the situation with regard to the implementation of the Declaration on the Granting of Independence to Colonial Countries and Peoples. The recommendation is in paragraph 184 of Document A/8723/Rev.1. Paragraph 184 indicates that Hong Kong should be removed from the list of non-self-governing territories.[83]

The approval of Document A/8723/Rev.1 is considered a watershed moment for the legal status of Hong Kong.[84] From the international law perspective, the legitimacy of the British administration of Hong Kong stood on precarious ground, but this was also true within the colony itself.[85] The British administration of Hong Kong also lacked democratic legitimacy.[86] The autocratic colony of Hong Kong's legal system was established by the 1843 Queen Victoria Letters of Patent.[87] The Letters of Patent were amended multiple times and these amendments established most of present-day Hong Kong's public insti-

---

[79] UNSC Res 3314 (14 December 1974) UN Doc A/RES/3314 (XXIX).
[80] Ng (n 1) 193.
[81] Howe (n 67) 512; Yiu-man (n 8) 299; Yew Chiew Ping and Kwong Kin-ming, 'Hong Kong Identity on the Rise' (2014) 54 Asian Survey 1088; Ng (n 1) 194.
[82] United Nations General Assembly (n 76).
[83] The UN General Assembly accepted the recommendation. 'The Special Committee also continued its review of the list of Territories to which the Declaration is applicable. In the light of the close examination of related matters, the Committee agreed that it should recommend to the General Assembly the exclusion of Hong Kong and Macau and dependencies from the list' (para 183).
[84] The legitimacy of the Chinese demands did not reduce the anxiety of Hong Kong residents and during the negotiation process Hong Kong experienced the effect of increase emigration toward Britain and North America. In 1997 and showing a level of extraordinary insight, Ronald Skeldon indicated that the rising emigration trends in Hong Kong will reduced the level cultural diversity within the city and that might promote a new emerging nationalism. Ronald Skeldon, 'Hong Kong: Colonial City to Global City to Provincial City?' (1997) 14 Cities 265, 270.
[85] United Nations General Assembly (n 76).
[86] Ng (n 1) 196.
[87] The Letters Patent (or The Hong Kong Charter) 1843 (CO129/2) 104.

tutions.[88] Section XIV of the Letters Patent allocated the power to the Governor to appoint the members of the Legislative Council (hereafter, LegCo).[89] This process, up until the handover to China, never included democratic elections.[90]

It was only after the Declaration and the enactment of the Basic Law that universal Sino–British suffrage was introduced in the HKSAR.[91] The schedule in which such a process should take place has attracted much controversy and is one of the reasons for the cycles of mass protests.[92] For instance, in 2007, the Standing Committee suggested that a reform of Hong Kong's electoral system should occur by 2017. The importance of the clarity of this decision is worth reporting verbatim.

> The session is of the view that appropriate amendments may be made to the specific method for selecting the fourth Chief Executive and the specific method for forming the fifth term Legislative Council of the Hong Kong Special Administrative Region in the year 2012; that the election of the fifth Chief Executive of the Hong Kong Special Administrative Region in the year 2017 may be implemented by the method of universal suffrage; that after the Chief Executive is selected by universal suffrage, the election of the Legislative Council of the Hong Kong Special Administrative Region may be implemented by the method of electing all the members by universal suffrage.[93]

Unfortunately, in 2014, the Standing Committee introduced limits on the possible development of Hong Kong's electoral system.[94] Between 2014 and 2015, the LegCo started a reform of the electoral system for the 2017 election, but the new bill, aligned with the will of the Standing Committee, did not

---

[88] The Letters Patent (or the principal Letters Patent) 1917 (118) 104, s XIII.
[89] Ng (n 1) 193.
[90] Tai (n 73) 352; Ng (n 1) 193, 196.
[91] 'Joint Declaration on the Question of Hong Kong (Adopted 19 December 1984, Entered into Force 12 June 1985) 1399 UNTS 33 1985' (n 50); Constitution of the Special Administrative Region of Hong Kong Articles: 45 (2), 51, 68, 70; Husa, 'Constitutional Biography of Hong Kong and Ambiguities of One Country, Two Systems Policy' (n 5) 271.
[92] Ngok Ma and Edmund W Cheng (eds), 'From Political Acquiescence to Civil Disobedience', in *The Umbrella Movement: Civil Resistance and Contentious Space in Hong Kong* (Amsterdam University Press 2020); Justin P Kwan, 'The Rise of Civic Nationalism: Shifting Identities in Hong Kong and Taiwan' (2016) 2 Contemporary Chinese Political Economy and Strategic Relations 941; Young (n 19); Simon Marsden, 'Autonomy, Sovereignty and Geography: What Does China Mean to Hong Kong?' in Kim Rubenstein and Mark Nolan (eds), *Alliance and Identity in a Globalised World* (Cambridge University Press 2012); Ng (n 1) 196.
[93] Standing Committee, Tenth National People's Congress, 'Decision on Hong Kong's Constitutional Development'.
[94] Standing Committee, Tenth Session of the Standing Committee of the Twelfth National People's Congress, 'Decision on Hong Kong's Constitutional Development'.

include arrangements for adopting universal suffrage. One of the effects of this was 75 days of civil unrest and the occupation of several central city sites.[95]

Why did the members of the Standing Committee change their mind? The historical inherited imperial system allowed an unelected British-appointed Governor to manage the SAR with limited oversight. This point is delivered in clear narrative by Ng.

> Beijing wanted to continue the so-called 'executive-dominant' system in the colonial era that gave the unelected governor dictatorial power ... For instance, the chief executive and his or her government can make most policies, appoint a wide range of public officials without the legislature's consent, propose most legislation, refuse to promulgate laws passed by the legislature, and dissolve the legislature when there is serious conflict between the executive and the legislature.[96]

Since 2006, NPCSC aided the expansion of Hong Kong executive powers and reduced its oversight by the LegCo by vetting candidates and disqualifying elected oppositions members.[97]

I will return to this point when I discuss the driver of change in the next section of this chapter, but Chinese central institutions have, since 2007, lost support in Hong Kong.[98] There are also minor social irritants. Chinese mainland residents are perceived as 'queue jumpers' and generally as 'untrustworthy'.[99] The unscheduled appearance of mainland Chinese mothers ready to give birth in Hong Kong's hospital emergency rooms is one of the many points of friction between residents and newcomers.[100] These are the so-called *anchor babies*.[101] The hostility manifested against the parents of anchor babies is one

---

[95] Ma and Cheng (n 1); Ma and Cheng (n 92); Ng (n 1).
[96] Ng (n 1) 197.
[97] ibid 198.
[98] Chui Ping Iris Kam, 'Personal Identity versus National Identity among Hong Kong Youths – Personal and Social Education Reform after Reunification' (2012) 18 Social Identities 649; Yu and Kwan (n 57); Husa, 'Constitutional Biography of Hong Kong and Ambiguities of One Country, Two Systems Policy' (n 5) 273.
[99] Young (n 19) 21; 'Hong Kong Advert Calls Chinese Mainlanders "Locusts"' *BBC News* (1 February 2012); Amie Tsang, 'Hong Kong Anger at Chinese "Locust" Shoppers Intensifies' *Financial Times* (16 February 2015).
[100] Bernard Yam, 'Cross-Border Childbirth Between Mainland China and Hong Kong: Social Pressures and Policy Outcomes' (2011) 8 PORTAL Journal of Multidisciplinary International Studies 1; Susanne YP Choi and Ruby YS Lai, 'Birth Tourism and Migrant Children's Agency: The "Double Not" in Post-Handover Hong Kong' (2020) 48(5) Journal of Ethnic and Migration Studies 1193.
[101] Yuen and Chung (n 6) 22.

of the many manifestations of 'them and us' narratives that are emerging as a part of Hong Kong nationalism.

> The rising purchasing power of Chinese citizens fuelled a spending spree on items ranging from daily goods to luxury merchandise to offshore properties ... but the increasing influx of capital and people has also brought and adverse impact on local livelihood, as manifested by the problem of tourism and parallel trading, which the HKSAR government has failed to address.[102]

Middle- and upper-class Chinese immigrants have an appetite for high-end products. The expanding luxury goods sector in Hong Kong fed by mainland Chinese tourism and newcomers displaced traditional shops and increased the cost of living in several areas in an already overcrowded Hong Kong.[103]

Economic localism and anti-gentrification movements can be found in most modern cities.[104] At a global level, the racist trope 'rich foreigners are buying out land and taking our women' is exploited by ethnocentric nationalists and political demagogues in multiple political systems.[105] In Hong Kong, given the compact size of the SAR, these xenophobic stances are currently identified with the term *localism*.[106] However, the ethnic element of the localist movement, which includes blatant racist narratives, is only a part of Hong Kong's identity-formation movement.[107]

Hong Kong localism, despite its ebb and flow, includes genuine support for democracy, the rule of law and human rights, which are all currently antithetical with the stances adopted by China. Simon Yuen and Sanho Chung, in their multi-factored analysis of the development of Hong Kong localism, show that from 2004 to 2018, mass demonstrations were due to multiple reasons.[108] In their analysis, which combined a large-spectrum quantitative analysis and a qualitative review of individual perceptions, Yuen and Chung showed

---

[102] ibid.

[103] ibid.

[104] 'Houses over Apartments: Chinese Overseas Buyers Tipped to Come Back for Land When Australia's Borders Open' *ABC News* (1 July 2021); Toby Helm and political editor, 'Stop Rich Overseas Investors from Buying up UK Homes, Report Urges' *The Observer* (1 February 2014).

[105] Mark Findlay, *Globalisation, Populism, Pandemics and the Law: The Anarchy and the Ecstasy* (Edward Elgar Publishing 2021); Andrej Zaslove, *The Re-Invention of the European Radical Right: Populism, Regionalism, and the Italian Lega Nord* (MQUP 2011); Randall Curren, 'Patriotism, Populism, and Reactionary Politics since 9.11', *Handbook of Patriotism* (Springer 2018).

[106] 'Houses over Apartments: Chinese Overseas Buyers Tipped to Come Back for Land When Australia's Borders Open' (n 104); Helm and editor (n 104).

[107] Yuen and Chung (n 6) 22.

[108] ibid.

that pragmatic individual concerns, such as the rising cost of living or the aforementioned phenomenon of anchor babies, were a few of the motivators for mass protests.[109] The study evaluated over 200 mass protests in the period between 2011 and 2018.[110] Thirty-one of these protests were against the central institutions and 186 were organised by pro-Chinese and Hong Kong institutions.[111] However, signs of the legitimate instability of the HKSAR–China arrangements could be seen much earlier.

On 1 July 2003, a march was attended by over 500 000 protesters (that is over 10 per cent of the over-16-year-old SAR population).[112] The first of July marked the first day of the 1987 handover to China, but in 2003, it was the catalyst for those who opposed the anti-sedition bill.[113] The bill was intended to implement Article 23 of the Basic Law, the text of which was agreed during the Sino–British negotiations.[114] In the years that followed, the First of July March continued to attract thousands of protesters until 2019.[115] In 2019, the First of July March coincided with a series of violent events that included the storming of the LegCo and violent clashes with the police.[116]

In relation to civic peace, between 2019 and 2020, Hong Kong experienced increasing instability that was stopped only by the approval of the Law of the People's Republic of China on Safeguarding National Security in the Hong Kong Special Administrative Region – which is normally referred to as the Hong Kong National Security Law (hereafter, NSL) – in July 2020 and the restrictions related to the COVID-19 pandemic.[117] For instance, the Fugitive Offenders and Mutual Legal Assistance in Criminal Matters Legislation

---

[109] ibid.

[110] ibid 19.

[111] ibid.

[112] National Bureau of Statistics (n 33); Ma and Cheng (n 1).

[113] The Hong Kong Special Administrative Region shall enact laws on its own to prohibit any act of treason, secession, sedition, subversion against the Central People's Government, or theft of state secrets, to prohibit foreign political organisations or bodies from conducting political activities in the Region, and to prohibit political organisations or bodies of the Region from establishing ties with foreign political organisations or bodies. Constitution of the Special Administrative Region of Hong Kong art 23; Ng (n 1) 193.

[114] Buckley and Roger (n 75).

[115] Simon Scarr, Manas Sharma and Marco Hernandez, 'Hong Kong Protests: How Many Protesters Took to the Streets on July 1?' (Reuter 2019).

[116] 'Hong Kong Protests: What LegCo Graffiti Tells Us – BBC News' (3 July 2019); Anne Marie Roantree, 'China Condemns Violent Hong Kong Protests as "Undisguised Challenge" to Its Rule' *Reuters* (2 July 2019).

[117] Shek (n 1) 1; Ismangil and Lee (n 1); Ng (n 1) 198; Law of the People's Republic of China on Safeguarding National Security in the Hong Kong Special Administrative Region 2020.

(Amendment) Bill 2019, which allowed for the extradition of suspected criminals from Hong Kong, was perceived as an attempt to reduce the autonomy of Hong Kong's criminal system.[118] The bill triggered 13 weeks of mass protests, which probably, without the COVID-19 restrictions, would have continued to the present day.[119] At the time of writing this chapter, COVID-19 restrictions have changed the nature of the protests.[120] 'Protesters meet in small groups or they appear as flash mobs in public areas that are "protester friendly" and they disappear before the authorities appear.'[121]

In short, there is a lingering mistrust of Hong Kong Chinese central institutions and disillusion with the power of regional institutions that have to be patriotically loyal to China.[122] Hong Kong's regional intuitions have limited recourse and have to walk a very narrow tightrope between an obligation to comply with central government and the demands of an increasingly frustrated population.[123] The crisis of legitimacy is linked to multiple factors, but in this chapter I will only focus on two: the diverging basis for the legitimacy of the SAR system and the development of Hong Kong localism as a new regional identity.

These are only a selection of social elements within a complex interaction that has direct repercussions on the territorial system of governance of Hong Kong. Drivers of change are, according to the Future Studies methodology, intended to be used as elements for forecasting scenarios.[124] As mentioned earlier, future scenarios require a multidisciplinary team of experts with a cluster of expertise that is beyond the scope of this chapter.[125] It is also important that the SAR in Hong Kong is a system of regional governance that is

---

[118] Secretary for Security, The Legislative Council. (2019). Fugitive Offenders and Mutual Legal Assistance in Criminal Matters Legislation (Amendment) Bill 2019 2019; Alex Yue Feng Zhu and Kee Lee Chou, 'Collective Action in the Anti-Extradition Law Amendment Bill Movement in Hong Kong: Two Integrative Group Identification Models' (2021) 21 Analyses of Social Issues and Public Policy 1033; Francis LF Lee and others, 'Hong Kong's Summer of Uprising: From Anti-Extradition to Anti-Authoritarian Protests' (2019) 19 China Review 1; Yanhong Yin and Irene Wieczorek, 'What Model for Extradition between Hong Kong and Mainland China? A Comparison between the 2019 (Withdrawn) Amendment to Hong Kong Extradition Law and the European Arrest Warrant' (2020) 11 New Journal of European Criminal Law 504.
[119] Ismangil and Lee (n 1).
[120] ibid.
[121] ibid.
[122] Husa, 'Constitutional Biography of Hong Kong and Ambiguities of One Country, Two Systems Policy' (n 5) 273.
[123] Zhu and Chou (n 118).
[124] Hazell (n 22).
[125] Agranoff and Glover (n 22).

due to lapse.[126] Given the current trend in the economic development of China – massive demographic disparity between the two (Hong Kong and Chinese) national identities and the possibility that hegemonic policies might be strictly and undemocratically enforced – a high level of assimilation is likely to occur.[127] In other words, the crisis of legitimacy that currently affects the SAR is, by way of comparison to others considered in this book, likely to end with the extinction of or a radical remodelling of the HKSAR.

There is an economic element of the crisis which will not be discussed in this chapter but is worth mentioning. Hong Kong by way of comparison to any of the other regions considered in this book, benefits from a very high level of fiscal and financial autonomy.[128] In addition to the protection of private initiatives for all Hong Kong residents, regional institutions can autonomously collect and distribute fiscal revenue.[129] At the time of the handover, the preservation of such a high level of economic autonomy was beneficial to both Hong Kong and to China.[130] In 1998, Hong Kong accounted for 18.4 per cent of Chinese GDP.[131] However, in 2020, the SAR contribution to the Chinese GDP was 2.3 per cent, and this share is rapidly diminishing.[132] Furthermore, China's decreasing dependency on Hong Kong's economic power was coupled with Hong Kong's increasing dependency on Chinese investments.[133] Since 2006, Hong Kong has been included in the Chinese five years plan and its development is a part of the Guangdong–Hong Kong–Macao Greater Bay Area meg-

---

[126] 'The Government of the People's Republic of China ... The above-stated basic policies of the People's Republic of China regarding Hong Kong and the elaboration of them in annex I to this Joint Declaration will be stipulated, in a Basic Law of the Hong Kong Special Administrative Region of the People's Republic of China, by the National People's Congress of the People's Republic of China, and they will remain unchanged for 50 years.' 'Joint Declaration on the Question of Hong Kong (Adopted 19 December 1984, Entered into Force 12 June 1985) 1399 UNTS 33 1985' (n 50) 3.

[127] Howe (n 67); Ng (n 1) 194.

[128] Constitution of the Special Administrative Region of Hong Kong 62, 73, 106, 108.

[129] 'Joint Declaration on the Question of Hong Kong (Adopted 19 December 1984, Entered into Force 12 June 1985) 1399 UNTS 33 1985' (n 50) Article 3(8); Leo F Goodstadt, 'Fiscal Freedom and the Making of Hong Kong's Capitalist Society' (2010) 24 China Information 273, 273; Constitution of the Special Administrative Region of Hong Kong art 7 , Chapter 4(1).

[130] Lin Hing Chan, 'Chinese Investment in Hong Kong: Issues and Problems' 15.

[131] The World Bank, 'GDP per Capita (Current US$) – Hong Kong SAR, China (1960–2020'.

[132] ibid; Ng (n 1) 194; Fong (n 3).

[133] Zhang Shidong, 'China's Investors Are Flooding Hong Kong's Capital Market in Search of Value as They Dodge US Sanctions' (*South China Morning Post*, 7 February 2021).

alopolis.[134] This dependency inversion that occurred relatively recently had multiple implications for the management of the regional cycle of governance crises in Hong Kong.[135] As for the rest of this book, the analysis of financial changes in the Hong Kong–China relationship are not intended to provide an economic evaluation or to forecast future scenarios.

It is, however, reasonable to argue that at the time of the handover, Hong Kong represented an economic asset from multiple perspectives.[136] In the 1990s, Hong Kong had world-class financial service infrastructure that helped the development of those Chinese businesses that wanted to amass capital in the global market.[137] That, in turn, allowed Hong Kong's companies to access the Chinese economy, which, at the time of writing this book, is the second largest in the world.[138] In the early 1990s, the Shanghai and Shenzhen stock markets could not compete with Hong Kong's financial sector.[139] The Shanghai and Shenzhen stock markets were over-regulated.[140] Hong Kong's financial market was, and still is, open, has a very low level of taxation and relatively transparent oversight regarding trading strategies.[141] This image of an efficient economic powerhouse has been dented by a series of unfortunate events. The 2007–09 global financial crisis, 2004's severe acute respiratory syndrome outbreak and the 2020 COVID-19 pandemic have impacted both Hong Kong and China,[142] yet the Chinese economy has navigated these events better. The Chinese economy is, by comparison to Hong Kong's economy, industrial and based on the export of goods.[143] Furthermore, the establishment of the Shanghai–Hong Kong Stock Connect in 2014 and the Shenzhen–Hong Kong Stock Connect in 2016 allow for a number of companies to move invest-

---

[134] Ng (n 1) 194.
[135] Shidong (n 133).
[136] Goodstadt (n 129).
[137] Hong Kong Monetary Authority, 'Hong Kong Monetary Authority – Dominant Gateway to China' <www.hkma.gov.hk/eng/key-functions/international-financial-centre/hong-kong-as-an-international-financial-centre/dominant-gateway-to-china/> accessed 24 November 2021.
[138] ibid.
[139] William Arthur Thomas, *Western Capitalism in China: A History of the Shanghai Stock Exchange* (Ashgate 2001) 61, 287.
[140] ibid.
[141] Goodstadt (n 129).
[142] Kang Hua Cao and others, 'Covid-19's Adverse Effects on a Stock Market Index' (2021) 28 Applied Economics Letters 1157, 1158.
[143] Marcus Richard Keogh-Brown and Richard David Smith, 'The Economic Impact of SARS: How Does the Reality Match the Predictions?' (2008) 88 Health Policy (Amsterdam, Netherlands) 110; Anya Khanthavit, 'Measuring COVID-19 Effects on World and National Stock Market Returns' (2021) 8 The Journal of Asian Finance, Economics and Business 1, 4.

ments between China and Hong Kong, thus reducing the distinctiveness of Hong Kong's stock market as a natural foothold for foreign investors in the Chinese economy.[144]

In addition, the Shanghai–Hong Kong Stock Connect in 2014 and the Shenzhen–Hong Kong Stock Connect in 2016 increased the dependence of Hong Kong's stock market on Chinese investments thus casting doubt on HK retaining its special legal status.[145] Both the Shanghai and Shenzhen stock markets are dominated by Chinese state-owned enterprises.[146] Given that Hong Kong's stock market revenues subsidise the HKSAR's economy and its institutions, there is an awareness among all members of Hong Kong civic society that any animosity against China will have financial and fiscal implications.

## DRIVER OF CHANGE: BRITISH CONSTITUTIONALISM VERSUS CHINESE LENINISM–MARXISM

In this section of the chapter, I will explain how two perceptions of what constitutionalism entails in Hong Kong and in China will continue to be a proxy for the crisis of legitimacy of the central institutions in Hong Kong.[147] In particular, the hierarchical approach of the CCP in interpreting the Basic Law motivated Hong Kong localist movements to distrust the CCP's control over Chinese institutions.[148]

China has been depicted as a country that has 'a material constitution without constitutionalism'[149] and 'democracy without contestation'.[150] Pragmatic rea-

---

[144] Rafaelita M Aldaba and Josef T Yap, 'Investment and Capital Flows: Implications of the ASEAN Economic Community' 49; Authority (n 137).

[145] Karen Jingrong Lin and others, 'State-Owned Enterprises in China: A Review of 40 Years of Research and Practice' (2020) 13 China Journal of Accounting Research 31.

[146] ibid; Ng (n 1) 198.

[147] Husa, '"Accurately, Completely, and Solemnly"' (n 5); Qianfan Zhang, 'A Constitution without Constitutionalism? The Paths of Constitutional Development in China' (2010) 8 International Journal of Constitutional Law 950.

[148] Kam Wong, 'Human Rights and Limitation of State Power: The Discovery of Constitutionalism in the People's Republic of China' (2006) 7 Asia-Pacific Journal on Human Rights and the Law 1; Peter K Yu, 'Digital Copyright and the Parody Exception in Hong Kong' (2014) 41 Media Asia 119; Husa, 'Constitutional Biography of Hong Kong and Ambiguities of One Country, Two Systems Policy' (n 5) 271.

[149] Zhang (n 147); Jerome Alan Cohen, 'China's Changing Constitution' (1978) 76 The China Quarterly 794; Husa, '"Accurately, Completely, and Solemnly"' (n 5); Wong (n 148); Andrew Peng, 'Sinicized Marxist Constitutionalism: Its Emergence, Contents, and Implications' (2011) 2 Global Discourse 83.

[150] Peng Hu, 'Popular Understanding of Democracy in Contemporary China' (2018) 25 Democratization 1441, 1446. For a theoretical view of polyarchies without contesta-

soning, rather than constitutionalism, is one of the dominant assumptions of Chinese constitutional thinking.[151] Pragmatic reasoning in China, as described in Randall Peerenboom, includes a combination of clientelism and the promotion of economic development.[152] The two elements are interdependent, but the preservation of the informal structure of the communist party has a logical priority.[153] This has positive and negative logical implications. The positive implication is that all Chinese economic development is directly linked to the CCP's policies.[154] In other words, it is only the Standing Committee that can claim to be the author of three decades of economic growth and of the day-to-day positive changes in the lives of millions of its subjects.[155] The negative implication is that no other theoretical assumption, such as the protection of the right to self-determination by a physical entity such as an individual entrepreneur, can claim that her activities contribute to the common good.[156]

Pragmatic reasoning is also part of the rule of law in all liberal democracies but its role is interstitial.[157] Reasonableness and proportionality are requirements of judicial reasoning that are used to qualify abstract rules in pragmatic decisions.[158] However, in China, the Standing Committee has the prerogative to trump any constitutional rule.[159] The Chinese rule of law is 'what a democratic dictatorship of the people decided to be'.[160] The CCP's management of state resources, which are equitably distributed in relation to the needs of the Chinese population, is both a normative justification and a paradigm limit on

---

tion see: Robert Alan Dahl, *Polyarchy: Participation and Opposition* (Yale University Press 1971).

[151] Zhang (n 147); Cohen (n 149); Husa, '"Accurately, Completely, and Solemnly"' (n 5); Wong (n 148); Peng (n 149).

[152] Randall Peerenboom, *China's Long March Toward Rule of Law* (Cambridge University Press 2009) ch 10.

[153] ibid 411; 521.

[154] ibid 455.

[155] Peng (n 149).

[156] ibid; Husa, 'Constitutional Biography of Hong Kong and Ambiguities of One Country, Two Systems Policy' (n 5) 278.

[157] Neil MacCormick, 'Reasonableness and Objectivity' (1998) 74 Notre Dame Law Review 1575; Neil MacCormick, *Legal Reasoning and Legal Theory* (Clarendon Press 1994) ch 2; FI Michelman, 'The Problem of Constitutional Interpretative Disagreement' in Mitchell Aboulafia, Myra Orbach Bookman and Cathy Kemp (eds), *Habermas & Pragmatism* (Routledge 2002).

[158] Aharon Barak, *Proportionality: Constitutional Rights and Their Limitations* (Cambridge University Press 2012); MacCormick, 'Reasonableness and Objectivity' (n 157).

[159] Zhang (n 147).

[160] Peerenboom (n 152).

the role of judges.[161] For instance, Peng argues that the legal system is one of the many technical devices that are necessary for the preservation of the status quo of the CCP, and indirectly, for the promotion of the commonwealth of Chinese people.[162] Husa reaches a similar conclusion.

> The crucial thing to understand in regard to the Chinese Constitution is that it is understood differently from common law or Western law; it grasps constitution and constitutionalism in a rather specific manner. In order to understand constitutionalism with a Chinese flavour one needs to acknowledge, on the one hand, that the PRC Constitution is a mixture of polity and the governing Chinese Communist Party's ideology, and on the other, is the machinery of the statecraft, that is the state apparatus.[163]

There are multiple implications arising from the amalgamation of clientelism, ideology and economic policies. For instance, Husa explains that the quasi-jurisdictional intervention by the Standing Committee in Hong Kong's electoral regulation should be considered to be aligned with Chinese legal assumptions.[164] In particular, the prerogative to intervene in any jurisdictional activity is derived from the doctrine of the 'Three Supremes': 'the supremacy of the business of the Chinese Communist Party, interests of the people, and the supremacy of constitutional law'.[165] As odd as the term the *Three Supremes* might sound, the hierarchical structure of the three values provides *de jure* justification for the dictatorship of the Standing Committee. The scope of these values is only partially reduced, and not limited, by the Hong Kong Basic Law.[166]

In contrast with the Chinese system, Hong Kong's legal system is heavily influenced by the British constitutional doctrine.[167] The autonomy of its institutions is guaranteed by Article 2 of the Basic Law.[168] The equality of all individuals, the respect of the rule of law and the right to self-determination can be traced from historical documents like the Magna Carta and the Declaration of Arbroath.[169] One of the many pragmatic implications of the combination of

---

[161] 'If judicial review is necessary for constitutionalism, and constitutionalism is good for the interests of the vast majority of people, then "the people themselves" are the ultimate driving force for constitutional progress.' Zhang (n 147) 951.

[162] Cohen (n 149) 838.

[163] Husa, '"Accurately, Completely, and Solemnly"' (n 5) 237.

[164] ibid.

[165] ibid 236.

[166] ibid.

[167] ibid 233; Constitution of the Special Administrative Region of Hong Kong Article 8.

[168] Constitution of the Special Administrative Region of Hong Kong.

[169] Martin Loughlin, *The Idea of Public Law* (Oxford University Press 2003) 245.

these principles is that institutions within Britain and in its colonies, such as Hong Kong, derived their legitimacy from a system of rules that is interpreted by judges such as those who populated the Privy Council.[170]

One of the British legacies of the Privy Council in Hong Kong, which acted as the final appellate jurisdiction in the SAR, is the establishment of a connection between the perceived legitimacy of a legal system and the existence of a specialised apolitical class of legal professionals.[171] However, Article 158 of the Basic Law gives a prerogative to the Standing Committee to take over such a role as the final interpreter of Hong Kong's law.[172] This power has since been confirmed by the Hong Kong Court of Final Appeal in *Lau Kong Yung and Others v the Director of Immigration*.[173]

The key point here is that; the power to interpret the Basic Law is not an exceptional prerogative given to a central institution. Article 158 (1) asserts the normative subordination of the Hong Kong law to the will of the Standing Committee.[174] The intervention, in its interpretative role, of the Standing Committee has been rare and only technical. In cases such as *Democratic Republic of the Congo and Others v FG Hemisphere Associates LLC,* the implication of immigration policies and the interpretative ambiguity of the legal material justified a reference to the Standing Committee of the National People's Congress of the People's Republic of China (hereafter NPCSC).[175] Yet, the power allocated in Article 158 has been used in more controversial cases that triggered popular unrest. For instance, in June 2014, the qualification of the rules regulating the selection process for the Hong Kong Chief Executive by the Standing Committee was perceived by a large part of the Hong Kong population as an unjustifiable interference in Hong Kong's autonomy.[176] The interpretation focused on Annex 1 of the Basic Law that set out the

---

[170] Oliver Jones, 'A Worthy Predecessor? The Privy Council on Appeal from Hong Kong, 1853 to 1997' in Simon Young and Yash Ghai (eds), *Hong Kong's Court of Final Appeal: The Development of the Law in China's Hong Kong* (Cambridge University Press 2013).

[171] Husa, 'Constitutional Biography of Hong Kong and Ambiguities of One Country, Two Systems Policy' (n 5) 286. In Hong Kong by the activity of the final appellate jurisdiction of the Judicial Committee of the Privy Council within the House of Lords. Jones (n 170) 94; Ng (n 1) 193.

[172] Constitution of the Special Administrative Region of Hong Kong; Husa, '"Accurately, Completely, and Solemnly"' (n 5) 240; Young (n 19).

[173] *Lau Kong Yung and others v the Director of Immigration* [1999] HKCFA 5 (Court of Final Appeal) [54].

[174] Constitution of the People's Republic of China (as amended) Article 67(4).

[175] *Democratic Republic of the Congo And Others v FG Hemisphere Associates LLC* [2011] HKCFA 43; Young (n 19).

[176] State Council (China), 'The Practice of the "One Country, Two Systems" Policy in the Hong Kong Special Administrative Region' s V(4) Young (n 19); Ma and Cheng (n 92) 44.

procedures for the election of the Chief Executive.[177] The clarification by the Standing Committee was one of the key catalysts for a 79-day occupation of the city by the Umbrella Movement.[178] While it is clear that multiple elements influenced the Umbrella Movement, the interpretation of Annex 1 of the Basic Law was perceived as an ideological attempt to reduce the level of autonomy in the region.[179] The enactment of the NSL in 2020 was one of the latest interpretations of the Basic Law by the Standing Committee.[180]

The Standing Committee instead perceived the interpretation of Annex 1 as one of the activities aimed at maintaining a stable and pacific transition of the former British colony into China.[181] It is particularly difficult for the Standing Committee to accept that pluralism, even when it is heavily manipulated by the interests of political parties (as it is in most liberal democracies), contributes to the common good.[182] Marxist–Leninist models like the one adopted by China assume that a segmented society based on class (that is, a pyramid-shaped capitalist society) will foster morally unjustifiable differences.[183]

The clash between the two ideological stances can only be accommodated at a pragmatic level.[184] It is unfortunate for the Hong Kong self-governing movement that the Standing Committee has little to gain ideologically from allowing the accommodation of the regionalists' demands that are attached to Hong Kong's capitalist society.[185] It has, in contrast, something to gain from showing that Hong Kong liberalism, where unruly protesters are protected by a system of rules made by an elite for an elite, fosters social instability.[186] It is from this perspective that the Chinese constitutional system will continue to

---

[177] Constitution of the Special Administrative Region of Hong Kong; Choi and Lai (n 100) 194; Ng (n 1) 194.

[178] Ma and Cheng (n 92) 38.

[179] Constitution of the Special Administrative Region of Hong Kong Annex 1.

[180] Law of the People's Republic of China on Safeguarding National Security in the Hong Kong Special Administrative Region.

[181] State Council (China) (n 176).

[182] James Tully, 'The Unfreedom of the Moderns in Comparison to Their Ideals of Constitutional Democracy' (2002) 65 Modern Law Review 204.

[183] General Office of the State Council of the People's Republic of China (n 18); Joseph (n 40); Brown, *Contemporary China* (n 58) 115; Husa, 'Constitutional Biography of Hong Kong and Ambiguities of One Country, Two Systems Policy' (n 5) 273.

[184] General Office of the State Council of the People's Republic of China (n 18); Joseph (n 40); Brown, *Contemporary China* (n 58) 115; Husa, 'Constitutional Biography of Hong Kong and Ambiguities of One Country, Two Systems Policy' (n 5) 274.

[185] Ng (n 1) 197–8.

[186] Lee and others (n 118); Roantree (n 116); Yuen and Chung (n 6); Ng (n 1) 197–8.

act as a negative driver of change in the crisis of the legitimation of its institutions in Hong Kong.

## DRIVER OF CHANGE: HONG KONG LOCALISM AND CHINESE HEGEMONIC IDENTITY

In this section, I will explain that rigid stances that promote both Hong Kong localism and Chinese national identity are fostering diverging processes of legal self-identification. These processes proxy for the current cycle of the legitimation crises.[187] In the previous section of this chapter, I explained that legal assumptions of communism and liberalism derive differing interpretations of the role of popular demonstrations in Hong Kong.[188] In this section, I will focus on the identity-formation processes that distinguish Chinese national and Hong Kong and regional identities. There are indications that the self-referential processes which distinguish Chinese and Hong Kong identities are related to fear and the intolerance of minute differences fuelled by state-sponsored propaganda and by social media.[189] This crisis cycle is a 'negative' driver of change since it is likely to continue to increase the scope and the depth of the legitimation crisis until the special status of the HKSAR lapses in 2047.[190]

**The Emergence of Ethnic Localism in Hong Kong**

Localism in Hong Kong is a complex and dynamic social phenomenon that is associated with a series of identity-based political demands.[191] One of these is the demand for independence.[192] The number of social indicators of an identity varies, but there is general consensus that over 90 per cent of the Hong Kong population is ethnically Chinese.[193] The relationship between China and Hong Kong is associated with the concept of Hong Kong localism, but it is, from a sociological perspective, a form of banal nationalism.[194] Michael Billing uses the term to describe the identity-formation process in societies in which

---

[187] Yuen and Chung (n 6); Young (n 19).
[188] Kerry Brown, *China* (1st edition, Polity 2020) ch 5.
[189] Yuen and Chung (n 6); Michael Billig, *Banal Nationalism* (Sage 1995); Michael Ignatieff, *The Warrior's Honor: Ethnic War and the Modern Conscience* (Vintage 1999); Veg (n 6).
[190] Young (n 19); Yiu-man (n 8) 304.
[191] Yuen and Chung (n 6) 20; Cheung (n 4); Yiu-man (n 8).
[192] ibid; ibid; ibid.
[193] National Bureau of Statistics (n 33); Fong (n 3); Centre for Communication and Public Opinion Survey (n 56).
[194] Billig (n 189); Veg (n 6); Yuen and Chung (n 6).

an external observer might find them to be socially homogenous.[195] However, relatively inconsequential elements of daily life, such as a variation in the use of an alphabet or a local phraseology, becomes a daily reminder of the difference between 'a communal imagined us' and the 'a-communal imagined us'.[196] These are minor differences and they might have a series of repercussions on the stability of a system of governance, as noted in two books by Sigmund Freud.[197]

Recent studies on the causes of conflicts show that ethnic similitudes are a significant factor that fosters group violence.[198] The conclusion appears counterintuitive. It would be logical to assume that social proximity will breed competition, allowing best practices to spread across communities. However, Polaore and Wacziarg have found evidence of the opposite.[199] Their paper focuses on the analysis of international conflicts between 1816 and 2001, and they concluded that linguistic, cultural and genetic similarities increased rather than reduced the possibility of international conflicts.[200] Similarities and proximity, in short, breed violence.[201] Michael Ignatieff's book *Warrior Honour* describes the perverting nature of banal nationalism that prepared the multinational state for civil war.[202] In his rendering of the reason for the Balkan conflict in the 1990s, he concluded that intolerance for small cultural differences divided cities, villages, neighbours and families.[203]

Hong Kong localism has not reached the level of the deeply ingrained hatred that was distinctive of the 1990s' war in the Balkans,[204] yet sociological analyses and statistical surveys show the emerging intolerance of small differences in the HKSAR.[205] For instance, Elaine Chan and Joseph Chan explain that

---

[195] Billig (n 189) 27; Anderson (n 32).

[196] Ignatieff (n 189). Sigmund Freud used the term 'narcissism minor differences' in *The Standard Edition of the Complete Psychological Works of Sigmund Freud: VOLUME 11 (1910): Five Lectures on Psycho-Analysis, Leonardo Da Vinci and Other Works* (Anna Freud and James Strachey eds, The Hogarth Press and the Institute of Psycho-Analysis 1957) 199; *Group Psychology and the Analysis of the Ego* (Lulu.com 2018) 31–32; *Civilization and Its Discontents* (Prabhat Prakashan 2015) V.

[197] Freud, *Civilization and Its Discontents* (n 196) V; Freud, *Group Psychology and the Analysis of the Ego* (n 196) 30–31.

[198] Enrico Spolaore and Romain Wacziarg, 'War and Relatedness' (2016) 98 The Review of Economics and Statistics 925, 925.

[199] ibid.

[200] ibid 938.

[201] ibid 925.

[202] Ignatieff (n 189) ch 2.

[203] ibid.

[204] Michael Ignatieff, *Blood & Belonging: Journeys into the New Nationalism* (Vintage 1994); Veg (n 6); Yuen and Chung (n 6).

[205] Ignatieff (n 204); Veg (n 6); Yuen and Chung (n 6).

Hong Kong localism has, in its current form, emerged as a reaction to multiple events that progressively increased the sense of intolerance towards Chinese mainland residents and the institutions that represent them.[206] Their analysis used a significant sample of Hong Kong residents and shows, for instance, that after the annexation with China and the creation of the SAR, a large part of the population perceived themselves as Chinese and Chinese Hong Kong residents.[207] From 2007, the process of self-identification stopped and, it is logical to assume, the same individuals who claimed to be Chinese started to indicate that Hong Kong was their cultural homeland.[208]

> This national consciousness redrew the communal barriers and excluded Mainlanders as members of their community, generating a distinct idea of a nation centring only on the locality of Hong Kong without concerning the rest of the PRC, whether Hong Kong is or is not envisioned to be an independent city-state.[209]

The process of identity formation included the adoption of a racist stance. The term locusts and *chee-na* are often used against tourists and pro-China Hong Kong residents.[210] The term *shina*, which has a similar sound and is still officially in use in Japan, is mispronounced as *chee-na* by localist supporters who know that it is a highly derogatory racist label.[211] One of the most controversial episodes in the recent history of the localism movement that is associated with the use of *chee-na* was during the LegCo oath ceremony of Sixtus Leung and Yau Wai-ching. The two newly elected legislative representatives, who were sponsored by an alliance of localist political parties, altered the wording of the oath in a way that included multiple mispronunciations of the word China as *chee-na*.[212] The oath-taking controversy was one of the reasons that led to the disqualification of six newly elected localist representatives and eventually to

---

[206] Yuen and Chung (n 6).
[207] Elaine Chan and Joseph Chan, 'Liberal Patriotism in Hong Kong' (2014) 23 Journal of Contemporary China 952, 959.
[208] Centre for Communication and Public Opinion Survey (n 56).
[209] Yiu-man (n 8) 300.
[210] Yuen and Chung (n 6) 21; Husa, '"Accurately, Completely, and Solemnly"' (n 5); Mark Ives, 'How a Word, "Chee-Na," Renewed a Crisis Between Beijing and Hong Kong – The New York Times' *The New York Times* (9 November 2006).
[211] Yuen and Chung (n 6) 21; Husa, '"Accurately, Completely, and Solemnly"' (n 5); 'How a Word, "Chee-Na," Renewed a Crisis Between Beijing and Hong Kong – The New York Times' (n 210).
[212] 'How a Word, "Chee-Na," Renewed a Crisis Between Beijing and Hong Kong – The New York Times' (n 210); *Youngspiration's Sixtus 'Baggio Leung' Takes His Oath at the Hong Kong Legislature* (Directed by Hong Kong Free Press, 2016).

the interpretative intervention of Article 104 of the Basic Law by the Standing Committee.[213]

Recall that less than two decades previously, most Hong Kong localists perceived themselves as part of the Chinese heritage that they currently denigrate.[214] The fact that national identities are dynamic social phenomena is a truism, yet in Hong Kong, its relatively small size, ethnic homogeneity and high population density escalated the speed of this change.[215] There is also an acute awareness by all political actors that public events, such as the oath takings at the LegCo or demonstrations, can rapidly trigger a spiral of actions which change attitudes in a large part of the population.[216]

In all the legal systems considered in this book, the identity-formation process is a complex phenomenon. Tully uses the term *multinationalism* to describe the Canadian experience and Smith uses polycentric nationalism in relation to the British identity.[217] What is distinctive about Hong Kong is that a large section of a regional community holds multiple attachments to multiple ideological views that are *prima facie* incompatible.[218] These stances are liberalism, Confucianism, Taoism and Buddhism.[219] Hong Kong Chinese nationalism is one of the few forms of nationalism where such a divergent meaning also provides some of the building blocks of a national identity.[220] This complex relationship and the rapid changes in attitudes towards one or another of these ideological stances have become more evident during the current cycle of crises.[221]

The paradox is that social scientists consider this distinctive Chinese tolerance for what are ultimately incompatible ideological stances as one of the distinctive features of pan-hegemonic Chinese culture.[222] Empirical studies confirm, for instance, that Chinese nationalism is multifaced and extreme

---

[213] Standing Committee, Tenth Session of the Standing Committee of the Twelfth National People's Congress (n 94); Constitution of the Special Administrative Region of Hong Kong; Husa, "'Accurately, Completely, and Solemnly'" (n 5) 232; Ng (n 1) 193.

[214] Ignatieff (n 204).

[215] Centre for Communication and Public Opinion Survey (n 56); Iris Kam (n 98).

[216] Yuen and Chung (n 6).

[217] James Tully, *Strange Multiplicity: Constitutionalism in an Age of Diversity* (CUP 1995); Smith (n 72).

[218] Ng (n 1) 197–8.

[219] Robert Bickers and Ray Yep, *May Days in Hong Kong: Riot and Emergency In 1967* (Hong Kong University Press 2009) 95; Chan and Chan (n 207) 959.

[220] Wang, Madson and Maleson (n 9) 28.

[221] Cheung (n 4) 323.

[222] Chi Kit Chan, 'China as "Other": Resistance to and Ambivalence toward National Identity in Hong Kong' (2014) 2014 China Perspectives 25, 26; Chan and Chan (n 207) 959; Wang, Madson and Maleson (n 9) 30.

xenophobic nationalism is relatively rare.[223] It is in the interstitial relationship between these multiple meaning providers that Hong Kong localism and strict Chinese nationalism develop their reciprocal narratives of mutual intolerance.[224] It is a matter of speculation as to whether an independent Hong Kong that is advocated for by localists might be inspired by the template of a multinational society provided by Singapore or tilt towards civil unrest à la Northern Ireland.[225] However, there are signs that the current leadership of the localist movement seeks to promote extreme positions that have reinforced the internal connection between localist supporters.[226] This stance is not propaedeutic for developing negotiations between identity groups that are essential for maintaining a perceived connection between the legitimacy of the legal system and the individuals who are ruled by it.[227]

The idea of a Hong Kong national identity that excludes and denigrates other identities is only partly a response to Chinese hegemonic claims over Hong Kong. The circular structure of the interaction 'you are Chinese and this land belongs to us' and its equally ideological answer 'we are not Chinese and we own our destiny' is part of an identity-based conflict. Without a change of course in the leadership of the localist movement, the interaction between the two apparently unreconciled attitudes (that is, localism and Chinese hegemonism) will continue to foster the perception of the illegitimacy of both stances until the two systems one country agreement lapses in 50 years' time.[228] From this perspective, the identity-formation process in Hong Kong will continue to be a negative driver of change. The CCP will continue to represent Hong Kong as rules breakers, whereas localists will continue to find reasons to be distinguished from mainlanders.

## Chinese National Identity: The Sons of the Dragon

In the previous section, I explained that Hong Kong localism is a new phenomenon in the HKSAR.[229] In this section, I will discuss the effect of having

---

[223] Yinxian Zhang, Jiajun Liu and Ji-Rong Wen, 'Nationalism on Weibo: Towards a Multifaceted Understanding of Chinese Nationalism' (2018) 235 The China Quarterly 758, 761, 768.

[224] Ignatieff (n 189); Freud, *Group Psychology and the Analysis of the Ego* (n 196).

[225] Centre for Communication and Public Opinion Survey, (n 56); Cheung (n 4).

[226] Yuen and Chung (n 6); Veg (n 6); Tsang (n 99); 'Hong Kong Advert Calls Chinese Mainlanders "Locusts"' (n 99).

[227] Donald Horowitz, 'Some Realism about Constitutional Engineering' in Andreas Wimmer (ed), *Facing Ethnic Conflicts: Toward a New Realism* (Rowman & Littlefield 2004).

[228] Kwan (n 92).

[229] Brown, *China* (n 188).

a ruling communist party that should, in theory, support universal values, but that in practice claims exclusive ownership of the Chinese identity.[230] I will explain how China has adopted an ethnic-collectivistic nationalism that is predominantly authoritarian and intolerant.[231]

The idea of a multinational state has been part of Chinese collective consciousness for over a millennium;[232] yet, modern Chinese identity relies on the connection between morality, social compliance and respect for the established hierarchy.[233] The three national features are derived directly from Confucianism, and their connection is explained in a clear narrative by Wang, Madson and Maleson.

> This idea of obedience and rigid application of hierarchical status also applied on a national scale ... This concept is reflected in the Chinese word 'nation/state' or guo jia. The first character means 'nation' and the second means 'family'. As within the family unit, loyalty and obedience to rulers were paramount virtues within society. In the analysis of Chinese identity that drives the series of crises in Hong Kong is the triadic relationship between CCP identity, Chinese national identity, and the commonwealth of the Chinese people. The commonwealth of Chinese people is constructed primarily by the CCP's own subjective interest.[234]

There is broad consensus on the interaction between the authority of the CCP and the normative implications of the rule of law.[235] Husa delivers a very similar point: '[b]asically, the doctrine of Three Supremes consists of three parallel constitutional principles: first is the supremacy of the business of the Chinese Communist Party, second is the supremacy of the interests of the people, and third is the supremacy of constitutional law.'[236] He also noted that there is a distinct lack of coherence regarding how the three elements are managed in the HKSAR.[237]

This lack of consistency has implications for the governance of Hong Kong, where the rational element of the British interpretation of the rule of law has

---

[230] Neo and Xiang (n 29); FA Schneider, 'Emergent Nationalism in China's Sociotechnical Networks: How Technological Affordance and Complexity Amplify Digital Nationalism' (2022) 28 Nations and Nationalism 267.

[231] Cheung (n 4) 321; Brown, *Contemporary China* (n 58) 230; Cheung (n 4) 428; Weiwei Zhang, *China Wave, the Rise of a Civilizational State* (World Scientific Publishing Company 2012) 134.

[232] Yiu-man (n 8) 298.

[233] Wang, Madson and Maleson (n 9) 28; Yiu-man (n 8); Brown, *China* (n 188); Neo and Xiang (n 29); Hu (n 150) 1442.

[234] Wang, Madson and Maleson (n 9) 28.

[235] Husa, '"Accurately, Completely, and Solemnly"' (n 5).

[236] My emphasis ibid 236.

[237] ibid. similar conclusion is in: Yiu-man (n 8) 300; Ng (n 1) 197–8.

established solid roots and where interference in such principles constantly produces anxiety and public outrage.[238] However, the mere existence of foreign values in Hong Kong has a triggering effect on the Chinese communal psyche.[239] The existence of Hong Kong as a liberal enclave is a reminder of the opium wars and the Japanese invasion, which are still part of national identity narratives.[240] Wang points out that foreign powers, during their colonial expansion, humiliated China.[241] This is a crucial aspect as the key thinking with Chinese identity. Being humiliated is a total 'loss of face', even if this happened many years ago.

It is unfortunate that, for the CCP and its official narrative, the legal status of the HKSAR is an ever-present reminder of a historical legacy in which China could not effectively control its borders.[242] There is little critical engagement with the fact that the current size of the population of China and the present political system are also the result of warfare in which minorities were marginalised and deported as it is the case for some Chinese minorities.[243] The humiliation at the hands of foreign powers is, instead, considered one of the sociological reasons for the assertion of the indivisibility of China.[244] Again, the idea that a territory is sacred (for whatever reason) is part of the stable nationalist diet of all modern nation states.[245] This claim of the sacred unity of the state that is associated with the Han ethnic group has pragmatic implications for Hong Kong. It reduces, for instance, the possibility that localist demands for self-determination will be considered as plausible political demands.[246] However, that is only a legal manifestation of an ideological stance that gives priority to the power of the Standing Committee and the normative values of the CCP over the political aspirations of a minority group.[247]

The CCP system in China acts as a syncretic meaning provider that has little tolerance for dissidents.[248] This authority is associated with meritocracy and

---

[238] Wong and Liu (n 19).
[239] Yiu-man (n 8) 296.
[240] The Government SAR (n 58).
[241] ibid.
[242] Brown, *Contemporary China* (n 58) 49; Yiu-man (n 8) 296.
[243] Fukuyama (n 32) 110–11.
[244] Brown, *Contemporary China* (n 58) 49; Yiu-man (n 8) 296.
[245] Liah Greenfeld, 'Introduction to the Research Handbook on Nationalism' in Liah Greenfeld and Zeying Wu (eds), *Research Handbook on Nationalism* (Edward Elgar Publishing 2020) 3.
[246] Kerry Brown, 'The EU, US and China: Hybrid Multilateralism and the Limits of Prioritizing Values' (2021) Global Summitry 14, para 65.
[247] Zhang (n 231) 134.
[248] ibid 114, 132; Hu (n 150) 1442.

the efficiency of CCP policies.[249] The effects of this pronominally authoritarian ethnic-collectivistic nationalism in the Hong Kong crisis are both internal and external to the HKSAR.[250] Within Hong Kong, residents who support Chinese nationalism perceive the localist movement as a manifestation of a cultural betrayal which has the potential to challenge the economic stability and prosperity of the SAR.[251] The CCP instead responds, in general, to the pleas for self-government by re-asserting its authority.[252] The Party's mission is to ensure that China is not weak and that it is not perceived as weak by international actors.[253] The mere existence of the open opposition that continues in Hong Kong is one of the reasons that has generated draconian responses by the CCP which are supported by the Chinese population.[254] The 'tightening of the grip' on Hong Kong, as Brown called it, appears excessive to those individuals in Hong Kong who do not support localism and to the international community.[255] It is perhaps a way for China to save face. Yet, it should be considered as a manifestation of the Chinese identity-formation process.

The CCP's interventions are counterproductive in Hong Kong.[256] The tightening of CCP control over Hong Kong, through, for example, the NSL, and the imposition of hegemonic views feed into the level of mistrust in Hong Kong regarding the CCP's leadership, but the Standing Committee has a very limited margin of discretion.[257] This point is made by Brown in a clear narrative: '[w]hy is Beijing obsessed with order? It fears the alternative.'[258] There is the possibility that Hong Kong's liberalism might spread to mainland China and that this might trigger the events that fostered the collapse of communist countries in Europe.[259] In an economically prosperous China, this is a highly

---

[249] Zhang (n 231) 131–34.

[250] Cheung (n 4).

[251] Liah Greenfeld and Zeying Wu, '"Liberate Hong Kong, the Revolution of Our Times": The Birth of the First Orient Nation in the Twenty-First Century' in Yuk-man Cheung (ed), *Research Handbook on Nationalism* (Edward Elgar Publishing 2020) 329.

[252] Greenfeld and Wu (n 251); Cheung (n 4).

[253] Kerry Brown, 'China's Ruling Creed at 100: The Party Never Stops' (*Engelsberg Ideas*, 1 July 2021).

[254] Kerry Brown, 'Why Is Beijing Obsessed with Order? It Fears the Alternative' *South China Morning Post* (28 April 2018); Brown, *Contemporary China* (n 58); Ng (n 1) 193.

[255] Brown, 'Why Is Beijing Obsessed with Order?' (n 254); Brown, *Contemporary China* (n 58).

[256] Zhang (n 231); Neo and Xiang (n 29).

[257] Law of the People's Republic of China on Safeguarding National Security in the Hong Kong Special Administrative Region.

[258] Brown, 'Why Is Beijing Obsessed with Order?' (n 254).

[259] Greenfeld and Wu (n 251).

improbable eventuality,[260] but the fear that such events might occur justify the CCP's draconian stance in Hong Kong. Fear of change is seldom a positive element in the identity-making process. It is particularly so when fear produces narratives for an authoritarian regime that is imposed on a regional minority.[261] There are, however, few very indications that the Chinese identity process will change, but until Hong Kong is no longer perceived as a potential danger for China, the CCP's political stance will continue to feed into Hong Kong localists' mistrust in central institutions.

## CONCLUSION

The series of mass demonstrations in Hong Kong against China that started in 2004 is the most obvious manifestation of the crisis of legitimacy of the CCP's institutions in the SAR.[262] COVID-19 restrictions led to the approval of the 2020 NSL to prevent mass protests, but the restrictions over public gatherings have simply shifted the public distrust in the institutions elsewhere.[263] In this chapter, it was argued that the regional crisis in Hong Kong is linked, among other factors, to two drivers of change.

The first driver of change is legal. The Standing Committee will continue to act as the final interpreter of the Hong Kong Basic Law.[264] The Standing Committee, by limiting political representation, culling freedom of speech and reducing the application of the rule of law will continue to foster the perception of it being an imperialist institution in the SAR.[265]

The interaction between national identities is the second driver of change that was considered.[266] The Chinese population includes multiple regional identities, but overall, it is culturally homogeneous.[267] With a population of over 1.3 billion, over 90 per cent of the population is part of one Han ethnic group.[268] Demographically, Hong Kong is a small multicultural enclave within China.[269] The majority of its residents identified themselves as culturally Chinese Hong Kong residents.[270] The similarity between the Chinese and Hong

---

[260] Brown, 'Why Is Beijing Obsessed with Order?' (n 254); Brown, *China* (n 188).
[261] Ng (n 1) 198.
[262] Veg (n 6).
[263] Ismangil and Lee (n 1); Husa, 'Constitutional Biography of Hong Kong and Ambiguities of One Country, Two Systems Policy' (n 5) 275; Ng (n 1) 197.
[264] Young (n 19).
[265] Greenfeld and Wu (n 251).
[266] Yiu-man (n 8).
[267] National Bureau of Statistics (n 33).
[268] ibid.
[269] Jessieca Leo, *Global Hakka: Hakka Identity in the Remaking* (Brill 2015).
[270] ibid.

Kong identity is one of the reasons for the development of a distinctive form of nationalism based on small differences.[271] Hong Kong also has a role in the formation of Chinese identity. The existence the HKSAR is a permanent reminder of national shame arising from a period in which China was subjected to European imperialism.[272] The fear that liberal values might spread from the former British colony to the rest of China has fostered the use of draconian measures such as the NSL. In turn, this has fed into the mistrust of localists, making the cycle of the crisis surrounding the legitimacy of central institutions self-sustaining.

---

[271] Yuen and Chung (n 6); Ignatieff (n 204); Freud, *Group Psychology and the Analysis of the Ego* (n 196).
[272] Ng (n 1) 192.

# 6. France: the end of New Caledonia's *sui generis* status

This chapter discusses the ongoing crisis of the legitimacy of French and regional institutions in New Caledonia.[1] New Caledonia, like Northern Ireland, is a deeply divided consociative regional democracy that has endured a high level of political violence.[2] A series of agreements ended the 1980s' civil war and set up a transitory constitutional regime.[3] The deliberative phase ended when the latest of three consultative referenda was also won by unionists.[4] In

---

[1] Parts of this chapter appeared in an article entitled 'New Caledonia: The Archipelago That Does Not Want to Be Freed' in the *Journal de Droit Comparé du Pacifique* (Vol XXIV, 2019). I am indebted to Chief Editor Prof Toni Angelo, Prof Jennifer Corrin and the *Journal de Droit Comparé du Pacifique*'s anonymous referees for their invaluable feedback. The author and the publisher would like to thank the University of Victoria in Wellington for the permission to reprint extracts from the article. As per usual, all errors are my own.

[2] John Connell, *New Caledonia of Kanaky: The Political History of a French Colony* (Development Studies Centre, The Australian National University 2017) 318–58; David A Chappell, *The Kanak Awakening: The Rise of Nationalism in New Caledonia* (University of Hawaii Press 2013) 223; François Doumenge, 'La dynamique géopolitique du Pacifique Sud (1965–1990)' (1990) 43 Les Cahiers d'Outre-Mer 113, 161.

[3] French Parliament, 'Accords de Matignon-Oudinot Du Juin 1988 in the Rapport Fait Au Nom de La Commission Des Lois Constitutionnelles, de Législation, Du Suffrage Universel, Du Règlement et d'administration Générale Sur Le Projet de Loi, Adopté Par l'Assemblée Nationale, Après Déclaration d'urgence, Portant Amnistie d'infractions Commises à l'occasion d'événements Survenus En Nouvelle-Calédonie, Annexes 1 & 2, Senat 7 of December 1989, Vol 112 47–52'. Accord sur la Nouvelle-Calédonie signé à Nouméa le 5 mai 1998; Loi n° 99-209 organique du 19 mars 1999 relative à la Nouvelle-Calédonie (consolidée au 07 janvier 2019) Article 99; Constitution du 4 octobre 1958 (version consolidée) 1958 Article 77, 78. Loi constitutionnelle no 98-610 du 20 juillet 1998 relative à la Nouvelle-Calédonie. Denise Fisher, *France in the South Pacific: Power and Politics* (ANU Press 2013) French and English versions available in Appendix 1 (p.311); Carine David and Manuel Tirard, 'La Nouvelle-Calédonie après le troisième référendum d'autodétermination du 12 décembre 2021: 40 ans pour rien ?' (2022) La Revue des droits de l'homme. 1.

[4] French Government–Haut-commissariat de la République en Nouvelle-Calédonie, 'Les Résultats – Élections Nouvelle-Calédonie' <www.elections-nc.fr/elections-2018-2020/referendum-2020/les-resultats> accessed 18 May 2022.

2023, the new negotiation phase of the transitory regime will decide the future status of New Caledonia within the French constitutional system.

However, the events surrounding the last of the three referenda has increased the tension in the archipelago. In December 2021, residents of New Caledonia were asked to vote for the third time in three years in a consultative referendum over independence from France.[5] For the third time, the majority favoured the status quo.[6] Of the votes cast, 96.5 per cent supported the union with the Republic of France (hereafter, France).[7] The result is, however, misleading. The Kanaks, who are the original inhabitants of the archipelago and who make up over 40 per cent of its population, boycotted the referendum and denounced its legitimacy.[8] The events surrounding the referendum are unfortunate for multiple reasons. Still, they are particularly regrettable because this plebiscite was established to stop protracted civil unrest.[9]

This chapter will discuss two drivers of change that sustain a perception of the illegitimacy of public institutions in New Caledonia. The first driver of change is the constitutional setting for the forthcoming 2023 negotiation process over the future status of the archipelago within the French Constitution.[10] The second driver of change focuses on the process of identity formation of both French and Kanak identities in New Caledonia.[11] According

---

[5] ibid.
[6] ibid.
[7] ibid.
[8] In the months that preceded the 2021 referendum there were concerns that the region would go back to a civil war and the term boycott, that was perceived too inflammatory, was avoided by representatives all political parties. David and Tirard (n 3) 7.
[9] Connell (n 2) 318–58; Chappell, *The Kanak Awakening* (n 2) 223; Doumenge (n 2) 161. 'Accord de Noumea' <www.mncparis.fr/uploads/accord-noumea.pdf> accessed 27 December 2018; David A Chappell, 'The Noumea Accord: Decolonization Without Independence in New Caledonia? (Accord with France)' (1999) 72 Pacific Affairs 373.
[10] David and Tirard (n 3) 8.
[11] A Stone Sweet, 'The Politics of Constitutional Review in France and Europe' (2007) 5 International Journal of Constitutional Law 69; David Marrani, *Dynamics in the French Constitution: Decoding French Republican Ideas* (Routledge 2013); Chappell, 'The Noumea Accord' (n 9); Chappell, *The Kanak Awakening* (n 2).

to the United Nations, New Caledonia is a non-self-governing territory[12] administered by France as a French autonomous collectivity.[13]

New Caledonia benefits from a constitutionally entrenched legislative and administrative autonomy.[14] The archipelago's landmass is 18,500 km$^2$, and it is composed of the island of Grand Terre, the archipelago of the Loyalty Islands and several smaller and sporadically inhabited islands and atolls.[15] The island of Gran Terre is the largest, and it includes the regional capital Noumea. The Pacific archipelago is isolated: Noumea is 539 km south of Port Villa in Vanuatu, 1472 km southwest of Brisbane and 1804 km north of Auckland.

Compared to metropolitan France, New Caledonia is rich in resources. The archipelago includes the fourth-largest reserve of nickel in the world.[16] The history of nickel mining, which still makes up 90 per cent of the exports of the archipelago, is also deeply intertwined with the political development of

---

[12] United Nations General Assembly, 'General Assembly Resolution n.1514 Declaration on the Granting of Independence to Colonial Countries and Peoples'; United Nations, 'Report of the Secretary-General – Information from Non-Self-Governing Territories Transmitted under Article 73 e of the Charter of the United Nations' 3; Stéphanie Graff, 'Quand combat et revendication kanak ou politique de l'État français manient indépendance, décolonisation, autodétermination et autochtonie en Nouvelle-Calédonie' (2012) Journal de la Société des Océanistes 61, 69.

[13] French Constitution 1958 (as revised 23/07/2008) 1958 Article 73, 74. Loi constitutionnelle n° 2008-724 du 23 juillet 2008 de modernisation des institutions de la Ve République Article 9, 11, 39, 40, 39, 40. David Chappell, 'Decolonisation and Nation-Building in New Caledonia: Reflections on the 2014 Elections' (2015) 67 Political Science 56, 57; Géraldine Giraudeau, 'Le Droit International et Les Transitions Constitutionnelles' in Françoise Cayrol (ed), *L'avenir institutionnel de la Nouvelle-Calédonie* (Presses universitaires de la Nouvelle-Calédonie 2018) 25; Graff (n 12) 74; Sophie Boyron, *The Constitution of France: A Contextual Analysis* (Hart Publishing 2013) 206, 214; David and Tirard (n 3) 1.

[14] David Marrani, 'Asia-Pacific: Insights from the Region: Will New Caledonia Be Another Tokelau?' (2006) 31 Alternative Law Journal 102, 102; Loi n° 99-209 organique du 19 mars 1999 relative à la Nouvelle-Calédonie (consolidée au 07 janvier 2019) Article 1.

[15] Émilie Dotte, 'Modes d'exploitation et d'intégration Au Sein Des Territoires Kanak Précoloniaux Des Ressources Végétales Forestières (IIe Millénaire Ap. J.-C.): Approche Ethno-Archéo-Anthracologique En Nouvelle-Calédonie' in Théophane Nicolas and Aurélie Salavert (eds), *Territoires et économies* (Éditions de la Sorbonne 2016) 155; Institut de la Statistique et des Études Économiques-Recensement, 'Résultats Du Recensement 2019 Institut de La Statistique et Des Études Économiques-Recensement' (2019).

[16] Séverine Blaise, 'The "Rebalancing" of New Caledonia's Economy' (2017) 52 Journal of Pacific History 194; Colin Filer and Pierre-Yves Le Meur, *Large-Scale Mines and Local-Level Politics: Between New Caledonia and Papua New Guinea* (ANU Press 2017) 4. Emily Schnebele, 'Nickel', *Mineral Commodity Summaries 2017* (US Govt PRINTING Office 2017).

the French colony.[17] The marine exclusive economic zone (hereafter EEZ) is also a current and potential source of revenue, since it covers a surface of over 1.4 million km$^2$.[18] In 2017, the economic support that New Caledonia received from France was estimated to account for 15 per cent of the regional GDP,[19] and the tertiary sector, made up largely of French civil servants, remains the highest contributor to the regional economy.[20] The effective contribution of the mining sector is notoriously difficult to evaluate since it is dependent on forecasted environmental costs that cannot be easily assessed. Still, mining revenues combined with the influx of wages for French public servants is estimated to make up over 90 per cent of the New Caledonian economy.[21]

Due to French immigration policies, most of the resident population currently has colonial or overseas ancestry; however, in the northern region, there is a relative local majority of Kanaks.[22] The Kanak ethnic group, is fragmented sociologically, politically and linguistically.[23] The grouping of a multinational society in a single taxonomy is the result of the colonisation process, which does not need to be discussed in this chapter, yet the sociological and political

---

[17] Pierre-Yves Le Meur and Claire Levacher, 'Mining and Competing Sovereignties in New Caledonia' (2022) 92 Oceania 74, 74; John Connell, 'The 2020 New Caledonia Referendum: The Slow March to Independence?' (2021) 56 The Journal of Pacific History 144, 147; Isabelle Leblic, 'Sovereignty and Coloniality in the French-Speaking Pacific: A Reflection on the Case of New Caledonia, 1980–2021' (2022) 92 Oceania 107, 115.

[18] C Le Visage and others, 'Inventory of the Economic Zones of the French Territories in the Pacific' (1998) 75 The International Hydrographic Review 108; Flanders Marine Institute (VLIZ), Belgium, 'Maritime Boundaries Geodatabase: Maritime Boundaries and Exclusive Economic Zones (200NM), Version 10.

[19] Filer and Meur (n 15) 8.

[20] Blaise (n 16) 204.

[21] Leah S Horowitz, 'Toward a Viable Independence? The Koniambo Project and the Political Economy of Mining in New Caledonia' (2004) 16 The Contemporary Pacific 287, 299, 303; Leblic, 'Sovereignty and Coloniality in the French-Speaking Pacific' (n 17) 114; Blaise (n 16) 214; Le Meur and Levacher (n 17); Henri Torre, 'Rapport d'information fait au nom de la Commission des finances, du contrôle budgétaire et des comptes économiques de la Nation sur la mission de contrôle effectuée en Nouvelle-Calédonie relative à la défiscalisation des usines de traitement de nickel' (Senat 2005).

[22] 'Institut de La Statistique et Des Études Économiques-Recensement' (n 15); Fisher (n 3) 107; Chappell, 'Decolonisation and Nation-Building in New Caledonia' (n 13); Raylene Ramsay, 'Telling the Past as Identity Construction in the Literatures of New Kanaky/New Caledonia' (2008) Journal of the Australasian Universities Language and Literature Association 113, 119; Horowitz (n 21) 289.

[23] Fisher (n 3) 121; Chappell, 'Decolonisation and Nation-Building in New Caledonia' (n 13) 58; Blaise (n 16) 197; Isabelle Leblic, 'Kanak Identity, New Citizenship Building and Reconciliation' (2007) Journal de la Société des Océanistes 271, 274; David and Tirard (n 3) 5.

heterogeneity of the Kanak nation also has constitutional implications for the future of New Caledonia.[24] The different perceptions within Kanak identity over the choices that define and will define the commonwealth of New Caledonia played out in the three referenda over independence.[25] In the 2018 referendum, the pro-independence movement collected 44 per cent of the votes cast, in 2020, that number increased to 47 per cent, and in 2021, it stood at only 3 per cent.[26] As mentioned earlier, the 2021 referendum was denounced as unrepresentative, and the insistence by the French Government that it should be considered as the final democratic element of archipelago independence process has cast a very dark shadow over the legitimacy of the 2023 constitutional negotiations.[27]

The Noumea Accord set up a temporary status for the archipelago via the related constitutional reform, which in theory prepared the region for decolonisation.[28] It was preceded by the Matignon–Oudinot Accord (hereafter, the Matignon Accord).[29] In this chapter, I will focus on the constitutional implications of the Noumea Accord and the effects of the process of recognition of the Kanak identity.[30]

Before these narratives are explored in more detail, a series of issues must be dealt with as part of preliminary discussions. First, Kanaks had inhabited the group of islands and atolls called New Caledonia for over a thousand years before the French Empire annexed their land in 1853.[31] We will not attempt to depict the pre-colonisation period with unproper mawkishness, yet it is

---

[24] Fisher (n 3) 58; Loi n° 99-209 organique du 19 mars 1999 relative à la Nouvelle-Calédonie (consolidée au 07 janvier 2019) 188.

[25] Horowitz (n 21) 299.

[26] Le Meur and Levacher (n 17) 89.

[27] David and Tirard (n 3) 8.

[28] Graff (n 12) 66–73; Kanak Agency for Development, 'United Nations: New Caledonia: Current Realities and Prospects for Decolonization under the Noumea Accord'; 'Accord de Noumea' (n 9); Loi n° 99-209 organique du 19 mars 1999 relative à la Nouvelle-Calédonie (consolidée au 07 janvier 2019); General Assembly United Nations, 'Resolution 35/118 Plan of Action for the Full Implementation of the Declaration on Granting of Independence to Colonial Countries and Peoples'; General Assembly United Nations, 'Resolution 41/41A Implementation of the Declaration on the Granting of Independence to Colonial Countries and Peoples'; Le Meur and Levacher (n 17) 89.

[29] For a detailed analysis of the economic implications of the Noumea Accord see: Blaise (n 16); Horowitz (n 21).

[30] David and Tirard (n 3).

[31] Isabelle Leblic, 'Chronologie de la Nouvelle-Calédonie' (2003) Journal de la Société des Océanistes 299; Connell (n 2) 6; Isabelle Leblic, 'Présentation : Nouvelle-Calédonie, 150 ans après la prise de possession' (2003) Journal de la Société des Océanistes 135; Dotte (n 15) 155.

safe to suggest that colonisation had a negative impact on the Kanak and their culture.[32] Pierre-Yves Le Meur and Claire Levacher describe the key phases of French Imperial Policy in a succinct narrative.

> The result was land spoliation, slow-motion/laisser faire genocide (until the 1930s), and strong racial, social and spatial segregation. Kanak Indigenous peoples were subjects, not citizens, of the empire under the indigénat disciplinary regime (1887–1946), confined in small and remote land reservations under the aegis of a neo-customary administrative chieftainship, the police force (gendarmerie) acting at the interface between Kanak tribes (an administrative qualification) and the colonial administration.[33]

The discovery of rich mining resources was directly coupled with government-promoted Asian and Pacific immigration, as these immigrants were perceived as 'better' than the Kanak.[34] Wallisian and Futunan forced immigration steered ethnic frictions with the Kanaks and further destabilised the socio-political structure of the archipelago.[35]

Second, the effect of the several decades of officially abetted immigration from France developed a divided society in which poor Kanaks lived in rural areas, forced immigrants were moved into shanty towns next to the city and the French inhabited the urban areas.[36] From the 1950s onwards, the oscillating economic cycles of the archipelago's mining sector exacerbated the already fragile relationship between the Kanak and the new residents, which is perceived as the starting point for the violent uprising.[37]

> The French response was to drown the Kanak demands of self-governance by increasing the number of immigrants. New Caledonia combined a loss of political autonomy and self-government (through various laws in 1963 and 1969) with a migratory boom encouraged by the French State to drown Kanak claims by number. Around 35,000–40,000 people arrived during a short-lived but intense nickel boom in less than ten years.[38]

---

[32] Horowitz (n 21) 301; Le Meur and Levacher (n 17) 79.

[33] Le Meur and Levacher (n 17) 80.

[34] Connell (n 2) 6; Yann Bencivengo, 'Naissance de l'industrie du nickel en Nouvelle-Calédonie et au-delà, à l'interface des trajectoires industrielles, impériales et coloniales (1875–1914)' (2014) Journal de la Société des Océanistes 137, 145.

[35] Connell (n 2) 97.

[36] Chappell, 'Decolonisation and Nation-Building in New Caledonia' (n 13) 60; Blaise (n 16) 207; 'Institut de La Statistique et Des Études Économiques-Recensement' (n 15).

[37] Horowitz (n 21) 291; 301; Le Meur and Levacher (n 17) 80 ; Connell (n 2) 318–58; Chappell, *The Kanak Awakening* (n 2) 223; Doumenge (n 2) 161.

[38] Le Meur and Levacher (n 17) 79.

The policy was effective, but it was met with violent resistance.[39] As with any sociological phenomenon, there are multiple explanations for politically motivated violence. In this instance, it was associated with the increasing awareness on the part of the political leaders of the Kanak, some of whom had graduated from French universities, that the colonies were tired of the ailing French Imperial power.[40] There was also an increasing awareness that moral pressure would not, in itself, be sufficient to bring about change.[41] It was, for instance, De Gaulle's impromptu policy that suppressed regional autonomy in Polynesia and New Caledonia which confirmed the view that France was committed to stay in the Pacific.[42] The French clawing back their Pacific territories was, it is reasonable to assume, one of the triggers for the Kanak revolt between 1984 and 1988.[43]

Third, the Matignon and Noumea Accords ended most of the hostilities but left a legacy of lingering politically motivated violence.[44] It is reasonable to suggest that they are bad agreements that set up a temporary autonomy.[45] We will return to the effects of the two accords later, yet it is important to say that the Noumea Accord was a proxy for a reform of the French Constitution.[46] The reform allocated a series of constitutionally protected competencies to New Caledonia, rebalanced the public expenditures to support Kanak communities[47]

---

[39] ibid.
[40] Graff (n 12) 66.
[41] ibid.; Howard Zinn, *A People's History of the United States* (Reissue edition, Harper 2017) eKindle location: 3317.
[42] Chappell, 'Decolonisation and Nation-Building in New Caledonia' (n 13) 59. Fisher (n 3) 57.
[43] Chappell, 'Decolonisation and Nation-Building in New Caledonia' (n 13) 59; Horowitz (n 21) 292; Graff (n 12) 66. Article 188 of the Loi 99-209 as restricting the electoral franchise to those who were resident in New Caledonia before 1998.
[44] Chappell, 'Decolonisation and Nation-Building in New Caledonia' (n 13) 59; 'Vale Nouvelle-Calédonie dénonce "une violence quotidienne", et renforcée, contre l'usine du Sud' (*Nouvelle-Calédonie la 1ère*); 'Kanak Groups Call For International Investigation Into Shooting By Police | Pacific Islands Report'; 'France Sends More Police to New Caledonia' (*RNZ*, 7 November 2016).
[45] Leblic, 'Sovereignty and Coloniality in the French-Speaking Pacific' (n 17) 115.
[46] Accord sur la Nouvelle-Calédonie signé à Nouméa le 5 mai 1998; Loi n° 99-209 organique du 19 mars 1999 relative à la Nouvelle-Calédonie (consolidée au 07 janvier 2019) Article 99; Constitution du 4 octobre 1958 (version consolidée) Article 77, 78. Loi constitutionnelle no 98-610 du 20 juillet 1998 relative à la Nouvelle-Calédonie. Fisher (n 3) 69; Loi n° 99-209 organique du 19 mars 1999 relative à la Nouvelle-Calédonie (consolidée au 07 janvier 2019) 99. Fisher (n 3) French and English versions available in Appendix 1.
[47] Blaise (n 16) 197.

and set the conditions under which its residents could vote in referenda over full sovereignty in the future.[48]

Fourth, the electoral roll for the referendum over independence has been particularly controversial. There are currently three electoral rolls in New Caledonia.[49] One electoral part designates who can vote in municipal elections (and that coincides with the list for the European Parliament election). An electoral roll decides who can vote for national elections (French Parliament and French President). One electoral roll sets the limit of the franchise for the referenda over independence (ex, Articles 76 and 77 of the 1958 Constitution).[50]

A series of regional commissions were set up to evaluate the requests to be listed in the electoral roll for the 2018 referendum, and the voting day was a relatively subdued affair.[51] A majority of the listed voters favoured the status quo, yet there were substantial regional variations.[52] Most voters in the northern provinces of La Gran Terre and the islands opted to support independence, whereas the southern provinces and Noumea voted for the status quo.[53] The 2018 referendum was the first of three, but the franchise for the other two was purposefully substantially changed to alter the results in way that favoured France.[54]

---

[48] Accord sur la Nouvelle-Calédonie signé à Nouméa le 5 mai 1998; Loi n° 99-209 organique du 19 mars 1999 relative à la Nouvelle-Calédonie (consolidée au 07 janvier 2019) Article 99; Constitution du 4 octobre 1958 (version consolidée) Article 77, 78. Loi constitutionnelle no 98-610 du 20 juillet 1998 relative à la Nouvelle-Calédonie. Fisher (n 3) 69; Loi n° 99-209 organique du 19 mars 1999 relative à la Nouvelle-Calédonie (consolidée au 07 janvier 2019) 99. Fisher (n 3) French and English versions available in Appendix 1 (p.311). 'Les Autres Textes Relatifs Aux Listes Électorales/Le Cadre Juridique/Référendum 2018/Elections 2018/Politiques Publiques/Accueil – Les Services de l'État En Nouvelle-Calédonie' (n 46).

[49] Chappell, 'Decolonisation and Nation-Building in New Caledonia' (n 13) 59.

[50] ibid.

[51] ibid 60; French Constitution 1958 (as revised 23/07/2008) Article 77; Loi organique n° 2018-280 du 19 avril 2018 relative à l'organisation de la consultation sur l'accession à la pleine souveraineté de la Nouvelle-Calédonie – Article 2. Accord sur la Nouvelle-Calédonie signé à Nouméa le 5 mai 1998; Loi n° 99-209 organique du 19 mars 1999 relative à la Nouvelle-Calédonie (consolidée au 07 janvier 2019) Article 99. Fisher (n 3) 69; Loi n° 99-209 organique du 19 mars 1999 relative à la Nouvelle-Calédonie (consolidée au 07 janvier 2019) 99. Fisher (n 3) French and English versions available in Appendix 1. 'Les Autres Textes Relatifs Aux Listes Électorales/Le Cadre Juridique/Référendum 2018/Elections 2018/Politiques Publiques/ Accueil – Les Services de l'État En Nouvelle-Calédonie' (n 46).

[52] La commission de contrôle de l'organisation et du déroulement de la consultation sur l'accession à la pleine souveraineté de la Nouvelle-Calédonie, 'Journal officiel de la République Française n.257 (7.11.2018)'.

[53] ibid.

[54] Constitution du 4 octobre 1958 (version consolidée) Article 77.

Fifth, New Caledonia is part of the Overseas Countries and Territories Association of the European Union (hereafter, OCTA).[55] New Caledonia is currently the second-highest beneficiary of European Union funding in the OCTA group.[56] The funding has allowed tertiary education students and staff to travel to and study in world-class European universities.[57] In addition, New Caledonia's currency is 'pegged' to the Euro, which, in the long term, reduces the currency fluctuation that affects all small Pacific nations.[58] In comparison to other small island states, a stable currency contributes to a greater inflow of foreign direct investments and, consequently, to the creation of more jobs.[59]

## A NEGATIVE DRIVER OF CHANGE: THE PARADIGM OF THE UNITY OF THE FRENCH REPUBLIC

The result of the 2021 referendum and the violence that preceded it signalled a change in New Caledonia's ongoing process of decolonisation.[60] In this section, I will discuss the effects that the 1958 constitutional principles, such as the unity of the Republic and decentralisation reforms, might have in the ongoing crisis in New Caledonia.[61]

It is reasonable to suggest that the boycotted 2021 referendum will have a negative effect on the 2023 negotiations and the recognition of the Kanaks' identity claims. The demands for recognition must be accommodated via a distinctively French idea of equality inserted into the paradigm of the unity of the Republic.[62] The most likely basis for the negotiation will be the text of the 1958

---

[55] 'Treaty Establishing the European Community (Consolidated Version 2002) OJ C 325, 24.12.2002, p. 33–184' Title 4, Annex II. For an extensive analysis of the status of New Caledonia see: RC Plachecki, 'EU and World Trade Law – Economic Partnership Agreements and Considerations for New Caledonia' (2008) 14 Revue Juridique Polynésienne 71.

[56] 'EEAS – European External Action Service – European Commission' (*EEAS – European External Action Service*) 'Pacific Regional Indicative Programme 2014–2020 – EEAS – European External Action Service – European Commission' (*EEAS – European External Action Service*); Blaise (n 16) 210.

[57] 'EEAS – European External Action Service – European Commission' (n 56); 'Pacific Regional Indicative Programme 2014–2020 – EEAS – European External Action Service – European Commission' (n 56); Blaise (n 16) 210.

[58] Fiona Murray, *The European Union and Member State Territories: A New Legal Framework Under the EU Treaties* (Springer Science & Business Media 2012) 77.

[59] Plachecki (n 55) 91–95.

[60] Loi n° 99-209 organique du 19 mars 1999 relative à la Nouvelle-Calédonie (consolidée au 07 janvier 2019) 99–209.

[61] Boyron (n 13) 23.

[62] Marrani (n 11) 112. Constitution du 4 octobre 1958 (version consolidée); Noumea Accord 1998 (2002) 7(1) Australian Indigenous Law Reporter 88; Loi n°56-619 du 23

Constitution (as amended) in *Titre XIII Dispositions transitoires relatives a la Nouvelle-Caledonie* of the 1958 Constitution.[63] Article 99 of Loi 99-209 lists the legislative competencies of the New Caledonia Congress. Congress has, for instance, a legislative competence in relation to symbols (Article 99(1)), customs (Article 99(5)) and land resources such as oil and nickel (Article 99(6)).[64] The introduction of the customary law has been a proxy for flourishing pluralistic jurisprudence across a range of New Caledonia's legal institutions.[65] The recognition of Kanak distinctiveness is mediated by the principle of legislative equivalence between the law approved in France and that approved in New Caledonia,[66] and the paradigm of the unity of the French Republic.[67]

The 'paradigm of unity' is considered the keystone of the French constitutional system.[68] The Noumea Accord and the related reform of the French Constitution derogates such a principle temporarily.[69] The text of the 1958 Constitution does not leave much room for debate over the recognition of sub-state national identities, and until the 1998 reforms that recognised the possibility of the transient special status of New Caledonia, the French con-

---

1956 juin mesures propres a assurer l'evolution des territoires relevant du Ministere de la France d'outre-mer 1956 (56-619); Loi n° 88-1028 du 9 novembre 1988 portant dispositions statutaires et préparatoires à l'autodétermination de la Nouvelle-Calédonie en 1998; Loi n° 99-209 organique du 19 mars 1999 relative à la Nouvelle-Calédonie (consolidée au 07 janvier 2019); Loi organique n° 2015-987 du 5 août 2015 relative à la consultation sur l'accession de la Nouvelle-Calédonie à la pleine souveraineté.

[63] Loi constitutionnelle no 98-610 du 20 juillet 1998 relative à la Nouvelle-Calédonie; Constitution du 4 octobre 1958 (version consolidée) Titre XIII .

[64] Marrani (n 14) 102; Loi n° 99-209 organique du 19 mars 1999 relative à la Nouvelle-Calédonie (consolidée au 07 janvier 2019) Article 99; Gustaaf van Nifterik, 'French Constitutional History, Garden or Graveyard?: Some Thoughts on Occasion of Les Grands Discours Parlementaires' (2007) 3 European Constitutional Law Review 476, 480.

[65] Pascale Deumier, 'Introduction: Présentation de la Base de Données' in Etienne Cornut, Pascale Deumier and Françoise Cayrol-Baudrillart (eds), *La coutume kanak dans le pluralisme juridique calédonien* (Presses universitaires de Nouvelle-Calédonie 2018) 26.

[66] Boyron (n 13) 213.

[67] Marrani (n 11) 106, 120–122. Constitution du 4 octobre 1958 (version consolidée) Article 75-1; Loi constitutionnelle n° 2008-724 du 23 juillet 2008 de modernisation des institutions de la Ve République Article 40.

[68] Marrani (n 11) 106.

[69] Jeremie Gilbert and David Keane, 'Equality versus Fraternity? Rethinking France and Its Minorities' (2016) 14 International Journal of Constitutional Law 883, 296; Marrani (n 14); Boyron (n 13) 214.

stitutional model was considered the archetype of the unitary state.[70] Overseas territories and communities were recognised, yet the acknowledgement was temporary and only indirectly linked to the recognition of sub-state identities.[71] The more recent 2008 constitutional reform recognised, for instance, the existence of regional languages as part of the process of the modernisation of the state's institutions.[72] Yet, French is the only official language.

French public institutions, for instance, must produce official documents in French.[73] Institutions might produce translated documents in Kanak, but they cannot be considered official documents.[74] David Marrani explains the normative implications that are associated with the use of a singular official language: 'Only the French language is the language of the French Republic. A few populations with different languages are recognised, as particular cultural identities and subordinated ethnicities.'[75] The image of a homogeneous linguistic community spills over into the normative debate on the protection of minorities, because French institutions, as a supernumerary elaboration, refuse to recognise the existence of minority groups within their population.[76] Again,

---

[70] David Avrom Bell, *The Cult of the Nation in France: Inventing Nationalism, 1680–1800* (Harvard University Press 2001) 198; X Philippe, 'France: The Amendment of the French Constitution "on the Decentralized Organization of the Republic"' (2004) 2 International Journal of Constitutional Law 691, 691; Michel Rosenfeld and Andras Sajo, 'Constitutional Identity' in Michele Rosenfeld and Andras Sajo (eds), *The Oxford Handbook of Comparative Constitutional Law* (Oxford University Press, USA 2012) 763.

[71] Loi constitutionnelle n° 2008-724 du 23 juillet 2008 de modernisation des institutions de la Ve République.

[72] Constitution du 4 octobre 1958 (version consolidée) Article 2 (1); Loi n° 99-209 organique du 19 mars 1999 relative à la Nouvelle-Calédonie (consolidée au 07 janvier 2019) 140; Loi organique n° 2013-1027 du 15 novembre 2013 portant actualisation de la loi organique n° 99-209 du 19 mars 1999 relative à la Nouvelle-Calédonie – Article 6.

[73] Marrani (n 11) 122.

[74] ibid. *Loi organique* (textually translated as Organic Law) have a special status and approval procedures within the hierarchy of French legal systems because they are intended to implement an aspect of the 1958 Constitution. Political debates over the constitutional accommodation of identity-based claims do not happen in a vacuum. The constitution normally sets the boundaries of both the 'reasonable' in relation, for instance, to the partaking of the sharing of public, and the 'possible' *vis-à-vis* the derogation to fundamental principles such as equality. It is perhaps more so in a codified constitutional system like the one adopted in France. Boyron (n 13) 32–53; Nifterik (n 64).

[75] Marrani (n 11) 121.

[76] Gilbert and Keane (n 69) 884; Connell (n 17) 147.

Marrani describes the manifestation of the paradigm of unity with a distinctive insight.

> Language is employed as the means to organise the world through an ideological order, it is a theatrical representation of a society; it is a theatrical representation of a society that believes it is what is represented: a society formed by language into a country (France), then into a Republic.[77]

In other words, the imposition of the French language is one of the manifestations of a French nationalist ideology that cannot accept the multinational nature of the French Republic.[78]

This insistence on giving priority to the idea of a French monolithic culture is, most probably, a manifestation of an eighteenth-century nation-building strategy that might have passed its sell-by date.[79] Bell describes it in a lucid narrative.

> Faced with this monumental task, the revolutionaries adopted the methods of the Reformation-era priesthood, proposing to send their well-drilled republican versions of the Jesuits out into the countryside to teach, persuade, and indoctrinate by every possible means, and to provide the diverse population with common education, a common set of allegiances, and a common language.[80]

Electing to use a common language is also part of social engineering imposed by a nationalist ideology.[81] Anderson refers to the concept of an *Imagined Community* in which strangers are gathered around a shared language as a sociological project favouring some ideological elements and omitting others.[82] *Loi constitutionnelle* n°2003-276 is one of the instances in which the principle of administrative decentralisation is asserted in the 1958 Constitution, yet the reallocation of political power from the central to the regional institutions

---

[77] Marrani (n 11) 113.

[78] Bell (n 70) 198; J Habermas, 'The European Nation State. Its Achievements and Its Limitations. On the Past and Future of Sovereignty and Citizenship' (1996) 9 Ratio Juris 125; Boyron (n 13) 27; Félicien Lemaire, *Le Principe d'indivisibilité de La République: Mythe et Réalité* (Presses universitaires de Rennes 2010) 186.

[79] Bell (n 70) 199; Michele Rosenfeld, Andras Sajo and Susanne Baer (eds), 'Equality' in Michele Rosenfeld and Andras Sajo (eds), *The Oxford Handbook of Comparative Constitutional Law* (Oxford University Press, USA 2012) 984, 993; Ernest Gellner, *Nationalism* (Phoenix 1998) 33; Benedict Anderson, *Imagined Communities: Reflections on the Origin and Spread of Nationalism* (Verso 1983).

[80] Bell (n 70) 201.

[81] Gellner (n 79).

[82] Anderson (n 79); Anthony D Smith, *Theories of Nationalism* (Duckworth 1971) 171; Vito Breda, *Constitutional Law and Regionalism: A Comparative Analysis of Regionalist Negotiations* (Edward Elgar Publishing 2018) ch 1.

is based on the assumption that the decentralisation of a selected number of administrative functions might increase the overall efficiency of the French public sector.[83] It is not a derogation of the superiority of French identity.

The specific status of the French Polynesian territories and New Caledonia, which have been allowed to adopt purposeful measures to benefit their local populations, is based on their distance from metropolitan France. However, extraordinary measures can occur only on the basis of administrative reasons. The fact that most residents in these areas are also part of an ethnic or religious group is not relevant to the model.[84]

The relocation of administrative powers is not related to a recognition of sub-state national identities, nor can it be constructed as an exception to the paradigm of the unity of the French nation.[85] There is, however, an element of flexibility in the formulation of the paradigm of unity that allows for the accommodation of specific regional needs.[86] The 1998 Noumea Accord is, according to Marrani and Fisher, one of the manifestations of that flexibility.[87] As mentioned earlier in this chapter, the Accords emerged after a period of political instability and ethnic violence.[88] This last stage of the development of the Kanak identity is associated with a troublesome period in the relationship between independence supporters and French institutions. *Les événements*, as the period of instability was called, was also a phase of negotiation. Still, in terms of forming the current development of New Caledonia, the watershed moment happened in the aftermath of the 1988 Gossanah Cave Crisis.[89]

The Matignon and Noumea Accords indicated the end of the violence and set out the areas of customary law.[90] They prepared the way for the establishing of the Customary Senate representing the different regional New Caledonian customary councils.[91] In addition, the French Government accepted that the electoral franchise was to be amended in such a way that it would reduce the effects of immigration, and, in exchange, the Kanak accepted postponing

---

[83] Boyron (n 13) 215; Loi constitutionnelle n°2003-276 du 28 mars 2003 relative à l'organisation décentralisée de la République – Article 1. Also relevant: Loi n° 82-213 du 2 mars 1982 relative aux droits et libertés des communes, des départements et des régions 82–213. For a general summary: Boyron (n 13) 32–37.
[84] Gilbert and Keane (n 69) 896.
[85] Philippe (n 70) 700.
[86] Stone Sweet (n 11).
[87] Fisher (n 3) French and English versions available in Appendix 1. Marrani (n 11) 119.
[88] Chappell, 'Decolonisation and Nation-Building in New Caledonia' (n 13) 59.
[89] Blaise (n 16) 195.
[90] ibid.
[91] Loi n° 99-209 organique du 19 mars 1999 relative à la Nouvelle-Calédonie (consolidée au 07 janvier 2019) 137.

an eventual referendum over independence.[92] It was, however, clear that a demographic majority of non-Kanak would continue to have a limited say on the administration of the archipelago, and having the opportunity to have scheduled referenda over secession was a profitless and transient prize for the Kanak.[93]

The French Parliament had to approve the Accord (it did so with Organic Law 99-209 1999),[94] amend the 1958 Constitution[95] and continue to pass statutory acts and regulations that maintained the Republic's commitment to the Noumea Accord throughout multiple political cycles in the French Government. One of the latest statutory activities linked to the Accord was the approval of Loi 2018-280, which dealt with some of the issues related to the limits of the referendum voting franchise.[96] There is limited space to discuss the administrative ramification of Loi 2018-280 for public institutions and private individuals, such as the management of customary land, in the period that followed the Noumea Accord. Yet, it is important to state that both agreements prepared the road map for collaboration between the central and regional administrations.[97]

What is distinctive about the Noumea Accord is the indirect recognition of the Kanak as a sub-state national identity within the constitutional endorsement of the paradigm of unity. For instance, the recognition of national symbols in Article 5 of Loi 99-209, the traditional law, and its jurisdictional implications in Title I of the same statute are manifestations of the existence of concurring national identities.[98] The administrative relocation of institutions, such as the Kanak Development Agency,[99] that actively promote the decolonisation process from France in the archipelago and within international organisations, such as the United Nations, are also indications of the recognition of a sub-state identity.[100] It might be a case of reality – (and necessity) in this instance – not only being the mother of constitutional transformation but also the first cousin to prescience. Perhaps the most obvious sign of a change of roles in the paradigm of unity within the French constitutional system is

---

[92] 'Institut de La Statistique et Des Études Économiques-Recensement' (n 15); Fisher (n 3) 68; Blaise (n 16) 210.
[93] Fisher (n 3) 69.
[94] Loi n° 99-209 organique du 19 mars 1999 relative à la Nouvelle-Calédonie.
[95] Loi constitutionnelle no 98-610 du 20 juillet 1998 relative à la Nouvelle-Calédonie.
[96] Loi organique n° 2018-280 du 19 avril 2018 relative à l'organisation de la consultation sur l'accession à la pleine souveraineté de la Nouvelle-Calédonie.
[97] For instance: Loi n° 99-209 organique du 19 mars 1999 relative à la Nouvelle-Calédonie (consolidée au 07 janvier 2019) Title II.
[98] ibid Article 23(4), 140, 143.
[99] ibid Article 23(4).
[100] United Nations (n 12); United Nations General Assembly (n 12).

the recognition of the Traditional Customs Senate: 'The Traditional Customs Senate has to be consulted, depending on the procedural requirements, by the president of the government, by the president of the congress or by the president of the provinces, on projects or bills that affect the Kanak identity.'[101] The consultative power is again limited, but there is explicit recognition of the Kanak identity.

It is the recognition of an imprecisely defined sociological group rather than a national identity. Yet, it is the combination of accepting a sociological fact (e.g., the existence of a concurring identity next to the French nation) and the recognition that a social group has an administrative power that gives an indication, among many, that France's paradigm of unity might allow for a degree of constitutional flexibility in the next phase of the decolonisation process.[102]

Recall that until recently, the recognition of a minority language in France was associated with an insistent denial of the possibility of a multinational French Republic[103] and that the French jurisprudence underpinning the paradigm of unity might continue to describe France as a single nation in which localised ethnic communities do speak a local patois.[104] However, the reference in Loi 99-209 to a Kanak identity indicates, at the very least, an increasing awareness of the limit of the paradigm of unity.[105]

It is a matter of speculation as to whether such a new awareness might be the first step towards the recognition of a multinational France. Most of France's adjacent European states do recognise official languages. The Spanish Constitution recognises its nationalities (e.g., Basque), and the Swiss,[106] Italian[107] and Belgian[108] Constitutions acknowledge their linguistic communities. However, the historical and institutional conditions upon which the Republic is founded are different. For instance, Marrani noted that imposing,

---

[101] Original: Le Sénat coutumier est consulté, selon les cas, par le président du gouvernement, par le président du congrès ou par le président d'une assemblée de province sur les projets ou propositions de délibération intéressant l'identité [K]anak. Loi n° 99-209 organique du 19 mars 1999 relative à la Nouvelle-Calédonie (consolidée au 07 janvier 2019) Article 143 (1).

[102] Yves Tanguy, 'La Motion de Défiance Dans Le Statut de La Corse: Vers Une Mise En Jeu de La Responsabilité Des Exécutifs Devant Les Assemblées Locales ?' (1992) 45 La Revue administrative 121, 121; Marrani (n 11) 92, 99, 105, 119.

[103] Marrani (n 11) 121.

[104] ibid 122.

[105] Loi n° 99-209 organique du 19 mars 1999 relative à la Nouvelle-Calédonie (consolidée au 07 janvier 2019) 143 (1).

[106] Federal Constitution of 18 April 1999 of the Swiss Confederation 2000 Article 4.

[107] Constitutional Law n. 4 26.02.1948.

[108] Belgian Parliament, 'Belgian Constitution as Updated Following the Constitutional Revision of 24 October 2017' Article 2.

by the use of violence if necessary, a local vernacular in substitution of Latin has been a crucial aspect in the formation of the Republic.[109] The French jurisprudence's current qualification of equality principles remains strongly associated with the paradigm of national unity. It will continue to add an element of inertia in the process of the constitutional recognition of the Kanak identity.

## NEGATIVE DRIVER OF CHANGE: THE DYNAMIC OF THE KANAK IDENTITY

In the previous section, we discussed the explicit and implicit constitutional limits of the process of the recognition of the Kanak identity. This section focuses instead on the Kanak communities and their political aspirations. Despite the 2021 referendum fiasco,[110] secession is high on the agenda of most political parties that represent the Kanak identity.[111] However, the Caledonia Union, which collects multi-ethnic franchises, favours a free association with France.[112]

As mentioned in the introduction, the Kanak Peoples are generally recognised as part of Melanesia.[113] However, Kanak society is highly diversified and fractured along political, tribal and clan lines.[114] The current identity has been affected by the European colonisation process in a way that had, at a general level, a negative impact on the size of the population and Kanak culture.[115] In relation to political claims that have constitutional significance, most political parties support decentralisation and a minority support independence. It is interesting to note that in the 1950s and after decentralisation started,[116] the Caledonian Union represented the interests of both Kanak and European residents. In the 1959 referendum, 98 per cent of the voters supported the union with France.[117] However, in 1963, New Caledonia's autonomy was reduced[118] via a series of statutory measures, and a new regulation was inserted to admin-

---

[109] Marrani (n 11) 118.
[110] David and Tirard (n 3).
[111] Chappell, 'Decolonisation and Nation-Building in New Caledonia' (n 13) 12, 63.
[112] Fisher (n 3) 56.
[113] Chappell, *The Kanak Awakening* (n 2) 16.
[114] Chappell, 'Decolonisation and Nation-Building in New Caledonia' (n 13) 62; Barbara A West, *Encyclopedia of the Peoples of Asia and Oceania* (Infobase Publishing 2010) 360.
[115] United Nations (n 12); United Nations General Assembly (n 12); Chappell, *The Kanak Awakening* (n 2) 21.
[116] Loi n°56-619 du 23 1956 juin mesures propres a assurer l'evolution des territoires relevant du Ministere de la France d'outre-mer.
[117] Fisher (n 3) 56.
[118] ibid 58.

ister the archipelago's recently discovered mining resources.[119] The transfer of administrative power over local mining resources also coincided with a revival of the Kanak identity.[120]

It is plausible to suggest that after World War II, increasing awareness of Kanak Peoples' cultural distinctiveness was coupled with the coordination of political demands by political parties like the Kanak and Socialist National Liberation Front.[121] In the 1970s, multiple parties claimed to represent the Kanak identity: 'LKS (Libération Kanak Socialiste, Socialist Kanak Liberation), FULK (Front Uni de la Libération Kanak, United Kanak Liberation Front), the UPM (Union Progressiste Mélanésienne, Popular Melanesian Union), and the PSC (Parti Socialiste Calédonie, [New] Caledonian Socialist Party).'[122] The whirlpool of New Caledonian politics will not be discussed in detail. However, it is notable that the frustration with the lack of decentration might have been a proxy for the degeneration of the political debate into violence.[123] Chappell, for instance, suggests an untrammelled relationship of causation between the centralist stance held by the French Government and New Caledonia's period of political violence.[124]

It is also important to note that immigration and the formation of the electoral roll were, and to some extent still are, perceived as one of the hot debates for the political parties representing Kanak identity, and the Europeans, Asians and Pacific Islanders who settled in New Caledonia.[125] Regarding the French policy of encouraging external migration for political reasons, French Prime Minister and former DOM-TOM Minister Pierre Messmer wrote to his DOM-TOM Secretary of State on 17 July 1972 that indigenous nationalist

---

[119] Loi n°69-4 du 3 janvier 1969 modifiant la reglementation miniere en nouvelle-caledonie 1969 (69-4).

[120] Chappell, *The Kanak Awakening* (n 2) 212; Le Meur and Levacher (n 17).

[121] Fisher (n 3) 58.

[122] ibid.

[123] ibid 61; Chappell, 'Decolonisation and Nation-Building in New Caledonia' (n 13) 60; Chappell, *The Kanak Awakening* (n 2) 212; T Hadden and K Boyle, 'Northern Ireland: Conflict and Conflict Resolution' in K Rupesinghe (ed), *Ethnic Conflict and Human Rights* (United Nations University Press 1988); Garth Stevenson, *Parallel Paths: The Development of Nationalism in Ireland and Quebec* (McGill-Queen's University Press 2006); Georg Grote, *The South Tyrol Question, 1866–2010: From National Rage to Regional State* (Peter Lang 2012); Professor Michael Keating, *Nations against the State: The New Politics of Nationalism in Quebec, Catalonia and Scotland* (Palgrave Macmillan 1996).

[124] Chappell, 'Decolonisation and Nation-Building in New Caledonia' (n 13) 60.

[125] Fisher (n 3) 59; Loi n° 99-209 organique du 19 mars 1999 relative à la Nouvelle-Calédonie (consolidée au 07 janvier 2019) Article 4.

claims could only be avoided if residents came from metropolitan France.[126] The policy was effective and, by the middle of the 1960s, had a significant impact on reducing the role that the Kanak could have as part of a minority group within New Caledonia's political arena and French national politics.[127]

A substantial step towards the normalisation of the relationship between the Kanak and France was the international recognition of the status of the Kanak identity.[128] In 1986, the General Assembly of the United Nations reintroduced New Caledonia onto the list of territories that might benefit from a process of decolonisation.[129] It is also apparent that, after the 1960s, French immigration policies transformed the role of the Kanak from a demographic majority to a heavily monitored minority.[130] In 1988, Fisher reported that over 6,000 military personnel were stationed for a platitudinous 'development reason' in the proximity of Kanak villages.[131] The Imperial orthopraxy might have been subsumed, yet the current demography of the archipelago continues to be a source of attrition between the Kanak and the residents who arrived in New Caledonia.

The Gossanah Cave Crisis is considered a turning point in French and Kanak relations.[132] A group of Kanak kidnapped and held hostage 29 French Gendarmes in a cave system in the island of Ouvéa. The hostages were liberated by a military operation which resulted in 21 deaths and attracted widespread international condemnation.[133] In the aftermath of the crisis, French central institutions, at least in practice, accepted that institutional violence might not stop the process of the recognition of the Kanak, and the Kanak accepted that they would continue their struggle without using violence. Two agreements marked this new stage of the process of negotiation. The first was the Matignon Accord.[134] The Noumea Accord was the second agreement, which arrived seven years after the Matignon Accord.[135] Compared to the Matignon

---

[126] Fisher (n 3) 59; Loi n° 99-209 organique du 19 mars 1999 relative à la Nouvelle-Calédonie (consolidée au 07 janvier 2019) Article 4.

[127] Fisher (n 3) 57; Le Meur and Levacher (n 17) 79.

[128] General Assembly United Nations, 'Resolution 41/41A Implementation of the Declaration on the Granting of Independence to Colonial Countries and Peoples' (n 28).

[129] ibid.

[130] 'Institut de La Statistique et Des Études Économiques-Recensement' (n 15); Fisher (n 3) 97.

[131] Fisher (n 3) 65.

[132] ibid 66.

[133] ibid.

[134] French Parliament (n 3).

[135] Loi n° 99-209 organique du 19 mars 1999 relative à la Nouvelle-Calédonie (consolidée au 07 janvier 2019); Loi organique n° 2015-987 du 5 août 2015 relative à la consultation sur l'accession de la Nouvelle-Calédonie à la pleine souveraineté; Loi

Accord, the Noumea Accord had stronger constitutional implications since it changed the status of New Caledonia from a region to a temporary autonomous territory with constitutionally entrenched legislative competencies.[136] More generally, the Matignon Accord signalled that French central institutions were willing to negotiate the recognition of local customs.[137]

The Matignon Accord should be considered, for instance, as one of the processes that fostered a considerable reduction in ethnic violence between the majority of the population, which has European ancestry, and the original inhabitants of New Caledonia.[138] It also prepared a plan for the redistribution of land and mining resources, like the one managed by the Société d'Economie Mixte de Développement Contrélée par la Province Nord, to the northern provinces that have a larger Kanak population.[139] So, the Matignon Accord and Noumea Accord might have indicated that the political parties representing French national interests and those supporting New Caledonian identities were accepting of the dynamic nature of identity-based political claims.[140] The importance of the agreement is described by Fisher:

> [i]ts [the Noumea Accord] ] key features include an acknowledgment of the 'shock' of colonisation both to the identity of the Kanak people and those who had come either for religious reasons or against their will; a future for all groups within a common destiny; and a continued commitment to economic rebalancing. In a new concept of shared sovereignty, the French State would transfer all but the central, or regalian, sovereign competencies (defence, foreign affairs, justice, law and order, and the currency) progressively to local institutions in a defined schedule.[141]

The economic and constitutional implications, Fisher notes, of the Noumea Accord are significant; it also indicated a new direction for the French nation-building strategy. The test of the Accord shows signs of a shared commitment to negotiating rational decisions rather than imposing nationalist and exclusionary assumptions on others. In addition, the long, perhaps too long-term schedule for the administrative transfer of powers and the referenda over independence (e.g., Title IX of Loi 99-209, which implemented the

---

organique n° 2018-280 du 19 avril 2018 relative à l'organisation de la consultation sur l'accession à la pleine souveraineté de la Nouvelle-Calédonie; Fisher (n 3) 69.

[136] Loi n° 99-209 organique du 19 mars 1999 relative à la Nouvelle-Calédonie (consolidée au 07 janvier 2019) 99.

[137] Fisher (n 3) 63; French Parliament (n 3).

[138] Fisher (n 3) 63.

[139] Blaise (n 16) 200; Fisher (n 3) 67–70; Horowitz (n 21) 294; Le Meur and Levacher (n 17).

[140] Fisher (n 3) 70.

[141] ibid.

Noumea Accord) reveals a distinctive awareness of the dynamic nature of the identity-making process.[142]

Furthermore, the two accords separated the political issue of managing the archipelago's resources from the debate over the protection of the Kanak identity, Kanak languages and traditional customs.[143] In 1988, for instance, the Agency for the Development of the Kanak Culture was one of the institutions that signalled a change in the interaction between French central institutions and Kanak Peoples.[144] The Agency for the Development of the Kanak Culture has a significant role in promoting tourism. Yet politically, it also increases the profile of the Kanak culture and ultimately provides a reference point for developing a national identity.[145] The Customary Senate of New Caledonia is, for instance, actively promoting the cultural implications of having a multilinguistic Kanak identity.[146]

The public support for developing a local culture has been an example of collaboration between the Kanak, New Caledonian immigrants and French institutions. However, diverging political and legal interpretations of previous agreements are expected in such a dynamic social environment. One of the most debated issues is the boundaries of the electoral franchise for the planned set of referenda over independence and, in 2021, the postponement of the date of the third referendum.[147]

The political parties representing the Kanak identity considered Article 188 of Loi 99-209 as restricting the electoral franchise to those who were resident in New Caledonia before 1998. The political parties that favoured the union with France interpreted Article 188 as having a less narrow ten-year residency

---

[142] Loi n° 99-209 organique du 19 mars 1999 relative à la Nouvelle-Calédonie (consolidée au 07 janvier 2019) 99.

[143] Chappell, 'Decolonisation and Nation-Building in New Caledonia' (n 13) 61; Leblic, 'Kanak Identity, New Citizenship Building and Reconciliation' (n 23) 275.

[144] Loi n° 88-1028 du 9 novembre 1988 portant dispositions statutaires et préparatoires à l'autodétermination de la Nouvelle-Calédonie en 1998 – Article 2 Article 93; 'Agence de développement de la culture kanak'; 'The Tjibaou Cultural centre and ADCK' <www.adck.nc/presentation/english-presentation/the-tjibaou-cultural-centre-and-adck> accessed 22 January 2019; French Parliament (n 3).

[145] Chappell, 'Decolonisation and Nation-Building in New Caledonia' (n 13) 61. For a general analysis of the identity building Z Bauman, 'Identity in the Globalising World' (2001) 9 Social Anthropology 121; Z Bauman, 'Right or Wrong – My Country?' (1997) 39 Argument 327; Zygmunt Bauman, *Community: Seeking Safety in an Insecure World* (Polity Press 2001).

[146] Chappell, 'Decolonisation and Nation-Building in New Caledonia' (n 13) 61.

[147] Cour de Cassation, Assemblée plénière, du 2 juin 2000, 99-60274, Publié au bulletin; *PY v France* [2005] European Court of Human Rights 66289/99.

restriction.[148] The unionists (e.g., Rassemblement, Nouvelles Caledoniennes) were concerned with the progressive undemocratic effect of reducing the electoral franchise to a list that is over 20 years old.[149] After a long gestation the act was amended to recognise the restriction of the franchise.[150] The process might appear long and convoluted, but deciding who can be part of a community is normally perceived as fundamental for a political entity.[151]

The saga over 'who can vote' in one the best example of the dynamic nature of the Kanak's identity-formation process and of the other identity groups in New Caledonia. The 2018 referendum did not register a change in France's identity-based politics, but the unexpected narrow defeat gave hope to the pro-independence movement.[152] The result confirmed deeply entrenched ethnic divisions: '96 percent of Kanaks voted for independence while 92 percent of Europeans voted against independence. Those who identified themselves as Caldoches or as "Other communities and not declared" voted 89 percent against independence. Wallisians and Futunans, something of a small balancing force, voted 57 percent against independence.'[153] After the 2018 referendum, an ethnic group of Wallisians and Futunans formed a political party and surprisingly decided to support independence.[154] Historically, both small immigrant communities had an uneasy relationship with the Kanaks, and they preferred to maintain the protection of the French Government.[155]

In 2020, the change in the political attitudes of Wallisians and Futunans towards secession, the collapse of the price of nickel which led, among other factors, to the sale of the Goro mine to foreign companies, and the COVID pandemic were all contributing factors to a volatile political situation that was preparing for the referendum.[156] 2020 was also marked by an increase in political violence.[157] As is the case of Northern Ireland discussed in Chapter 1,

---

[148] Loi n° 99-209 organique du 19 mars 1999 relative à la Nouvelle-Calédonie (consolidée au 07 janvier 2019) 99; Fisher (n 3) 103, 107.

[149] Fisher (n 3) 101.

[150] Fisher (n 3) 103. Loi organique n° 2015-987 du 5 août 2015 relative à la consultation sur l'accession de la Nouvelle-Calédonie à la pleine souveraineté; Loi organique n° 2018-280 du 19 avril 2018 relative à l'organisation de la consultation sur l'accession à la pleine souveraineté de la Nouvelle-Calédonie – Article 2.

[151] Connell (n 17) 150.

[152] French Government (n 4); Connell (n 17) 150; Alexander Dayant, 'The Demographic Influence in New Caledonia's next Referendum' <www.lowyinstitute.org/the-interpreter/demographic-influence-new-caledonia-s-next-referendum> accessed 18 May 2022.

[153] Connell (n 17) 150.

[154] ibid 152; Leblic, 'Chronologie de la Nouvelle-Calédonie' (n 31) 125.

[155] Connell (n 17) 152.

[156] ibid 151; David and Tirard (n 3) 7–8.

[157] 'France Sends More Police to New Caledonia' (n 44).

political violence in New Caledonia did not cease entirely with the enactment of the a peace agreement.[158]

Despite all the changes, the result of the 2020 referendum changed little from the result in 2018 in which 53.3 per cent of casted votes supported the union with France.[159] Most individuals voted along the same ethnic boundaries set in the 2018 elections,[160] making the change in the political attitudes of Wallisians and Futunans not a significant factor in the final result.[161] The data for the 2021 referendum might have been the same, but secessionist parties decided to boycott the referendum.[162]

In the lead-up to the referendum, Nouvelle Caledonia experienced a sharp increase in COVID-related fatalities, and the Kanak communities who were in mourning asked for the political campaign to be postponed.[163] The decision to hold a referendum was not part of the regional government's prerogative and the French Government refused to postpone it.[164] The result was unrepresentative of the franchise.[165] Only 45 per cent of the franchise voted, and 97 per cent of the voters supported the union with France.[166] The Kanak communities considered the referendum void and asked for another opportunity to vote.[167]

This is problematic for the future development of an identity-based relationship in the archipelago. In compliance with the Noumea Accord, the representatives of all political parties should start the negotiation process for a reform of the statute of New Caledonia.[168] As mentioned earlier, Loi n° 99-209 (and its related constitutional reform) was intended as a temporary measure to give the time to New Caledonians to negotiate a common destiny with or without France.[169] The date for the start of the transition process set by the French Government is 30 June 2023. Given the results of the three referenda, logic

---

[158] ibid.
[159] Connell (n 17) 155.
[160] ibid.
[161] ibid.
[162] ibid 157; David and Tirard (n 3) 5.
[163] David and Tirard (n 3) 7; ibid 5.
[164] David and Tirard (n 3) 7.
[165] French Government – Haut-commissariat de la République en Nouvelle-Calédonie (n 4).
[166] ibid; David and Tirard (n 3) 7.
[167] 'À leurs yeux, en effet, le troisième scrutin prévu par l'accord de Nouméa n'a pas "réellement" eu lieu.' 'From their point of view [pro-independence political parties] the third referendum did not take place.' (My translation.) David and Tirard (n 3) 8.
[168] ibid; French Constitution 1958 (as revised 23/07/2008) Title XIII; Loi n° 99-209 organique du 19 mars 1999 relative à la Nouvelle-Calédonie (consolidée au 07 janvier 2019) 99–209.
[169] Loi n° 99-209 organique du 19 mars 1999 relative à la Nouvelle-Calédonie (consolidée au 07 janvier 2019).

would imply that Nouvelle Caledonia should relinquish its *sui generis* status of a territorial collective and move to 'classic' overseas territory status, as per Article 74 of the French Constitution.[170] As discussed throughout the book, it is outside the scope of this endeavour to forecast future scenarios. Still, there are strong indications that Kanaks will perceive the 2023 negotiations as illegitimate, and a reduction in the archipelago's autonomy as demeaning to their national identity.[171]

There is also a possibility that politically motivated violence lingering inside of French–Kanak identity-based interactions will increase, further stopping the negotiation and making another constitutional accord necessary.[172] Independently from whether representatives of Kanak political parties will participate in the 2023 negotiations, it is clear that current identity interactions have a negative bearing on the perception of the legitimacy of the current and future territorial governance of New Caledonia.

## CONCLUSION

This chapter discussed a selection of constitutional and political factors that are likely to influence the perception of the legitimacy of New Caledonia's current and future institutions. I discussed the effect of the paradigm of unity of the French Constitutional system, the constitutional requirement of having French as the only official language and the implications for Kanak Peoples' status. It was argued that while the Matignon Accord and Noumea Accord have constitutionally entrenched New Caledonia's autonomy, the paradigm of unity will continue to add an element of inertia to the process of the recognition of New Caledonian identities.[173]

A second driver of change considered in this chapter was the interaction between Kanak identity and French identity in reshaping the constitutional status of the archipelago. The Noumea Accord set the referenda over independence, like the one in 2021, as a requirement for constitutional negotiation over the future of the archipelago, which is currently set for 2023.[174] Referenda that seek to change the status of a political unity are not apotropaic devices. They should be inserted into a process that is perceived as legitimate by all

---

[170] David and Tirard (n 3) 8–9; French Constitution 1958 (as revised 23/07/2008).
[171] David and Tirard (n 3) 8.
[172] 'France Sends More Police to New Caledonia' (n 44); 'Kanak Groups Call For International Investigation Into Shooting By Police | Pacific Islands Report' (n 44); 'Vale Nouvelle-Calédonie dénonce "une violence quotidienne", et renforcée, contre l'usine du Sud' (n 44).
[173] David and Tirard (n 3) 8; Marrani (n 11).
[174] David and Tirard (n 3) 8.

involved,[175] and the 2021 referendum fell short of that requirement. I explained that the increasing ethnic tension culminating in the boycott of the 2021 referendum is part of the degrading interaction between the Kanak and French identities, which is likely to continue to have negative effects on the Kanak perception of the legitimacy of the regional and central institutions in New Caledonia.

---

[175] James Tully, 'The Unfreedom of the Moderns in Comparison to Their Ideals of Constitutional Democracy' (2002) 65 Modern Law Review 204; Stephen Tierney, 'Popular Constitutional Amendment: Referendums and Constitutional Change in Canada and the United Kingdom' (2015) 41 Queen's Law Journal 41; Stephen Tierney, 'Constitutional Referendums: A Theoretical Enquiry' (2009) 72 Modern Law Review 360.

# 7. Australia and the Northern Territory: an unfortunate intervention

This chapter discusses the Australian federal policies in the Northern Territory. In particular it focuses on Northern Territory National Emergency Response, hereafter the Intervention, and its follow-up set of policies called Stronger Futures. It is, by comparison to other cases discussed in this book, an atypical regional crisis. The rest of the book analyses cases of extreme tension between regional and central institutions which are related to identity-based crises. This chapter instead focuses on the Northern Territory Intervention and its follow-up set of policies called Stronger Futures which racially targeted Aboriginal Peoples and Torres Strait Islanders residing in the Northern Territory.[1] The analysis will show that among the many drivers of change, there are three significant factors that contributed to the cycle of distrust in Australian institutions by these Indigenous communities.[2] The first driver of change considered in this chapter is a constitutional system that allows the Federal Parliament to pass laws that target racial groups without consultation with either regional institutions or representatives of Aboriginal Peoples and

---

[1] Northern Territory National Emergency Response Act 2007; Stronger Futures in the Northern Territory (Consequential and Transitional Provisions) Act 2012; Appropriation (Northern Territory National Emergency Response) (NO. 1) 2007–2008; Social Security and Other Legislation Amendment (Welfare Payment Reform) Act 2007; Appropriation (Northern Territory National Emergency Response) (NO. 2) 2007–2008; Stronger Futures in the Northern Territory Act 2012; Stronger Futures in the Northern Territory (Consequential and Transitional Provisions) Act 2012. Appropriation (Northern Territory National Emergency Response) (NO. 1) 2007–2008; Appropriation (Northern Territory National Emergency Response) (NO. 2) 2007–2008.

[2] Tim Rowse, 'The National Emergency and Indigenous Jurisdictions' in Jon C Altman and Melinda Hinkson (eds), *Coercive Reconciliation: Stabilise, Normalise, Exit Aboriginal Australia* (Arena Publications Association 2007); Stan Grant, 'Stan Grant: A Decade after the NT "Intervention", the "torment of Powerlessness" Lives On' *ABC News* (21 June 2017); Daphne Habibis, Penny Skye Taylor and Bruna S Ragaini, 'White People Have No Face: Aboriginal Perspectives on White Culture and the Costs of Neoliberalism' (2020) 43 Ethnic and Racial Studies 1149; Ben Doherty, '"Unacceptable": UN Committee Damns Australia's Record on Human Rights' (2017) The Guardian (17 October 2017).

Torres Strait Islanders.[3] The second driver of change of this crisis is related to values held by Aboriginal Peoples that are significantly different from those of non-Indigenous Australians.[4] The third driver of change is related to the level of poverty and the remoteness of the Territorial Aboriginal communities that allow the crisis of legitimacy to linger.[5]

The Commonwealth of Australian Constitution Act 1900,[6] hereafter the Australian Constitution, provides a system of territorial governance that includes six Federal States, three internal territories and seven external territories.[7] The Australian Capital Territory (hereafter the ACT) is an autonomous region that includes the national capital of Canberra.[8] The list of external territories includes, among others, Norfolk Island and the Australian Antarctic Territory. The six States are New South Wales, Queensland, South Australia, Tasmania, Victoria and Western Australia.[9] States benefit from a level of parliamentary sovereignty, which grants substantial autonomy.[10] Since the enactment of the Federal Constitution, the level of State self-government has been progressively reduced by the jurisprudence of the Hight Court and by a fiscal imbalance that renders States dependent on Federal grants.[11]

---

[3] Marcia Langton, 'Trapped in the Aboriginal Reality Show [The Howard Government Intervention in Northern Territory Aboriginal Communities. Paper in: Re-Imagining Australia. Schultz, Julianne (Ed.).]' (2008) Griffith Review 143; Marcia Langton, 'Indigenous Exceptionalism and the Constitutional "Race Power"' (2013) Space, Place and Culture 1; Nicholas Pengelley, 'The Hindmarsh Island Bridge Act: Must Laws Based on the Race Power Be for the "Benefit" of Aborigines and Torres Strait Islanders?' (1998) 20 Sydney Law Review 144.

[4] Habibis, Taylor and Ragaini (n 2); Kaine Grigg and Lenore Manderson, 'The Australian Racism, Acceptance, and Cultural-Ethnocentrism Scale (RACES): Item Response Theory Findings' (2016) 15 International Journal for Equity in Health 49.

[5] 'Poverty and Child Abuse and Neglect' (*Child Family Community Australia*); Jon Altman, 'Deepening Indigenous Poverty in the Northern Territory'; Australian Government, 'Indigenous Australians Data' (*Australian Institute of Health and Welfare*).

[6] Commonwealth of Australia Constitution Act 1900 c.12 s 122. Hereafter Australian Constitution.

[7] Jennifer Clarke and others, *Hanks Australian Constitutional Law Materials and Commentary* (LexisNexis Butterworths 2012) chs 3–6.

[8] The Australian Constitution s 125; The Seat of Government Act 1908.

[9] Clarke and others (n 7) ch 3.

[10] Vito Breda, *Constitutional Law and Regionalism: A Comparative Analysis of Regionalist Negotiations* (Edward Elgar Publishing 2018) 206.

[11] Nicholas Aroney and James Allan, 'An Uncommon Court: How the High Court of Australia Has Undermined Australian Federalism' (2008) 30 Sydney Law Review 245.

This chapter focuses on, as mentioned earlier, the implications of the Intervention and the Stronger Futures Policies in the Northern Territory.[12] The system of governance of the Northern Territory is analogous to the one adopted in Australian States, with the notable exception that the Commonwealth can pass any type of law that it considers fit.[13] The size and the low population density had direct negative implications on the governance of the Aboriginal Peoples and Torres Strait Islander communities, which will be discussed later in the penultimate section of this chapter.[14]

The effects of the Intervention officially commenced on 7 August 2007.[15] The bulk of the Intervention's administrative policies were anchored to three statutes: the Appropriation (Northern Territory National Emergency Response) 2007–2008 1–2,[16] the Northern Territory National Emergency Response Act 2007[17] and the Social Security and Other Legislation Amendment (Welfare Payment Reform) 2007.[18] These statutes amended a series of acts that specifically regulated the interaction between Aboriginal communities and public institutions, such as the Northern Territory Self-Government Act 1978,[19] and suspended the application of others, such as the Racial Discrimination Act 1975.[20] There were substantial changes to the Aboriginal Land Rights (Northern Territory) Act 1976[21] and the Native Title Act 1993.[22] Many of the elements included in the Intervention were decanted, so to speak, in the Stronger Futures Policy, which included the Stronger Futures Act 2012[23] and

---

[12] Australia Government, 'Area of Australia – States and Territories' (15 May 2014).
[13] The Australian Constitution.
[14] Altman (n 5).
[15] Melinda Hinkson, 'Introduction: In the Name of the Child' in Jon C Altman and Melinda Hinkson (eds), *Coercive Reconciliation: Stabilise, Normalise, Exit Aboriginal Australia* (Arena Publications Association 2007); Jon Altman and Susie Russell, 'Too Much "Dreaming": Evaluations of the Northern Territory National Emergency Response Intervention 2007–2012' (2012) Evidence Base: A Journal of Evidence Reviews in Key Policy Areas 1; Megan Davis and others, 'International Human Rights Law, Women's Rights and the Intervention' (2009) 7 Indigenous Law Bulletin 11.
[16] Appropriation (Northern Territory National Emergency Response) (NO. 1) 2007–2008; Appropriation (Northern Territory National Emergency Response) (NO. 2) 2007–2008.
[17] Northern Territory National Emergency Response Act 2007.
[18] Social Security and Other Legislation Amendment (Welfare Payment Reform) Act 2007.
[19] Northern Territory (Self-government) Act 1978.
[20] Racial Discrimination Act 1975.
[21] Aboriginal Land Rights (Northern Territory) Act 1976.
[22] Native Title Act 1993 n 110.
[23] Stronger Futures in the Northern Territory Act 2012.

the Stronger Futures (Consequential and Transitional Provisions) Act 2012.[24] The effects of these statutes on the Territorian Aboriginal Peoples will be discussed as part of an analysis of the drivers of change that have contributed to an ongoing crisis of legitimacy of the public institutions within the Aboriginal and Torres Strait Islander communities.

Before discussing the three drivers of change selected for this chapter, a number of points need to be clarified as a part of a preliminary discussion. First, the term *Aboriginal Peoples and Torres Strait Islanders* (or Aboriginal Peoples) is used in this chapter in a way that includes a very large cluster of Aboriginal and Islander communities.[25] Aboriginal Peoples and Torres Straits Islanders are among the oldest continuum cluster of living civilisations.[26] In this chapter, I will focus on the Aboriginal Peoples and Torres Strait Islander communities located in the Northern Territory.[27] Aboriginal Peoples and Torres Strait Islanders are composed of 96 per cent of Aboriginal Peoples, 1 per cent of Torres Strait Islanders and 3 per cent of individuals who define themselves as both Aboriginal and as a Torres Strait Islander.[28] Second, I will use the term *the rest of the Australian population* to identify the population that is not Aboriginal. The rest of the Australian population, like other mass economic immigration nations, is composed of multiple layers of immigrants from all over the world.[29] Over 50 per cent of the current Australian population have British and Irish heritage.[30]

Third, the term *the Intervention* will include the set of measures within the Northern Territory National Emergency Response and its successive changes. The Act was amended multiple times leading up to its replacement in 2012 by the Stronger Futures Policy.[31] Fourth, the preparation for the Stronger Futures Policy commenced before the series of events that triggered the

---

[24] Stronger Futures in the Northern Territory (Consequential and Transitional Provisions) Act 2012.

[25] Henry Reynolds, *Dispossession: Black Australians and White Invaders* (2nd edition, 1996).

[26] Jo McDonald and others, 'Karnatukul (Serpent's Glen): A New Chronology for the Oldest Site in Australia's Western Desert' (2018) 13 Plos One 2.

[27] Australian Government, 'Indigenous Australians Data' (n 5).

[28] Louise Markus, 'Aboriginal and Torres Strait Islander Health Performance Framework 2020 Key Health Indicators – Northern Territory' (2020) 24, 1; Australian Institute of Health and Welfare, 'Profile of Indigenous Australians' (2021).

[29] Commonwealth of Australia – Australian Bureau of Statistics, 'Census: Aboriginal and Torres Strait Islander Population' (2017).

[30] 'Overseas Migration, 2020–21 Financial Year | Australian Bureau of Statistics' (17 December 2021); Australian Bureau of Statistics, 'The Average Australian' (10 April 2013).

[31] Northern Territory National Emergency Response Act 2007; Stronger Futures in the Northern Territory Act 2012.

National Emergency Response, but it was enacted afterwards.[32] It included a ten-year 'sunset clause' following its enactment.[33] Fifth, the Northern Territory Intervention and the Stronger Futures Policy partially overlap with the Closing the Gap Policy.[34] Closing the Gap, like the two regional policies, sets targets that encompass the Northern Territory as well as the entire nation of Australia. It will not be discussed in this chapter.

## A FALSE START: THE INTERVENTION

The set of policies included in the Intervention were part of a reaction to the *Ampe Akelyernemane Meke Mekarle: Little Children Are Sacred* Report, hereafter the *Little Children Are Sacred* Report, commissioned by and then submitted to the Northern Territory Government on the 30 April 2007.[35] The report indicates a high level of sexual abuse of Aboriginal children, and it recommended coordinated State and Federal actions.[36]

The report was made public in June 2007, and by July, the Federal Government announced its intention to pass a series of measures that were designed to protect Australian Aboriginal children from abuse.[37] The Federal Government did not attempt to consult with Aboriginal communities, nor did it make any attempt to consult with other experts.[38] This failure to take a more cooperative approach to the alleged crisis was coupled with a lack of a critical review of the data.[39] Two years after the Intervention, the Australian Human

---

[32] Altman and Russell (n 15).
[33] Stronger Futures in the Northern Territory Act 2012 s 118(1).
[34] Australian Government, 'Closing the Gap on Indigenous Disadvantage: The Challenge for Australia – Indigenous Justice Clearinghouse' <www.indigenousjustice.gov.au/resources/closing-the-gap-on-indigenous-disadvantage-the-challenge-for-australia/> accessed 16 March 2022.
[35] Northern Territory and others, *Ampe Akelyernemane Meke Mekarle: Little Children Are Sacred* (Dept of the Chief Minister, Office of Indigenous Policy 2007).
[36] ibid 9; Commonwealth of Australia 2008, NTER Review Board, 'Northern Territory Emergency Response: Report of the NTER Review Board' (2008) Report 9.
[37] Hinkson (n 15) 1; Diana Perche, 'Ten Years on, It's Time We Learned the Lessons from the Failed Northern Territory Intervention' (*The Conversation*, 26 June 2017); Altman and Russell (n 15).
[38] Sally Hunter, 'Child Maltreatment in Remote Aboriginal Communities and the Northern Territory Emergency Response: A Complex Issue' (2008) 61 Australian Social Work 372, 372; Nick McKenzie, 'Pedophile Ring Claims Unfounded' *The Sydney Morning Herald (Sydney, Australia)* (7 May 2009).
[39] Australian Human Rights Commission, 'A Statistical Overview of Aboriginal and Torres Strait Islander Peoples in Australia: Social Justice Report 2008' 309 <https://humanrights.gov.au/our-work/statistical-overview-aboriginal-and-torres-strait-islander-peoples-australia-social> accessed 5 March 2022; McKenzie (n 38).

Rights Commission evaluated the evidence that supported the recommendations put forward in the *Little Children Are Sacred* Report.[40] The Australian Human Rights Commission concluded that the number of cases of sexual abuse among Aboriginal children was significant, but not to a level that could be described as an urgent national emergency.[41]

The significant differences between Aboriginal children and non-Aboriginal children could have been explained by the level of economic and social deprivation among Aboriginal regional communities.[42] There was, at the time in which the Intervention's policies were implemented, a general concern that poverty and sexual abuse were corelated, but experts were ignored.[43] Sally Hunter, in her analysis of the evidence that triggered the National Emergency Response, concluded: 'Unfortunately, there has been little Australian research conducted to date on the causes of overrepresentation of Indigenous children and families.'[44] Recent analyses confirmed that data on child abuse, like that considered in the *Little Children Are Sacred* Report, should have been adjusted on the basis of the level of economic depression of the Aboriginal families in rural areas of the Northern Territory.[45]

There are strong indications, for instance, that poverty increases the level of stress and stress-related violence within the family.[46] Domestic violence, alcohol and drug abuse, and mental illness, especially depression and anxiety disorders, are all correlated to some degree with poverty.[47] There is also – albeit a less explored – connection between family violence experienced by women and children through financial abuse and control. Leaving these relationships is difficult due to threat of poverty that the mother may experience if

---

[40] Australian Human Rights Commission (n 39) 309.

[41] Likewise in the Northern Territory, in 2005 (the year prior to the Northern Territory Emergency Response (NTER)) 4.2 per cent of Indigenous children substantiations were for sexual abuse compared to 9.3 per cent of other Territorian children, a figure that does not appear to support the allegations of endemic child abuse in NT remote communities that was the rationale for the NTER. However, the possibility of significant under-reporting must be considered as an explanatory factor, particularly in the light of the findings of the *Little Children are Sacred* Report (n 35).

[42] Hinkson (n 15) 9, 11.

[43] Altman and Russell (n 15) 3.

[44] Hunter (n 38) 274.

[45] Frank Ainsworth, 'The Social and Economic Origins of Child Abuse and Neglect' (2020) 45 Children Australia 202, 203; Maxia Dong and others, 'The Interrelatedness of Multiple Forms of Childhood Abuse, Neglect, and Household Dysfunction' (2004) 28 Child Abuse & Neglect 771.

[46] Ainsworth (n 45); National Research Council (U.S.) (ed), *Understanding Child Abuse and Neglect* (National Academy Press 1993); Anandi Mani and others, 'Poverty Impedes Cognitive Function' (2013) 341 Science 976.

[47] Ainsworth (n 45) 203.

she does attempt to leave.[48] Similar conclusions are found in Hunter's article. He reviewed the Intervention, and concluded that the key factors in the comparative were not the existence of a high number of paedophiles: 'There are ... correlations between poverty, family violence, and alcohol abuse, with 92% of victims of family violence being female, 90% of offenders being male, 87% of offenders being influenced by alcohol at the time, and 78% of both victims and offenders being Indigenous.'[49] It is currently clear that the premises of the Intervention were not sufficiently analysed: 'Despite the rhetoric and the research evidence, the Federal Government intervention in the Northern Territory does not appear to be based on current knowledge.'[50]

The most damaging statement of the unsupported deduction was, unfortunately, from the Federal Indigenous Affairs Minister, who claimed that:

> Everybody who lives in those communities knows who runs the paedophile rings, they know who brings in the (sniffable) petrol, they know who sells the ganja ... They need to be taken out of the community and dealt with, not by tribal law, but by the judicial system that operates throughout Australia.[51]

The allegation that multiple networks of paedophiles were operating within Territorian Aboriginal communities arrived a few weeks before the enactment of the National Emergency legislation that singled out those communities.[52]

The current Australian data on unreported cases of child sexual abuse makes the assumption that networks of paedophiles were more prevalent in the Northern Territory unplausible.[53] New data shows, instead, that a concertation of reported cases of child sexual abuse in certain communities could be related to a single individual or to overreporting.[54] Recent anonymous data collection on child abuse also indicates a high endemic level of unreported cases in both

---

[48] Ainsworth (n 45); Dan Brown and Elisabetta De Cao, 'The Impact of Unemployment on Child Maltreatment in the United States' (University of Essex, Institute for Social and Economic Research 2018) 15; Hunter (n 38) 379.

[49] Hunter (n 38) 376.

[50] ibid 383.

[51] 'No Evidence of Indigenous Paedophile Rings: Martin' *The Sydney Morning Herald (Sydney, Australia)* (17 June 2006).

[52] Northern Territory and others (n 35) 247.

[53] ibid. Xiaojing Lei and others, 'Prevalence and Correlates of Sexual Harassment in Australian Adolescents' (2020) 19 Journal of School Violence 349; Michelle Rodino-Colocino, 'Me Too, #MeToo: Countering Cruelty with Empathy' (2018) 15 Communication and Critical/Cultural Studies 96. 'Australia's Children, Child Abuse and Neglect' (*Australian Institute of Health and Welfare*) March 2022; McKenzie (n 38); 'No Evidence of Indigenous Paedophile Rings: Martin' (n 51).

[54] Hunter (n 38) 379.

male and female children across Australia.⁵⁵ In a nutshell, the drafters of the *Little Children Are Sacred* Report acted in good faith but made the comparative situation of the Aboriginal community look worse than it was.⁵⁶

This point is delicate, therefore I must be precise; the suggestion that crimes related to molested children were unreported was most probably accurate, but that is a general problem in patriarchal societies.⁵⁷ For instance, and based on recent history, there are clear indications from the #MeToo movement that males who have a power role within particular professions (like Hollywood film producers or high-ranking academics) or are providers of sought-after goods (like illicit drugs) have historically abused their positions of gatekeepers.⁵⁸ It is true that these people are predators; however, this is not a reason to limit freedoms, like the access to alcohol, for an entire category of individuals.⁵⁹ In the aftermath of the #MeToo movement, no one has suggested, as far as I know, sending the US Army to Hollywood or reducing the flow of alcohol within elite groups of individuals who abused their professional gatekeeper roles.

There is also an indication that the *Little Children Are Sacred* Report was read selectively by the Federal Government.⁶⁰ The report recommended a set of policies that were to be prepared in consultation with Aboriginal communities.⁶¹ This point is worth repeating, because whilst the Intervention morphed over the years into the Stronger Futures Policy, which is specific to the Northern Territory, the Closing the Gap package consists of policies that are nationwide.⁶² However, the *Little Children Are Sacred* Report pointed out that all policies that affect Aboriginal Peoples and Torres Strait Islanders should be negotiated.⁶³ The Commonwealth Government, unfortunately, refused to have a dialogue with any of the Aboriginal institutions or community representatives, while claiming that it would engage directly with the 'people'.⁶⁴

---

⁵⁵ Lei and others (n 53); Rodino-Colocino (n 53). 'Australia's Children, Child Abuse and Neglect' (n 53).
⁵⁶ Lei and others (n 53). 'Australia's Children, Child Abuse and Neglect' (n 53).
⁵⁷ Lei and others (n 53) 350.
⁵⁸ Rodino-Colocino (n 53).
⁵⁹ ibid.
⁶⁰ Hinkson (n 15) 3; Perche (n 37); Altman and Russell (n 15).
⁶¹ Hinkson (n 15) 3.
⁶² Stronger Futures in the Northern Territory Act 2012; Stronger Futures in the Northern Territory (Consequential and Transitional Provisions) Act 2012; Altman and Russell (n 15); Australian Government, 'Closing the Gap on Indigenous Disadvantage: The Challenge for Australia – Indigenous Justice Clearinghouse' (n 34).
⁶³ Northern Territory and others (n 35) 9.
⁶⁴ Tim Rowse, 'The National Emergency and Indigenous Jurisdictions' in Jon C Altman and Melinda Hinkson (eds), *Coercive Reconciliation: Stabilise, Normalise, Exit Aboriginal Australia* (Arena Publications Association 2007) 54.

The interaction between the Government and representatives of the Territorian Aboriginal Peoples, which preceded Stronger Futures, was, instead, described as tokenistic.[65]

The selective reading of the *Little Children Are Sacred* Report was coupled with the adoption of statutory policies that are unrelated to the condition of children.[66] The most notorious of them was an amendment to the Aboriginal Land Rights (Northern Territory) Act 1976 that allowed the Federal Government to take control of community leases.[67] Community leases were part of the Aboriginal Land Rights (Northern Territory) Act 1976, which was the first statute that recognised the communal ownership of the traditional land in the Northern Territory. The Aboriginal communities, once their occupation was recognised, had an unalienable freehold on their traditional land. However, the 2007 Intervention includes measures that permitted the compulsory acquisition of 'Aboriginal Townships and [the] winding back of the permit system'.[68]

There is no mention in the *Little Children Are Sacred* Report that such a policy might be needed. There is an orthogonal argument for having logistical bases for representatives of the Federal Government and the Armed Forces in the communities to be included, but that did not require a reform of the communal land system.[69]

It is worth mentioning that in 2006, the Federal Parliament passed an Aboriginal Land Rights (Northern Territory) Amendment which, among other changes, allowed for the leasing of community assets to Government institutions.[70] The process of leasing, however, crucially included a 'negotiation stage' that was curtailed by the Intervention.[71] Furthermore, the amendment of Section 19 of the Aboriginal Land Rights (Northern Territory) Act 1976 inserted the possibility of having a lease system for communal land held by Aboriginal communities for 'any purpose' that is consistent with the Intervention Policy.[72] This is a 'carte blanche' transfer of power from

---

[65] Social Policy Connections, 'Statement by Northern Territory Elders and Community Representatives – No More! Enough Is Enough!'; Altman and Russell (n 15).

[66] Pat Turner and Nicole Watson, 'The Trojan Horse' in Jon C Altman and Melinda Hinkson (eds), *Coercive Reconciliation: Stabilise, Normalise, Exit Aboriginal Australia* (Arena Publications Association 2007).

[67] Northern Territory National Emergency Response Act 2007 pt 4; Aboriginal Land Rights (Northern Territory) Act 1976.

[68] Turner and Watson (n 66) 205; Altman and Russell (n 15) 3; Northern Territory National Emergency Response Act 2007 pt 2, div. 2.

[69] Turner and Watson (n 66).

[70] ibid 205.

[71] Aboriginal Land Rights (Northern Territory) Act 1976.

[72] ibid.

Aboriginal Peoples to the Government. In their analysis of the changes to the Aboriginal Land Rights (Northern Territory) Act 1976 brought about by the Intervention, Nicole Watson and Pat Tuner use the trope 'Trojan horse' to describe the insertion of unrelated Federal policy into a national emergency package of reforms.[73] However, they point out that Northern Territory Aboriginal Peoples, unlike the residents of ancient Troy, were aware of the ruse and probably would never accept such an insidious present.[74]

Even without the cost in terms of the significant violation of human rights,[75] the Intervention was a substantial failure.[76] Many of its policies were infective, and a few were damaging to the healthcare of children.[77] By 2008, the Northern Territory Emergency Response Board (NTER Board), which commissioned the Intervention, indicated many of its inherent flaws.

> There is a strong sense of injustice that Aboriginal people and their culture have been seen as exclusively responsible for problems within their communities that have arisen from decades of cumulative neglect by governments in failing to provide the most basic standards of health, housing, education and ancillary services enjoyed by the wider Australian community.[78]

The NTER Board conducted widespread consultations with over 30 communities and collected over 200 submissions.[79] The feedback was overwhelmingly critical of the Intervention: 'the significant government investment associated with the NTER was a historic opportunity wasted because of its failure to galvanise the partnership potential of the Aboriginal community.'[80] The Australian Government engaged with the report and, in 2008, reinstated the Racial Discrimination Act 1975, but that reduced rather than eliminated the discriminatory element of the Intervention.[81]

---

[73] Turner and Watson (n 66) 205.
[74] ibid 210.
[75] Commonwealth of Australia 2008, NTER Review Board (n 36) 46.
[76] ibid 9.
[77] Hunter (n 38).
[78] Commonwealth of Australia 2008, NTER Review Board (n 36) 9.
[79] ibid.
[80] ibid 10.
[81] 'While noting that the State party will complete the reinstatement of the Racial Discrimination Act in December 2010, the Committee is concerned by the continuing difficulties in using the Act to challenge and provide remedies for racially discriminatory NTER measures (arts. 1, 2 and 5).' United Nations, Committee on the Elimination of Racial Discrimination, 'Concluding Observations of the Committee on the Elimination of Racial Discrimination – Australia. CERD/C/AUS/CO/15-17'.

A change of Government did not lead to any substantial alterations to the measures set out in the Intervention until 2012.[82] The Stronger Futures Policy included a new set of statutes that decanted some aspects of the Intervention and increased the level of consultation with Aboriginal communities.[83] However, the Stronger Futures Policy was generally perceived as being 'too little' and 'too late'. The Northern Territory Elders and Community Representatives response to the new policy left little space for discussion: 'We will not support an extension of the Intervention legislation ... The recent consultations report shows that Government has failed to take seriously our concerns and feelings. This report is simply a reflection of pre-determined policy decisions.'[84] The pre-legislative consultation was perceived as a tokenistic process that did not search for a consensus.[85] Furthermore, rebranding of previous policies and the changes in targets made it very difficult for external observers to evaluate whether there was any significant impact from the Intervention and, consequently, to assess the effectiveness of the Stronger Futures Policy.[86]

In short, the statutory and administrative policies that created the Intervention and Stronger Futures Polices were derived from an exaggerated crisis, left the pathogenic effects of two centuries of racial discrimination partly untreated and entrenched a perception among Territorian Aboriginal Peoples that they were administrative subjects instead of citizens with unalienable rights.[87] In the next section, I will discuss the Australian constitutional system as one of the factors that contributes to a lingering crisis of the legitimacy of public institutions in the Northern Territory.

---

[82] Stronger Futures in the Northern Territory Act 2012.

[83] ibid; Stronger Futures in the Northern Territory (Consequential and Transitional Provisions) Act 2012; Australia, Australia and Housing Department of Families Community Services and Indigenous Affairs, *Stronger Futures in the Northern Territory: A Ten Year Commitment to Aboriginal People in the Northern Territory* (Dept of Families, Housing, Community Services and Indigenous Affairs 2012); Aboriginal Peak Organisations of the Northern Territory, 'Stronger Futures and Customary Law (Briefing Paper 2012)'.

[84] Connections (n 65).

[85] Emma Partridge, Sarah Maddison and Hon Alastair Nicholson, 'Human Rights Imperatives and the Failings of the Stronger Futures Consultation Process' (2012) 18 Australian Journal of Human Rights 21, 29, 32.

[86] Altman and Russell (n 15) 3.

[87] Connections (n 65); Megan Davis, 'A Culture of Disrespect: Indigenous Peoples and Australian Public Institutions' (2006) 8 UTS Law Review 135.

## THE CONSTITUTIONAL RACE POWER: A NEGATIVE DRIVER OF CHANGE

The legitimisation crisis that affects the Northern Territory Aboriginal population is dissimilar to the regional crises that are described in the rest of this book. The lack of trust in public institutions by Aboriginal Peoples is due, among many other factors, to a historically ingrained suspicion of the organisations that should represent a multinational constitutional system.[88] In other words, the Australian Constitution does not represent the diversity of its constituency.[89] The identity crisis, so to speak, is more acute and has more implications in the Northern Territory where there is a higher concentration of Aboriginal communities.[90] The Intervention and the Stronger Futures Policies, which lapsed in 2022, are manifestations of a precarious legal fiction which assumes that these policies regulate a uniform population yet, ironically, single out a 'race' for being unable to care for the welfare of its children.[91]

A lack of recognition combined with the power to discriminate is one of the negative drivers, among a gamut of contextual factors, that sustains the cycle of disrespect towards Aboriginal Peoples and fosters their mistrust in public institutions.[92] There are historical reasons that make such a process extremely difficult.[93] A rigid constitutional system,[94] the popular misconception over the implications of recognising a sociological fact[95] and lingering racist assumptions among a large section of the population[96] are a few of the elements that

---

[88] Murray Goot and Tim Rowse, *Divided Nation?: Indigenous Affairs and the Imagined Public* (Melbourne Univ Publishing 2007) 150.

[89] Goot and Rowse (n 88); George Williams, 'Removing Racism from Australia's Constitutional DNA' (2012) 37 Alternative Law Journal 151.

[90] Australian Government, 'Indigenous Australians Data' (n 5); Davis (n 87); Altman and Russell (n 15).

[91] Altman and Russell (n 15); Rowse (n 2); Northern Territory and others (n 35).

[92] Megan Davis, 'Political Timetables Trump Workable Timetables: Indigenous Constitutional Recognition and the Temptation of Symbolism over Substance' in Simon Young, Jeremy Patrick and Jennifer Nielsen (eds), *Constitutional Recognition of First Peoples in Australia: Theories and Comparative Perspectives* (Federation Press 2016); Australian Parliament, Joint Select Committee on Constitutional Recognition of Aboriginal and Torres Strait Islander Peoples, *Final Report* (2015); Australian Indigenous Leadership Centre, 'Submission to Joint Select Committee on Constitutional Recognition of Aboriginal and Torres Strait Islander Peoples' (Australian Indigenous Leadership Centre 2014) 062.

[93] Australian Indigenous Leadership Centre (n 92); Davis (n 92); Breda (n 10) ch 8.

[94] The Australian Constitution s 128; Clarke and others (n 7) 142.

[95] Davis (n 92); Goot and Rowse (n 88) 78.

[96] Anne Pedersen and others, 'Attitudes toward Aboriginal Australians in City and Country Settings' (2000) 35 Australian Psychologist 109; Grigg and Manderson (n 4) 32.

make the process of the recognition of Aboriginal Peoples improbable.[97] This is unfortunate, because the lack of recognition and the related institutional structures to negotiate changes in status have a detrimental effect on the perception of the legitimacy of a legal system that is axiologically multinational.[98] Recall that in multinational legal systems, constitutional law sets the boundaries within which identity-based demands are negotiated.[99]

Independently from the reasons for the lack of recognition, Australia is an oddity in the family of English-speaking mass immigration democracies.[100] Canada,[101] the United States[102] and New Zealand[103] have all adopted a mechanism to recognise First Nations' identity-based claims.[104] There is also international pressure to recognise Aboriginal Peoples and Torres Strait Islanders. The United Nations Committee on the Elimination of Racial Discrimination call upon signatory States, like Australia, to '[e]nsure that members of indigenous peoples have equal rights in respect of effective participation in public life and that no decisions directly relating to their rights and interests are taken without their informed consent'.[105]

The Australian constitutional system has not adopted either the recommendation of United Nations Committee on the Elimination of Racial Discrimination or put in place a system to ensure the recognition of Aboriginal

---

[97] Davis (n 92); Breda (n 10) 215.

[98] Goot and Rowse (n 88); Australian Indigenous Leadership Centre (n 92); James Tully, 'The Unfreedom of the Moderns in Comparison to Their Ideals of Constitutional Democracy' (2002) 65 Modern Law Review 204; Vito Breda, 'An Odd Partnership: Identity-Based Constitutional Claims' in Fiona Jenkins, Mark Nolan and Kim Rubenstein (eds), *Allegiance and Identity in a Globalised World* (Cambridge University Press 2014).

[99] Jürgen Habermas, 'On the Relation Between the Nation, the Rule of Law and Democracy' in Pablo De Greiff and Ciaran Cronin (eds), *The Inclusion of the Other: Studies in Political Theory* (The MIT Press 2000).

[100] Dominic O'Sullivan, 'The Treaty of Waitangi in Contemporary New Zealand Politics' (2008) 43 Australian Journal of Political Science 317; Frank Pommersheim, 'At the Crossroads: A New and Unfortunate Paradigm of Tribal Sovereignty' (2010) 55 South Dakota Law Review 48; James Tully, *Strange Multiplicity: Constitutionalism in an Age of Diversity* (CUP 1995).

[101] Government of Canada; Indigenous and Northern Affairs Canada; Communications Branch, 'The Government of Canada's Approach to Implementation of the Inherent Right and the Negotiation of Aboriginal Self-Government' (3 November 2008).

[102] Pommersheim (n 100).

[103] Amy L Catalinac, 'The Establishment and Subsequent Expansion of the Waitangi Tribunal: The Politics of Agenda Setting' (2004) 56 Political Science 5.

[104] Tully (n 100).

[105] United Nations Committee on the Elimination of Racial Discrimination, 'General Recommendation 23: Indigenous Peoples , 1997.A/52/18, Annex V' 23.

Peoples and Torres Strait Islanders' identity-based rights.[106] Megan Davis, one of the leading experts on the analysis of the ongoing process of the constitutional recognition of Aboriginal Peoples and Torres Strait Islanders reports that the Australian legal and political system has an entrenched fundamental disrespect for Indigenous Peoples.[107] The disrespect is, as mentioned earlier, met with contempt by Aboriginal Peoples and Torres Strait Islanders.[108]

The Australian Government, during the few months taken to draft the Intervention and Stronger Futures Policies, assumed the Aboriginal communities would be reluctant to cooperate, and thus acted either without or with very limited consultations.[109] The lack of deliberative engagement increased the perception that such policies were, at the very best, alien to the Aboriginal culture, and at the worst, deliberately put in place to hamper identity-based rights.[110] That perception increased the mutual mistrust and, we can reasonably assume, reduced the level of compliance.[111]

The concerns surrounding a lack of potential cooperation were most probably connected to claims of widespread corruption among the leadership of Aboriginal communities.[112] There are indications of complacency and unfairness in the way 'big men' were allocating resources to favour family members.[113] There was no indication that corruption was associated with claims of the systematic abuse of children.[114] In other words, there were no indications that Aboriginal leaders would not cooperate to reduce the level of child abuse in their communities.[115] Aboriginal leaders were not involved, and both the Intervention and Stronger Futures Policies increased the level of oversight of Aboriginal institutions that were beneficiaries of Federal money.[116]

Other elements of the Intervention were tangential to its stated aims. The insertion of compulsory lease agreements on the communities established by the Land Reform Act 1976, the forced acquisition of community sites by the Government (75 were acquired), the administratively unchallengeable demolition of settlements and the insertion of a market-based economy on Aboriginal land indicated ulterior motives.[117] The suspension of the Racial Discrimination

---

[106] Davis (n 92).
[107] Davis (n 87) 138.
[108] Habibis, Taylor and Ragaini (n 2).
[109] Altman and Russell (n 15); Rowse (n 2) 54.
[110] Connections (n 65); Partridge, Maddison and Nicholson (n 85).
[111] Partridge, Maddison and Nicholson (n 85).
[112] Rowse (n 2).
[113] ibid.
[114] ibid.
[115] ibid.
[116] Turner and Watson (n 66).
[117] Altman and Russell (n 15) 3.

Act and the use of Armed Forces personnel to provide logistic and security to civil servants sent to deliver the Intervention gave the impression that an invading force was making excuses for exploiting Aboriginal Peoples and Torres Strait Islander resources.[118]

It is worth repeating that by 2007, Aboriginal Peoples and Torres Strait Islanders had been on the receiving end of racist policies since the beginning of colonisation.[119] Even at the time of writing this book, the Australian Constitution is, as far as I know, unique among the family of Western-style constitutional systems as it allows the enactment of racist law.[120] It permits the Federal Parliament to pass statutes for the benefit of '[t]he people of any race for whom it is deemed necessary to make special laws'.[121] The prerogative is commonly called the 'race power' since it allows the enactment of statutory material that targets a racial group.[122] The idea that a formal principle of equality could be derogated on the basis of a racist distinction was linked to a Darwinian assumption, shared by some of the drafters, which considered inferior races to be destined for extinction.[123] The current text is the result of a 1967 amendment to the Constitution's text.[124] The assumption was that after the amendment, laws could still be passed using a racial reference, but only in favour of a particular group.[125] Such a prerogative was tested in the Hight Court in the case of *Kartinyeri v Commonwealth*.[126] The Court accepted the argument

---

[118] Davis (n 87); Altman and Russell (n 15) 3; Racial Discrimination Act.

[119] Reynolds (n 25) 10; Australian Parliament, Joint Select Committee on Constitutional Recognition of Aboriginal and Torres Strait Islander Peoples (n 93) 4; Ciaran O'Faircheallaigh, 'Aborigines, Mining Companies and the State in Contemporary Australia: A New Political Economy or "Business as Usual"?' (2006) 41 Australian Journal of Political Science 1; Clarke and others (n 7) 33; Australian Parliament – Human Rights and Equal Opportunity Commission, *Bringing Them Home: Report of the National Inquiry into the Separation of Aboriginal and Torres Strait Islander Children from Their Families* (Human Rights and Equal Opportunity Commission 1997).

[120] Langton, 'Indigenous Exceptionalism and the Constitutional "Race Power"' (n 3).

[121] *The Australian Constitution* 51 (xxvi).

[122] Williams (n 89) 151; Ambelin Kwaymullina, 'Recognition, Referendums and Relationships: Indigenous Worldviews, Constitutional Change, and the "Spirit" of 1967' in Simon Young, Jeremy Patrick and Jennifer Nielsen (eds), *Constitutional Recognition of First Peoples in Australia: Theories and Comparative Perspectives* (Federation Press 2016) 29, 31.

[123] Geoffrey Sawer, 'Australian Constitution and the Australian Aborigine' (1966) 2 Federal Law Review 17, 18.

[124] Williams (n 89).

[125] ibid 151; Goot and Rowse (n 88) 27.

[126] *Kartinyeri v Commonwealth* [1998] HCA 22, 195 CLR 337.

that Section 51 xxvi did not restrict the prerogative of the Commonwealth to pass discriminatory legislation.

> Given the limited nature of the purposes thus disclosed and given, also, that as a matter of language and syntax, the amendment was apt to achieve those purposes, and only those purposes, it is not possible, in my view, to treat s 51(xxvi) as *limited to laws which benefit Aboriginal Australians* if it is not similarly limited with respect to the people of other races.[127]

The power to discriminate, confirmed in *Kartinyeri v Commonwealth*, had indirect ramifications for the Aboriginal Peoples and the communities that were directly targeted by the Intervention. Given the suspension of the Racial Discrimination Act 1975 and the wide statutory discretion granted to the Federal Parliament in *Kartinyeri v Commonwealth*, it was very difficult for Aboriginal Peoples to challenge the legitimacy of the Intervention.[128] Even the change to the lease system in Part 4 of the Northern Territory National Emergency Response Act 2007 that was unrelated to the dubious national emergency could not reasonably be challenged in court.[129] After *Kartinyeri v Commonwealth*, the Parliament is, put simply, within its power to pass legislation that can damage the interests of Aboriginal communities.

It is beyond doubt that Aboriginal Peoples considered the Intervention and Stronger Futures Policies as representing non-Aboriginal values.[130] The Intervention and Stronger Futures are instead one of the manifestations of a legal system that is not designed to be multinational.[131] The lack of recognition of multinational social structures within the Australian constitutional system and the related absence of negotiation processes will continue to feed the cycle of the perceived disrespect of and suspicion by Aboriginal Peoples.[132]

---

[127] My emphasis: *Kartinyeri v Commonwealth* [1998] HCA 22, 195 CLR 337, 361 para 30.

[128] Northern Territory National Emergency Response Act 2007; Appropriation (Northern Territory National Emergency Response) (NO. 2) 2007–2008.

[129] Turner and Watson (n 66).

[130] Altman and Russell (n 15); Connections (n 65).

[131] Michael Keating, 'So Many Nations, so Few States: Territory and Nationalism in the Global Era' in James Tully and Alain-G Gagnon (eds), *Multinational Democracies* (CUP 2001).

[132] Davis (n 92); Davis (n 87).

## NEGATIVE DRIVER OF CHANGE: GEOGRAPHICAL POVERTY

The policies that are derived from the Intervention[133] and Stronger Futures[134] might not have, it is reasonable to assume, increased the perception of the legitimacy of public institutions among Aboriginal Peoples in the Northern Territory. The repeated failures to achieve Government targets revealed to the wider public the dramatic level of poverty among Northern Territory Aboriginal communities.[135] In 2017, a decade after the Intervention, Jong Altman explains that in the Northern Territory, over 40 per cent of all Aboriginal households lived below the Australian poverty line.[136] In this section, I will explain how that paucity of resources and the spread out rural Aboriginal communities contribute to the perception of abandonment and exploitation among Aboriginal Peoples that sustains the crisis concerning the legitimacy of public institutions in the Northern Territory. I use the term *poverty* as a compressive of the lack of resources (e.g., household incomes) and opportunities (e.g., jobs and accessible service providers).

The Northern Territory covers a large landmass, and it is sparsely populated. It is one-sixth of the size of the United States and seven times the size of the United Kingdom, but with a population of only 250,000.[137] The comparative poverty of Aboriginal Peoples and Torres Strait Islanders in Australia is a statistical fact.[138] The gap is more evident in the Northern Territory where Aboriginal Peoples and Torres Strait Islanders make up more than half of the residents of geographically large rural areas.[139] For instance, over 40 per cent of Northern Territory Aboriginal Peoples and Torres Strait Islanders live in 'overcrowded dwellings with major structural problems'.[140] Within the limit of the Federal and State dichotomy, Federal institutions seek to bring the same level of opportunities to Aboriginal communities across the Northern Territory as is expected in the rest of Australia.[141] There are, however, substantial differences between the effect of distributive justice policies among the Aboriginal

---

[133] Northern Territory National Emergency Response Act 2007.
[134] Stronger Futures in the Northern Territory Act 2012.
[135] 'Poverty and Child Abuse and Neglect' (n 5); Altman (n 5); Australian Government, 'Indigenous Australians Data' (n 5).
[136] Altman (n 5).
[137] Commonwealth of Australia – Australian Bureau of Statistics (n 29).
[138] Australian Government, 'Indigenous Australians Data' (n 5).
[139] ibid Table HH 4b.
[140] ibid Tables HH 4b, HH 10.
[141] Australian Government, 'Closing the Gap on Indigenous Disadvantage: The Challenge for Australia – Indigenous Justice Clearinghouse' (n 34).

population. Even before the Intervention, reports such as the 2005 Social Justice Report by the Human Rights Commission, also known as Tom Calma's Report, indicated a gap between Aboriginal Peoples and Torres Strait Islanders in areas such as life expectancy,[142] infant and child health,[143] education[144] and employment.[145] The Closing the Gap social justice campaign that followed Tom Calma's Report was one of the factors that motivated the Australian Government to set a series of policies aimed at reducing the substantive inequality between Aboriginal Peoples and Torres Strait Islanders and the rest of Australia. The set of policies that took the same name as the social campaign focuses on multiple areas, but six targets were adopted by the Council of Australian Governments (currently called the National Cabinet). That is the Government forum that is intended to coordinate the territorial governance policies between Federal and regional governments in Australia.

> 1. close the life expectancy gap within a generation 2. halve the gap in mortality rates for Indigenous children under five within a decade 3. ensure access to early childhood education for all Indigenous four years olds in remote communities within five years 4. halve the gap in reading, writing and numeracy achievements for children within a decade 5. halve the gap for Indigenous students in year 12 attainment or equivalent attainment rates by 2020, and 6. halve the gap in employment outcomes between Indigenous and non-Indigenous Australians within a decade.[146]

None of the targets have been met within the timeframes. The level of mortality for four-year-old children and under is almost three times higher among Aboriginal communities than for the rest of Australia.[147] The life expectancy is shorter by more than three years, the level of education is lower and the level of unemployment for Northern Territory Aboriginal Peoples and Torres Strait Islanders is over 50 per cent.[148] The average income of a Northern Territory Aboriginal Household is $613 per week, whereas the average income of non-Indigenous households is $1,450.[149] The level of criminal supervision of young Aboriginal individuals and the level of imprisonment are over eight times the level of young adult supervision and detention for the non-Aboriginal

---

[142] Human Rights and Equal Opportunity Commission, 'Social Justice Report 2005' 18.
[143] ibid.
[144] ibid 78.
[145] ibid 151.
[146] Australian Government, 'Closing the Gap on Indigenous Disadvantage: The Challenge for Australia – Indigenous Justice Clearinghouse' (n 34) 6.
[147] Markus (n 28) 10.
[148] ibid 11.
[149] ibid.

population.[150] The analysis of the drivers of change provided by the Australian Department of Families, Housing, Community Services and Indigenous Affairs gives a clear indication of the future obstacles that policies like Closing the Gap and Stronger Futures might encounter.[151]

The Australian Department of Families, Housing, Community Services and Indigenous Affairs (hereafter ADFHCSIA) data suggests a link of causation, for instance, between the level of wealth, mental health and family violence.[152] The drivers of change that are used by the ADFHCSIA to prepare statistically-based Future Scenarios is the methodology that is also adopted in this book.[153] For instance, remoteness, as a driver of change, increases the levels of poverty and mental illness that are proxies for forecasting future levels of mental illness, substance addiction and family violence.[154]

There is no reason to doubt that the Government and Parliament will continue to act based on data and on the drivers of change published by the ADFHCSIA.[155] The level of poverty is, however, so significant that it continues to reduce the effect of ambitious policies. The ineffectiveness and the unhelpful setting of overambitious targets that are constantly reworded or postponed increase the level of scepticism in Northern Territory Aboriginal Peoples and Torres Strait Islanders.[156] This has a compounding effect on other negative drivers of change noted in the previous section. The persistence of a constitutional race power, the refusal to concede an overdue constitutional recognition, which was discussed as the first driver of change, and the infectiveness of policies that focus on the symptoms rather than on the causes of

---

[150] ibid 12.

[151] ibid 11.

[152] Anton Isaacs and others, 'Lower Income Levels in Australia Are Strongly Associated With Elevated Psychological Distress: Implications for Healthcare and Other Policy Areas' (2018) 9 Frontiers in Psychiatry; 'Poverty and Child Abuse and Neglect' (n 5); Roselinde Kessels and others, 'A Distributional Regression Approach to Income-Related Inequality of Health in Australia' (2020) 19 International Journal for Equity in Health 102; Richard G Wilkinson and Kate E Pickett, 'Income Inequality and Social Dysfunction' (2009) 35 Annual Review of Sociology 493.

[153] Australian Human Rights Commission, *National Anti-Racism Strategy Consultation Report July 2012* (Australian Human Rights Commission 2012); Williams (n 89); United Nations Committee on the Elimination of Racial Discrimination, 'Concluding Observations on the Eighteenth to Twentieth Periodic Reports of Australia'.

[154] Australian Government, 'Indigenous Australians Data, Australian Burden of Disease Study: Drivers of Change in Risk Factor Attributable Burden Indigenous Australians 2018' (Australian Institute of Health and Welfare).

[155] Australia, Australia and Department of Families (n 83).

[156] Altman and Russell (n 15).

social malaise are creating a loop of detachment between Aboriginal Peoples and Australian institutions.

## NEGATIVE DRIVER OF CHANGE: MODERN RACISM AND THE IDENTITY CHASM

The unhelpful constitutional setting and untreated causes of poverty are two, among many, of the negative drivers of change that reduce the process of the identification of a relationship between Aboriginal Peoples and public institutions. In this section, I will add that differences between the identity formation of Aboriginal Peoples and non-Aboriginal Australians have a hindering effect on the lingering crisis of the legitimacy of the public institutions in the Northern Territory.[157]

Daphne Habibis and others, in their article titled 'White people have no face: Aboriginal perspectives on White culture and the costs of neoliberalism', reported the existence of a cultural gap between 'White Australians' and Aboriginal Peoples in the Northern Territory.[158] The research methodology combined questionnaires and semi-structured interviews aimed at assessing Aboriginals' perceptions of non-Aboriginal people. The data collected by Habibis and others indicates that, at a general level, Aboriginal Peoples perceived non-Aboriginal people as shallow, egoistical and uncaring.[159] The sample shows that Aboriginal Peoples who are placed at different levels of the socioeconomic hierarchy perceive non-Aboriginals as being obsessed with material goods. The article reports the results of the study using an evocative narrative that is worth reporting verbatim: 'Dollar dreaming is linked to perceptions of competitiveness, individualism and selfishness. Many respondents appreciate the value of discipline and hard work but observe how these tend to be linked with selfishness.'[160]

In relation to those policies that seek to manage communal land, it is very much a case of dollar dreaming.[161] Consistently, the responders noted how material goods and short-term gains were given priority over family ties, communal values and the environment.[162] This commitment to liberalism is in line with a society made of mass economic immigrants.[163] Non-Aboriginal people

---

[157] Goot and Rowse (n 88); Habibis, Taylor and Ragaini (n 2).
[158] Habibis, Taylor and Ragaini (n 2) 1155.
[159] ibid 1158.
[160] ibid.
[161] Stronger Futures in the Northern Territory (Consequential and Transitional Provisions) Act 2012 Schedule 2; O'Faircheallaigh (n 119).
[162] Habibis, Taylor and Ragaini (n 2) 1161.
[163] ibid 1162.

are perceived to hold an eschewed set of moral values. The priority of profit over family also affects public commitment, which supports land expropriation for urban development and mining concessions over the preservation of natural assets for futures generations.[164]

Research on the effect of materialism in family relations in Australia appears to confirm the perceptions collected in Habibis and others' article.[165] Data on racist attitudes towards Aboriginal Peoples also shows that a large part of the Australian population considers this minority to be affected by alcoholism and, in general, as unwilling to work.[166]

In *Constitutional Law and Regionalism*, I discussed the effect of lingering racism in Australia as one of the sociological factors that is currently reducing the possibility of a successful constitutional referendum over the constitutional recognition of Aboriginal Peoples and Torres Strait Islanders.[167] The argument that was defended in *Constitutional Law and Regionalism*, among many others, was that racism still affects a large part of the population who might vote against a constitutional reform, thus making the reform improbable.[168] The argument posed here is, instead, that racist attitudes towards Aboriginal Peoples aliment mutual distrust between Territorial Aboriginal Peoples and the rest of the population.[169]

For instance, Goot and Rowse noted in their analysis of media commission polls taken from 1947 to 2007 that data on Australian racism is difficult to assess.[170] The scope of the analysis in the commissioned polls has shifted over the years with the increasing awareness of the role of fairness and equality.[171] The stereotype of Aboriginal Peoples as primitive, nomadic, passive, lazy and alcoholics is still reported in the polls.[172] However, there has been a recent shift in emphasis among Australians regarding the reasons for differentiating Aboriginal Peoples and Torres Strait Islanders. References to responsibility, equality and culture are emerging as the new reasons for holding negative

---

[164] ibid 1162; John Connell and Richard Howitt, *Mining and Indigenous Peoples in Australasia* (Sydney University Press in association with Oxford University Press 1993); Ben Cubby, 'Mining Licences Would Reap Aborigines Millions' *The Sydney Morning Herald (Sydney, Australia)* (Sydney, NSW, 9 March 2012) 1.

[165] Shaun A Saunders, 'A Snapshot of Five Materialism Studies in Australia' (2007) 1 Journal of Pacific Rim Psychology 14.

[166] Pedersen and others (n 96) 100; Goot and Rowse (n 88) 170.

[167] Breda (n 10) 221; Australian Parliament, Joint Select Committee on Constitutional Recognition of Aboriginal and Torres Strait Islander Peoples (n 92); Davis (n 92).

[168] Breda (n 10) 234.

[169] Pedersen and others (n 96) 100; Goot and Rowse (n 88) 170.

[170] Goot and Rowse (n 88) 19.

[171] ibid 168.

[172] ibid 170.

attitudes towards others.[173] However, the new sematic game among Australian mainstream media which replaced the term *race* with *culture*, and *ignorance* with the *inability to manage public resources* has not altered the underlying racism towards Aboriginal Peoples.[174]

As a large scope meta-analysis of the polls found, old-school racism, which is segregationist, and punitive policies are still present both in major cities and in small towns in Western Australia.[175] That is, for instance, true for 25 per cent of the responders in Perth (1.2 million residents).[176] However, Pedersen and others provide an indication that over 60 per cent of city and rural dwellers bear 'modern prejudices' towards Aboriginal Peoples.[177] The three common beliefs about Aboriginal Peoples that were reported were: 'that they receive more welfare payments than non-Aboriginal people, that the Commonwealth Government helps them make loan repayments on cars, and that Aboriginal people are more likely to drink alcohol than are non-Aboriginal people.'[178] A long-term analysis of individual attitudes delivered similar results across Australia and in individual States.[179] The most troubling results are reported in Islam; Mir Rabiul and Jahjah Mirna's article titled 'Predictors of young Australians' attitudes toward Aboriginals, Asians and Arabs'.[180] The sample of White Anglo-Saxon university students indicated that modern prejudice (which they called symbolic prejudice) is present in young and relatively privileged adults.[181]

There is a general indication that racist attitudes towards Aboriginal Peoples might be rebranding to look more egalitarian, but that they are here to stay.[182]

In short, Aboriginal Peoples consider both the institutions and a large part of the population as shallow, exploitative and focused on short-term gains.[183] Instead, a large part of the non-Aboriginal population hold on to 'old-school'

---

[173] Yuval Noah Harari, *Sapiens: A Brief History of Humankind* (Vintage 2015) ch 11.
[174] Goot and Rowse (n 88) 171.
[175] Pedersen and others (n 96) 112.
[176] ibid.
[177] ibid.
[178] ibid 109.
[179] Grigg and Manderson (n 4); Mir Rabiul Islam and Mirna Jahjah, 'Predictors of Young Australians 'Attitudes Toward Aboriginals, Asians and Arabs' (2001) 29 Social Behavior and Personality: An International Journal 569; David Mellor, 'Contemporary Racism in Australia: The Experiences of Aborigines' (2003) 29 Personality and Social Psychology Bulletin 474.
[180] Islam and Jahjah (n 179).
[181] ibid 577.
[182] ibid.
[183] ibid.

racism and new modern prejudices that approve of discriminatory policies that are very similar to those included in the Intervention and Stronger Futures.[184] These are also the policies that confirm the lingering mistrust in the Federal and regional institutions in the Northern Territory.[185] Research shows that racist attitudes tend to change very little after the formative school years and the current data indicates that a substantial shift is required to bring Aboriginal Peoples and the rest of Australia closer together.[186] It is from this perspective that the chasm between identity perceptions will continue to be a negative driver of change in the crisis of the legitimacy of public institutions that affects the perceptions of Aboriginal Peoples in the Northern Territory.

## CONCLUSION

In the winter of 2007, whilst Australian Army personnel in civilian cars rolled into remote communities in the Northern Territories and their settlements were demolished, Aboriginal Peoples and Torres Strait Islander parents sent their children to hide in the bushland, terrified that they might be taken away again.[187] The Intervention and Stronger Futures Policies were rightly perceived as morally unjustifiable.[188] This chapter discusses the crisis of legitimacy affecting regional and Federal institutions operating in the Northern Territory.

The crisis discussed in this chapter is an atypical regional crisis. It started with a report to the Northern Territory Government that suggested an higher than 'normal' level of sexual abuse among Aboriginal children.[189] The data, we now know, was accurate but open to misinterpretation. A series of Federal Governments used the report to support a string of policies. A few of these policies had little to do with child welfare,[190] and in general entrenched the historical mistrust in public institutions among Aboriginal Peoples and Torres Strait Islanders.[191]

I explained how the analysis on the *Little Children Are Sacred* Report that triggered the National Emergency Response was probably alarmistic. Based on the current awareness of the level of sexual harassment endemic in most

---

[184] Altman and Russell (n 15).
[185] ibid; Davis (n 87).
[186] Kevin M Dunn and others, 'Constructing Racism in Australia' (2004) 39 Australian Journal of Social Issues 409, 413; Islam and Jahjah (n 179).
[187] Hinkson (n 15) 3.
[188] Altman and Russell (n 15); Connections (n 65).
[189] Northern Territory and others (n 35).
[190] Turner and Watson (n 66).
[191] Grigg and Manderson (n 4); Altman and Russell (n 15); Habibis, Taylor and Ragaini (n 2).

patriarchal societies, Aboriginal Peoples and Torres Strait Islanders residing in the Northern Territory report a comparatively higher level of sexual abuse.[192] However, that is probably related to the level of extreme deprivation experienced by those who reside in remote areas in the Northern Territory.[193]

Independently from the reasons that motivated the Intervention, the chapter provided an analysis of three drivers of change. They all had, and continue to have, a hindering effect on the perception of the legitimacy of Federal and regional institutions in the Northern Territory by Aboriginal Peoples and Torres Strait Islanders. The first negative driver of change is the legal setting that allows Federal institutions to impose the policies set in the Intervention without consultation with Territorian institutions and, more importantly, with Aboriginal Peoples.[194] The Intervention included a series of measures on land management that had little to do with the welfare of Aboriginal Peoples, which probably would have been strongly opposed.[195] The Stronger Futures Policy remedied many of the shortcomings of the Intervention.[196] The policy was, for instance, from the outset, in compliance with the Racial Discrimination Act 1975, but the damage had already been done.[197]

The second driver of change considered in the chapter focused on the effects of extreme poverty and the isolation of rural Aboriginal Peoples and Torres Strait Islander communities.[198] There are substantial gaps between Aboriginal Peoples and the rest of Australia in terms of life expectancy,[199] infant and child health,[200] education[201] and employment.[202] The lack of a systematic and negotiated engagement with a paucity of resources in rural areas of the Northern Territory has negative effects on the perception of legitimacy of both the

---

[192] Northern Territory and others (n 35); 'Australia's Children, Child Abuse and Neglect' (n 53).

[193] Australian Government, 'Indigenous Australians Data, Australian Burden of Disease Study: Drivers of Change in Risk Factor Attributable Burden Indigenous Australians 2018' (n 154); Commonwealth of Australia 2008, NTER Review Board (n 36); Hunter (n 38); Ainsworth (n 45) 203; Dong and others (n 45).

[194] Hinkson (n 15) 3.

[195] Habibis, Taylor and Ragaini (n 2); Turner and Watson (n 66); Altman and Russell (n 15) 3.

[196] Stronger Futures in the Northern Territory (Consequential and Transitional Provisions) Act 2012 Schedule 1.

[197] Stronger Futures in the Northern Territory Act 2012 s 4; Racial Discrimination Act; Connections (n 65).

[198] 'Poverty and Child Abuse and Neglect' (n 5); Altman (n 5); Australian Government, 'Indigenous Australians Data' (n 5).

[199] Human Rights and Equal Opportunity Commission (n 142) 18.

[200] ibid.

[201] ibid 78.

[202] ibid 151.

Intervention and the Stronger Futures Policies.[203] The Stronger Futures Policy lapsed in the middle of 2022.[204] It is axiological that ineffective Government action bred disillusionment, but in a situation in which institutions had an history of discrimination, mistrust among Aboriginal Peoples has also been fostered.

Distrust between Aboriginal Peoples and non-Aboriginal people is one of the defining elements of the identity-making process that is discussed as the third driver of change. Historically, Aboriginal Peoples and Torres Strait Islanders have suffered the effects of colonisation, which included policies aimed at cultural and physical genocide.[205] However, there is more at play than just this transgenerational trauma.[206] There are indications that Aboriginal Peoples and Torres Strait Islanders in the Northern Territory are unreceptive to many of the individualist values that are distinctive of Australian society.[207] There is, in short, a cultural chasm between the identity groups, which makes the process of self-identification between rules and groups extremely difficult.[208] In a situation in which communities hold different values, the imposition – instead of negotiation – of policies like the Intervention and Stronger Futures is likely to decrease rather than enhance the perception of the legitimacy of public institutions in the Northern Territory by Aboriginal Peoples and Torres Strait Islanders.

---

[203] Altman (n 5).
[204] Stronger Futures in the Northern Territory Act 2012 118 (1).
[205] Williams (n 89); Langton, 'Indigenous Exceptionalism and the Constitutional "Race Power"' (n 3); Bain Attwood, *Telling the Truth About Aboriginal History* (Allen & Unwin 2005).
[206] Goot and Rowse (n 88).
[207] Habibis, Taylor and Ragaini (n 2); Saunders (n 165).
[208] Pedersen and others (n 96) 100; Goot and Rowse (n 88) 170.

# 8. Papua New Guinea and Bougainville: civil war and a new sovereign state

Bougainville is an autonomous region of Papua New Guinea that is likely to become independent before 2028.[1] The newly established Bougainville Constitutional Planning Commission might set an even earlier schedule for secession.[2] Independence is the last step in a process that commenced with a regional civil war.[3] In 2019, a consultative referendum was held and the result indicated that a majority of 97 per cent of Bougainville residents supported independence.[4] The referendum was part of the process that granted constitutionally entrenched autonomy to Bougainville and prepared the conditions for the work of the Bougainville Constitutional Planning Commission.[5]

This chapter analyses the three drivers of change of the process that led Bougainville out of a crisis of governance and into a new institutional system. The first positive driver of change considers the role of hybrid institutions. The perception of legitimacy in Bougainville is heavily dependent on balancing traditional customs with liberal values. The second positive driver of change is the role of women in hybrid institutions. The third driver of change looks into the role of managing the extractive sector in a post-conflict Bougainvillean society.

The Independent State of Papua New Guinea (hereafter, PNG), with its seven million inhabitants, is one of the largest Pacific nations.[6] Its land mass,

---

[1] Autonomous Bougainville Government, 'Special JSB Meeting Endorses Era Kone Covenant' <www.abg.gov.pg accessed 8 July 2022>.

[2] Autonomous Bougainville Government, 'ABG Press Release: Consultations for New Independence Constitution Underway' <www.abg.gov.pg accessed 9 July 2022>.

[3] Joanne Wallis, *Constitution Making During State Building* (Reprint edition, Cambridge University Press 2016).

[4] Kerryn Baker and Thiago Oppermann, 'The Bougainville Referendum: Lessons for the Future' Department of Pacific Affairs in brief series: 2020/16 2; Anthony J Regan, 'Bougainville: Origins of the Conflict, and Debating the Future of Large-Scale Mining' in Colin Filer and Pierre-Yves Le Meur (eds), *Large-scale Mines and Local-level Politics: Between New Caledonia and Papua New Guinea* (ANU Press 2017).

[5] Wallis, *Constitution Making During State Building.* (n 3).

[6] National Statistical Office, *2011 National Population & Housing Census: Ward Population Profile: Islands Region* (2014); Central Intelligence Agency, 'Papua New

which is roughly double the size of the United Kingdom, is composed of a series of Pacific islands and atolls.[7] To the east, PNG shares a border with the Republic of Indonesia, to the Southeast, it is separated from Australia by the Torres Strait, and to the Southwest, by the Solomon Islands. In the past few decades, the country has experienced strong economic growth and was only marginally affected by the 2008 economic crisis; however, COVID-19 had a disproportionally negative effect on PNG.[8] PNG's institutions were unprepared for the COVID-19 pandemic, and the striking level of vaccine hesitancy led to a comparatively high number of fatalities in the economically deprived urban areas.[9]

The institutional structure of PNG is considered, in relation to international standards, to be weak.[10] The current PNG Constitution was enacted in 1975 following independence from Australia.[11] It adopts the flexible Westminster model with an explicit amendment system.[12] Division three of the Constitution includes an extensive list of unqualified and qualified rights.[13] There is, however, the possibility of suspending these rights during national emergen-

---

Guinea – The World Factbook –'; Francis Fukuyama, *Political Order and Political Decay: From the Industrial Revolution to the Globalisation of Democracy* (Profile Books 2014) 167.

[7] Anthony Regan, 'Bougainville, Papua New Guinea: Lessons from a Successful Peace Process' (2018) 163 The RUSI Journal 44, 8.

[8] Xinshen Diao and others, 'Effects of COVID-19 on Papua New Guinea's Food Economy: A Multi-Market Simulation Analysis' (International Food Policy Research Institute 2020); Paul Flanagan, 'The Distorting Effects of the Resource Sector on National Economies: A Case Study from Papua New Guinea' in Christina Hill and Luke Fletcher (eds), *Growing Bougainville's Future* (Jubilee Australia Research Centre 2018) 42; 'UNDP 2019 Human Development Report: Human Development in Asia-Pacific Region Advances Dramatically, but Unevenly | UNDP in Papua New Guinea' (*UNDP*).

[9] 'Papua New Guinea COVID-19 Response' (*Australian Government Department of Foreign Affairs and Trade*); Diao and others (n 8).

[10] Elsina Wainwright, *Our Failing Neighbour: Australia and the Future of Solomon Islands* (Australian Strategic Policy Institute 2003); Fukuyama (n 6) 306; Jared Diamond, *Collapse: How Societies Choose to Fail or Succeed: Revised Edition* (Penguin Group US 2011) 352, 566, 499; 'Transparency International – Papua New Guinea' <www.transparency.org/country/PNG> accessed 12 February 2020.

[11] Constitution of the Independent State of Papua New Guinea – National Parliament of Papua New Guinea 1975 (consolidated version) 1975.

[12] ibid 13–17, 346; Wallis, *Constitution Making During State Building.* (n 3) 262; Richard Albert, 'The Structure of Constitutional Amendment Rules' (2014) 49 Wake Forest Law Review 913, 940.

[13] Constitution of the Independent State of Papua New Guinea – National Parliament of Papua New Guinea 1975 (consolidated version); Justice Collier, 'The Influence of the Magna Carta on Papua New Guinea Law' (25 June 2015) 95; Vito Breda, 'The Australian Offshore Detention Regime: A Constitutional Reflection'

cies like the COVID-19 Pandemic.[14] Another legal transplant from the United Kingdom is the system of territorial governance. PNG is a unitary state where the Autonomous Region of Bougainville (hereafter, Bougainville) has a *sui generis* status.[15] Bougainville has its own constitution that is considered a part of the PNG Constitution.[16]

The 2021 Era Kone Covenant concluded the first phase of the post-2019 referendum negotiation between the Autonomous Bougainville Government (hereafter, ABG) and the PNG Government.[17] The currently agreed schedule for secession indicates that Bougainville might become independent by 2027, and a new set of negotiations between representatives of the central and regional governments is underway.[18] Similar to the rest of the cases discussed within this book, there are multiple elements that influenced the development of the relationship between Bougainville's and PNG's institutions. This chapter will discuss three among many factors that might be informative for further comparative constitutional studies. The three drivers of change considered in this chapter are the role of hybrid custom-liberal institutions, gender and the institutional management of the extractive sector.[19]

---

(2016) Quaderni costituzionali; *Namah v Pato* [2016] PGSC 13; SC1497 (26 April 2016).

[14] Constitution of the Independent State of Papua New Guinea – National Parliament of Papua New Guinea 1975 (consolidated version) ss 40, Part X.; Breda, 'The Australian Offshore Detention Regime' (n 13).

[15] The Constitution of the Autonomous Region of Bougainville 2004 ss 300, Division II; The Constitution of the Autonomous Region of Bougainville 2004.

[16] Constitution of the Independent State of Papua New Guinea – National Parliament of Papua New Guinea 1975 (consolidated version) 332 (c).

[17] Steven Kolova, 'The Bougainville Independence Referendum Consultations Impasse' (2022) 37 Contemporary PNG Studies: DWU Research Journal 7. Autonomous Bougainville Government, 'Bougainville Referendum Declared Petition-Free'.

[18] Autonomous Bougainville Government (n 2); Autonomous Bougainville Government, 'Governments to Establish Treaty Commission to Oversee Consultation Process'; Autonomous Bougainville Government, 'ABG Passes 2020 Budget of over K400 Million' <www.abg.gov.pg> accessed 14 February 2020.

[19] A general analysis of the peace process is in Regan who describes 25 elements that affected the peace process in Bougainville. Anthony Regan, *Light Intervention: Lessons from Bougainville* (United States Institute of Peace Press 2010) 134. Wallis' comparative analysis, instead, focuses the elements that differentiated the decentralisation in East Timor from Bougainville. Wallis, *Constitution Making During State Building* (n 3) pt 3.

# REGIONALISM IN A POST-COLONIAL PACIFIC NATION

PNG's social context is, even within Oceania, distinctive, and before I discuss the role of the selected drivers of change, a series of analyses has to be dealt with as part of a preparatory explanation of Bougainville's secession process. Bougainville is a relatively small archipelago, representing less than 3 per cent of the PNG landmass, located between PNG's mainland and the Solomon Islands.[20] Within the margin of error that is inherent in any ethnic classification, Bougainville residents are considered Melanesians, like the majority of the PNG population.[21] What is characteristic of the Bougainville population, by comparison to most of the PNG population, is a darker skin palette.[22] Bougainville has only 260,000 residents, which accounts for 3.6 per cent of the PNG population.[23] This is one of the smallest regions considered in this book, yet it includes 25 linguistic communities that are also subdivided into even smaller linguistic enclaves.[24] The small size of the Bougainville population is not an impediment for independence.[25] There are states with a smaller population both in Oceania and in Europe,[26] yet the level of linguistically fuelled ethnic divisions in Bougainvillean society was one of the contributory factors in the civil war.[27]

Bougainvillean residents have a claim to distinctiveness from the rest of the PNG population, but the historical development of PNG's and Bougainville's institutions is intertwined.[28] Buka and Bougainville were first sighted by

---

[20] Regan, 'Bougainville, Papua New Guinea' (n 7) 8; Wallis, *Constitution Making During State Building* (n 3) 235.

[21] Regan, 'Bougainville, Papua New Guinea' (n 7) 8; Wallis, *Constitution Making During State Building* (n 3) 235.

[22] Regan, *Light Intervention* (n 19) 8.

[23] National Statistical Office, 'Population' <www.nso.gov.pg/index.php/population-and-social/other-indicators> accessed 14 February 2020; National Statistical Office (n 6) 28; Regan, 'Bougainville, Papua New Guinea' (n 7) 7.

[24] Regan, 'Bougainville, Papua New Guinea' (n 7) 8; Darell Tryon, 'The Languages of Bougainville' in Anthony Regan and Helga Griffin (eds), *Bougainville before the Conflict* (ANU Press 2015).

[25] Regan, 'Bougainville, Papua New Guinea' (n 7) 8; Tryon (n 24).

[26] Resina Katafono (ed), *A Sustainable Future for Small States: Pacific 2050* (The Commonwealth 2017); Anthony Payne and Paul Sutton, 'Towards a Security Policy for Small Island and Enclave Developing States' in Anthony Payne and Paul Sutton (eds), *Size and Survival* (Routledge 2014).

[27] Tryon (n 24); Regan, 'Bougainville' (n 4).

[28] Regan, 'Bougainville, Papua New Guinea' (n 7); Wallis, *Constitution Making During State Building* (n 3); Lorraine Garasu and Andy Carl (eds), *Weaving Consensus: The Papua New Guinea-Bougainville Peace Process* (Conciliation Resources 2002).

a British vessel, but it was a French sailor, Luis de Bougainville, who, in 1768, named the archipelago.[29] Bougainville and PNG passed through the hands of several colonial powers until the United Nations appointed the Government of Australia as the trustee of PNG and Bougainville.[30]

PNG is, according to anthropologists, one of the most multicultural nations in the world.[31] In a relatively small area, a multitude of ethnic groups speak thousands of languages that do not share any linguistic affinity.[32] Historically, the clan, rather than the nation, has been the most common form of political association.[33] Among many elements that distinguish PNG's variegated clan life, there are practices that might be associated with a patrimonial society.[34] This has multifarious implications for PNG's system of governance.[35] For instance, Transparency International ranks PNG within the 'highly corrupt' states.[36] Patrimonialism is one of the distinctive features of Italian regionalism (as discussed in Chapter 3) and Italy is one of the most corrupt political systems in Europe. Yet Italy, with a large section of its territory controlled by organised crime syndicates, is only ranked 42nd on the list of the most corrupt countries in the world out of 180 political systems.[37] PNG is, by way of comparison to Italy, currently classified as 142nd out of 180.[38] Furthermore, the level of corruption since 2011 has been linearly increasing.[39] There is a limited

---

Whether such a distinctiveness is a legitimate ground for secession is not under review in this book. See: David Haljan, *Constitutionalising Secession* (Hart Publishing 2014) ch 6.

[29] Regan, *Light Intervention* (n 19) 167.
[30] ibid 168.
[31] National Statistical Office (n 23); Regan, *Light Intervention* (n 19) 7; Wallis, *Constitution Making During State Building* (n 3) 237; Tryon (n 24); William A Foley, 'The Languages of New Guinea' (2000) 29 Annual Review of Anthropology 357.
[32] Foley (n 31) 357.
[33] Regan, *Light Intervention* (n 19) 8.
[34] Albert Ayius and Ronald James May, *Corruption in Papua New Guinea: Towards an Understanding of Issues* (National Research Institute 2007); Malama Meleisea and Penelope Schoeffel, 'Forty-Five Years of Pacific Island Studies: Some Reflections' (2017) 87 Oceania 337; Terence Wesley-Smith, 'Self-Determination in Oceania' (2007) 48 Race & Class 29; 'UNDP 2019 Human Development Report: Human Development in Asia-Pacific Region Advances Dramatically, but Unevenly | UNDP in Papua New Guinea' (n 8); 'Transparency International – Papua New Guinea' (n 10).
[35] Wallis, *Constitution Making During State Building* (n 3) 262–73.
[36] 'Transparency International – Papua New Guinea' (n 10).
[37] Mario Caciagli, 'The Long Life of Clientelism in Southern Italy' in Jun'ichi Kawata (ed), *Comparing Political Corruption and Clientelism* (Ashgate 2006); 'Italy' (*Transparency.org*).
[38] 'Transparency International – Papua New Guinea' (n 10).
[39] ibid.

level of transparency, which makes civil servants unaccountable, and this, coupled with an ineffectual criminal law system, ensures a reasonable level impunity for those involved in fraudulent practices.[40]

However, the political structure of PNG, as in many other Pacific States, cannot be compared with the model adopted in modern liberal states.[41] Expensive gifts and patronages are part of daily life in villages and urban areas.[42] In PNG, liberal institutions struggle to take roots and there are indications that a new hybrid model that combines customary law and some of the liberal criteria of good governance is developing.[43] The implications of the hybrid model will be discussed later.[44]

PNG and Bougainville are both rich in resources, but the distribution of wealth has increased inequalities, which in turn has been a proxy for corruption, civil instability and violence.[45] There are strong indications that society is suffering from many of the negative effects of the so-called resource curse.[46] PNG is the site of, for instance, several world-class mining operations, and new sites are discovered every year.[47] The revenue from the commodity

---

[40] Sinclair Dinnen, *Law and Order in a Weak State* (Center for Pacific Islands Studies, School of Hawaiian, Asian, and Pacific Studies, University of Hawai'i Press 2001); Sinclair Dinnen, 'Lending a Fist? Australia's New Interventionism in the Southwest Pacific' (ANU Dept of Pacific Affairs (DPA) formerly State, Society and Governance in Melanesia (SSGM) Program 2004) Working/Technical Paper.

[41] Wainwright (n 10); Dinnen, 'Lending a Fist?' (n 40) 6; Fukuyama (n 6); Ramona Boodoosingh and Penelope Schoeffel, 'Community Law-Making and the Codification of Customary Laws – Social and Gender Issues in Samoa' (2018) Department of Pacific Affairs in brief series: 2018/19; Michael Goldsmith, 'Codes of Governance in the Pacific' in Elise Huffer and Asofou So'o (eds), *Governance in Samoa pulega i Samoa* (Asia Pacific Press 2000).

[42] Vito Breda, 'Samoa: Constitutional Governance and Customary Law' (2019) 23 Comparative Law Journal of the Pacific 163.

[43] Christina Hill and Luke Fletcher (eds), 'Growing Bougainville's Future 2018'; Regan, 'Bougainville' (n 4); Wallis, *Constitution Making During State Building* (n 3); Joanne Wallis, 'The Role of "Uncivil" Society in Transitional Justice: Evidence from Bougainville and Timor-Leste' (2019) 31 Global Change, Peace & Security 159; Dinnen, 'Lending a Fist?' (n 40) 6; Francis Fukuyama, *The Origins of Political Order: From Prehuman Times to the French Revolution* (Profile Books 2012) 312; Breda, 'Samoa: Constitutional Governance and Customary Law' (n 42); Vito Breda, *Constitutional Law and Regionalism: A Comparative Analysis of Regionalist Negotiations* (Edward Elgar Publishing 2018) 168–74.

[44] Ayius and May (n 34).

[45] 'UNDP 2019 Human Development Report: Human Development in Asia-Pacific Region Advances Dramatically, but Unevenly | UNDP in Papua New Guinea' (n 8); United Nations Development Programme, '2014 Human Development Report PNG'.

[46] United Nations Development Programme (n 45) 5.

[47] Michael Main, 'Australia Can Help Ensure the Biggest Mine in PNG's History Won't Leave a Toxic Legacy' (*The Conversation*) <http://theconversation.com/

sectors, however, has not been fully exploited by national enterprises due to a lack of financial and technological know-how.[48] Multinational companies have taken on the task of extracting resources, thus transferring the economic benefits from the added value of their activities to foreign shareholders.[49] It is up to PNG's institutions to ensure that such companies act in ways that do not impact negatively on human rights,[50] that comply with national policies[51] and that respect customary laws.[52] However, the high level of corruption mentioned earlier and the intersection between customary traditions and liberal assumptions makes the enforcement of environmental policies and the protection of human rights extremely difficult.[53] For instance, in his analysis of the proposed Frieda River Mine Project, experts, such as Michael Main, suggest that the Australian Government should help the PNG Government in ensuring that Pan Aust operations, an Australian-based company that is due to develop the mining site, are environmentally sound.[54] Main's recommendations are admirable, yet it is unlikely that the PNG Government will be willing to accept help. Pacific communities have been, in general, particularly unresponsive to the efforts of developed agencies and foreign states.[55] As discussed in the case of Sicily, in a patrimonial society, corruption and the mismanagement of

---

australia-can-help-ensure-the-biggest-mine-in-pngs-history-wont-leave-a-toxic-legacy-185580> accessed 8 July 2022; Kristian Lasslett, 'The Crisis Began in 1886: A Long View of Bougainville's Decolonisation Struggle' in Christina Hill and Luke Fletcher (eds), *Growing Bougainville's Future* (Jubilee Australia Research Centre 2018); Regan, 'Bougainville' (n 4); Flanagan (n 8) 43; Charlotte Lundgren, Thomas Alun and Robert York, 'Boom, Bust, or Prosperity? Managing Sub-Saharan Africa's Natural Resource Wealth' ch 2; United Nations Development Programme (n 45) 14.

[48] United Nations Development Programme (n 45) 15; Diamond (n 10) 443.

[49] ibid; ibid.

[50] United Nations Development Programme (n 45) 20; Constitution of the Independent State of Papua New Guinea – National Parliament of Papua New Guinea 1975 (consolidated version) Division 3.

[51] Mining Act 1992; Oil and Gas Act 1998.

[52] Main (n 47); United Nations Development Programme (n 45) 20; Constitution of the Independent State of Papua New Guinea – National Parliament of Papua New Guinea 1975 (consolidated version) ss 53–54.

[53] United Nations Development Programme (n 45) 4, 21; Diamond (n 10) 16, 349, 352.

[54] Main (n 47).

[55] David Kinley, 'Bendable Rules The Development Implications of Human Rights Pluralism' in Brian Z Tamanaha, Caroline Sage and Michael Woolcock (eds), *Legal Pluralism and Development: Scholars and Practitioners in Dialogue* (Cambridge University Press 2012); Goldsmith (n 41); Don Matheson, Kunhee Park and Taniela Sunia Soakai, 'Pacific Island Health Inequities Forecast to Grow Unless Profound Changes Are Made to Health Systems in the Region' (2017) 41 Australian Health Review 590, 4–9.

resources are perceived as the rationale that underpins the system of territorial governance.[56] Endemic corruption and the mismanagement of resources are not, in other words, perceived as a pathology of the system, and an external intervention by a foreign government is unlikely to have a positive effect on the development of PNG.[57]

The lack of understanding of PNG's informal institutional system is one of the reasons behind the civil war in Bougainville and the current plan for secession.[58] In 1965, a mining company controlled by British and Australian Rio Tinto discovered a copper and gold deposit in an area of Bougainville called Panguna.[59] It was a pivotal moment in the history of PNG. From the start of production to its closure in 1989 (due to the mounting civil unrest), the mining operation in Panguna provided 17 per cent of PNG's inland revenue and over a third of State exports.[60] In 1975, PNG declared its independence from Australia. In the same year, Bougainville proclaimed itself independent from Australia and PNG.[61] However, the Bougainville proclamation was not recognised by PNG nor by the international community; instead, PNG's Parliament, in 1976, granted a level of autonomy to the region.[62] Crucially, PNG's Parliament allocated the regional mining royalties to the newly formed North Solomon Provincial Government.[63]

It was too little, too late. In 1989, the disparity in the process that allocated resources was the catalyst for a violent uprising that officially ended in 2001 with the Peace Agreement.[64] The regional civil war was brutal and established

---

[56] Antonella Coco, 'Neopatrimonialism and Local Elite Attitudes. Similarities and Differences Across Italian Regions' (2015) 3 Territory, Politics, Governance 167; Veronica Ronchi, 'The Hybrid State Destatization and Neopatrimonialism' (Fondazione Eni Enrico Mattei 2020) 13; Paolo Buonanno and others, 'Poor Institutions, Rich Mines: Resource Curse in the Origins of the Sicilian Mafia' (2015) 125 Economic Journal F175.
[57] 'UNDP 2019 Human Development Report: Human Development in Asia-Pacific Region Advances Dramatically, but Unevenly | UNDP in Papua New Guinea' (n 8).
[58] Regan, *Light Intervention* (n 19) 26, 168; Wallis, *Constitution Making During State Building* (n 3) 196.
[59] Lasslett (n 47) 8; Regan, 'Bougainville' (n 4).
[60] Regan, *Light Intervention* (n 19) 26, 168; Wallis, *Constitution Making During State Building* (n 3) 196.
[61] Wallis, *Constitution Making During State Building* (n 3) 196.
[62] Regan, *Light Intervention* (n 19) 169.
[63] ibid 15; Wallis, *Constitution Making During State Building* (n 3) 197.
[64] Wallis, *Constitution Making During State Building* (n 3) 197; '"Bougainville Peace Agreement", Arawa, 30 August 2001'; Regan, 'Bougainville, Papua New Guinea' (n 7); Regan, 'Bougainville' (n 4); Mary O'Callaghan, 'The Origins of the Conflict' in Lorraine Garasu and Andy Carl (eds), *Weaving Consensus: The Papua New Guinea-Bougainville Peace Process* (Conciliation Resources 2002).

a regional mistrust of PNG's institutions that lingers on to the present day.[65] For instance, the PNG Government ordered the withdrawal of all institutions from Bougainville and the establishment of air and sea blockades around the archipelago which clearly indicate an intention to starve the island.[66] Bougainville descended into a state of anarchy, with multiple localised conflicts between opposing factions.[67] The PNG blockade, whilst not stopping the internal fighting, had the effect of depriving Bougainville of food and medicines, which decimated the most vulnerable members of the community.[68] The number of civilian casualties is contested, but it is likely to be over 20,000.[69] It was, as in other cases discussed in this book, genocide with cognition through starvation and lack of medical support. The majority of the population was displaced in camps or was forced to seek refuge on remote parts of the island.[70]

By 1997, Bougainvilleans were tired of the stalemate. The women formed local groups and regional associations and demanded peace.[71] I will discuss the role of women in Bougainville's system of governance when I analyse the role of gender in Bougainville's hybrid regional institutions. At this point, is important to note that the civil war was a conflict over mining resources, and that communal land titles in Bougainville pass through a matriarchal line, giving women a distinctive role in the peace process.[72] In 1998, PNG and Bougainville embarked on a normalisation process with the establishment of the Lincoln Agreement.[73]

---

[65] Regan, 'Bougainville' (n 4).
[66] Regan, *Light Intervention* (n 19) 13–15; O'Callaghan (n 64) 9.
[67] Wallis, *Constitution Making During State Building* (n 3) 199; Lasslett (n 47) 20.
[68] Regan, *Light Intervention* (n 19) 35, 170; O'Callaghan (n 64) 10.
[69] Regan, *Light Intervention* (n 19) 35, 170; O'Callaghan (n 64) 10.
[70] O'Callaghan (n 64) 9.
[71] Josephine Tankunani Sirivi, Marilyn Taleo Havini and Australian National University (eds), *As Mothers of the Land: The Birth of the Bougainville Women for Peace and Freedom* (Pandanus Books, Research School of Pacific and Asian Studies, Australian National University 2004); Dr Ruth Saovana-Spriggs, 'Women's Contributions to Bougainville's Past, Present and Future'; 'Meaningful Participation: Women and Peacebuilding in the Pacific' <www.lowyinstitute.org/the-interpreter/meaningful-participation-women-and-peacebuilding-pacific> accessed 3 February 2020; Lorraine Garasu and Volker Boege, 'Bougainville' in Morgan Brigg and Roland Bleiker (eds), *Mediating Across Difference: Oceanic and Asian Approaches to Conflict Resolution* (University of Hawai'i Press 2011) 175–77.
[72] Wallis, *Constitution Making During State Building* (n 3) 248; Regan, *Light Intervention* (n 19) 139; Christina Hill and Luke Fletcher, 'Introduction' in Christina Hill and Luke Fletcher (eds), *Growing Bougainville's Future* (Jubilee Australia Research Centre 2018) 4.
[73] Anthony Regan, 'Resolving Two Dimension of Conflict: The Dynamics of Consent, Consent and Compromise' in Lorraine Garasu and Andy Carl (eds), *Weaving*

Peace officially arrived in the form of the 2001 Arawa Peace Agreement.[74] The Peace Agreement was followed by a reform of the PNG Constitution, which established the Autonomous Region of Bougainville and provided for a referendum over independence.[75] The years that followed were marked by sporadic episodes of armed violence, but there are strong indications that the peace process is holding a steady course.[76] New Zealand and the Australian Government helped with the normalisation process.[77] At the time of writing this chapter, the Bougainville Constitutional Planning Commission is preparing the schedule for Bougainville's secession from PNG.[78] This is just a skeleton analysis of a convoluted process, yet it provides enough information for the analysis of a selection of drivers of change during the civil war that are still affecting the secession process.

## A POSITIVE DRIVER OF CHANGE: A HYBRID CONSTITUTIONAL CONSENSUS

In the previous section, I explained that the process of Bougainville's decentralisation, like the devolution in Northern Ireland, happened as a side effect of a civil war.[79] In this section, I discuss a selection of drivers of change that help with normalisation processes and that are likely to change the future institutional assets of Bougainville. As for the other chapters of this book, it is left up to the reader to allocate different weights to these factors or to forecast future scenarios for Bougainville.[80]

PNG is a unitary state with limited experience of dealing with decentralised institutions.[81] Regional and local institutions are poorly financed, and rural

---

*Consensus: The Papua New Guinea-Bougainville Peace Process* (Conciliation Resources 2002).

[74] '"Bougainville Peace Agreement", Arawa, 30 August 2001' (n 64).

[75] Regan, *Light Intervention* (n 19) 22, 174; Garasu and Carl (n 28); Lorraine Garasu, 'Women Promoting Peace and Reconciliation' in Lorraine Garasu and Andy Carl (eds), *Weaving Consensus: The Papua New Guinea-Bougainville Peace Process* (Conciliation Resources 2002).

[76] Regan, *Light Intervention* (n 19) 176–77.

[77] Regan, 'Bougainville, Papua New Guinea' (n 7); Wallis, *Constitution Making During State Building* (n 3) pt III.

[78] Autonomous Bougainville Government (n 2).

[79] Wallis, *Constitution Making During State Building* (n 3); Regan, 'Bougainville, Papua New Guinea' (n 7).

[80] Robert Agranoff and Mark Glover, 'Introduction: Forecasting Constitutional Futures' in Robert Hazell (ed), *Constitutional Futures Revisited: Britain's Constitution to 2020* (Palgrave Macmillan 2008); Robert Hazell, *Constitutional Futures: A History of the Next Ten Years* (Oxford University Press 1999).

[81] Garasu and Carl (n 28) 8.

areas tend to be attached to customary practices managed by village councils.[82] Furthermore, there is, in relation to the secessionist aspirations of Bougainville, a reasonable concern that other areas of PNG might demand independence.[83] Despite all these hindering factors, the Bougainville peace process delivered an articulated constitutional reform, a peaceful referendum and a negotiated path towards independence.[84] The result of the 2019 referendum, in which 97 per cent of the Bougainvillean voters opted for independence, indicates that the perceived future of the archipelago is for it to be a new country. This is remarkable, because constitutional systems with a well-established democratic tradition, a high level of education and well-founded regional and central institutions, such as Spain and the United Kingdom, have recently struggled to maintain a linear decentralisation process based on institutional cooperation and deliberation.[85] The difficulties of establishing a perception of legitimacy of the central intuitions in the Basque Country and Northern Ireland are discussed at length in the respective chapters of this book.

PNG is, by comparison to the United Kingdom and Spain, poor, and liberal institutions were transplanted.[86] One of the positive drivers of change for the normalisation process of Bougainville is related to the hybridisation of liberal institutions. As part of the customary tradition, Bougainvilleans expect an elevated level of consultation in all processes that might change the status of the local population.[87] The perceived entitlement to be listened to, combined with a flexible constitutional amendment process, is likely to continue to affect the

---

[82] ibid.

[83] Regan, 'Bougainville, Papua New Guinea' (n 7) 59.

[84] Hill and Fletcher (n 43); Regan, *Light Intervention* (n 19); Wallis, *Constitution Making During State Building* (n 3); Autonomous Bougainville Government (n 2).

[85] Hector Lopez Bofill, 'Hubris, Constitutionalism, and "the Indissoluble Unity of the Spanish Nation": The Repression of Catalan Secessionist Referenda in Spanish Constitutional Law' (2019) 17 International Journal of Constitutional Law 943; Breda, *Constitutional Law and Regionalism* (n 43) 62; Vito Breda and Andreja Mihailovic, 'New Caledonia: The Archipelago That Does Not Want to Be Freed' (2019) 24 Comparative Law Journal of the Pacific 69; Alan Berman, 'Future Kanak Independence in New Caledonia: Reality or Illusion?' (1998) 34 Stanford Journal of International Law 287.

[86] United Nations Development Programme (n 45).

[87] Papua New Guinea: Constitution of the Independent State of Papua New Guinea (rev. 2014) 1975 Preamble 5 (1), section 332 3 (b); 'TIPNG Hosts Democracy Workshop for 45 Youths' (*Post Courier*, 16 December 2019) <https://postcourier.com.pg/tipng-hosts-democracy-workshop-for-45-youths/> accessed 6 February 2020; Regan, 'Resolving Two Dimension of Conflict: The Dynamics of Consent, Consent and Compromise' (n 73).

future constitutional status of the region within the PNG Constitution or, in the case of secession, the constitution of the new country.[88]

Bougainville has a special position within the PNG Constitution.[89] First, constitutional norms that regulated the status of Bougainville are subjected to a double-lock mechanism (regional and national) that prevents the National Parliament of Papua New Guinea (hereafter, the PNG Parliament or the Parliament) from unilaterally changing the status of Bougainville.[90] Second, residual matters not explicitly covered by constitutions cannot be exercised without the assent of both the PNG Government and the ABG.[91] Third, in case of a dispute, the parties must initiate an arbitration procedure.[92] The Joint Supervisory Body (hereafter, JSB) monitors the implementation of the Bougainville devolution process and provides dispute-resolution services.[93] Fourth, PNG's central institutions collect taxes from the region that are then redistributed. Bougainville is not, at the time of authoring this book, fiscally self-sufficient.[94] Fiscal self-sufficiency is one of the conditions for regional secession.[95]

The allocation of fiscal revenues to the region was also included in the 1976 Bougainville Agreement,[96] but it was the 2002 constitutional reform that entrenched the legislative competencies of the newly formed regional government.[97] The allocations include, for instance, the prerogative to manage

---

[88] Wallis, *Constitution Making During State Building* (n 3) 205; Regan, 'Resolving Two Dimension of Conflict: The Dynamics of Consent, Consent and Compromise' (n 73).

[89] Constitution of the Independent State of Papua New Guinea – National Parliament of Papua New Guinea 1975 (consolidated version) pt XIV; Graham Hassall and Cheryl Saunders, *Asia-Pacific Constitutional Systems* (Cambridge University Press 2002) 223, 233.

[90] Constitution of the Independent State of Papua New Guinea – National Parliament of Papua New Guinea 1975 (consolidated version) s 345; Regan, *Light Intervention* (n 19) 92, 94.

[91] Constitution of the Independent State of Papua New Guinea – National Parliament of Papua New Guinea 1975 (consolidated version) s 292 (2).

[92] ibid 292 (3), 333, 334.

[93] ibid 343; Regan, 'Bougainville, Papua New Guinea' (n 7) 49.

[94] '"Bougainville Peace Agreement", Arawa, 30 August 2001,' (n 64) ss 135, 149–59.

[95] ibid.

[96] Wallis, *Constitution Making During State Building* (n 3) 197.

[97] The Organic Law on Peace-building in Bougainville – Autonomous Bougainville Government and Bougainville Referendum 2002 Division II; Papua New Guinea: Constitution of the Independent State of Papua New Guinea (rev. 2014) Section 349 (2) the Constitutional Amendment No.23 2001; Constitution of the Independent State of Papua New Guinea – National Parliament of Papua New Guinea 1975 (consolidated version) pt 14.

commodity resources (oil and gas, section 290 2 (*zo*) and mining section 290 2 (*zm*)). Also, one part of the new competences includes clusters of heads of power that are related to the extractive sector. These are the management of the environment (*o*), forestry (*s*), marine areas (*u*), heritage (*w*) and wildlife preservation (*zze*).[98]

The benefits that these areas might provide to the region are extensive, but the ABG must avoid the pitfalls of managing an economy that is dependent on the extractive sector. I will discuss this point in the last section of this chapter, where the 'curse of resources' is discussed in detail.[99] There is, in general, an extensive level of administrative and fiscal autonomy.[100] The ABG has the prerogative to exploit its resources and to retain a substantial proportion of the financial revenues that these resources produce.[101] There is an argument to be made in relation to the effect of pre-conflict foreign exploitation of the island but this narrative has not find its way on the negotiation process. Sections 348 to 343 of the Constitution regulated the consultative referendum over Bougainville independence that took place in 2019.[102] The result of the referendum indicated unequivocally that the majority of the Bougainvillean population supported secession.[103]

The peace process and the institutional activity that followed cannot be easily summarised, yet it is reasonable clear that customary practices did contribute to the current constitutional assets of the region.[104] For instance, in describing the series of debates that took place during the consultation process, Wallis points out the connection between deliberation and social practices. 'Overall, public participation in constitution making in Bougainville was

---

[98] Papua New Guinea: Constitution of the Independent State of Papua New Guinea (rev. 2014).

[99] Jeffrey D Sachs and Andrew M Warner, 'The Curse of Natural Resources' (2001) 45 European Economic Review 827; Buonanno and others (n 56).

[100] The Organic Law on Peace-building in Bougainville – Autonomous Bougainville Government and Bougainville Referendum 2002 ss 35–51.

[101] Autonomous Bougainville Government, 'ABG Vice President Applauds State Negotiation Team on P'Nyang Project' <www.abg.gov.pg/index.php/news/read/abg-vice-president-applauds-state-negotiation-team-on-pnyang-project> accessed 15 February 2020.

[102] Constitution of the Independent State of Papua New Guinea – National Parliament of Papua New Guinea 1975 (consolidated version) 342 (1); '"Bougainville Peace Agreement", Arawa, 30 August 2001' (n 64) ss 309–324.

[103] Autonomous Bougainville Government, 'Bougainville Referendum: 97% Vote for Independence' <www.abg.gov.pg/> accessed 14 February 2020; Autonomous Bougainville Government, 'Governments to Establish Treaty Commission to Oversee Consultation Process' (n 18); Autonomous Bougainville Government, 'Bougainville Referendum Declared Petition-Free' (n 17); Kolova (n 17) 21.

[104] Wallis, 'The Role of "Uncivil" Society in Transitional Justice' (n 43).

extensive ... the consultation process was highly inclusive, transparent, and participatory, managing to have a wide reach throughout Bougainville and to Bougainvilleans living elsewhere in Papua New Guinea.'[105] Bougainvilleans are, again within the limit of reasonableness that is part of any social assertion, culturally compelled to participate in all deliberative activities that they perceive will affect their status in a fundamental way.[106] They also hold a reasonable expectation that political decisions might be the proxy for laws to change.[107] There are positive and negative side effects of having a constitutional system in which much of the population perceive that they have a participatory entitlement to political processes.[108] One of the positive side effects is a strong connection between laws and social perceptions. Deliberative practices in which groups of individuals or their representatives share their pollical opinions tend to develop a sense of ownership over the outcomes of such deliberative processes.[109] This is the so-called normative spill-over effect of the deliberation process in which both the winners and losers in a debate accept the fairness of the deliberative procedure and the legitimacy of its outcome.[110]

This is in theory. In practice, most large democracies tend to have a low level of public involvement.[111] This low level of engagement might be due to an ever-increasing political apathy or to the acceptance that periodic elections are sufficient for ensuring a form of political accountability.[112] However, low levels of engagement and the expectation that citizens must accept the effects of indirect political representation is problematic in a political system with minorities that have fundamental cultural differences.[113] For instance, the

---

[105] Wallis, *Constitution Making During State Building* (n 3) 223.

[106] Regan, 'Resolving Two Dimension of Conflict: The Dynamics of Consent, Consent and Compromise' (n 73).

[107] Wallis, *Constitution Making During State Building* (n 3) 323.

[108] ibid; Regan, 'Resolving Two Dimension of Conflict: The Dynamics of Consent, Consent and Compromise' (n 73) 39.

[109] Joshua Cohen, 'Deliberation and Democracy' in William Rehg (ed), *Deliberative Democracy: Essays on Reason and Politics* (MIT 1997); Joshua Cohen and Charles Sabel, 'Directly-Deliberative Polyarchy' (1997) 3 European Law Journal 313.

[110] Vito Breda, 'Constitutional Patriotism' in Mortimer Sellers and Stephan Kirste (eds), *Encyclopedia of the Philosophy of Law and Social Philosophy* (Springer Netherlands 2017).

[111] Patrick Macklem, 'Militant Democracy, Legal Pluralism, and the Paradox of Self-Determination' (2006) 4 International Journal of Constitutional Law 488.

[112] Breda, 'Constitutional Patriotism' (n 110); Macklem (n 111).

[113] James Tully, 'The Imperialism of Modern Constitutional Democracy' in Martin Loughlin and Neil Walker (eds), *The Paradox of Constitutionalism: Constituent Power and Constitutional Form* (Oxford University Press 2007); James Tully, *Strange Multiplicity: Constitutionalism in an Age of Diversity* (Cambridge University Press 1995).

refusal to change the constitutional status of a minority language might be perceived as a reasonable cost-cutting public policy, yet for a minority, it might be perceived as another attempt at the hegemonic suppression of its identity.[114] Tully, in his analysis of Canadian multinationalism, provides one of the most persuasive explanations of the normative connection between proposed constitutional changes and the entitlement to negotiate those modifications by all those affected.[115]

In the case of Bougainville, the level of the ethnic and linguistic fragmentation of the archipelago is currently not as relevant as the management of local resources.[116] In Bougainville, it is expected that radical changes within a village are agreed by all the families represented in the village within the Council of Elders.[117] This assumption is interwoven within a general perception of the legitimacy of communally agreed constitutional reforms.[118]

The expected high level of involvement has a stabilising effect on the polity, but it is time consuming.[119] For instance, the numerous attempts to stop the civil war were perceived as failures because the different factions failed to agree over the terms of the peace process.[120] However, Regan noted that failing to obtain a consensus over substantive issues related to civil war should not be perceived as a catastrophe in a hybrid society like Bougainville.[121] It is axiomatic that debates over traumatic events, like the effect of an ongoing civil war and the attempt of the central government to starve the island into submission, take time to deliver agreements, and these debates take even more time when there is a cultural expectation that unanimous consensus is perceived as a requirement for the legitimacy of the decision taken in a deliberative arena.[122]

For instance, it is logical to assume that the Bougainville Constitutional Planning Commission is currently grappling with the implications of the requirement for the unanimity of its decisions.[123] Recall that unanimous consensus is part of customary expectations and is not an institutional

---

[114] Dominique Arel, 'Political Stability in Multinational Democracies.' in Alain Gagnon and James Tully (eds), *Multinational Democracies* (Cambridge University Press 2001); Michael Keating, 'So Many Nations, so Few States: Territory and Nationalism in the Global Era' in James Tully and Alain Gagnon (eds), *Multinational Democracies* (Cambridge University Press 2001).

[115] Tully, *Strange Multiplicity: Constitutionalism in an Age of Diversity* (n 113).

[116] Regan, 'Bougainville' (n 4); Hill and Fletcher (n 43).

[117] Wallis, *Constitution Making During State Building* (n 3) 323.

[118] ibid.

[119] ibid 350.

[120] Regan, 'Bougainville' (n 4).

[121] ibid.

[122] Garasu and Carl (n 28); Kolova (n 17).

[123] Autonomous Bougainville Government (n 2).

requirement.[124] However, the expectation that 'all must agree over changes in the status' of the region will continue to alter the works of the Bougainville Constitutional Planning Commission. This elevated level of participation or unanimity will also drive, it is fair to expect, the institutional development of an independent or autonomous Bougainville region. This is a time-consuming political practice that has a distinctive advantage; it anchors agreements in stable political ground. It is, and it will continue to be, a costly but positive driver of change in the future development of Bougainville's institutions.

## A POSITIVE DRIVER OF CHANGE: THE ROLE OF WOMEN IN BOUGAINVILLE

In the previous section of this chapter, I explained that Bougainville's clans have developed hybrid institutions that manage resources, solve conflicts and devise policies.[125] In this section, I will discuss the role of gender in the Bougainvillean political system. I will explain that women had, and will continue to have, a leading role in the institutional development of Bougainville.

In Bougainville, land titles pass thought matriarchal lines,[126] and hybrid institutions recognise the distinctive role of women as political negotiators.[127] The land economic exploitation will be discussed in the next part of this chapter as it is connected to the development of a fiscally independent Bougainville;[128] however, gender has a role in the management of the institutional crisis and it can be discussed as a standalone driver of change. There are, for instance, three seats reserved for women in the House of Representatives.[129] Each Bougainville village has a Council of Elders, and the members are selected using customary law (e.g. the so-called big man system). The Council is dominated by men, but the Village Assembly is a new institution, and it works as a hybrid liberal and customary institution.[130] There is no division based on political parties, as such parties are perceived as unfit in terms of traditional practices.[131] Gender is, however, considered as one element that helps in forming a political consensus over contentious issues.[132]

---

[124] Wallis, 'The Role of "Uncivil" Society in Transitional Justice' (n 43).
[125] Breda, 'Samoa: Constitutional Governance and Customary Law' (n 42).
[126] Wallis, *Constitution Making During State Building* (n 3) 239.
[127] Bougainville House of Representatives, 'The Constitution of the Autonomous Region of Bougainville 2004' s 28; Wallis, *Constitution Making During State Building* (n 3) 276.
[128] Wallis, *Constitution Making During State Building* (n 3) 239.
[129] Bougainville House of Representatives (n 127) s 55 (b) ii.
[130] Wallis, *Constitution Making During State Building* (n 3) 271.
[131] ibid 325.
[132] ibid.

There is an overlapping element between the role of the clan and the role of gender in Bougainvillean politics.[133] Men tend to have leading roles in political debates, yet women's views can be inserted into local debates indirectly or, in the case of managing property resources, directly, by imposing a veto on policies that negatively impact on their role as custodians of the land.[134] A mining company may find a way to get around this veto, but doing so would be downplaying the function of customary law, which would have, as was previously mentioned, serious consequences. In addition, Bougainvillean women have traditionally been perceived, within the margin of error that is distinctive of any description of a highly diversified society, as the peacemakers and political negotiators within the community.[135] This role assumed regional relevance during the peace process. Women acted as mediators between clans that were engaged in violent feuds.[136]

One of promoters of the peace process described the expected role and the demands of women in a clear narrative: 'We, the women, hold custodial rights of our land by clan inheritance. We insist that women leaders must be party to all stages of the political process in determining the future of Bougainville.'[137] Wallis considers this requirements as an indication of the advanced stage of deliberative democracy.[138] A tangential effect of the customary role of women in Bougainville society appeared during the peace process, when a sizeable number of ANZAC military personnel who monitored the truce (the so-called Truce Monitoring Groups) were women.[139] The presence of female military personnel, combined with the decision not to arm the Truce Monitoring Groups, confirmed the perception among Bougainvilleans of the exclusive peace-making intent of foreign military personnel.[140] This was perhaps a small marketing victory for a military task force sent into a former colony. Whether that was intentional or not is irrelevant to this analysis. It had the effect of making the Truce Monitoring Groups fit in with Bougainvillean cultural perceptions.[141]

---

[133] ibid 271.

[134] ibid 239.

[135] ibid 248; Regan, *Light Intervention* (n 19) 139; Hill and Fletcher (n 72) 4.

[136] Regan, *Light Intervention* (n 19) 139.

[137] Garasu (n 75).

[138] Wallis, 'The Role of "Uncivil" Society in Transitional Justice' (n 43).

[139] Regan, *Light Intervention* (n 19) 69.

[140] Erika J Techera, 'Samoa: Law, Custom and Conservation' (2006) 10 New Zealand Journal of Environmental Law 361; Breda, 'Samoa: Constitutional Governance and Customary Law' (n 42); Breda and Mihailovic (n 85).

[141] Wallis, *Constitution Making During State Building* (n 3) 248.

Bougainville's public institutions are expected to be hybrid.[142] As mentioned earlier, policy and institutional changes are expected to be discussed by all and approved by all.[143] Women, whilst the road to equality in Bougainville might be exceedingly long, had and have a distinctive *quasi*-institutional role.[144] Recall that within village institutions, like the Councils of Elders, there is no distinction between customary law and constitutional law.[145] Evidence of this hybridisation process can be found in several Pacific nations, such as New Zealand, Samoa, Guam, Hawaii and New Caledonia.[146] In these legal systems, like in Bougainville, hybridisation adds a level of complexity that has the tendency to reduce the speed of economic and institutional development.[147] However, in post-conflict societies like Bougainville, customary female participation in institutional development has a positive effect since it allows an open channel of dialogue during times of political impasse.[148] These impasses occur often because unanimity is, as discussed in the previous section, perceived as a requirement for legitimacy.[149]

## A NEUTRAL DRIVER OF CHANGE: THE DEVELOPMENT OF THE EXTRACTIVE SECTOR

In the previous two parts of this chapter, I explained how Bougainville's hybrid institutions have a special constitutional role within the PNG system of governance.[150] Bougainville's legislative and administrative prerogatives were constitutionally entrenched in 2006.[151] The protection of these prerogatives was part of the 2001 peace settlement that formally ended the regional civil

---

[142] United Nations Development Programme (n 45).
[143] Regan, 'Bougainville' (n 4).
[144] Bougainville House of Representatives (n 127) s 55 (b) ii.
[145] ibid.
[146] Techera (n 140); Breda, 'Samoa: Constitutional Governance and Customary Law' (n 42); Breda, *Constitutional Law and Regionalism* (n 43) 150, 170, 178.
[147] United Nations Development Programme (n 45).
[148] Wallis, 'The Role of "Uncivil" Society in Transitional Justice' (n 43).
[149] Regan, 'Resolving Two Dimension of Conflict: The Dynamics of Consent, Consent and Compromise' (n 73); Regan, *Light Intervention* (n 19) 139, 143; Wallis, *Constitution Making During State Building* (n 3) 350.
[150] '"Bougainville Peace Agreement", Arawa, 30 August 2001' (n 64); Wallis, 'The Role of "Uncivil" Society in Transitional Justice' (n 43) 167; Regan, 'Bougainville, Papua New Guinea' (n 7) 47; Garasu and Carl (n 28).
[151] '"Bougainville Peace Agreement", Arawa, 30 August 2001,' (n 64); Wallis, 'The Role of "Uncivil" Society in Transitional Justice' (n 43) 167; Regan, 'Bougainville, Papua New Guinea' (n 7) 47; Garasu and Carl (n 28).

war.[152] I also explained that women have a special status in Bougainville. In this part of the chapter, I will discuss the role of the extractive sector.[153] Mining has a pivotal role in the institutional development of Bougainville, but its contribution to the development of Bougainville's institutions cannot easily be qualified as positive or negative. Historically, mining brings an element of risk to the political stability of small nations,[154] and it normally reduces economic development and might foster corruption.[155] These are a few of the effects of the so-called curse of resources.[156] In Bougainville, the dispute over the control of a gold mine was one of the reasons for the civil war,[157] and it is a source of the lingering tension between the regional and central institutions.[158] As for the rest of this book, it is outside the scope of this chapter to discuss future scenarios and, in the case of the extractive sector, it is very difficult to suggest whether it might be a positive or negative driver of change. There is a possibility that Bougainvillean institutions might escape the 'curse of resources' by adopting exactly the deliberative policies that led the region out of the civil war.

Recall that the past decade has seen a remarkable decentralisation process in Bougainville.[159] The process of constitutional decentralisation normally requires trained negotiators, a sophisticated knowledge of the workings of multi-layered administrative systems to reduce the possibility of future

---

[152] '"Bougainville Peace Agreement", Arawa, 30 August 2001' (n 64); Wallis, 'The Role of "Uncivil" Society in Transitional Justice' (n 43) 167; Regan, 'Bougainville, Papua New Guinea' (n 7) 47; Garasu and Carl (n 28).

[153] Regan, 'Bougainville' (n 4) 404; Regan, *Light Intervention* (n 19); Wallis, *Constitution Making During State Building* (n 3) pt III; Saovana-Spriggs (n 71); Garasu and Carl (n 28); Luke Fletcher, 'Can Panguna Save Bougainville?' in Christina Hill and Luke Fletcher (eds), *Growing Bougainville's Future* (Jubilee Australia Research Centre 2018).

[154] Sachs and Warner (n 99) 837; Buonanno and others (n 56).

[155] Sachs and Warner (n 99).

[156] ibid 837; Buonanno and others (n 56).

[157] Regan, 'Bougainville' (n 4) 404; Regan, *Light Intervention* (n 19); Wallis, *Constitution Making During State Building* (n 3) pt III; Saovana-Spriggs (n 71); Garasu and Carl (n 28); Fletcher (n 153).

[158] Autonomous Bougainville Government, 'ABG Vice President Applauds State Negotiation Team on P'Nyang Project' (n 101); Fletcher (n 153); 'Bougainville's Panguna Copper Mine Looks Closer to Reopening Following 1989 Closure after Deal between Landowners & Autonomous Government' (*International Mining*, 16 February 2022).

[159] Papua New Guinea: Constitution of the Independent State of Papua New Guinea (rev. 2014) s 290; The Organic Law on Peace-building in Bougainville – Autonomous Bougainville Government and Bougainville Referendum 2002.

conflicts, and effective state and regional institutions.[160] It is a complex and hazardous activity for the most advanced constitutional systems like those discussed in this book. It requires a sophisticated knowledge of the effects of decentralisation processes and their pragmatic implications.[161]

By the end of the civil war, Bougainville did not have any fully functional representative institutions based on written rules.[162] Political factions were represented by individuals, who had limited or no experience of political negotiations and limited knowledge of regionalism.[163] What is unique to the Bougainvillean process of decentralisation was the ability to form a large consensus regarding complex policies.[164] Women had a unique role on the deliberative process the prepared the road to peace. The question is whether such an asset might solve conflicts over the distribution of resources in Bougainville.[165]

The archipelago is blessed with higher, by comparison to many other Pacific nations, levels of raw materials and gas, which, in theory, can increase the level of wealth of the population.[166] There are, as elsewhere, environmental and societal costs associated with the establishment of large extractive operations in a community that is divided along ethnic lines.[167] For instance, the Panguna Mine has left a permanent awareness of the disruptive effects of industrial operations in a community where most of the population is unskilled.[168] The debate over the potential re-opening of the Panguna Mine, given the multiple interests that are at stake, is far from over.[169] For instance, in 2015, the PNG Government tried to buy a share of Rio Tinto's stake in the Panguna Mine Project.[170] The Regional Government opposed the transaction because it would give the PNG Government control over Bougainvillean mining resources that

---

[160] Donald Horowitz, 'Some Realism about Constitutional Engineering' in Andreas Wimmer (ed), *Facing Ethnic Conflicts: Toward a New Realism* (Rowman & Littlefield 2004); Breda, *Constitutional Law and Regionalism* (n 43).

[161] Breda, *Constitutional Law and Regionalism* (n 43).

[162] Regan, 'Resolving Two Dimension of Conflict: The Dynamics of Consent, Consent and Compromise' (n 73).

[163] Wallis, *Constitution Making During State Building* (n 3).

[164] Regan, 'Bougainville' (n 4).

[165] ibid.

[166] Hill and Fletcher (n 43) 6; National Statistical Office (n 6); Garasu and Carl (n 28) 8.

[167] National Statistical Office (n 23); Regan, 'Bougainville' (n 4) 362.

[168] Regan, 'Bougainville' (n 4) 357, 366. Hill and Fletcher (n 43); Regan, 'Bougainville' (n 4) 365, 372, 404.

[169] Regan, 'Bougainville' (n 4).

[170] ibid 395; Cathal Doyle, 'Free Prior and Informed Consent, Development and Mining on Bougainville: Choice and the Pursuit of Self-Determined Development' in Christina Hill and Luke Fletcher (eds), *Growing Bougainville's Future* (Jubilee Australia Research Centre 2018).

were explicitly devolved in the 2001 Peace Agreement.[171] In the immediate future, there are no guarantees that local institutions might have the ability to manage tribal expectations over Panguna or other areas. The Council of Elders, which might perceive itself as having exclusive rights over whatever resources might be present on its traditional lands, has to convince its members to partake local mining or oil resources.[172] There are no indications that Bougainville's regional institutions have reached this level of foresight.[173]

In parallel to a debate over the beneficial and hindering effects of the mining sector, there are discussions over the possibility of developing other areas of the economy. The agricultural economy is moving, albeit slowly, from subsistence to exports,[174] with high-quality organic products being sold in Australia and Europe.[175] The idea of a low environmental impact agricultural sector has already been evaluated elsewhere in the Pacific, and Bougainville's land mass makes its agriculture sector one of the larger of the Pacific Islands.[176]

In short, the crucial dilemmas over whether 'to mine or not to mine' or whether 'to drill or not to drill' are historically part of the debate over the legitimacy of Bougainville's autonomous institutions.[177] It is perceived that the mismanagement of the mining sector was the reason for the civil war that fuelled secessionist aspirations.[178] There is also an awareness that the future stability of the autonomous institutions is dependent on the fairness of their mining policies and their ability to deliver public services.[179] As mentioned earlier, the aim of the book is not to project future scenarios. However, given that the development of Bougainville's bid for independence is dependent on the ability to cover, at least partially, the large gap between expenditures and fiscal revenues, the development of the extractive sector will be one of the drivers of change of the future institutional partnership between Bougainville and PNG.

---

[171] Regan, 'Bougainville' (n 4) 396.

[172] ibid 358, 389, 404.

[173] Autonomous Bougainville Government, 'ABG Vice President Applauds State Negotiation Team on P'Nyang Project' (n 101); Regan, 'Bougainville' (n 4) 398; 'Bougainville Copper Limited's Panguna Mine Hits Roadblock from Protesters – ABC News (Australian Broadcasting Corporation)' (17 June 2007).

[174] Hill and Fletcher (n 43).

[175] ibid; Wesley Morgan, 'Growing Island Exports: High Value Crops and the Future of Agriculture in the Pacific' in Christina Hill and Luke Fletcher (eds), *Growing Bougainville's Future* (Jubilee Australia Research Centre 2018).

[176] Techera (n 140).

[177] Hill and Fletcher (n 43) 7.

[178] Regan, 'Bougainville' (n 4).

[179] Séverine Blaise, 'The "Rebalancing" of New Caledonia's Economy' (2017) 52 Journal of Pacific History 194.

However, mining resources do not help the development of political systems.[180] A single event, such as a dispute over who is entitled to what, the allocation of jobs within an extractive operation or a collapse in the price of commodities, might destabilise a small country.[181] The social effect of the curse of resources is not easy to manage.[182] Yet, an institutionally effective extractive sector in a resource thirsty Asia can create the conditions for the development of a highly prosperous society, as has been the case for Australia.[183] The question is whether Bougainvilean hybrid institutions have learned from the debacle of the Panguna Mine.[184] If the answer is positive, the rich extractive sector would be a positive driver of change in the development of regional institutions.

## CONCLUSION

At the time of writing this chapter, the Bougainville Constitutional Planning Commission is preparing the document for the eventual secession of Bougainville.[185] The relationship between Bougainville and PNG is distinctive, yet it shows that a high level of participation might help to reduce the effect of the regional governance crisis.[186] There are still lingering effects of the humanitarian, political and constitutional crises that affected both PNG and Bougainville.[187] In this chapter, I focused on the drivers of change that influenced, and that might continue to develop, the relationship between Bougainville and PNG. The first driver of change considered in the chapter was the role of high-level popular participation and the consensus expected by Bougainvilleans.[188]

Most citizens in liberal democracies tend to be reasonably satisfied with periodic and indirect involvement with the political process.[189] Bougainvillean residents have a tendency to accept the lengthy timelines involved in political

---

[180] Sachs and Warner (n 99).
[181] William H Sewell, 'Historical Events as Transformations of Structures: Inventing Revolution at the Bastille' (1996) 25 Theory and Society 841.
[182] Sachs and Warner (n 99).
[183] Sewell (n 181); Sachs and Warner (n 99) 833.
[184] Fletcher (n 153).
[185] Autonomous Bougainville Government (n 2).
[186] Wallis, *Constitution Making During State Building* (n 3); Regan, *Light Intervention* (n 19).
[187] Regan, *Light Intervention* (n 19).
[188] Garasu and Carl (n 28); Wallis, *Constitution Making During State Building* (n 3) 277.
[189] Macklem (n 111); Gerald F Gaus, 'Reason, Justification, and Consensus: Why Democracy Can't Have It All' in James Bohman and William Rehg (eds), *Deliberative*

engagement because customs impose a higher level of participation in the decision-making process. Laws are perceived as legitimate only if they were a manifestation of popular consensus.[190] Similar expectations are found in other Pacific nations.[191]

The demands for policies to be anchored to a widespread consensus are indications of a distinctive hybrid pollical culture.[192] Deliberation and consensus were, for instance, distinctive elements of the peace process and of the constitutional reforms that followed.[193] There are also strong indications that participation and consensus will continue to affect the constitutional future of the partnership between Bougainville and PNG. This will be the case, independently from the result of the current negotiations over independence.[194]

The second driver of change discussed the effect of the hybridisation of customary law with liberal institutions, which, among many other effects, recognised the distinctive contribution of women to Bougainville's public life.[195] It is a combination of traditional practices and a demand for equality that allows women to be one of the drivers of change of the future constitutional assets of Bougainville.[196]

The last driver of change considered in this chapter is the relationship between institutional development and the extractive sector.[197] The curse of resources is a sociological fact, and the history of Bougainville is one of the many cases that confirms the negative impact of extractive wealth.[198] The process that finds the right balance between developing fiscally responsible institutions and the environmental impact of large-scale extractive operations is likely to affect the constitutional structure of both PNG and Bougainville.[199]

---

*Democracy: Essays on Reason and Politics* (MIT 1997); Diao and others (n 8); 'Papua New Guinea COVID-19 Response' (n 9).

[190] Garasu and Carl (n 28).

[191] Elise Huffer and Asofou So'o, 'Consensus versus Dissent: Democracy, Pluralism and Governance in Sāmoa' (2003) 44 Asia Pacific Viewpoint 281; Iati Iati, 'The Good Governance Agenda for Civil Society: Implications for the Fa'a Samoa' in Elise Huffer and Asofou So'o (eds), *Governance in Samoa pulega i Samoa* (Asia Pacific Press 2000).

[192] Thomas D Grant, 'Aid as an Instrument for Peace; a Civil Society Perspective' (2015) 109 The American Journal of International Law 68, 85.

[193] Garasu and Carl (n 28).

[194] Autonomous Bougainville Government (n 2).

[195] Joanne Wallis, *Hybridity on the Ground in in Peacebuilding and Development: Critical Conversations* (ANU Press 2018).

[196] Saovana-Spriggs (n 71).

[197] United Nations Development Programme (n 45); Regan, 'Bougainville' (n 4); Doyle (n 170).

[198] Sachs and Warner (n 99).

[199] Hill and Fletcher (n 43); Fletcher (n 153).

However, it is difficult to qualify the role that regional institutional development might have in relation to the extractive sector. A single event might tilt the current balance of power within the region and trigger another civil war, or it might foster the development of a prosperous, independent and less patrimonial Bougainville.[200]

---

[200] Fletcher (n 153); 'Bougainville's Panguna Copper Mine Looks Closer to Reopening Following 1989 Closure after Deal between Landowners & Autonomous Government' (n 158).

# Conclusion to *Constitutional Crises and Regionalism*

A regional constitutional crisis is sparked in a multinational society when a significant portion of its residents no longer think that central legal institutions should govern them.[1] Social factors may support this perception, but in every case examined in this book, constitutional rules have had a key positive or negative influence on each regional crisis.

At the beginning of the book, I quoted Horowitz. He notes, with a level of candour that often escapes comparative public lawyers, how '[m]ost divided societies have crafted no institutions at all to attend to their ethnic problems [and] some have crafted counterproductive provisions'.[2] For instance, during the Bougainville crisis (Chapter 8), these ill-devised rules contributed to the escalation of the crisis to the point where secession is currently unavoidable.[3] However, the majority of situations considered in this book reported on inadequate constitutional arrangements, such as those in Northern Ireland (Chapter

---

[1] The Northern Ireland Act 1998 c 47; Constitutional Law n. 2 26.02.1948; Ley Orgánica 3/1979, de 18 de diciembre, de Estatuto de Autonomía para el País Vasco. 1979; The Constitution Act 1982; U.S. Const. art 1 § 8 cl.3; Basic Law of the Hong Kong Special Administrative Region of the People's Republic of China OCW CD 825 (HK) 1997; Loi constitutionnelle no 98-610 du 20 juillet 1998 relative à la Nouvelle-Calédonie; The Australian Constitution art 51 (xxvi); The Organic Law on Peace-building in Bougainville – Autonomous Bougainville Government and Bougainville Referendum 2002.

[2] Donald Horowitz, 'Some Realism about Constitutional Engineering' in Andreas Wimmer (ed), *Facing Ethnic Conflicts: Toward a New Realism* (Rowman & Littlefield 2004) 252.

[3] Constitution of the Independent State of Papua New Guinea – National Parliament of Papua New Guinea 1975 (consolidated version) 1975 s 336 (c); Anthony Regan, *Light Intervention: Lessons from Bougainville* (United States Institute of Peace Press 2010) 170.

1),[4] the Basque Country (Chapter 2),[5] Northern Territory (Chapter 7),[6] as well as partially ineffective institutions, such as those in Sicily (Chapter 3)[7] and Hong Kong (Chapter 5).[8] Except for the Quebec October Crisis analysis (Chapter 4),[9] all instances in this book are examples of active crises.[10] Quebec might also be the only case in this book in which a regional community is not currently experiencing the effects of transgenerational trauma.[11]

Transgenerational trauma, like individual trauma, does not disappear overnight.[12] The Basque Country, Northern Ireland's sectarian communities, Alaskan Natives and Aboriginal Peoples and Torres Strait Islanders have, for centuries, been at the receiving end of policies that could be equated to an attempt at cultural and physical genocide.[13] These communities cannot

---

[4] Henry Jarrett, 'Northern Ireland A Place Apart?' in Brian CH Fong and Atsuko Ichijo (eds), *The Routledge Handbook of Comparative Territorial Autonomies* (Taylor & Francis Group 2022).

[5] Ley 12/1981, de 13 de mayo por la que se aprueba el Concierto Economico con la Comunidad Autónoma del Pais Vasco 1981; Rogelio Alonso, 'Why Do Terrorists Stop? Analyzing Why ETA Members Abandon or Continue with Terrorism' (2011) 34 Studies in Conflict & Terrorism 696.

[6] Jon Altman and Susie Russell, 'Too Much "Dreaming": Evaluations of the Northern Territory National Emergency Response Intervention 2007–2012' (2012) Evidence Base: A Journal of Evidence Reviews in Key Policy Areas 1.

[7] Daron Acemoglu, Giuseppe De Feo and Giacomo Davide De Luca, 'Weak States: Causes and Consequences of the Sicilian Mafia' (2020) 87 The Review of Economic Studies 537.

[8] Cora Chan, 'The Legal Limits on Beijing's Powers to Interpret Hong Kong's Basic Law' (*HKU Legal Scholarship Blog*, 3 November 2016).

[9] The Constitution Act, 1867, 30 & 31 Vict, c 3 (renamed from the British North America Act 1867 by the Constitution Act 1982 s.53 (2) s 51; Alain Gagnon, 'Empowerment through Different Means Nationalism and Federalism in the Canadian Context' in Alain-G Gagson and José María Sauca (eds), *Negotiating Diversity: Identity, Pluralism, and Democracy* (PIE Peter Lang 2014) 42; 'HC (Can) 27 November 2006 Vol 141, 39'.

[10] The Constitution Act 1982.

[11] Lisa Wexler, 'Looking across Three Generations of Alaska Natives to Explore How Culture Fosters Indigenous Resilience' (2014) 51 Transcultural Psychiatry 73; Michael Dudley, 'Contradictory Australian National Policies on Self-Harm and Suicide: The Case of Asylum Seekers in Mandatory Detention' (2003) 11 Australasian Psychiatry S102.

[12] F Hogman, 'Trauma and Identity through Two Generations of the Holocaust' (1998) 85 Psychoanalytic Review 551.

[13] Jesús Casquete, 'Commemorative Calendar and Reproduction of Radical Basque Nationalism' (2013) 14 Politics, Religion & Ideology 21; Duncan Morrow, *Sectarianism – A Review* (Ulster University 2019); Teresa Evans-Campbell, 'Historical Trauma in American Indian/Native Alaska Communities: A Multilevel Framework for Exploring Impacts on Individuals, Families, and Communities' (2008) 23 Journal of Interpersonal Violence 316; Altman and Russell (n 6).

and, more importantly, do not want to forget their pasts.[14] The transgenerational memory of trauma is periodically revisited in all these historically discriminated-against groups during the celebration of their martyrs. The book described how depictions of slain ETA members at a local festival and of Ulster Volunteers on suburban walls in East Belfast have the same identity-making purpose as the Tomb of the Unknown Soldier in Arlington, the London Cenotaph, the Altar of the Fatherland in Rome and the ANZAC Monument in Sydney's Hyde Park.[15]

Who merits our 'lest we forget'? To which king should we pledge our allegiance, and under what banner should we do so? Despite being short of presenting a coherent theory of regionalism, the cases included in this book demonstrate that multinational states are composed of dynamic social groups. If the constitutions of these countries were to be considered legitimate by all social communities that comprise contemporary societies, territorial systems of governance must allow for such dynamism.[16] Sociological analyses have repeatedly confirmed that sub-state nationalism is one of the many drivers of change in modern constitutional systems.[17]

It was argued that, in a situation where multiple national identities make up a constituency, a constitution could not be assumed to be ethnically neutral.[18]

---

[14] William A Douglass, *Basque Politics and Nationalism on the Eve of the Milennium* (University of Nevada Press 1999).

[15] Benedict Anderson, *Imagined Communities: Reflections on the Origin and Spread of Nationalism* (Verso 1983).

[16] Jarrett (n 4); Ludger Mees, 'Ethnogenesis in the Pyrenees: The Contentious Making of a National Identity in the Basque Country (1643–2017)' (2018) 48 European History Quarterly 462; Theodoros Rakopoulos, 'Divided by Land: Mafia and Anti-Mafia Proximity', *From Clans to Co-ops*, vol 4 (Berghahn Books 2018); Geneviève Zubrzycki, *Beheading the Saint: Nationalism, Religion, and Secularism in Quebec* (University of Chicago Press 2016); Daniel M Cobb, *Say We Are Nations: Documents of Politics and Protest in Indigenous America Since 1887* (University of North Carolina Press 2015); David Chappell, 'Decolonisation and Nation-Building in New Caledonia: Reflections on the 2014 Elections' (2015) 67 Political Science 56; Daphne Habibis, Penny Skye Taylor and Bruna S Ragaini, 'White People Have No Face: Aboriginal Perspectives on White Culture and the Costs of Neoliberalism' (2020) 43 Ethnic and Racial Studies 1149; Anthony J Regan, 'Bougainville: Origins of the Conflict, and Debating the Future of Large-Scale Mining' in Colin Filer and Pierre-Yves Le Meur (eds), *Large-scale Mines and Local-level Politics: Between New Caledonia and Papua New Guinea* (ANU Press 2017).

[17] Liah Greenfeld (ed), *Advanced Introduction to Nationalism* (Edward Elgar Publishing 2016); Liah Greenfeld and Zeying Wu (eds), *Research Handbook on Nationalism* (Edward Elgar Publishing 2020).

[18] Michael Keating, 'So Many Nations, So Few States: Territory and Nationalism in the Global Era' in James Tully and Alain-G Gagnon (eds), *Multinational Democracies* (CUP 2001).

A constitution is, among other elements, a manifestation of its constituency's aspirations.[19] Put another way; a constitution should express the ideal type of society that individuals aspire to belong. That is, among other elements, a society that cares for its diversity. Sociological studies across the globe have reported, with unusual consistency, that the current ethnic revival and populism may be linked to the collapse of other hegemonic meaning providers.[20] That is, socialism as a proxy for a communitarian society,[21] and liberalism as a prosaic device for individual self-realisation.[22] Whether these ideologies are collapsing or there is a farrago of reasons for populism around the globe is largely irrelevant for constitutional lawyers concerned with the effects of regional governance crises. The awareness that the constitution cannot be regarded as ethnically neutral is sufficient to establish constitutional institutions that accommodate, as needed, negotiations over language, symbols and resources.[23] Moreover, these institutions should adroitly stimulate cross-national identity collaboration, acknowledge regional and state majorities as having the same normative significance and have processes that safeguard human dignity.[24] There are more elements but this triangle, let us call it the righteous triangle, formed by the connections between these three elements (cross-group cooperation, respect for the majority will by the minority and human dignity), has

---

[19] Michel Rosenfeld and Andras Sajo, 'Constitutional Identity' in Michele Rosenfeld and Andras Sajo (eds), *The Oxford Handbook of Comparative Constitutional Law* (Oxford University Press, USA 2012).

[20] Anderson (n 15); Anthony D Smith, 'The Origins of Nations' in John Hutchinson and Anthony D Smith (eds), *Nationalism* (Oxford University Press 1994); Ernest Gellner, *Nationalism* (Phoenix 1998); Greenfeld (n 17); Vicki A Spencer, '"Communitarianism" and Patriotism' in Mitja Sardoc (ed), *Handbook of Patriotism* (Springer Cham 2018); Daniel Druckman, 'Nationalism, Patriotism, and Group Loyalty: A Social Psychological Perspective' (1994) 38 Mershon International Studies Review 43.

[21] Paul Gomberg, 'Against Patriotism, for Internationalism: A Marxist Critique of Patriotism' in Mitja Sardoc (ed), *Handbook of Patriotism* (Springer Cham 2018).

[22] Zygmunt Bauman, 'Identity in the Globalising World' (2001) 9 Social Anthropology 121; Zygmunt Bauman, *In Search of Politics* (Polity Press 1999).

[23] Jonathan Hearn and others, 'Debate on Bernard Yack's Book Nationalism and the Moral Psychology of Community' (2014) 20 Nations and Nationalism 395, 412.

[24] Horowitz (n 2); Giacomo Delledonne and Giuseppe Martinico (eds), *The Canadian Contribution to a Comparative Law of Secession: Legacies of the Quebec Secession Reference* (Springer International Publishing 2019); Vito Breda and Matteo Frau, 'Balancing Competing Dignity Claims: Insights from the United Kingdom and Italy' in Barry Bussey and Angus Menuge (eds), *The Inherence of Human Dignity: Foundations of Human Dignity, Volume 2* (Anthem Press 2021).

a compounding effect on societal perceptions of the legitimacy of a constitutional system.[25]

A constitution is one of the essential elements, among other factors, for the development of a modern society. It is, however, reasonably clear that externally imposed constitutional values might not create a halo of legitimacy around constitutional norms. In Hong Kong, there is little support for Chinese constitutionalism, which assumes 'the supremacy of the Chinese Communist Party's business, the supremacy of the people's interests, and the supremacy of constitutional law'.[26] The hierarchical structure of the three values provides a legal basis for the dictatorship of the Standing Committee over China, including the Hong Kong Special Administrative Region.[27] In contrast to a substantial part of the population of Hong Kong, the Standing Committee of the Chinese Communist Party perceives Hong Kong's liberal enclave (in which unruly demonstrators are flagrantly protected by a set of norms created by an elite for an elite) as a local nuisance that is potentially hindering the common good of Chinese people. This perception reinforces, rather than reduces, support in China for a new gamut of authoritarian policies in Hong Kong.[28]

Regionalism, at least the version defended in this book, does not reduce constitutionalism to political pragmatism.[29] The cases presented in this book provide a substantial critique of using expedients or a Panglossian legalistic manipulation of meanings.[30] For instance, it was argued that insisting that the

---

[25] Alain-G Gagnon and James Tully (eds), *Multinational Democracies* (Cambridge University Press 2001).

[26] Jaakko Husa, '"Accurately, Completely, and Solemnly": One Country, Two Systems and an Uneven Constitutional Equilibrium' (2017) 5 The Chinese Journal of Comparative Law 231, 236.

[27] 'Joint Declaration on the Question of Hong Kong (Adopted 19 December 1984, Entered into Force 12 June 1985) 1399 UNTS 33 1985'.

[28] Husa (n 26); Kerry Brown, 'China's Ruling Creed at 100: The Party Never Stops' (*Engelsberg Ideas*, 1 July 2021) 1; Kerry Brown, *Contemporary China* (Macmillan International Higher Education 2019).

[29] Horowitz (n 2).

[30] Daniel Wincott, Gregory Davies and Alan Wager, 'Crisis, What Crisis? Conceptualizing Crisis, UK Pluri-Constitutionalism and Brexit Politics' (2021) 55 Regional Studies 1528; Stuart A Durkin, 'Advancing Peace Culture in the Basque Autonomous Community: The Basque Education Plan for Peace and Human Rights (2008–2011)' (2013) 13 Studies in Ethnicity and Nationalism 342; Acemoglu, De Feo and De Luca (n 7); Dominique Clément, 'The October Crisis of 1970: Human Rights Abuses Under the War Measures Act' (2008) 42 Journal of Canadian Studies 160; Jaakko Husa, 'Constitutional Biography of Hong Kong and Ambiguities of One Country, Two Systems Policy' (2021) 9 The Chinese Journal of Comparative Law 268; Vito Breda and Andreja Mihailovic, 'New Caledonia: The Archipelago That Does Not Want to Be Freed' (2019) 24 Comparative Law Journal of the Pacific 69; Altman

concept of the Spanish nation is a unifying force for all nationalities residing on the Iberian Peninsula because the Constitution of 1978 says so[31] is both normatively incoherent and pragmatically counterproductive.[32] In the long term, the constitution cannot prevent social change, like a deranged King Canute who seeks to stop the waves from crashing on the shores of England.[33] Nor should it be used as a cudgel to enforce a sanctimonious perception of legitimacy that abases people's beliefs. Imposing, rather than retrieving, democratic legitimacy at the regional level often brings about the paroxysm of anger and disillusionment.

It is axiological that the constitution impacts its associated social system. In most instances, the effects are positive. One of the premises of this book is that a constitution, depending on the circumstances, might also influence the development of a crisis of legitimacy. Indeed, some of the situations reported in this monograph were resolved either because the crises themselves reinforced the existence of common constitutional values, as was the case during the Quebec October Crisis,[34] or because both central and regional institutions commonly agreed to go their separate ways, as was the case with the ongoing secession plan of Bougainville.[35] These experiences reveal a direct relationship between the ability of a constitution to regulate a diversified community and the capacity of its institutions to manage a crisis. For instance, a constitution enumerates, expressly or implicitly, the parameters within which different political groups at the central and regional levels can negotiate their understanding of what constitutes the common good with equanimity.[36] This is an ideal situation where the reference to an unidentified 'we' becomes a receptacle for the trope 'we the people'. The connection between such a trope and the constitution allows for the funnelling of the idiosyncratic ideals of millions of individuals – who have almost nothing in common with one another – into a single endeavour that we call the nation-state.[37]

However, this book also shows that a minimal level of administrative efficiency is necessary for establishing the process of self-identification between

---

and Russell (n 6); Anthony Regan, 'Bougainville, Papua New Guinea: Lessons from a Successful Peace Process' (2018) 163 The RUSI Journal 44.

[31] Hèctor López Bofill, 'Hubris, Constitutionalism, and "the Indissoluble Unity of the Spanish Nation": The Repression of Catalan Secessionist Referenda in Spanish Constitutional Law' (2019) 17 International Journal of Constitutional Law 943.

[32] Horowitz (n 2).

[33] It should be noted that King Canute was attempting to reprimand the syncopates.

[34] Garth Stevenson, *Parallel Paths: The Development of Nationalism in Ireland and Quebec* (McGill-Queen's University Press 2006) 274.

[35] Regan, 'Bougainville, Papua New Guinea' (n 30).

[36] Rosenfeld and Sajo (n 19).

[37] Jan-Werner Müller, *Constitutional Patriotism* (Princeton University Press 2007).

people and their constitutional systems.[38] Kelsen's evaluation of the connection between normativity and efficacy is just as applicable today as in 1947. He stated that a legal order is valid only if the behaviours to which this order refers are, by and large, in conformity with the legal order: 'This conformity ... is termed effectiveness, then effectiveness is a condition of the validity of the law.'[39] This also applies to multinational states. To have a multinational constitutional system that is representative of a highly diversified constituency, regional and state institutions need to be effective within the parameters of what can be considered reasonable. More importantly, modern constitutional institutions need to be seen as having the capacity to be effective.[40] Losing the perception of effectiveness curtails most, if not all, debates over legitimacy and the rule of law.

Institutional ineffectiveness is one of the *malae radices* of the crises in Northern Ireland and Sicily. Using the examples of Northern Ireland and Sicily, it was argued that some constitutional crises are directly tied to inefficient territorial governance.[41] In Northern Ireland, for instance, the Belfast Agreement brought the informal end to an unrecognised civil war and established the institutions of a regional consociative democracy.[42] Unfortunately, the system is not sophisticated enough to foster robust cross-community collaboration.[43] Similar arrangements can be found in the Noumea Accord, which set up the consociative government of New Caledonia (Chapter 6).[44]

---

[38] Arcangelo Dimico, Alessia Isopi and Ola Olsson, 'Origins of the Sicilian Mafia: The Market for Lemons' (2017) 77 The Journal of Economic History 1083; Wincott, Davies and Wager (n 30).

[39] Hans Kelsen, 'Law, State and Justice in the Pure Theory of Law' (1947) 57 Yale Law Journal 377, 378. See also David Haljan, *Constitutionalising Secession* (Hart Publishing 2014) 2.

[40] Anthony Spencer and Stephen Croucher, 'Basque Nationalism and the Spiral of Silence: An Analysis of Public Perceptions of ETA in Spain and France' (2008) 70 International Communication Gazette 137; Sebastian Veg, 'The Rise of "Localism" and Civic Identity in Post-Handover Hong Kong: Questioning the Chinese Nation-State' (2017) 230 The China Quarterly (London) 323; Louise I Shelley, 'Mafia and the Italian State: The Historical Roots of the Current Crisis' (1994) 9 Sociological Forum 661.

[41] Mary C Murphy and Jonathan Evershed, 'Contesting Sovereignty and Borders: Northern Ireland, Devolution and the Union' (2021) 10(5) Territory, Politics, Governance 661, 664; Jane Schneider and Peter Schneider, 'Mafia, Antimafia, and the Plural Cultures of Sicily' (2005) 46 Current Anthropology 501.

[42] Vito Breda and Erin Wolfe O'Rourke, 'Northern Ireland and South Tyrol: Constitutional Boundaries in Consociational Democracies' in Vito Breda and Matteo Frau (eds), *La contrattazione costituzionale dei livelli di autonomia: modelli per una comparazione* (Editoriale Scientifica 2020).

[43] The Northern Ireland (St Andrews Agreement) Act 2006 c 53 s 4.

[44] Constitution du 4 octobre 1958 (version consolidée) 1958; Noumea Accord 1998 (2002) 7(1) Australian Indigenous Law Reporter 88; Loi n°56-619 du 23 1956 juin

*Conclusion* 227

Regrettably, in Northern Ireland, the leadership of the sectarian communities that control large sections of Belfast has very little to gain from having an effective regional government that might curb the criminal activities of its associates.[45] Instead, sectarian leaders are interested in moving from one crisis of regional administration to another.[46] The instability of the system of governance is 'used' as support to demand more resources from the Central State. Since the Belfast Agreement in 1998, Northern Ireland has had the St Andrews Agreement of 2006, the Hillsborough Castle Agreement of 2010, the Stormont House Agreement of 2014 and the Fresh Start Agreement of 2015, 2020 New Decade, New Approach Agreement, in addition to the most recent Windsor Framework: A New Way Forward. None of these agreements has successfully established effective regional governance nor reduced the ongoing sectarian violence.[47]

It was explained that Brexit is an additional driver of change, contributing to rising civil unrest and sectarian violence. It was argued that Northern Irish institutions rely on money from the European Union and the UK Government, yet this aid reduces the incentive for sectarian groups to devise mediation strategies.[48] In other words, the flow of assistance to Northern Ireland constitutes an effort to find a solution to a problem that is exacerbated by the flow of resources.

Institutions are perhaps even less effective in Sicily (Chapter 3), where Mafia families dominate substantial portions of the territory.[49] In exchange for public procurement contracts and employment opportunities for Mafia associ-

---

mesures propres a assurer l'evolution des territoires relevant du Ministere de la France d'outre-mer 1956 (56-619); Loi n° 88-1028 du 9 novembre 1988 portant dispositions statutaires et préparatoires à l'autodétermination de la Nouvelle-Calédonie en 1998; Loi n° 99-209 organique du 19 mars 1999 relative à la Nouvelle-Calédonie (consolidée au 07 janvier 2019); Loi organique n° 2015-987 du 5 août 2015 relative à la consultation sur l'accession de la Nouvelle-Calédonie à la pleine souveraineté.

[45] Wincott, Davies and Wager (n 30).
[46] ibid.
[47] Murphy and Evershed (n 41); Wincott, Davies and Wager (n 30); Northern Ireland Statistics and Research Agency, 'Police Recorded Security Situation Statistics 1 December 2020 to 30 November 2021' (PSNI Statistics Branch 2021).
[48] European Union – European Regional Development Fund, 'A Review of PEACE III and Considerations for PEACE IV'; Northern Ireland Assembly, Department for Public Leadership and Social Enterprise, 'Briefing Note: The Consequences for the Northern Ireland Economy from a United Kingdom Exit from the European Union'.
[49] Direzione Nazionale Antimafia e Antiterrorismo Antimafia, 'Relazione Annuale Sulle Attività Svolte Dal Procuratore Nazionale Antimafia e Dalla Direzione Nazionale Antimafia Nonché Sulle Dinamiche e Strategie Della Criminalità Organizzata Di Tipo Mafioso Nel Periodo 1° Luglio 2018 – 31 Dicembre 2019' (Ministero dell'Interno 2020).

ates, corrupt politicians demand bribes and votes. This relationship is referred to as the 'golden triangle', in which the three sides of the trigon are composed of Mafia bosses, politicians and public officials.[50] All three sides of the trigon are busy feasting on the public purse. Unlike in Northern Ireland, Mafia bosses do not try to cover up their greed and narcissism with an ideological veneer. Bosses harvest their fiefdoms. They openly exploit, for their financial benefit, the corruption of Italian institutions and the lack of development of the population in southern Italy.

The Mafia is akin to a hemiparasitic plant. Families with ties to the Mafia are interested in ensuring a steady flow of resources from the Central State to Sicily, which guarantees employment for their associates and lucrative public contracts.[51] An extraordinary number of Italian inhabitants (2.4 million) officially reside in municipalities where police have found evidence that Mafia families control the majority of local political representatives.[52] There are probably more cases, but in these city councils, after a magistrate has deemed them to be owned by the Mafia, they are put under a forced central administration. That often proves a profitless and transient success for the Italian State. One or more representatives of the Central State, who may be corrupt or inept (quite possibly both), take over the day-to-day management of these Mafia-infiltrated city councils.[53] In the elections that follow the disbandment of Mafia-controlled city councils, residents of the city councils under administration often prefer to have Mafia-affiliated politicians re-elected.[54] They do that with cognition. There is a perception that Mafia syndicates are, by comparison to the kleptocracy of inept public servants and corrupt politicians, dependable and accountable security providers for all transactions.[55]

Sicily and – to a lesser extent – Northern Ireland are experiencing the effects of a circular institutional crisis in which institutions struggle to guarantee constitutional rights and liberties because criminal syndicates control the market

---

[50] European Commission, Directorate-General for Justice, Freedom and Security. and Center for the Study of Democracy, *Examining the Links between Organised Crime and Corruption* (CSD 2011).

[51] Shelley (n 40).

[52] Direzione Investigativa Antimafia, 'Semester Report 2019 Semester II'.

[53] John D'Attona, 'Explaining Italian Tax Compliance. A Historical Analysis' in Sven Steinmo (ed), *The Leap of Faith: The Fiscal Foundations of Successful Government in Europe and America* (Oxford University Press 2018) 108.

[54] Diego Gambetta, *The Sicilian Mafia: The Business of Private Protection* (Harvard University Press 1996) 65, 68, 79.

[55] Antonella Coco, 'Neopatrimonialism and Local Elite Attitudes. Similarities and Differences Across Italian Regions' (2015) 3 Territory, Politics, Governance 167, 20. The World Bank Group and The European Commission, 'Doing Business in the European Union 2020: Greece, Ireland and Italy'.

for violence. One of the many general lessons of these governance crises is that a patrimonial system of governance cannot be displaced through the allocation of resources. That, it was argued, is a solution that is part of the problem.

Based on the various cases presented here, it is possible to venture a few generalisations about which drivers were more significant in regional crises; however, these generalisations fall short of providing a genuine predictive theory. On a broader level, this book explained instead how greed, ideological stubbornness, legalist lucubrations, ethnic nationalism and self-centred sociopathic leadership (within or outside a regional community, as was the case of the invasion of Donbas and Crimea) might serve as a dais for a crisis of governance. The examples also show that once things have fallen apart, it can take a long time to regain a sense of attachment to a constitution and its values.

This sense of attachment might, however, be re-established if a few conditions are met. First, a constitution must have deliberative and administrative institutions that stimulate cross-national identity collaboration. Second, there is an explicit constitutional acknowledgement that regional and state majorities have the same normative significance. Third, there is a process that safeguards human dignity. In conclusion, it was argued that democratic and constitutionally entrenched institutions must find a complex balance between the requirement of coherence in a modern deliberative system and the practical needs of a multinational society. There is no simple mechanism for maintaining such an equilibrium, but comparative investigations, such as those provided in this book, should at least lessen the probability that analogous mistakes will be repeated.

# References

## INTERNATIONAL TREATIES

Consolidated Version of the Treaty on European Union [2008] OJ C115/13
Joint Declaration on the Question of Hong Kong 1399 UNTS 33 198 Signed 19/12/1984, ratified 25/5/1985
King of Great Britain and King of France, 'The Definitive Treaty of Peace and Friendship between His Britannick Majesty, the Most Christian King, and the King of Spain (The Treaty of Paris)' 1763 ESTC T32300 Signed 10/2/1763
Treaty between Great Britain and Ireland 626 LNTS 6, 9–19 Signed 6 December 1921, ratified 31/3/1922
U.S. Congress and Majesty the Emperor of all the Russias, 'Treaty Concerning the Cession of the Russian Possessions in North America by His Majesty the Emperor of All the Russias to the United States of America Treaty of Cession, 15 Stat. 539' Signed 20/3/1867, ratified 28/5/1867

## BIBLIOGRAPHY

Acemoglu D, De Feo G and De Luca GD, 'Weak States: Causes and Consequences of the Sicilian Mafia' (2020) 87 The Review of Economic Studies 537
Adams M, Husa J and Oderkerk M (eds), *Comparative Law Methodology* (Edward Elgar Publishing 2017)
Agranoff R and Glover M, 'Introduction: Forecasting Constitutional Futures' in Robert Hazell (ed), *Constitutional Futures Revisited: Britain's Constitution to 2020* (Palgrave Macmillan 2008)
Ahu Sandal N, 'Religious Actors as Epistemic Communities in Conflict Transformation: The Cases of South Africa and Northern Ireland' (2011) 37 Review of International Studies 929
Ainsworth F, 'The Social and Economic Origins of Child Abuse and Neglect' (2020) 45 Children Australia 202
Albert R, 'The Structure of Constitutional Amendment Rules' (2014) 49 Wake Forest Law Review 913
Alonso R, 'Pathways Out of Terrorism in Northern Ireland and the Basque Country: The Misrepresentation of the Irish Model' (2004) 16 Terrorism and Political Violence 695
Alonso R, 'Why Do Terrorists Stop? Analyzing Why ETA Members Abandon or Continue with Terrorism' (2011) 34 Studies in Conflict & Terrorism 696
Altman R and Russell S, 'Too Much "Dreaming": Evaluations of the Northern Territory National Emergency Response Intervention 2007–2012' (2012) Evidence Base: A Journal of Evidence Reviews in Key Policy Areas 1

Anderson B, *Imagined Communities: Reflections on the Origin and Spread of Nationalism* (Verso 1983)

Angeli A, Grazzini L, Lattarulo P, Macchi M, Petretto A and Irpet U, 'Differenze territoriali e autonomie regionali: come migliorare l'offerta di servizi nel paese?' XXXIX Conferenza scientifica annuale AISRe, Bolzano, 17 September 2018

Antonini L, *Federalismo all'italiana: Dietro le quinte della grande incompiuta. Quello che ogni cittadino dovrebbe sapere* (Marsilio Editori 2013)

Aparicio Rodríguez V, 'The Basque Country', *The Routledge Handbook of Comparative Territorial Autonomies* (Routledge 2022)

Arachi G and Santoro A, 'Tax Enforcement for SMEs: Lessons from the Italian Experience' (2007) 5 eJournal of Tax Research 225

Arel D, 'Political Stability in Multinational Democracies' in Alain Gagnon and James Tully (eds), *Multinational Democracies* (Cambridge University Press 2001)

Arnett J, *Between Empires and Frontiers: Alaska Native Sovereignty and U.S. Settler Imperialism* (ProQuest Dissertations Publishing 2018)

Arnett JL, 'Unsettled Rights in Territorial Alaska: Native Land, Sovereignty, and Citizenship from the Indian Reorganization Act to Termination' (2017) 48 Western Historical Quarterly 233

Aroney N and Allan J, 'An Uncommon Court: How the High Court of Australia Has Undermined Australian Federalism' (2008) 30 Sydney Law Review 245

Attwood B, *Telling the Truth About Aboriginal History* (Allen & Unwin 2005)

Ayius A and May RJ, *Corruption in Papua New Guinea: Towards an Understanding of Issues* (National Research Institute 2007)

Azuelos-Atias S, 'Semantically Cued Contextual Implicatures in Legal Texts' (2010) 42 Journal of Pragmatics 728

Babcock HM, 'A Civic-Republican Vision of Domestic Dependent Nations in the Twenty-First Century: Tribal Sovereignty Re-Envisioned, Reinvigorated, and Re-Empowered' (2005) 2005 Utah Law Review 443

Bach DC, 'Patrimonialism and Neopatrimonialism: Comparative Trajectories and Readings' (2011) 49 Commonwealth & Comparative Politics 275

Baker K and Oppermann T, 'The Bougainville Referendum: Lessons for the Future' Department of Pacific Affairs in Brief Series: 2020/16 2

Balasko Y, 'Economic Equilibrium and Catastrophe Theory: An Introduction' (1978) 46 Econometrica 557

Balfour S and Quiroga A, *The Reinvention of Spain: Nation and Identity since Democracy* (Oxford University Press 2007)

Barak A, *Proportionality: Constitutional Rights and Their Limitations* (Cambridge University Press 2012)

Barbera A and Fusaro C, *Corso di diritto pubblico. Nuova ediz.* (11th edn, Il Mulino 2020)

Bartl M, 'The Way We Do Europe: Subsidiarity and the Substantive Democratic Deficit' (2015) 21 European Law Journal 23

Basta K, 'The State between Minority and Majority Nationalism: Decentralization, Symbolic Recognition, and Secessionist Crises in Spain and Canada' (2018) 48 Publius: The Journal of Federalism 51

Bauman Z, 'Right or Wrong – My Country?' (1997) 39 Argument 327

Bauman Z, 'Identity: Then, Now, What For?' (1998) 123 Polish Sociological Review 205

Bauman Z, *In Search of Politics* (Polity Press 1999)

Bauman Z, *Community: Seeking Safety in an Insecure* World (Polity Press 2001)

Bauman Z, 'Identity in the Globalising World' (2001) 9 Social Anthropology 121

Beech M, 'Brexit and the Decentred State' (2022) 37(1) Public Policy and Administration 67

Behiels MD, *Prelude to Quebec's Quiet Revolution: Liberalism versus Neo-Nationalism, 1945–1960* (McGill-Queen's University Press – MQUP 1985)

Bel G, *Disdain, Distrust and Dissolution: The Surge of Support for Independence in Catalonia* (Sussex Academic Press 2015)

Bell DA, *The Cult of the Nation in France: Inventing Nationalism, 1680–1800* (Harvard University Press 2001)

Bencivengo Y, 'Naissance de l'industrie du nickel en Nouvelle-Calédonie et au-delà, à l'interface des trajectoires industrielles, impériales et coloniales (1875–1914)' (2014) Journal de la Société des Océanistes 137

Berman A, 'Future Kanak Independence in New Caledonia: Reality or Illusion?' (1998) 34 Stanford Journal of International Law 287

Biagini EF (ed), 'Home Rule as a "Crisis of Public Conscience"', in *British Democracy and Irish Nationalism 1876–1906* (Cambridge University Press 2007)

Bickers R and Yep R, *May Days in Hong Kong: Riot and Emergency in 1967* (Hong Kong University Press 2009)

Bieber F, 'Is Nationalism on the Rise? Assessing Global Trends' (2018) 17 Ethnopolitics 519

Billig M, *Banal Nationalism* (Sage 1995)

Blaise S, 'The "Rebalancing" of New Caledonia's Economy' (2017) 52 Journal of Pacific History 194

Bogdanor V, *Devolution in the United Kingdom* (Oxford University Press 1999)

Bogdanor V, *Devolution in the United Kingdom* (Oxford University Press 2001)

Bogdanor V, *The New British Constitution* (Hart 2009)

Boyle J, 'The Politics of Reason: Critical Legal Theory and Local Social Thought' (1985) 133 University of Pennsylvania Law Review 685

Boyle K and Hadden T, 'The Peace Process in Northern Ireland' (1995) 71 International Affairs 269

Boyron S, *The Constitution of France: A Contextual Analysis* (Hart 2013)

Breda V, 'Balancing Secularism with Religious Freedom: In Lautsi v Italy the European Court of Human Rights Evolved' in Angus JL Menuge (ed), *Legitimizing Human Rights* (Ashgate 2013)

Breda V, 'An Odd Partnership: Identity-Based Constitutional Claims' in Fiona Jenkins, Mark Nolan and Kim Rubenstein (eds), *Allegiance and Identity in a Globalised World* (Cambridge University Press 2014)

Breda V, 'How to Reverse the Italian Brain Drain: A Master Class from Australia' (2014) 52 International Migration 64

Breda V, 'The Australian Offshore Detention Regime: A Constitutional Reflection'(2016) 4 Quaderni Costituzionali 813

Breda V, 'Constitutional Patriotism' in Mortimer Sellers and Stephan Kirste (eds), *Encyclopaedia of the Philosophy of Law and Social Philosophy* (Springer Netherlands 2017)

Breda V, *Constitutional Law and Regionalism: A Comparative Analysis of Regionalist Negotiations* (Edward Elgar Publishing 2018)

Breda V, 'Samoa: Constitutional Governance and Customary Law' (2019) 23 Comparative Law Journal of the Pacific 163

Breda V and Mihailovic A, 'New Caledonia: The Archipelago That Does Not Want to Be Freed' (2019) 24 Comparative Law Journal of the Pacific 69

Brewer JD and Hayes BC, 'Victims as Moral Beacons: Victims and Perpetrators in Northern Ireland' (2011) 6 Contemporary Social Science 73

Brown D and De Cao E, 'The Impact of Unemployment on Child Maltreatment in the United States' (University of Essex, Institute for Social and Economic Research 2018) 15

Brown K, *Contemporary China* (Macmillan International Higher Education 2019)

Brown K, *China* (1st edn, Polity 2020)

Brown K, 'The EU, US and China: Hybrid Multilateralism and the Limits of Prioritizing Values' (2021) Global Summitry 14

Bruce S, *God Save Ulster: The Religion and Politics of Paisleyism* (Clarendon Press 1986)

Buckley R and Roger B, *Hong Kong: The Road to 1997* (Cambridge University Press 1997)

Buehn A and Schneider F, 'Size and Development of Tax Evasion in 38 OECD Coutries: What Do We (Not) Know?' (2016) 3 Journal of Economics and Political Economy 1

Buonanno P and others, 'Poor Institutions, Rich Mines: Resource Curse in the Origins of the Sicilian Mafia' (2015) 125 Economic Journal F175

Caciagli M, 'The Long Life of Clientelism in Southern Italy' in Jun'ichi Kawata (ed), *Comparing Political Corruption and Clientelism* (Ashgate 2006)

Cantor D and Land KC, 'Unemployment and Crime Rate Fluctuations: A Comment on Greenberg' (2001) 17 Journal of Quantitative Criminology 329

Cao KH and others, 'Covid-19's Adverse Effects on a Stock Market Index' (2021) 28 Applied Economics Letters 1157

Carrozza P, Giovine AD and Ferrari GF, *Diritto costituzionale comparato* (Laterza 2009)

Case DS and Voluck DA, *Alaska Natives and American Laws: Third Edition* (University of Alaska Press 2012)

Castells M and Jauregui G, 'Political Autonomy and Conflict Resolution: The Basque Case' in Kumar Rupesinghe and VA Tishkov (eds), *Ethnicity and Power in the Contemporary World* (United Nations University Press 1996)

Catalinac AL, 'The Establishment and Subsequent Expansion of the Waitangi Tribunal: The Politics of Agenda Setting' (2004) 56 Political Science 5

Chambers J, *A Belfast Child: My True Story of Life and Death in the Troubles* (John Blake 2020)

Chan CK, 'China as "Other": Resistance to and Ambivalence toward National Identity in Hong Kong' (2014) China Perspectives 25

Chan E and Chan J, 'Liberal Patriotism in Hong Kong' (2014) 23 Journal of Contemporary China 952

Chan LH, 'Chinese Investment in Hong Kong: Issues and Problems' (1995) 35 Asian Survey 941

Chappell D, 'The Kanak Awakening of 1969–1976: Radicalizing Anti-Colonialism in New Caledonia' (2003) Journal de la société des océanistes 187

Chappell D, 'Decolonisation and Nation-Building in New Caledonia: Reflections on the 2014 Elections' (2015) 67 Political Science 56

Chappell DA, 'The Noumea Accord: Decolonization Without Independence in New Caledonia? (Accord with France)' (1999) 72 Pacific Affairs 373

Chappell DA, *The Kanak Awakening: The Rise of Nationalism in New Caledonia* (University of Hawai'i Press 2013)

Chen T-F, 'Transplant of Civil Code in Japan, Taiwan, and China: With the Focus of Legal Evolution' (2011) 6 National Taiwan University Law Review 389

Chen AH-y, *The Changing Legal Orders in Hong Kong and Mainland China: Essays on 'One Country, Two Systems'* (City University of Hong Kong Press 2021)

Cheung Y-m, 'Liberate Hong Kong, the Revolution of Our Times: The Birth of the First Orient Nation in the Twenty-First Century' in Liah Greenfeld and Zeying Wu (eds), *Research Handbook on Nationalism* (Edward Elgar Publishing 2020)

Choi SYP and Lai RYS, 'Birth Tourism and Migrant Children's Agency: The "Double Not" in Post-Handover Hong Kong' (2020) 48(5) Journal of Ethnic and Migration Studies 1193

Choudhry S, 'Secession and Post-Sovereign Constitution-Making after 1989: Catalonia, Kosovo, and Quebec' (2019) 17 International Journal of Constitutional Law 461

Chung SY, *Hong Kong's Journey to Reunification: Memoirs of Sze-Yuen Chung* (Chinese University Press 2001)

Clarke J and others, *Hanks Australian Constitutional Law Materials and Commentary* (LexisNexis Butterworths 2012)

Clément D, 'The October Crisis of 1970: Human Rights Abuses Under the War Measures Act' (2008) 42 Journal of Canadian Studies 160

Coakley J, 'Adjusting to Partition: From Irredentism to "Consent" in Twentieth-Century Ireland' (2017) 25 Irish Studies Review 193

Coaldrake P, 'Reflections on the Repositioning of the Government's Approach to Higher Education, or I'm Dreaming of a White Paper' 22, Part 1 Journal of Higher Education Policy and Management 9

Cochrane F, *Northern Ireland: The Reluctant Peace* (Yale University Press 2013)

Coco A, 'Neopatrimonialism and Local Elite Attitudes. Similarities and Differences Across Italian Regions' (2015) 3 Territory, Politics, Governance 167

Cohen J, 'Deliberation and Democracy' in William Rehg (ed), *Deliberative Democracy: Essays on Reason and Politics* (MIT 1997)

Cohen J and Sabel C, 'Directly-Deliberative Polyarchy' (1997) 3 European Law Journal 313

Cohen JA, 'China's Changing Constitution' (1978) 76 The China Quarterly 794

Cohen-Almagor R, 'The Terrorists' Best Ally: The Quebec Media Coverage of the FLQ Crisis in October 1970' (2000) 25 Canadian Journal of Communication

Colla LL, 'Health Worker Gap in Italy: The Untold Truth' (2019) 394 The Lancet 561

Connell J, *New Caledonia of Kanaky: The Political History of a French Colony* (Development Studies Centre, The Australian National University 2017)

Connell J, 'The 2020 New Caledonia Referendum: The Slow March to Independence?' (2021) 56 The Journal of Pacific History 144

Connell J and Howitt R, *Mining and Indigenous Peoples in Australasia* (Sydney University Press in association with Oxford University Press 1993)

Corso G and Lopilato V, *Il diritto amministrativo dopo le riforme costituzionali. Parte generale* (Giuffrè Editore 2006)

Cox H, 'ICRA Habeas Corpus Relief: A New Habeas Jurisprudence for the Post-Oliphant World?' (2017) 5 American Indian Law Journal 597

Creel HG, 'The Beginnings of Bureaucracy in China: The Origin of the Hsien' (1964) 23 The Journal of Asian Studies 155

Curren R, 'Patriotism, Populism, and Reactionary Politics since 9.11', in Mitja Sardoc (ed), *Handbook of Patriotism* (Springer Cham 2018)

D'Attona J, 'Explaining Italian Tax Compliance. A Historical Analysis' in Sven Steinmo (ed), *The Leap of Faith: The Fiscal Foundations of Successful Government in Europe and America* (Oxford University Press 2018)

D'Attoma J, 'What Explains the North–South Divide in Italian Tax Compliance? An Experimental Analysis' (2019) 54 Acta Politica 104

David C and Tirard M, 'La Nouvelle-Calédonie après le troisième référendum d'autodétermination du 12 décembre 2021 : 40 ans pour rien ?' (2022) La Revue des droits de l'homme 1.

Davies RR, 'Colonial Wales' (1974) Past & Present 3

Davis M, 'A Culture of Disrespect: Indigenous Peoples and Australian Public Institutions' (2006) 8 UTS Law Review 135

Davis M, 'Political Timetables Trump Workable Timetables: Indigenous Constitutional Recognition and the Temptation of Symbolism over Substance' in Simon Young, Jeremy Patrick and Jennifer Nielsen (eds), *Constitutional Recognition of First Peoples in Australia: Theories and Comparative Perspectives* (Federation Press 2016)

Davis M and others, 'International Human Rights Law, Women's Rights and the Intervention' (2009) 7 Indigenous Law Bulletin 11

Delledonne G and Martinico G (eds), *The Canadian Contribution to a Comparative Law of Secession: Legacies of the Quebec Secession Reference* (Springer International Publishing 2019)

Deumier P, 'Introduction: Présentation de la Base de Données' in Etienne Cornut, Pascale Deumier and Françoise Cayrol-Baudrillart (eds), *La coutume kanak dans le pluralisme juridique calédonien* (Presses universitaires de Nouvelle-Calédonie 2018)

Di Gregorio S, *L'autonomia finanziaria della regione siciliana: il contenzioso con lo stato ed il ruolo della Corte costituzionale nell'attuazione della disciplina statutaria* (Jovene 2014)

Diamond J, *Collapse: How Societies Choose to Fail or Succeed: Revised Edition* (Penguin 2011)

Dicey AV, *Introduction to the Study of the Law of the Constitution* (Macmillan 1889)

Dickie J, *Cosa Nostra: A History of the Sicilian Mafia* (Hodder & Stoughton 2009)

Dinnen S, *Law and Order in a Weak State* (University of Hawai'i Press 2001)

Dinnen S, 'Lending a Fist? Australia's New Interventionism in the Southwest Pacific' Working/Technical Paper. Canberra: ANU Dept. of Pacific Affairs (DPA) formerly State, Society and Governance in Melanesia (SSGM) Program, 2004

Dixon R and Ginsburg T (eds), *Comparative Constitutional Law in Asia* (Edward Elgar Publishing 2014)

Dong M and others, 'The Interrelatedness of Multiple Forms of Childhood Abuse, Neglect, and Household Dysfunction' (2004) 28 Child Abuse & Neglect 771

Dotte É, 'Modes d'exploitation et d'intégration Au Sein Des Territoires Kanak Précoloniaux Des Ressources Végétales Forestières (IIe Millénaire Ap. J.-C.): Approche Ethno-Archéo-Anthracologique En Nouvelle-Calédonie' in Théophane Nicolas and Aurélie Salavert (eds), *Territoires et économies* (Éditions de la Sorbonne 2016)

Doumenge F, 'La dynamique géopolitique du Pacifique Sud (1965–1990)' (1990) 43 Les Cahiers d'Outre-Mer 113

Doyle C, 'Free Prior and Informed Consent, Development and Mining on Bougainville: Choice and the Pursuit of Self-Determined Development' in Christina Hill and Luke

Fletcher (eds), *Growing Bougainville's Future* (Jubilee Australia Research Centre 2018)

Dunn KM and others, 'Constructing Racism in Australia' (2004) 39 Australian Journal of Social Issues 409

Duran E and Duran B, *Native American Postcolonial Psychology* (SUNY Press 1995)

Echeverria B, 'Schooling, Language, and Ethnic Identity in the Basque Autonomous Community' (2003) 34 Anthropology & Education Quarterly 351

Edwards W, *Sovereignty and Land Rights of Indigenous Peoples in the United States* (Palgrave Macmillan US 2020)

Einaudi M, 'The Constitution of the Italian Republic' (1948) 42 The American Political Science Review 661

Eisenstadt SN, *Traditional Patrimonialism and Modern Neopatrimonialism* (SAGE Publications Ltd 1973)

Elliott M and Thomas R, *Public Law* (4th edn, Oxford University Press 2020)

Erdmann G and Engel U, 'Neopatrimonialism Reconsidered: Critical Review and Elaboration of an Elusive Concept' (2007) 45 Commonwealth & Comparative Politics 95

Erez L, 'Patriotism, Nationalism, and the Motivational Critique of Cosmopolitanism', in Mitja Sardoc (ed), *Handbook of Patriotism* (Springer Cham 2018)

Espadaler Fossas E, 'El principio dispositivo en el Estado autonómico' (2008) 71–72 Revista de Derecho Político 151

Espadaler Fossas E, 'El Control de Constitucionalitat Dels Estatuts d'autonomia' (2011) Revista catalana de dret públic 21

Evans-Campbell T, 'Historical Trauma in American Indian/Native Alaska Communities: A Multilevel Framework for Exploring Impacts on Individuals, Families, and Communities' (2008) 23 Journal of Interpersonal Violence 316

Feige C and Miron JeffreyA, 'The Opium Wars, Opium Legalization and Opium Consumption in China' (2008) 15 Applied Economics Letters 911

Felice E, *Perché Il Sud è Rimasto Indietro* (Il Mulino 2013)

Filer C and Meur P-YL, *Large-Scale Mines and Local-Level Politics: Between New Caledonia and Papua New Guinea* (ANU Press 2017)

Findlay M, *Globalisation, Populism, Pandemics and the Law: The Anarchy and the Ecstasy* (Edward Elgar Publishing 2021)

Fisher D, *France in the South Pacific: Power and Politics* (ANU Press 2013)

Flanagan P, 'The Distorting Effects of the Resource Sector on National Economies: A Case Study from Papua New Guinea' in Christina Hill and Luke Fletcher (eds), *Growing Bougainville's Future* (Jubilee Australia Research Centre 2018)

Foley WA, 'The Languages of New Guinea' (2000) 29 Annual Review of Anthropology 357

Fombad CM and Steytler N (eds), *Corruption and Constitutionalism in Africa* (Oxford University Press 2020)

Fong BCH, 'One Country, Two Nationalisms: Center-Periphery Relations between Mainland China and Hong Kong, 1997–2016' (2017) 43 Modern China 523

Fong BCH and Ichijo A (eds), *The Routledge Handbook of Comparative Territorial Autonomies* (Taylor & Francis Group 2022)

Freud S, *The Standard Edition of the Complete Psychological Works of Sigmund Freud: VOLUME 11 (1910): Five Lectures on Psycho-Analysis, Leonardo Da Vinci and Other Works* (Anna Freud and James Strachey eds, The Hogarth Press and the Institute of Psycho-Analysis 1957)

Freud S, *Civilization and Its Discontents* (Prabhat Prakashan 2015)

Freud S, *Group Psychology and the Analysis of the Ego* (Lulu 2018)
Fukuyama F, *The Origins of Political Order: From Prehuman Times to the French Revolution* (Profile Books 2012)
Freud S, *Political Order and Political Decay: From the Industrial Revolution to the Globalisation of Democracy* (Profile Books 2014)
Gagnon A, 'Québec-Canada's Constitutional Dossier' in Alain-G Gagnon (ed), *Quebec: State and Society* (University of Toronto Press 2004)
Gagnon A, 'Empowerment through Different Means Nationalism and Federalism in the Canadian Context' in Alain-G Gagson and José María Sauca (eds), *Negotiating Diversity: Identity, Pluralism, and Democracy* (Peter Lang 2014)
Gagnon A, 'Preface' in Gregory Baum (ed), *Le nationalisme: perspectives éthiques et religieuses* (Les Editions Fides 1998)
Gagnon A-G and Dionne X, 'Historiographies et Fédéralisme Au Canada' (2009) Revista d'estudis autonòmics i federals 10
Gagnon A-G and Tully J (eds), *Multinational Democracies* (Cambridge University Press 2001)
Galiana LAC, 'Constitutional Justice in Spain: Appeals to the Spanish Constitutional Court' (2013) 5 Revista de Estudos Constitucionais, Hermenêutica e Teoria do Direito 2
Gambetta D, *The Sicilian Mafia: The Business of Private Protection* (Harvard University Press 1996)
Ganapathy S, 'Alaskan Neo-Liberalism Conservation, Development, and Native Land Rights' (2011) 55 Social Analysis 113
Garasu L, 'Women Promoting Peace and Reconciliation' in Lorraine Garasu and Andy Carl (eds), *Weaving Consensus: The Papua New Guinea-Bougainville Peace Process* (Conciliation Resources 2002)
Garasu L and Boege V, 'Bougainville' in Morgan Brigg and Roland Bleiker (eds), *Mediating Across Difference: Oceanic and Asian Approaches to Conflict Resolution* (University of Hawai'i Press 2011)
Garasu L and Carl A (eds), *Weaving Consensus: The Papua New Guinea-Bougainville Peace Process* (Conciliation Resources 2002)
Garrido A and Llamas MR (eds), *Water Policy in Spain* (1st edn, CRC Press 2009)
Gary JE and von der Gracht HA, 'The Future of Foresight Professionals: Results from a Global Delphi Study' (2015) 71 Futures 132
Gaus GF, 'Reason, Justification, and Consensus: Why Democracy Can't Have It All' in James Bohman and William Rehg (eds), *Deliberative Democracy: Essays on Reason and Politics* (MIT 1997)
Gellner E, *Nationalism* (Phoenix 1998)
Gerston LN, *American Federalism: A Concise Introduction* (ME Sharpe 2007)
Ghaleigh NS, 'Neither Legal Nor Political? Bureaucratic Constitutionalism in Japanese Law' (2015) 26 King's Law Journal 193
Gilbert A and Mujanović J, 'Dayton at Twenty: Towards New Politics in Bosnia-Herzegovina' (2015) 15 Southeast European and Black Sea Studies 605
Gilbert J and Keane D, 'Equality versus Fraternity? Rethinking France and Its Minorities' (2016) 14 International Journal of Constitutional Law 883
Ginsburg T and Dixon R (eds), *Comparative Constitutional Law* (Paperback edn, Edward Elgar Publishing 2012)
Giovannini A and Vampa D, 'Towards a New Era of Regionalism in Italy? A Comparative Perspective on Autonomy Referendums' (2019) Territory, Politics, Governance 1

Giraudeau G, 'Le Droit International et Les Transitions Constitutionnelles' in Françoise Cayrol (ed), *L'avenir institutionnel de la Nouvelle-Calédonie* (Presses universitaires de la Nouvelle-Calédonie 2018)

Goddard S, *Indivisible Territory and the Politics of Legitimacy: Jerusalem and Northern Ireland* (Cambridge University Press 2009)

Goldsmith M, 'Codes of Governance in the Pacific' in Elise Huffer and Asofou So'o (eds), *Governance in Samoa pulega i Samoa* (Asia Pacific Press 2000)

Goodstadt LF, 'Fiscal Freedom and the Making of Hong Kong's Capitalist Society' (2010) 24 China Information 273

Goot M and Rowse T, *Divided Nation?: Indigenous Affairs and the Imagined Public* (Melbourne Univ Publishing 2007)

Gormley-Heenan C and Aughey A, 'Northern Ireland and Brexit: Three Effects on "the Border in the Mind"' (2017) 19 The British Journal of Politics and International Relations 497

Gounev P and Bezlov T, 'Examining the Links between Organised Crime and Corruption' (2010) 13 Trends in Organized Crime 326

Graff S, 'Quand combat et revendication kanak ou politique de l'État français manient indépendance, décolonisation, autodétermination et autochtonie en Nouvelle-Calédonie' (2012) Journal de la Société des Océanistes 61

Graham H, *War and Its Shadow: Spain's Civil War in Europe's Long Twentieth Century* (Sussex Academic Press 2012)

Greenfeld L (ed), *Advanced Introduction to Nationalism* (Edward Elgar Publishing 2016)

Greenfeld L, 'Introduction to the Research Handbook on Nationalism' in Liah Greenfeld and Zeying Wu (eds), *Research Handbook on Nationalism* (Edward Elgar Publishing 2020)

Greenfeld L and Wu Z (eds), *Research Handbook on Nationalism* (Edward Elgar Publishing 2020)

Grigg K and Manderson L, 'The Australian Racism, Acceptance, and Cultural-Ethnocentrism Scale (RACES): Item Response Theory Findings' (2016) 15 International Journal for Equity in Health 49

Grote G, *The South Tyrol Question, 1866–2010: From National Rage to Regional State* (Peter Lang 2012)

Guelke A, 'Northern Ireland's Flags Crisis and the Enduring Legacy of the Settler-Native Divide' (2014) 20 Nationalism and Ethnic Politics 133

Guerra LL and others, *Derecho Constitucional Vol. I El ordenamiento constitucional Derechos y deberes de los ciudadanos* (Editorial Tirant lo Blanch 2010)

Habermas J, 'The European Nation State. Its Achievements and Its Limitations. On the Past and Future of Sovereignty and Citizenship' (1996) 9 Ratio Juris 125

Habermas J, *Between Facts and Norms: Contributions to a Discourse Theory of Law and Democracy* (The MIT Press 1998)

Habermas J, 'On the Relation Between the Nation, the Rule of Law and Democracy' in Pablo De Greiff and Ciaran Cronin (eds), *The Inclusion of the Other: Studies in Political Theory* (The MIT Press 2000)

Habermas J, 'Democracy in Europe: Why the Development of the EU into a Transnational Democracy Is Necessary and How It Is Possible' (2015) 21 European Law Journal 546

Haljan D, *Constitutionalising Secession* (Hart 2014)

# References

Habibis D, Taylor PS and Ragaini BS, 'White People Have No Face: Aboriginal Perspectives on White Culture and the Costs of Neoliberalism' (2020) 43 Ethnic and Racial Studies 1149

Hadden T and Boyle K, 'Northern Ireland: Conflict and Conflict Resolution' in K Rupesinghe (ed), *Ethnic Conflict and Human Right* (United Nations University Press 1988)

Hall A, 'Incomplete Peace and Social Stagnation: Shortcomings of the Good Friday Agreement' (2018) 4 Open Library of Humanities 1

Harari YN, *Sapiens: A Brief History of Humankind* (Vintage 2015)

Hart HLA, *The Concept of Law* (Penelope A Bulloch and Joseph Raz eds, 3rd edn, Oxford University Press 2012)

Hassall G and Saunders C, *Asia-Pacific Constitutional Systems* (Cambridge University Press 2002)

Hayward K and McManus C, 'Neither/Nor: The Rejection of Unionist and Nationalist Identities in Post-Agreement Northern Ireland' (2019) 43 Capital & Class 139

Hazel K-J, 'The Media and Nationalism in Quebec: A Complex Relationship' (2001) 2 Journalism Studies 93

Hazell R, *Constitutional Futures: A History of the Next Ten Years* (Oxford University Press 1999)

Hazell R, *Constitutional Futures Revisited: Britain's Constitution to 2020* (Palgrave Macmillan 2008)

Hazell R, 'Constitutional Reform in the United Kingdom: Past, Present and Future' in Caroline Morris, Jonathan Boston and Petra Butler (eds), *Reconstituting the Constitution* (Springer 2011)

Hazell R, *Devolution and the Future of the Union* (The Constitution Unit 2015)

Hazell R and others, 'Answering the English Question' in Robert Hazell (ed), *Constitutional Futures Revisited: Britain's Constitution to 2020* (Palgrave Macmillan 2008)

Hazell R and Sandford M, 'English Question or Union Question? Neither Has Easy Answers' (2015) 86 Political Quarterly 16

Hemingway E, *The Sun Also Rises* (Hemingway Library ed edition, Scribner Book Company 2016)

Henderson A and others, 'England, Englishness and Brexit' (2016) 87 The Political Quarterly 187

Hien J, 'Tax Evasion in Italy. A God Given Right' in Sven Steinmo (ed), *The Leap of Faith: The Fiscal Foundations of Successful Government in Europe and America* (1st edn, Oxford University Press 2018)

Hinkson M, 'Introduction: In the Name of the Child' in Jon C Altman and Melinda Hinkson (eds), *Coercive Reconciliation: Stabilise, Normalise, Exit Aboriginal Australia* (Arena Publications Association 2007)

Hippler AE, 'Patterns of Sexual Behavior: The Athabascans of Interior Alaska' (1974) 2 Ethos 47

Hirschfield M, 'The Alaska Native Claims Settlement Act: Tribal Sovereignty and the Corporate Form' (1992) 101 The Yale Law Journal 1331

Hobsbawm E, *Nations and Nationalism since 1780: Programme, Myth, Reality* (Cambridge University Press 1992)

Hobsbawm E, *Age Of Empire: 1875–1914* (Hachette 2010)

Hogg PW, *Constitutional Law of Canada* (Carswell 2009)

Hooper A, *Culture and Sustainable Development in the Pacific* (ANU Press and Asia Pacific Press 2005)

Horowitz D, 'Some Realism about Constitutional Engineering' in Andreas Wimmer (ed), *Facing Ethnic Conflicts: Toward a New Realism* (Rowman & Littlefield 2004)

Horowitz LS, 'Toward a Viable Independence? The Koniambo Project and the Political Economy of Mining in New Caledonia' (2004) 16 The Contemporary Pacific 287

Howe C, 'Growth, Public Policy and Hong Kong's Economic Relationship with China' (1983) 95 The China Quarterly 512

Hu P, 'Popular Understanding of Democracy in Contemporary China' (2018) 25(8) Democratization 1441

Huffer E and So'o A, 'Consensus versus Dissent: Democracy, Pluralism and Governance in Sāmoa' (2003) 44 Asia Pacific Viewpoint 281

Human Rights and Equal Opportunity Commission, 'Social Justice Report 2005'

Hunter S, 'Child Maltreatment in Remote Aboriginal Communities and the Northern Territory Emergency Response: A Complex Issue' (2008) 61 Australian Social Work 372

Husa J, '"Accurately, Completely, and Solemnly": One Country, Two Systems and an Uneven Constitutional Equilibrium' (2017) 5 The Chinese Journal of Comparative Law 231

Husa J, 'Constitutional Biography of Hong Kong and Ambiguities of One Country, Two Systems Policy' (2021) 9 The Chinese Journal of Comparative Law 268

Husa J, *Interdisciplinary Comparative Law: Rubbing Shoulders with the Neighbours or Standing Alone in a Crowd* (Edward Elgar Publishing 2022)

Hutchinson J and Smith AD, 'Introduction' in John Hutchinson and Anthony D Smith (eds), *Nationalism* (Oxford University Press 1994)

Iati I, 'The Good Governance Agenda for Civil Society: Implications for the Fa'a Samoa' in Elise Huffer and Asofou So'o (eds), *Governance in Samoa pulega i Samoa* (Asia Pacific Press 2000)

Ichijo A, 'What Are Territorial Autonomies and Why the Handbook?' in Brian CH Fong and Atsuko Ichijo (eds), *The Routledge Handbook of Comparative Territorial Autonomies* (Routledge 2022)

Ignatieff M, *Blood & Belonging: Journeys into the New Nationalism* (Vintage 1994)

Ignatieff M, *The Warrior's Honor: Ethnic War and the Modern Conscience* (Vintage 1999)

Iris Kam CP, 'Personal Identity versus National Identity among Hong Kong Youths – Personal and Social Education Reform after Reunification' (2012) 18 Social Identities 649

Isaacs A and others, 'Lower Income Levels in Australia Are Strongly Associated With Elevated Psychological Distress: Implications for Healthcare and Other Policy Areas' (2018) 9 Frontiers in Psychiatry

Islam MR, 'Secession Crisis in Papua New Guinea: The Proclaimed Republic of Bougainville in International Law' (1991) 13 University of Hawaii Law Review 453

Islam MR and Jahjah M, 'Predictors of Young Australians' Attitudes Toward Aboriginals, Asians And Arabs' (2001) 29 Social Behavior and Personality: An International Journal 569

Ismangil M and Lee M, 'Protests in Hong Kong during the Covid-19 Pandemic' (2021) 17 Crime, Media, Culture: An International Journal 17

Itçaina X, 'Catholic Mediation in the Basque Peace Process: Questioning the Transnational Dimension' (2020) 11 Religions 216

Jackson A, *Home Rule: An Irish History, 1800–2000* (1st edn, Oxford University Press 2004)

Jacobsohn G and Schor M (eds), *Comparative Constitutional Theory* (Edward Elgar Publishing 2018)

Jarrett H, 'Northern Ireland A Place Apart?' in Brian CH Fong and Atsuko Ichijo (eds), *The Routledge Handbook of Comparative Territorial Autonomies* (Taylor & Francis Group 2022)

Jeffes E, 'Who Knows Best? Paternalism in Aboriginal Policy' (2020) 5 New: Emerging Scholars in Australian Indigenous Studies <https://epress.lib.uts.edu/au/student-journals/index.php/NESAIS/article/view/1554> accessed 8 March 2022

Jones O, 'A Worthy Predecessor? The Privy Council on Appeal from Hong Kong, 1853 to 1997' in Simon Young and Yash Ghai (eds), *Hong Kong's Court of Final Appeal: The Development of the Law in China's Hong Kong* (Cambridge University Press 2013)

Joseph WA, *Politics in China: An Introduction* (Oxford University Press 2014)

Joseph WA, 'Studying Chinese Politics' (2014) Politics in China 36

Katafono R (ed), *A Sustainable Future for Small States: Pacific 2050* (The Commonwealth 2017)

Keating M, 'So Many Nations, so Few States: Territory and Nationalism in the Global Era' in James Tully and Alain Gagnon (eds), *Multinational Democracies* (Cambridge University Press 2001)

Keating M, *The New Regionalism in Western Europe: Territorial Restructuring and Political Change* (Paperback ed repr, Edward Elgar Publishing 2003)

Keating M, 'Stateless Nations or Regional States?' in *Quebec* (University of Toronto Press 2004)

Keating M, 'Rethinking Sovereignty: Independence-Lite, Devolution-Max and National Accommodation' (2012) 16 Revista d'Estudis Autonòmics i Federals 9

Keating M and Bray Z, 'Renegotiating Sovereignty: Basque Nationalism and the Rise and Fall of the Ibarretxe Plan' (2006) 5 Ethnopolitics 347

Keating PM, *Nations against the State: The New Politics of Nationalism in Quebec, Catalonia and Scotland* (Palgrave Macmillan 1996)

Kedourie E, *Nationalism* (Hutchinson 1960)

Keil S and Kudlenko A, 'Bosnia and Herzegovina 20 Years after Dayton: Complexity Born of Paradoxes' (2015) 22 International Peacekeeping 471

Kelsen H, 'Law, State and Justice in the Pure Theory of Law' (1947) 57 Yale Law Journal 377

Kennedy-Pipe C, *The Origins of the Present Troubles in Northern Ireland* (Routledge 2014)

Kenny M and Sheldon J, 'When Planets Collide: The British Conservative Party and the Discordant Goals of Delivering Brexit and Preserving the Domestic Union, 2016–2019' (2021) 69 Political Studies 965

Keogh-Brown MR and Smith RD, 'The Economic Impact of SARS: How Does the Reality Match the Predictions?' (2008) 88 Health Policy 110

Kessels R and others, 'A Distributional Regression Approach to Income-Related Inequality of Health in Australia' (2020) 19 International Journal for Equity in Health 102

Khanthavit A, 'Measuring COVID-19 Effects on World and National Stock Market Returns' (2021) 8 The Journal of Asian Finance, Economics and Business 1

Kinley D, 'Bendable Rules The Development Implications of Human Rights Pluralism' in Brian Z Tamanaha, Caroline Sage and Michael Woolcock (eds), *Legal Pluralism and Development: Scholars and Practitioners in Dialogue* (Cambridge University Press 2012)

Kleinig J, *On Loyalty and Loyalties: The Contours of a Problematic Virtue* (Oxford University Press 2014)

Kolova S, 'The Bougainville Independence Referendum Consultations Impasse' (2022) 37 DWU Research Journal 7

Kwan JP, 'The Rise of Civic Nationalism: Shifting Identities in Hong Kong and Taiwan' (2016) 2 Contemporary Chinese Political Economy and Strategic Relations 941

Kwaymullina A, 'Recognition, Referendums and Relationships: Indigenous Worldviews, Constitutional Change, and the "Spirit" of 1967' in Simon Young, Jeremy Patrick and Jennifer Nielsen (eds), *Constitutional Recognition of First Peoples in Australia: Theories and Comparative Perspectives* (Federation Press 2016)

Kymlicka W, 'Multinational Federalism in Canada; Rethinking the Parnership' in Roger Gibbins and Guy Laforest (eds), *Beyond the Impasse: Towards Reconciliation* (McGill-Queen's University Press 1998)

La Spina A, 'The Fight against the Italian Mafia' in Letizia Paoli (ed), *The Oxford Handbook of Organized Crime* (Oxford University Press 2014)

Lafaye CG and Brochard P, 'Methodological Approach to the Evolution of a Terrorist Organisation: ETA, 1959–2018' (2021) Quality & Quantity 18

Lang AF and Wiener A (eds), *Handbook on Global Constitutionalism* (Edward Elgar Publishing 2017)

Langton M, 'Trapped in the Aboriginal Reality Show [The Howard Government Intervention in Northern Territory Aboriginal Communities. Paper in: Re-Imagining Australia. Schultz, Julianne (Ed.).]' (2008) Griffith Review 143

Langton M, 'Indigenous Exceptionalism and the Constitutional "Race Power"' (2013) Space, Place and Culture 1

Lantschner E, 'History of the South Tyrol Conflict and Its Settlement' in Jens Woelk, Francesco Palermo and Joseph Marko (eds), *Tolerance Through Law: Self Governance and Group Rights in South Tyrol* (Brill 2007)

Larson MS, *The Rise of Professionalism: Monopolies of Competence and Sheltered Markets* (Routledge 2017)

Lasslett K, 'The Crisis Began in 1886: A Long View of Bougainville's Decolonisation Struggle' in Christina Hill and Luke Fletcher (eds), *Growing Bougainville's Future* (Jubilee Australia Research Centre 2018)

Le Meur P-Y and Levacher C, 'Mining and Competing Sovereignties in New Caledonia' (2022) 92 Oceania 74

Le Sueur A, Sunkin M and Murkens JE, *Public Law: Text, Cases, and Materials* (Oxford University Press 2016)

Leblic I, 'Chronologie de la Nouvelle-Calédonie' (2003) Journal de la Société des Océanistes 299

Leblic I, 'Présentation : Nouvelle-Calédonie, 150 ans après la prise de possession' (2003) Journal de la Société des Océanistes 135

Leblic I, 'Kanak Identity, New Citizenship Building and Reconciliation' (2007) Journal de la Société des Océanistes 271

Leblic I, 'Sovereignty and Coloniality in the French-Speaking Pacific: A Reflection on the Case of New Caledonia, 1980–2021' (2022) 92 Oceania 107

Lee FLF and others, 'Hong Kong's Summer of Uprising: From Anti-Extradition to Anti-Authoritarian Protests' (2019) 19 China Review 1

Legrand P, 'Against a European Civil Code' (1997) 60 The Modern Law Review 44

Lei X and others, 'Prevalence and Correlates of Sexual Harassment in Australian Adolescents' (2020) 19 Journal of School Violence 349

Lemaire F, *Le Principe d'indivisibilité de La République: Mythe et Réalité* (Presses Universitaires de Rennes 2010)

Leo J, *Global Hakka: Hakka Identity in the Remaking* (Brill 2015)

Levinson S, *Pragmatics* (Cambridge University Press 1983)

Levinson S, 'Recursion in Pragmatics' (2013) 89 Language 149

Leyland P, 'The Multifaceted Constitutional Dynamics of U.K. Devolution' (2011) 9 International Journal of Constitutional Law 251

Lin KJ and others, 'State-Owned Enterprises in China: A Review of 40 years of Research and Practice' (2020) 13 China Journal of Accounting Research 31

Llera FJ, Leonisio R and Pérez Castaños S, 'The Influence of the Elites' Discourse in Political Attitudes: Evidence from the Basque Country' (2017) 19 National Identities 367

Llera FJ, Mata JM and Irvin CL, 'ETA: From Secret Army to Social Movement – the Post-Franco Schism of the Basque Nationalist Movement' (1993) 5 Terrorism and Political Violence 106

Lopez Bofill H, 'Hubris, Constitutionalism, and "the Indissoluble Unity of the Spanish Nation": The Repression of Catalan Secessionist Referenda in Spanish Constitutional Law' (2019) 17 International Journal of Constitutional Law 943

López Bofill H, 'Hubris, Constitutionalism, and "the Indissoluble Unity of the Spanish Nation": A Rejoinder to Antonio Bar' (2019) 17 International Journal of Constitutional Law 984

López Bofill H, 'A Nation of Nations? A Reply to Joseph H. H. Weiler' (2019) 17 International Journal of Constitutional Law 1315

Loughlin M, *The Idea of Public Law* (Oxford University Press 2003)

Loughlin M, 'Reflection on the Idea of Public Law' in Emilios Christodoulidis and Stephen Tierney (eds), *Public Law and Politics: The Scope and Limits of Constitutionalism* (Ashgate 2008)

Loveland I, *Constitutional Law, Administrative Law, and Human Rights: A Critical Introduction* (Oxford University Press 2018)

Lupo S, 'The Allies and the Mafia' (1997) 2 Journal of Modern Italian Studies 21

Lynn R, 'In Italy, North–South Differences in IQ Predict Differences in Income, Education, Infant Mortality, Stature, and Literacy' (2010) 38 Intelligence 93

Ma N and Cheng EW (eds), *The Umbrella Movement: Civil Resistance and Contentious Space in Hong Kong* (Revised edition, Amsterdam University Press 2020)

Ma N and Cheng EW (eds), 'From Political Acquiescence to Civil Disobedience', in *The Umbrella Movement: Civil Resistance and Contentious Space in Hong Kong* (Amsterdam University Press 2020)

MacCormick N, *Legal Reasoning and Legal Theory* (Clarendon Press 1994)

MacCormick N, 'Reasonableness and Objectivity' (1998) 74 Notre Dame Law Review 1575

Macklem P, 'Militant Democracy, Legal Pluralism, and the Paradox of Self-Determination' (2006) 4 International Journal of Constitutional Law 488

Mahoney J, 'Path Dependence in Historical Sociology' (2000) 29 Theory and Society 507

Mallonee M, 'Selective Justice: A Crisis of Missing and Murdered Alaska Native Women Notes' (2021) 38 Alaska Law Review 93

Mani A and others, 'Poverty Impedes Cognitive Function' (2013) 341 Science 976

Markus L, 'Aboriginal and Torres Strait Islander Health Performance Framework 2020 Key Health Indicators – Northern Territory' (2020) 24

Marrani D, 'Asia-Pacific: Insights from the Region: Will New Caledonia Be Another Tokelau?' (2006) 31 Alternative Law Journal 102

Marrani D, *Dynamics in the French Constitution: Decoding French Republican Ideas* (Routledge 2013)

Marsden S, 'Autonomy, Sovereignty and Geography: What Does China Mean to Hong Kong?' in Kim Rubenstein and Mark Nolan (eds), *Alliance and Identity in a Globalised World* (Cambridge University Press 2012)

Matheson D, Park K and Soakai TS, 'Pacific Island Health Inequities Forecast to Grow Unless Profound Changes Are Made to Health Systems in the Region' (2017) 41 Australian Health Review 590

McCulloch A, 'Consociational Executives: Power-Sharing Governments Between Inclusion and Functionality' in Ferran Requejo and Marc Sanjaume-Calvet (eds), *Defensive Federalism* (Routledge 2022)

McDonald J and others, 'Karnatukul (Serpent's Glen): A New Chronology for the Oldest Site in Australia's Western Desert' (2018) 13 Plos One

McEwen N and others, 'Intergovernmental Relations in the UK: Time for a Radical Overhaul?' (2020) 91 The Political Quarterly 632

Mees L, 'Nationalist Politics at the Crossroads: The Basque Nationalist Party and the Challenge of Sovereignty (1998–2014)' (2015) 21 Nationalism & Ethnic Politics 44

Mees L, 'Ethnogenesis in the Pyrenees: The Contentious Making of a National Identity in the Basque Country (1643–2017)' (2018) 48 European History Quarterly 462

Meierhenrich J and Loughlin M (eds), *The Cambridge Companion to the Rule of Law* (Cambridge University Press 2021)

Meleisea M and Schoeffel P, 'Forty-Five Years of Pacific Island Studies: Some Reflections' (2017) 87 Oceania 337

Mellor D, 'Contemporary Racism in Australia: The Experiences of Aborigines' (2003) 29 Personality and Social Psychology Bulletin 474

Michelman FI, 'The Problem of Constitutional Interpretative Disagreement' in Mitchell Aboulafia, Myra Orbach Bookman and Cathy Kemp (eds), *Habermas & Pragmatism* (Routledge 2002)

Mikheieva O, 'Motivations of Pro-Russian and Pro-Ukrainian Combatants in the Context of the Russian Military Intervention in the Donbas' in David R Marples (ed), *The War in Ukraine's Donbas* (Central European University Press 2022)

Milton E, 'Ethnic Pluralism; Strategies for Conflict Managmement' in Andreas Wimmer (ed), *Facing Ethnic Conflicts: Toward a New Realism* (Rowman & Littlefield 2004)

Molina F and Quiroga A, 'Mixed Feelings: Identities and Nationalisations in Catalonia and the Basque Country (1980–2015)' (2019) 21 National Identities 93

Moore C, Jacoby W and Gunlicks AB, 'German Federalism in Transition?' (2008) 17 German Politics 393

Morano Foadi S, 'Key Issues and Causes of the Italian Brain Drain' (2006) 19 Innovation: The European Journal of Social Science Research 209

Morata F and Popartan L, 'Spain' in Michael J Baun and Dan Marek (eds), *EU Cohesion Policy after Enlargement* (Palgrave Macmillan 2008)

Morgan W, 'Growing Island Exports: High Value Crops and the Future of Agriculture in the Pacific' in Christina Hill and Luke Fletcher (eds), *Growing Bougainville's Future* (Jubilee Australia Research Centre 2018)

Murphy MC and Evershed J, 'Contesting Sovereignty and Borders: Northern Ireland, Devolution and the Union' (2021) 10(5) Territory, Politics, Governance 661

Murray F, *The European Union and Member State Territories: A New Legal Framework Under the EU Treaties* (Springer Science & Business Media 2012)

Nagle J, 'Between Conflict and Peace: An Analysis of the Complex Consequences of the Good Friday Agreement' (2018) 71 Parliamentary Affairs 395

Nairn T, *The Break-up of Britain: Crisis and Neonationalism* (NLB and Verso Editions 1981)

Nardin L and others, 'Simulating Protection Rackets: A Case Study of the Sicilian Mafia' (2016) 30 Autonomous Agents and Multi-Agent Systems 1117

National Research Council (U.S.) (ed), *Understanding Child Abuse and Neglect* (National Academy Press 1993)

Nelken D, 'Legitimate Suspicions? Berlusconi and the Judges' (2002) 18 Italian Politics 112

Nespor S, *La Fabbrica Dei Nullafacenti* (il Mulino 2019)

Ng H-Y, 'Hong Kong: Autonomy in Crisis' in Brian CH Fong and Atsuko Ichijo (eds), *The Routledge Handbook of Comparative Territorial Autonomies* (Routledge 2022)

Nifterik G van, 'French Constitutional History, Garden or Graveyard?: Some Thoughts on Occasion of Les Grands Discours Parlementaires' (2007) 3 European Constitutional Law Review 476

O'Callaghan M, 'The Origins of the Conflict' in Lorraine Garasu and Andy Carl (eds), *Weaving Consensus: The Papua New Guinea-Bougainville Peace Process* (Conciliation Resources 2002)

O'Callaghan M, 'Genealogies of Partition; History, History-Writing and "the Troubles" in Ireland' (2006) 9 Critical Review of International Social and Political Philosophy 619

O'Faircheallaigh C, 'Aborigines, Mining Companies and the State in Contemporary Australia: A New Political Economy or "Business as Usual"?' (2006) 41 Australian Journal of Political Science 1

Offe C, *Varieties of Transition: The East European and East German Experience* (MIT Press 1997)

Offe C, '"Homogeneity" and Constitutional Democracy: Coping with Identity Conflicts through Group Rights' (1998) 6 Journal of Political Philosophy 113

Oklopcic Z, 'Constitutional (Re)Vision: Sovereign Peoples, New Constituent Powers, and the Formation of Constitutional Orders in the Balkans' (2012) 19 Constellations 81

O'Leary B, 'Debating Consociational Politics: Normative and Explanatory Arguments' in Sidney John Roderick Noel (ed), *From Power Sharing to Democracy: Post-conflict Institutions in Ethnically Divided Societies* (McGill-Queen's University Press 2005)

O'Leary B and McGarry J, *The Politics of Antagonism: Understanding Northern Ireland* (Bloomsbury Publishing 1996)

O'Sullivan D, 'The Treaty of Waitangi in Contemporary New Zealand Politics' (2008) 43 Australian Journal of Political Science 317

'Overseas Migration, 2020–21 Financial Year | Australian Bureau of Statistics' (17 December 2021)

'Pacific Regional Indicative Programme 2014–2020 – EEAS – European External Action Service – European Commission' (EEAS – European External Action Service)

Palmer B, 'The Bell Curve Review: IQ Best Indicates Poverty' (2018) *EC970, Department of Economics, Harvard University* 22.

Paoli L, *Mafia Brotherhoods: Organized Crime, Italian Style* (Oxford University Press 2008)

Paoli L, 'The Italian Mafia' in Letizia Paoli (ed), *The Oxford Handbook of Organized Crime* (Oxford University Press 2014)

Paoli L (ed), *The Oxford Handbook of Organized Crime* (Oxford University Press 2014)

Partridge E, Maddison S and Nicholson HA, 'Human Rights Imperatives and the Failings of the Stronger Futures Consultation Process' (2012) 18 Australian Journal of Human Rights 21

Payne A and Sutton P, 'Towards a Security Policy for Small Island and Enclave Developing States' in Anthony Payne and Paul Sutton (eds), *Size and Survival* (Routledge 2014)

Pedersen A and others, 'Attitudes toward Aboriginal Australians in City and Country Settings' (2000) 35 Australian Psychologist 109

Peerenboom R, *China's Long March Toward Rule of Law* (Cambridge University Press 2009)

Peng A, 'Sinicized Marxist Constitutionalism: Its Emergence, Contents, and Implications' (2011) 2 Global Discourse 83

Pengelley N, 'The Hindmarsh Island Bridge Act: Must Laws Based on the Race Power be for the "Benefit" of Aborigines and Torres Strait Islanders?' (1998) 20 Sydney Law Review: 144

Peterson JB, *Maps of Meaning: The Architecture of Belief* (1st edn, Routledge 2002)

Philippe X, 'France: The Amendment of the French Constitution "on the Decentralized Organization of the Republic"' (2004) 2 International Journal of Constitutional Law 691

Pickel A (ed), *Handbook of Economic Nationalism* (Edward Elgar Publishing 2022)

Ping YC and Kin-ming K, 'Hong Kong Identity on the Rise' (2014) 54 Asian Survey 1088

Pizzi WT and Marafioti L, 'New Italian Code of Criminal Procedure: The Difficulties of Building an Adversarial Trial System on a Civil Law Foundation' (1992) 17 The Yale Journal of International Law 1

Plachecki RC, 'EU and World Trade Law – Economic Partnership Agreements and Considerations for New Caledonia' (2008) 14 Revue Juridique Polynésienne 71

Plank G, *Rebellion and Savagery: The Jacobite Rising of 1745 and the British Empire* (University of Pennsylvania Press 2015)

Pola G, *Principles and Practices of Fiscal Autonomy: Experiences, Debates and Prospects* (Routledge 2016)

Pommersheim F, *Braid of Feathers: American Indian Law and Contemporary Tribal Life* (University of California Press 1997)

Pommersheim F, 'At the Crossroads: A New and Unfortunate Paradigm of Tribal Sovereignty' (2010) 55 South Dakota Law Review 48

Posner RA, 'Creating a Legal Framework for Economic Development' (1998) 13 The World Bank Research Observer 1

Pritchett L and Woolcock M, 'Solutions When the Solution Is the Problem: Arraying the Disarray in Development' (Center for Global Development 2002) 10

Quiroga A and Molina F, 'National Deadlock. Hot Nationalism, Dual Identities and Catalan Independence (2008–2019)' (2020) 4 Genealogy 15

Rakopoulos T, 'Façade Egalitarianism? Mafia and Cooperative in Sicily' (2017) 40 Political and Legal Anthropology Review 104

Rakopoulos T, *From Clans to Co-Ops: Confiscated Mafia Land in Sicily* (Berghahn 2018)

Rakopoulos T, 'The Limits of "Bad Kinship": Sicilian Anti-Mafia Families' in *From Clans to Co-ops*, vol 4 (Berghahn Books 2018)

Ramsay R, 'Telling the Past as Identity Construction in the Literatures of New Kanaky/ New Caledonia' (2008) Journal of the Australasian Universities Language and Literature Association 113

Regan A, 'Resolving Two Dimension of Conflict: The Dynamics of Consent, Consent and Compromise' in Lorraine Garasu and Andy Carl (eds), *Weaving Consensus: The Papua New Guinea-Bougainville Peace Process* (Conciliation Resources 2002)

Regan A, *Light Intervention: Lessons from Bougainville* (United States Institute of Peace Press 2010)

Regan A, 'Bougainville, Papua New Guinea: Lessons from a Successful Peace Process' (2018) 163 The RUSI Journal 44

Regan AJ, 'Bougainville: Origins of the Conflict, and Debating the Future of Large-Scale Mining' in Colin Filer and Pierre-Yves Le Meur (eds), *Large-scale Mines and Local-level Politics: Between New Caledonia and Papua New Guinea* (ANU Press 2017)

Reinares F, 'Nationalist Separatism and Terrorism in Comparative Perspective' in Tore Bjorge (ed), *Root Causes of Terrorism: Myths, Reality and Ways Forward* (Taylor & Francis Group 2005)

Renan E, *What Is a Nation?* (Presses-Pocket 1882)

Reynolds H, *Dispossession: Black Australians and White Invaders* (Allen & Unwin 1996)

Roberts CL, 'A Desert Grows between Us – The Sovereignty Paradox at the Intersection of Tribal and Federal Courts The Washington and Lee Law Alumni Association Student Notes' (2008) 65 Washington and Lee Law Review 347

Robinson W, 'The Benefits of a Benefit Corporation Statute for Alaska Native Corporations' (2016) 33 Alaska Law Review 329

Rodino-Colocino M, 'Me Too, #MeToo: Countering Cruelty with Empathy' (2018) 15 Communication and Critical/Cultural Studies 96

Rojo-Labaien E, 'Football and the Representation of Basque Identity in the Contemporary Age' (2017) 18 Soccer & Society 63

Ronchi V, 'The Hybrid State Destatization and Neopatrimonialism' (Milan: Fondazione Eni Enrico Mattei 2020)

Rosay A, 'Violence Against American Indian and Alaska Native Women and Men' (2016) NIJ Journal 38–45

Rosenfeld M, *The Identity of the Constitutional Subject* (Routledge 2010)

Rosenfeld M and Sajo A, 'Constitutional Identity' in Michele Rosenfeld and Andras Sajo (eds), *The Oxford Handbook of Comparative Constitutional Law* (Oxford University Press, USA 2012)

Rosenfeld M, Sajo A and Baer S (eds), 'Equality' in Michele Rosenfeld and Andras Sajo (eds), *The Oxford Handbook of Comparative Constitutional Law* (Oxford University Press, USA 2012)

Rosenthal P, 'The New Emergencies Act: Four Times the War Measures Act' (1991) 20 Manitoba Law Journal 563.

Rowse T, 'The National Emergency and Indigenous Jurisdictions' in Jon C Altman and Melinda Hinkson (eds), *Coercive Reconciliation: Stabilise, Normalise, Exit Aboriginal Australia* (Arena Publications Association 2007)

Russell M and Gover D, *Legislation at Westminster: Parliamentary Actors and Influence in the Making of British Law* (Oxford University Press 2017)

Rutherford P, *When Television Was Young: Primetime Canada 1952–1967* (University of Toronto Press 1990)

Sachs JD and Warner AM, 'The Curse of Natural Resources' (2001) 45 European Economic Review 827

Saovana-Spriggs DR, 'Women's Contributions to Bougainville's Past, Present and Future'

Sargiacomo M and others, 'Accounting and the Fight against Corruption in Italian Government Procurement: A Longitudinal Critical Analysis (1992–2014)' (2015) 28 Critical Perspectives on Accounting 89

Saunders C and Stone A (eds), *The Oxford Handbook of the Australian Constitution* (Oxford University Press 2018)

Saunders SA, 'A Snapshot of Five Materialism Studies in Australia' (2007) 1 Journal of Pacific Rim Psychology 14

Sawer G, 'Australian Constitution and the Australian Aborigine' (1966) 2 Federal Law Review 17

Schneider FA, 'Emergent Nationalism in China's Sociotechnical Networks: How Technological Affordance and Complexity Amplify Digital Nationalism' (2022) 28(1) Nations and Nationalism 267

Schütze R, 'Subsidiarity After Lisbon: Reinforcing the Safeguards of Federalism?' (2009) 68 The Cambridge Law Journal 525

Schwartz A, 'The Changing Concepts of the Constitution' (2022) Oxford Journal of Legal Studies (first online)

Sewell WH, 'Historical Events as Transformations of Structures: Inventing Revolution at the Bastille' (1996) 25 Theory and Society 841

Seymour M, 'La Nation Québécoise Peut-Elle Se Donner La Constitution de Son Choix?' (2015) Revue québécoise de droit international 6 241

Shek DTL, 'Protests in Hong Kong (2019–2020): A Perspective Based on Quality of Life and Well-Being' (2020) 3 Applied Research in Quality of Life 1 (online)

Sirivi JT, Havini MT and Australian National University (eds), *As Mothers of the Land: The Birth of the Bougainville Women for Peace and Freedom* (Pandanus Books 2004)

Skeldon R, 'Hong Kong: Colonial City to Global City to Provincial City?' (1997) 14 Cities 265

Skoczeń I, 'Minimal Semantics and Legal Interpretation' (2016) 29 International Journal for the Semiotics of Law 615

Smith A, 'Not an Indian Tradition: The Sexual Colonization of Native Peoples' (2003) 18 Hypatia 70

Smith A, *The Ethnic Revival* (1st edn, Cambridge University Press 2010)

Smith AD, *Theories of Nationalism* (Duckworth 1971)

Smith AD, *The Ethnic Revival* (CUP 1981)

Smith AD, 'The Origins of Nations' in John Hutchinson and Anthony D Smith (eds), *Nationalism* (Oxford University Press 1994)

Smith AD, *Nationalism: Theory, Ideology, History* (Polity Press; Blackwell 2001)

Soler Alemany M, 'Catalonia from Autonomy to Self-Determination' in Brian Fong and Atsuko Ichijo (eds), *The Routledge Handbook of Comparative Territorial Autonomies* (Routledge 2022)

Spencer A and Croucher S, 'Basque Nationalism and the Spiral of Silence: An Analysis of Public Perceptions of ETA in Spain and France' (2008) 70 International Communication Gazette 137

Spolaore E and Wacziarg R, 'War and Relatedness' (2016) 98 The Review of Economics and Statistics 925

Stevenson G, *Parallel Paths: The Development of Nationalism in Ireland and Quebec* (McGill-Queen's University Press 2006)

Stone Sweet S, 'The Politics of Constitutional Review in France and Europe' (2007) 5 International Journal of Constitutional Law 69

Tai BY, 'Stages of Hong Kong's Democratic Movement' (2019) 4 Asian Journal of Comparative Politics 352

Tanguy Y, 'La Motion de Défiance Dans Le Statut de La Corse: Vers Une Mise En Jeu de La Responsabilité Des Exécutifs Devant Les Assemblées Locales ?' (1992) 45 La Revue administrative 121

Tannam E, 'Intergovernmental and Cross-Border Civil Service Cooperation: The Good Friday Agreement and Brexit' (2018) 17 Ethnopolitics 243

Taylor A, *American Colonies: The Settling of North America* (The Penguin History of the United States, Volume 1) (Penguin 2002)

Techera EJ, 'Samoa: Law, Custom and Conservation' (2006) New Zealand Journal of Environmental Law 361

Tetley W, *The October Crisis, 1970 an Insider's View* (McGill-Queen's University Press 2007)

'The October Crisis of 1970' (1975) 33 The Advocate 218

Thomas D. Grant, 'Aid as an Instrument for Peace; a Civil Society Perspective' (2015) 109 The American Journal of International Law 68

Thomas WA, *Western Capitalism in China: A History of the Shanghai Stock Exchange* (Ashgate 2001)

Thompson BW, 'The De Facto Termination of Alaska Native Sovereignty: An Anomaly in an Era of Self-Determination' (1999) 24 American Indian Law Review 421

Tierney S, *Constitutional Law and National Pluralism* (Oxford University Press 2004)

Tierney S, 'Towards a Federal United Kingdom? Lessons from America' (2015) 6 Political Insight 16

Tierney S, '"We the People": Constituent Power and Constitutionalism in Plurinational States' in Martin Loughlin and Neil Walker (eds), *The Paradox of Constitutionalism: Constituent Power and Constitutional Form* (Oxford University Press 2007)

Tierney S, 'Constitutional Referendums: A Theoretical Enquiry' (2009) 72 Modern Law Review 360

Tierney S, 'Popular Constitutional Amendment: Referendums and Constitutional Change in Canada and the United Kingdom' (2015) 41 Queen's Law Journal 41

Tierney S, 'Federalism and Constitutional Theory' in Gary Jacobsohn and Miguel Schor (eds), *Comparative Constitutional Theory* (Edward Elgar Publishing 2018)

Tilley J and Evans G, 'Political Generations in Northern Ireland' (2011) 50 European Journal of Political Research 583

Trench A, 'Scotland and Wales: The Evolution of Devolution' in Robert Hazell (ed), *Constitutional Futures Revisited: Britain's Constitution to 2020* (Palgrave Macmillan 2008)

Trench A, 'Tying the UK Together?' in Robert Hazell (ed), *Constitutional Futures Revisited: Britain's Constitution to 2020* (Palgrave Macmillan 2008)

Trumbore PF and Owsiak AP, 'Brexit, the Border, and Political Conflict Narratives in Northern Ireland' (2019) 30 Irish Studies in International Affairs 195

Tryon D, 'The Languages of Bougainville' in Anthony Regan and Helga Griffin (eds), *Bougainville before the Conflict* (ANU Press 2015)

Tully J, *Strange Multiplicity: Constitutionalism in an Age of Diversity* (Cambridge University Press 1995)

Tully J, 'Introduction' in Alain-G Gagnon and James Tully (eds), *Multinational Democracies* (Cambridge University Press 2001)

Tully J, 'The Unfreedom of the Moderns in Comparison to Their Ideals of Constitutional Democracy' (2002) 65 Modern Law Review 204

Tully J, 'The Imperialism of Modern Constitutional Democracy' in Martin Loughlin and Neil Walker (eds), *The Paradox of Constitutionalism: Constituent Power and Constitutional Form* (Oxford University Press 2007)

Turner P and Watson N, 'The Trojan Horse' in Jon C Altman and Melinda Hinkson (eds), *Coercive Reconciliation: Stabilise, Normalise, Exit Aboriginal Australia* (Arena Publications Association 2007)

Uibopuu H-J, 'Soviet Federalism under the New Soviet Constitution' (1979) 5 Review of Socialist Law 171

Van der Hoek P, 'Enlarging the European Union: Taxation and Corruption in the New Member States' in Robert W McGee (ed), *Taxation and Public Finance in Transition and Developing Economies* (Springer US 2008)

Vazquez CG, 'A Business Entity by Any Other Name: Corporation: Community and Kinship' (2016) 33 Alaska Law Review 353

Veg S, 'The Rise of "Localism" and Civic Identity in Post-Handover Hong Kong: Questioning the Chinese Nation-State' (2017) 230 The China Quarterly 323

Visage CL and others, 'Inventory of the Economic Zones of the French Territories in the Pacific' (1998) 75 The International Hydrographic Review 1

Viver C, 'Spain's Constitution and Statutes of Autonomy: Explaining the Evolution of Political Decentralization' in Michael Burgess and G Alan Tarr (eds), *Constitutional Dynamics in Federal Systems: Sub-national Perspectives* (MQUP 2012)

Wainwright E, *Our Failing Neighbour: Australia and the Future of Solomon Islands* (Australian Strategic Policy Institute 2003)

Wallis J, *Constitution Making during State Building* (Cambridge University Press 2016)

Wallis J, *Hybridity on the Ground in Peacebuilding and Development: Critical Conversations* (ANU Press 2018)

Wallis J, 'The Role of "Uncivil" Society in Transitional Justice: Evidence from Bougainville and Timor-Leste' (2019) 31 Global Change, Peace & Security 159

Wang C, Madson N and Maleson A, *Inside China's Legal System* (Elsevier Science & Technology 2013)

Wang H, Rodríguez-Pose A and Lee N, 'The Long Shadow of History in China: Regional Governance Reform and Chinese Territorial Inequality' (2021) 134 Applied Geography 1025

Warleigh-Lack A and Langenhove LV, 'Rethinking EU Studies: The Contribution of Comparative Regionalism' (2010) 32 Journal of European Integration 541

Warne D and Frizzell LB, 'American Indian Health Policy: Historical Trends and Contemporary Issues' (2014) 104 American Journal of Public Health S263

Watts RL, 'Daniel J. Elazar: Comparative Federalism and Post-Statism' (2000) 30 Publius 155

Weber M, *Economy and Society: A New Translation* (Harvard University Press 2019)

Weber M, Roth G and Wittich C, *Economy and Society: An Outline of Interpretive Sociology* (University of California Press 1978)

Weiler J, 'A Nation of Nations?' (2019) 17 International Journal of Constitutional Law 1301

Welsh F, *A History of Hong Kong* (Harper Collins 1993)

Wesley-Smith T, 'Self-Determination in Oceania' (2007) 48 Race & Class 29

West BA, *Encyclopedia of the Peoples of Asia and Oceania* (Infobase Publishing 2010)

Wexler L, 'Looking across Three Generations of Alaska Natives to Explore How Culture Fosters Indigenous Resilience' (2014) 51 Transcultural Psychiatry 73

Wilkinson RG and Pickett KE, 'Income Inequality and Social Dysfunction' (2009) 35 Annual Review of Sociology 493

Williams G, 'Removing Racism from Australia's Constitutional DNA' (2012) 37 Alternative Law Journal 151

Williams G, Brennan S and Lynch A, *Blackshield and Williams Australian Constitutional Law and Theory* (Federation Press 2018)

Wilson R and Wilford R, 'Northern Ireland: Polarisation or Normalisation?' in Robert Hazell (ed), *Constitutional Futures Revisited: Britain's Constitution to 2020* (Palgrave Macmillan 2008)

Wincott D, Davies G and Wager A, 'Crisis, What Crisis? Conceptualizing Crisis, UK Pluri-Constitutionalism and Brexit Politics' (2021) 55 Regional Studies 1528

Wisthaler V, Prackwieser J and Röggla M, 'South Tyrol' in Brian CH Fong and Atsuko Ichijo (eds), *The Routledge Handbook of Comparative Territorial Autonomies* (Routledge 2022)

Woelk J, 'South Tyrol is (not) Italy: A Special Case in a (De)federalizing system' (2013) 369 L'Europe en Formation 126

Woelk J, Palermo F and Marko J, *Tolerance through Law* (Martinus Nijhoff Publishers 2008)

Wolff S, 'The Institutional Structure of Regional Consociations in Brussels, Northern Ireland, and South Tyrol' (2004) 10 Nationalism and Ethnic Politics 387

Wong HT and Liu S-D, 'Cultural Activism during the Hong Kong Umbrella Movement' (2018) 13 Journal of Creative Communications 157

Wong K, 'Human Rights and Limitation of State Power: The Discovery of Constitutionalism in the People's Republic of China' (2006) 7 Asia-Pacific Journal on Human Rights and the Law 1

Woodwell D, 'The "Troubles" of Northern Ireland: Civil Conflict in an Economically Well-Developed State' in Paul Collier and Nicholas Sambanis (eds), *Understanding Civil War (Volume 2: Europe, Central Asia, & Other Regions): Evidence and Analysis* (The World Bank 2005)

Woodworth P, *Dirty War, Clean Hands: ETA, the GAL and Spanish Democracy* (Cork University Press 2001)

Wyn Jones R and Scully R, *Wales Says Yes: Devolution and the 2011 Welsh Referendum* (University of Wales Press 2012)

Yam B, 'Cross-Border Childbirth Between Mainland China and Hong Kong: Social Pressures and Policy Outcomes' (2011) 8 PORTAL Journal of Multidisciplinary International Studies

Yin Y and Wieczorek I, 'What Model for Extradition between Hong Kong and Mainland China? A Comparison between the 2019 (Withdrawn) Amendment to Hong Kong Extradition Law and the European Arrest Warrant' (2020) 11 New Journal of European Criminal Law 504

Yiu-man TL, 'Mapping the Matrix of Nationalisms in Hong Kong: On the Six Generations of Hongkonger Identities from the 1920s to 2020 and Their Generational Conflicts' in Liah Greenfeld and Zeying Wu (eds), *Research Handbook on Nationalism* (Edward Elgar Publishing 2020)

Yu F-LT and Kwan DS, 'Social Construction of National Reality: Chinese Consciousness versus Hong Kong Consciousness' (2017) 3 Contemporary Chinese Political Economy and Strategic Relations 657

Yu PK, 'Digital Copyright and the Parody Exception in Hong Kong' (2014) 41 Media Asia 119

Yuen S and Chung S, 'Explaining Localism in Post-Handover Hong Kong: An Eventful Approach' (2018) 2018 China Perspectives 19

Zabalo J and Odriozola Irizar O, 'The Importance of Historical Context: A New Discourse on the Nation in Basque Nationalism?' (2017) 23 Nationalism & Ethnic Politics 134

Zabalo J and Iraola I, 'Current Discourses and Attitudes in Favour of the Independence of the Basque Country' (2022) 32 Regional & Federal Studies 73

Zalewski M and Barry J, *Intervening in Northern Ireland: Critically Re-Thinking Representations of the Conflict* (Routledge 2014)

Zaslove A, *The Re-Invention of the European Radical Right: Populism, Regionalism, and the Italian Lega Nord* (MQUP 2011)

Zhang Q, 'A Constitution without Constitutionalism? The Paths of Constitutional Development in China' (2010) 8 International Journal of Constitutional Law 950

Zhang W, *China Wave, The Rise of a Civilizational State* (World Scientific Publishing Company 2012)

Zhang Y, Liu J and Wen J-R, 'Nationalism on Weibo: Towards a Multifaceted Understanding of Chinese Nationalism' (2018) 235 The China Quarterly 758–83

Zhu AYF and Chou KL, 'Collective Action in the Anti-Extradition Law Amendment Bill Movement in Hong Kong: Two Integrative Group Identification Models' (2021) 1 Analyses of Social Issues and Public Policy 1033

Zinn H, *A People's History of the United States* (Reissue edn, Harper 2017)

Zirk-Sadowski M, 'Interpretation of Law and Judges Communities' (2012) 25 International Journal for the Semiotics of Law – Revue internationale de Sémiotique juridique 473

Zubrzycki G, 'Aesthetic Revolt and the Remaking of National Identity in Québec, 1960–1969' (2013) 42 Theory and Society 423

Zubrzycki G, *Beheading the Saint: Nationalism, Religion, and Secularism in Quebec* (University of Chicago Press 2016)

# CASE LAW

Alaska Chapter, Associated General Contractors of America v Pierce, 694 F2d 1162 (9th Cir 1982

Bernardo Provenzano v Italy (Application no 55080/13)

Cherokee Nation v Georgia, 30 US 1 (1831)

Constitutional Court Decision n 31 28/06/2010 172 (Suplemento 11409) BOE 1

Cour de Cassation, Assemblée plénière, du 2 juin 2000, 99-60274, Publié au bulletin

Cour de cassation, civile, Chambre civile 2, 8 mars 2018, 17-60275, Publié au bulletin [2018] Cour de cassation 17-60.275

Decision 76/1983, de 5 de agosto (BOE núm 197, de 18 de agosto de 1983)

Decision n4032 Tribunal of Palermo 17/7/2013
Democratic Republic of the Congo and Others v FG Hemisphere Associates LLC [2011] HKCFA 43
Johnson v M'Intosh 21 US 543 (1823)
Kartinyeri v Commonwealth [1998] HCA 22, 195 CLR 337
Lau Kong Yung and others v the Director of Immigration [1999] HKCFA 5 (Court of Final Appeal)
McGuinness v United Kingdom (Application no 39511/98; decision of 8 June 1999)
Namah v Pato [2016] PGSC 13; SC1497 (26 April 2016)
Native Title Act 1993 n110
Oliphant v Suquamish Indian Tribe (1978) 435 US 191
PY v France [2005] European Court of Human Rights 66289/99
Recurso: 1638–2017 (5 July 2017) Constitutional Court (Spain)
Reference Re Secession of Quebec [1998] 2 SCR 217 [1998] 217
Standing Committee, Decision on Hong Kong's Constitutional Development' 29.12.2007
Standing Committee, 'Decision on Hong Kong's Constitutional Development' 31.08.2014
United States v Wheeler 435 US 313 (1978)
Worcester v State of Georgia (1831) 31 US 515

# STATUTES

Aboriginal Land Rights (Northern Territory) Act 1976
Aboriginal Land Rights (Northern Territory) Regulations 2007
Alaska Native Claims Settlement Act (ANCSA) [1971] 43 U.S.C. (2012).
Appropriation (Northern Territory National Emergency Response) (NO. 1) 2007–2008
Basic Law of the Hong Kong Special Administrative Region of the People's Republic of China OCW CD 825 (HK) 1997
Belgian House of Representatives. Belgian Constitution as updated following the constitutional revision of 24 October 2017 (2017).
British North America Act 1867 (C3)
Canadian Charter of Rights and Freedoms, s 7, Part I of the Constitution Act, 1982, being Schedule B to the Canada Act 1982 (UK), 1982, c 11
Commonwealth of Australia Constitution Act 1900 c 12
Consolidated versions of the Treaty on European Union and the Treaty on the Functioning of the European Union (TFEU) [2016] OJ C202/1.
Constitution du 4 octobre 1958 (version consolidée) 1958
Constitution (Fundamental law) of the Union of Soviet Socialist Republics 1936
Constitution of Ireland (Bunreacht na hÉireann) 1937
Constitution of the Independent State of Papua New Guinea – National Parliament of Papua New Guinea 1975 (consolidated version) 1975
Constitution of the Italian Republic 1948
Constitution of the People's Republic of China (as amended) 1982
Constitutional Law n. 2 26.02.1948
Constitutional Law n. 3 26.02.1948
Constitutional Law n. 4 26.02.1948
Constitutional Law n. 5 26.02.1948
Constitutional Law n. 1 31.1963

Constitutional Law n. 3 18.10.2001
Constitutional Reform Act 2005 Ch 4
Council Decision (EU) 2020/135 on the conclusion of the Agreement on the withdrawal of the United Kingdom of Great Britain and Northern Ireland from the European Union and the European Atomic Energy Community [2020] OJ L029/1
European Union (Withdrawal Agreement) Act 2020 c.1 2020
Federal Constitution of 18 April 1999 of the Swiss Confederation 2000
French Constitution 1958 (as revised 23/07/2008) 1958
Government of Ireland Act 1920 c 67
Government of Wales Act 1998 c 38
Human Rights Act 1998 c 42
Indian Reorganization Act 1934 Pub.L. 73–383 2022
Law n. 5 21.05.2009
Law n. 5 21.12.1971
Law n. 64 2.2.1974
Law n. 646 25.09.1982
Law n. 1684 25.11.1962
Law n. 1086 5.11.1971
Law of the People's Republic of China on Safeguarding National Security in the Hong Kong Special Administrative Region 2020
Ley 12/1983, de 14 de octubre, del Proceso Autonómico 1985
Ley 7/2014, de 21 de Abril, Por La Que Se Modifica La Ley 12/2002, de 23 de Mayo, Por La Que Se Aprueba El Concierto Económico Con La Comunidad Autónoma Del País Vasco 2014
Ley Orgánica 3/1979, de 18 de diciembre, de Estatuto de Autonomía Para El País Vasco 1979
Ley Orgánica 6/1981, de 30 de diciembre, de Estatuto de Autonomía para Andalucía 1982
Ley Orgánica 7/1982 30 de julio, de Armonización del Proceso Autonómico (LOAPA) 1982
Ley Orgánica 6/2002, de 27 de junio, de Partidos Políticos 2002
Ley Orgánica 1/2006, de 10 de abril, de Reforma de la Ley Orgánica 5/1982, de 1 de julio, de Estatuto de Autonomía de la Comunidad Valenciana 2006
Loi n°69-4 du 3 janvier 1969 modifiant la reglementation miniere en nouvelle-caledonie 1969
Loi constitutionnelle n° 2008-724 du 23 juillet 2008 de modernisation des institutions de la Ve République
Loi constitutionnelle n°2003-276 du 28 mars 2003 relative à l'organisation décentralisée de la République
Loi constitutionnelle no 98-610 du 20 juillet 1998 relative à la Nouvelle-Calédonie
Loi n° 82-213 du 2 mars 1982 relative aux droits et libertés des communes, des départements et des régions
Loi n° 88-1028 du 9 novembre 1988 portant dispositions statutaires et préparatoires à l'autodétermination de la Nouvelle-Calédonie en 1998
Loi n° 99-209 organique du 19 mars 1999 relative à la Nouvelle-Calédonie (consolidée au 07 janvier 2019)
Loi n°56-619 du 23 1956 juin mesures propres a assurer l'evolution des territoires relevant du Ministere de la France d'outre-mer 1956
Loi organique n° 2013-1027 du 15 novembre 2013 portant actualisation de la loi organique n° 99-209 du 19 mars 1999 relative à la Nouvelle-Calédonie

Loi organique n° 2015-987 du 5 août 2015 relative à la consultation sur l'accession de la Nouvelle-Calédonie à la pleine souveraineté
Loi organique n° 2018-280 du 19 avril 2018 relative à l'organisation de la consultation sur l'accession à la pleine souveraineté de la Nouvelle-Calédonie
Loi organique n° 2018-280 du 19 avril 2018 relative à l'organisation de la consultation sur l'accession à la pleine souveraineté de la Nouvelle-Calédonie
Marine (Scotland) Act 2010 Asp 5
Mining Act 1992
Nineteenth Amendment of the Constitution Act 1998
Northern Territory National Emergency Response Act 2007
Northern Territory (Self-government) Act 1978
Official Languages Act (1969) 1970, R.S.C, c 0-2
Oil and Gas Act 1998
Papua New Guinea: Constitution of the Independent State of Papua New Guinea (rev. 2014) 1975
Racial Discrimination Act 1975
Social Security and Other Legislation Amendment (Welfare Payment Reform) Act 2007
Spanish Constitution 1978
Stronger Futures in the Northern Territory Act 2012
Stronger Futures in the Northern Territory (Consequential and Transitional Provisions) Act 2012
Terrorism Act 2000 (as revised) c 11
The Letters Patent (or The Hong Kong Charter) 1843 (CO129/2) 104
The Letters Patent (or the principal Letters Patent) 1917 (118) 104
The Australian Constitution 1901
The Constitution Act, 1867, 30 & 31 Vict, c 3 (renamed from the British North America Act 1867 by the Constitution Act 1982 s.53 (2)
The Constitution Act 1982
The Constitution of the Autonomous Region of Bougainville 2004
The Criminal Law Amendment Act S.C. 1968–69, c 38
The Northern Ireland Act 1998 c 47
The Northern Ireland (St Andrews Agreement) Act 2006 c 53
The Organic Law on Peace-building in Bougainville, Autonomous Bougainville Government and Bougainville Referendum 2002
The Quebec Act 1774 14 Geo. III c 83
The Seat of Government Act 1908
The War Measures Act 5 1914 c 2
To update the online data entry format for federal databases relevant to cases of missing and murdered indigenous women (MMIW Act of Savanna's Act) Pub.L 116-165
Violence Against Women Act Reauthorization Act of 2022 (as a part of the Consolidated Appropriations Act, 2022) Pub.L. 117–103) 2022
Violence Against Women Act Reauthorization Act of 2022 Pub.L. 117–103 2022
Wales Act 2017 c 4
War Measures Act 1970 c W.-2

## DOCUMENTS AND REPORTS

Aboriginal Peak Organisations of the Northern Territory, 'Stronger Futures and Customary Law (Briefing Paper 2012)' Darwin 2012

Accord sur la Nouvelle-Calédonie signé à Nouméa le 5 mai 1998 Numea 1998

Agreement on the withdrawal of the United Kingdom of Great Britain and Northern Ireland from the European Union and the European Atomic Energy Community [2020] OJ L029/7 [2020] OJ L029/1 Brussels 2020

Alaska Legal Services Corporation., 'Tribal Court Jurisdiction in Alaska 2012' Anchorage 2012

Alaska Native Women's Resource Center, 'Missing and Murdered Indigenous Women: An Action Plan for Alaska Native Communities 2021' Fairbanks 2021

Australian Institute of Family Studies, 'Poverty and Child Abuse and Neglect' Canberra 2019

Australia and Department of Families Community Services and Indigenous Affairs, Stronger Futures in the Northern Territory: A Ten Year Commitment to Aboriginal People in the Northern Territory, Dept of Families, Housing, Community Services and Indigenous Affairs Canberra 2012

Australian Bureau of Statistics, 'Census: Aboriginal and Torres Strait Islander Population' Canberra 2021

Australian Bureau of Statistics. 'The Average Australian' Canberra 2013

Australian Human Rights Commission, 'A Statistical Overview of Aboriginal and Torres Strait Islander Peoples in Australia: Social Justice Report 2008' Canberra 2009

Australian Human Rights Commission, 'National Anti-Racism Strategy Consultation Report' Canberra 2012

Australian Indigenous Leadership Centre, 'Submission to Joint Select Committee on Australian Indigenous Leadership Centre Constitutional Recognition of Aboriginal and Torres Strait Islander Peoples' Kingston 2014

Australian Institute of Health and Welfare 'Australia's Children, Child Abuse and Neglect'. Canberra 2020

Australian Parliament, Joint Select Committee on Constitutional Recognition of Aboriginal and Torres Strait Islander Peoples, 'Final Report' Canberra 2015

Banca d 'Italia, 'Economie Regionali L'economia Delle Regioni Italiane Dinamiche Recenti e Aspetti Strutturali' Rome 2014

Canadian Museum of History 'Gallup Poll 1970: Justification for Invoking the WarMeasures Act' Gatineau 1970

Census Bureau 'American Indian Alaska Native Population Growth'. Washington 2019

Center for Security and Crime Science 'Predictive Modelling Combining Short and Long-Term Crime Risk Potential: Final Report' Philadelphia 2010

CERM, 'La spesa sanitaria delle Regioni in Italia' Siena 2017

Central Intelligence Agency. 'The World Factbook: Hong Kong'. US Government Printing Office Washington 2017

Central Intelligence Agency, 'The World Factbook Papua: New Guinea' US Government Printing Office Washington 2017

Centre for Communication and Public Opinion Survey, The Chinese University of Hong Kong 'The Identity and National Identification of Hong Kong People Survey Results' Hong Kong 2015

Connections, 'Statement by Northern Territory Elders and Community Representatives – No More! Enough Is Enough!' Melbourne, 2011

Commisione Parlamentare di Inchiesta Sule fenomeno della mafia, 'Audizione Del Collaboratore Della Giustizia Antonino Calderone-Presidenza Del Presidente Luciano Violante' Rome 2018

Commisione Parlamentare di Inchiesta Sule fenomeno della mafia, 'Report by the Procuratore Nazionale Antimafia' Rome 2014

Commisione Parlamentare di Inchiesta Sule fenomeno della mafia, 'Report by the Procuratore Nazionale Antimafia' Rome 2019

Conservative and Unionist Party, 'The Conservative and Unionist Party Manifesto 2019' London 2019

Diao X and others, 'Effects of COVID-19 on Papua New Guinea's Food Economy: A Multi-Market Simulation Analysis' International Food Policy Research Institute Washington 2020

Declaration on the Rights of Indigenous Peoples (GA Res 61/295, UN Doc A/RES/47/1 (2007))

Departamento de Seguridad, Gobierno Basco 'Archivo de resultados electorales'. Vitoria Gasteiz 2019

Department for Public Leadership and Social Enterprise, 'Briefing Note: The Consequences for the Northern Ireland Economy from a United Kingdom Exit from the European Union' Belfast 2015

Department of Families, Housing, Community Services and Indigenous Affairs 'Closing the Gap on Indigenous Disadvantage: The Challenge for Australia' Canberra 2009

Department of Foreign Affairs and Trade 'Papua New Guinea COVID-19 Response' Canberra 2022

Department of Justice, Annual Government-to-Government and Violence Against Women Tribal Consultation, '2021 Update on the Status of Tribal Consultation Recommendations'

Department of the Chief Minister, Office of Indigenous Policy 'Northern Territory and others, Ampe Akelyernemane Meke Mekarle: Little Children Are Sacred' Darwin 2007

Department of Pacific Affairs Australian Government 'Community Law Making and the Codification of Customary Laws' in brief series: 2018/19 Canberra 2019

Direzione Nazionale Antimafia e Antiterrorismo, 'Relazione Annuale Sulle Attività Svolte Dal Procuratore Nazionale Antimafia e Dalla Direzione Nazionale Antimafia Nonché Sulle Dinamiche e Strategie Della Criminalità Organizzata Di Tipo Mafioso Nel Periodo 1° Luglio 2018 – 31 Dicembre 2019.' Rome 2020

Direzione Nazionale Antimafia e Antiterrorismo, Relazione Annuale Sulle Attività Svolte Dal Procuratore Nazionale Antimafia e Dalla Direzione Nazionale Antimafia Nonché Sulle Dinamiche e Strategie Della Criminalità Organizzata Di Tipo Mafioso Nel Periodo 2° Luglio 2018 – 31 Dicembre 2019.' Rome 2020

European Commission, Irish Government and UK Government, 'HM Government, Financing Agreement between the United Kingdom of Great Britain and Northern Ireland, Ireland and the European Commission on the PEACE PLUS Programme 2021–2027, CP 823' (as revised March 2023)

European Commission and UK Government, 'Joint Declaration of the Union and the United Kingdom in the Joint Committee Established by the Agreement on the Withdrawal of the United Kingdom of Great Britain and Northern Ireland from the European Union and the European Atomic Energy Community of 24 March 2023 on Article 13(3a) of the Windsor Framework (See Joint Declaration No 1/2023)' PUB/2023/435 [2023] OJ L102/90

European Commission, Directorate-General for Justice, Freedom and Security, 'Competitiveness in Low-Income and Low-Growth Regions – The Lagging Regions Report 2017' Brussels 2017

European Commission, and Center for the Study of Democracy, 'Examining the Links between Organised Crime and Corruption' Brussels 2011

European Parliamentary Research Service, 'Regional Inequalities in the EU' European Parliamentary Research Service, Brussels 2009

Flanders Marine Institute (VLIZ), Belgium, 'Maritime Boundaries Geodatabase: Maritime Boundaries and Exclusive Economic Zones Version 10, Ostend 2018

French Republic, FranceArchives, 'Visite Officielle Du Général de Gaulle à Montréal, Exposition Universelle de Montréal', Paris 1967

French Parliament, 'Accords de Matignon-Oudinot Du Juin 1988 in the Rapport Fait Au Nom de La Commission Des Lois Constitutionnelles, de Législation, Du Suffrage Universel, Du Règlement et d'administration Générale Sur Le Projet de Loi, Adopté Par l'Assemblée Nationale, Après Déclaration d'urgence, Portant Amnistie d'infractions Commises à l'occasion d'événements Survenus En Nouvelle-Calédonie, Annexes 1 & 2, Senat 7 of December 1989, Vol 112 47-52' Paris 1989

Fondazione Eni Enrico Mattei, 'The Hybrid State Destatization and Neopatrimonialism': Milan 2020

Front de Libération du Québec, 'Le manifeste du FLQ'. *La Presse*, Montreal 2009

General Assembly United Nations, 'Resolution 35/118 Plan of Action for the Full Implementation of the Declaration on Granting of Independence to Colonial Countries and Peoples' New York 1980

General Assembly United Nations, 'Resolution 41/41A Implementation of the Declaration on the Granting of Independence to Colonial Countries and Peoples' New York 1986

General Office of the State Council of the People's Republic of China, 'The Socialist System of Laws with Chinese Characteristics' Beijing 2011

Hayward, Katy, David Phinnemore, and Milena Komarova. 'Anticipating and Meeting New Multilevel Governance Challenges in Northern Ireland after Brexit'. The UK in a Changing Europe – Queen's University Belfast, London 2020

Haut-commissariat de la République en Nouvelle-Calédonie, 'Les Résultats Du Référendum 2018 – Élections Nouvelle-Calédonie' Noumea 2021

Hong Kong Monetary Authority. 'Dominant Gateway to China' Hong Kong 2019

Human Rights and Equal Opportunity Commission, 'Bringing Them Home: Report of the National Canberra 1987

Indigenous and Northern Affairs, 'The Government of Canada's Approach to Implementation of the Inherent Right and the Negotiation of Aboriginal Self-Government' Paonia 2008

Philippine Institute for Development Studies, 'Investment and Capital Flows: Implications of the ASEAN Economic Community' Makati 2009

Inquiry into the Separation of Aboriginal and Torres Strait Islander Children from Their Families' Canberra 1997

IRES Piemonte and others, 'La Finanza Territoriale' Siena 2018

Istituto Nazionale di Statistica, 'Dati Statistici per Il Territorio: Regione Sicilia' Rome, 2020

Istituto Nazionale di Statistica, 'Delitti Denunciati Dalle Forze Di Polizia All'autorità Giudiziaria' Rome 2010

La commission de contrôle de l'organisation et du déroulement de la consultation sur l'accession à la pleine souveraineté de la Nouvelle-Calédonie, 'Journal officiel de la République Française n.257 Paris 2018

International Monetary Fund, Lundgren C, Alun T and York R, 'Boom, Bust, or Prosperity? Managing Sub-Saharan Africa's Natural Resource Wealth' Washington 2013

National Bureau of Statistics, 'Main Data of the Seventh National Population Census 2020' Washington 2021

National Inquiry into Missing and Murdered Indigenous Women and Girls (Canada), 'Executive Summary of the Final Report: Reclaiming Power and Place: The Final Report of the National Inquiry into Missing and Murdered Indigenous Women and Girls' Quebec City 2019

National Statistical Office '2011 National Population & Housing Census: Ward Population Profile: Islands Region' Port Moresby 2014

NTER Review Board, 'Northern Territory Emergency Response: Report of the NTER Review Board' Canberra 2008

Northern Ireland Statistics and Research Agency, 'Police Recorded Security Situation Statistics 1 December 2020 to 30 November 2021' Belfast 2021

Northern Ireland Statistics and Research Agency, 'Incidents and Crimes with a Hate Motivation Recorded by the Police in Northern Ireland Update to 30th September 2021' Belfast 2021

OECD 'Skills Matter: Further Results from the Survey of Adult Skills' Paris 2016

Office of the First Minister and, Report on the Inquiry Into Building a United Community 'Fifteenth Report, Written Submissions' Belfast 2015

Politics Science Resources 'Labour Party Manifesto, General Election 1997' London 2012

PSNI Statistics Branch, 'Police Recorded Security Situation Statistics' Belfast 2017

Public Opinions Programme, 'National Issues. People's Ethnic Identity' Hong Kong 2018

Scottish Government 'Community Experiences of Sectarianism' Edinburgh 2015

Scottish Ministers, the Welsh Ministers and the Northern Ireland Executive Committee., 'Devolution: Memorandum of Understanding and Supplementary Agreements' London 2013

Sénat 'Rapport d'information fait au nom de la Commission des finances, du contrôle budgétaire et des comptes économiques de la Nation sur la mission de contrôle effectuée en Nouvelle-Calédonie relative à la défiscalisation des usines de traitement de nickel' Paris 2005

The Department of Public Safety, 'Felony Level Sex Offenses, Crime in Alaska Supplemental Report 2017' Anchorage 2017

The Electoral Office of Northern Ireland 'UK Parliamentary Election 2019 – Results' Belfast 2019

The Government SAR, 'Basic Education Curriculum Guide – Building on Strengths: Four Key Tasks – Achieving Learning to Learn – 3A Moral and Civic Education' Hong Kong 2002

The Government of the Republic of Slovenia, Statistical Office, 'SiStat Database' Ljubljana 2021

The School of Regulation and Global Governance (RegNet). 'Deepening Indigenous Poverty in the Northern Territory' Canberra 2017

The UK Government and the Government of Ireland, 'The Belfast Agreement: An Agreement Reached at the Multi-Party Talks on Northern Ireland 1998' Belfast 1998

The United Nations 'Joint Declaration on the Question of Hong Kong (Adopted 19 December 1984, Entered into Force 12 June 1985) New York 1985
The World Bank, 'GDP per Capita (Current US$) – Hong Kong SAR, China (1960–2020)' Washington 2020
The World Bank Group and The European Commission, 'Doing Business in the European Union 2020: Greece, Ireland and Italy' Washington 2020
Tribunal of Palermo, 'Witness Transcript of Tommaso Buscetta to Judge G. Falcone' Palermo 1984
United Nations, 'Concluding Observations of the Committee on the Elimination of Racial Discrimination – Australia' New York 2010
United Nations, General Recommendation 23: Indigenous Peoples, 1997.A/52/18, Annex V' New York 1997
United Nations, 'Report of the Secretary-General – Information from Non-Self-Governing Territories Transmitted under Article 73 e of the Charter of the United Nations' New York 2017
United Nations, 'New Caledonia: Current Realities and Prospects for Decolonizaion under the Noumea Accord' New York 2012
United Nations Development Program, 'UNDP 2019 Human Development Report: Human Development in Asia-Pacific Region Advances Dramatically, New York 2022
United Nations Development Programme, '2014 Human Development Report PNG' New York 2014
United Nations General Assembly, 'General Assembly Resolution n.1514 Declaration on the Granting of Independence to Colonial Countries and Peoples' New York 1960
United Nations General Assembly, 'UNGA Res 2908 (1972) GAOR 27th Session Supp 29, 08 New York 1972
U.S. Department of Justice/Department of the Interior, 'Report to the President: Activities and Accomplishments of the First Year of Operation Lady Justice' Washington 2020
U.S. Department of Justice/Department of the Interior, Office on Violence Against Women, 'Annual Report Proceedings, Government-to-Government Violence Against Women Tribal Consultation' Washington 2020
U.S. Department of Justice/Department of the Interior, Tribal Consultations & Advisory Groups, 'Tribal Consultation Reports' Washington 2014
U.S. Department of Justice/Department of the Interior, 'Consultation on Public Safety and Missing or Murdered Indigenous Persons' (16 March 2022) Washington 2022
Violence Policy Center, 'When Men Murder Women: An Analysis of 2017 Homicide Data' Washington 2019

# NEWS REPORTS

AFFAIRS SHI and Cubby B, 'Mining Licences Would Reap Aborigines Millions' The Sydney Morning Herald (Sydney, Australia) (Sydney, NSW, 9 March 2012) 1
Aizpeolea LR, 'ETA pone fin a 43 años de terror' El País (20 October 2011)
Allison W, 'Native American Women Are Missing and Murdered. Will the Federal Government Act?' The Colorado Independent (18 February 2020)
Barry J, 'From Power Sharing to Power Being Shared Out' Green European Journal (1 July 2017)

Bartosch J, 'Why Are So Many Indigenous Women in Alaska Coming Up Missing and Murdered?' A&E (26 January 2019)

'Berlusconi Masterminded Tax Evasion Plan, Italian Court Says' Reuters (29 August 2013)

Brown K, 'Why Is Beijing Obsessed with Order? It Fears the Alternative' South China Morning Post (28 April 2018)

'Can Northern Ireland Survive Brexit?' Politico (29 August 2013)

Cochrane F, 'How Northern Ireland's Government Went from Mutual Suspicion to Collapse' The Conversation (18 January 2017)

Coleman M, 'Fighting an Election Only to Refuse a Seat: Sinn Féin and Westminster Abstention' The Conversation (2 May 2017)

'Concorsi nelle Forze dell'ordine truccati, 8 misure cautelari' Agenzia Italia (12 July 2020)

Dayant A, 'The Demographic Influence in New Caledonia's next Referendum' Lowy Institute (30 August 2020)

Doherty B, '"Unacceptable": UN Committee Damns Australia's Record on Human Rights' *The Guardian* (17 October 2017)

Discours de Montréal 'Vive le Québec libre' Panorama – (28 July 1967)

'Disoccupazione giovanile record: la Sicilia in coda alla classifica europea' La Repubblica (30 April 2019)

'Eta: Basque Separatists Begin Weapons Handover' BBC News (8 April 2017)

'France Sends More Police to New Caledonia' RNZ (7 November 2016)

Gardner D, 'Why Basques and Catalans See Independence Differently' Financial Times (12 July 2019)

Grant S, 'Stan Grant: A Decade after the NT "Intervention", the "torment of Powerlessness" Lives On' ABC News (21 June 2017)

Helm T and editor political, 'Stop Rich Overseas Investors from Buying up UK Homes, Report Urges' The Observer (1 February 2014)

'Hong Kong Advert Calls Chinese Mainlanders "Locusts"' BBC News (1 February 2012)

'Hong Kong Protests: What LegCo Graffiti Tells Us' BBC News (3 July 2019)

'Hong Kong Protests: What Is the "Umbrella Movement"?' CBBC Newsround (28 September 2019)

'Houses over Apartments: Chinese Overseas Buyers Tipped to Come Back for Land When Australia's Borders Open' ABC News (1 July 2021)

'How a Word, "Chee-Na," Renewed a Crisis Between Beijing and Hong Kong' The New York Times (10 November 2016)

'Italian Regions of Lombardy and Veneto Vote for More Autonomy' The New York Times (22 October 2017)

'Kanak Groups Call For International Investigation Into Shooting By Police', Pacific Islands Report (17 January 2017)

'La banda dei giudici corrotti: l'inchiesta che sta sconvolgendo la magistratura' l'Espresso (19 February 2019)

Lieto GD, 'What's the Deal (or No-Deal) with Brexit? Here's Everything Explained' The Conversation (17 January 2019)

Liz H, 'Domestic Violence, Sexual Violence and MMIW' Alaska Native News (3 May 2021) Main M, 'Australia Can Help Ensure the Biggest Mine in PNG's History Won't Leave a Toxic Legacy' The Conversation (29 June 2022)

McKenzie N, 'Pedophile Ring Claims Unfounded' The Sydney Morning Herald (7 May 2009)

'Meaningful Participation: Women and Peacebuilding in the Pacific' Lowy Institute (12 November 2018)
Murphy MC, 'What Sinn Féin's Election Success Means for Irish Relations with the EU – and Brexit' The Conversation (13 February 2020)
'No Evidence of Indigenous Paedophile Rings: Martin' The Sydney Morning Herald (17 June 2006)
Perche D, 'Ten Years on, It's Time We Learned the Lessons from the Failed Northern Territory Intervention' (The Conversation, 26 June 2017)
Phinnemore D, 'Brexit and Northern Ireland: The Latest Commitments Explained' The Conversation (1 November 2019)
Roantree AM, 'China Condemns Violent Hong Kong Protests as "Undisguised Challenge" to Its Rule' Reuters (2 July 2019)
'Salgono a 201 i comuni attualmente sciolti in Italia' Openpolis (23 March 2020)
Scarr S, Sharma M and Hernandez M, 'Hong Kong Protests: How Many Protesters Took to the Streets on July 1?' Reuters (4 July 2019)
Scuola R, 'Augusto Fantozzi e i 7 Arrestati: Ecco Chi Sono i Docenti Dello Scandalo Concorsi Truccati' Corriere della Sera (25 September 2017)
Shidong Z, 'China's Investors Are Flooding Hong Kong's Capital Market in Search of Value as They Dodge US Sanctions' South China Morning Post (7 February 2021)
State Council (China), 'The Practice of the "One Country, Two Systems" Policy in the Hong Kong Special Administrative Region'
Tarantino F, 'Sicilia, commissari in 278 Comuni che non hanno approvato il bilancio: c'è anche Palermo' Giornale di Sicilia (10 August 2022)
'The Hong Kong Protests Explained in 100 and 500 Words' BBC News (28 November 2019)
Truett Jerue, Tami 'A Tribal Perspective on the Crisis of Alaska Native Women and MMIW | NIWRC' (27 April 2017)
Tsang A, 'Hong Kong Anger at Chinese "Locust" Shoppers Intensifies' Financial Times (16 February 2015)
Vale Nouvelle-Calédonie dénonce "une violence quotidienne", et renforcée, contre l'usine du Sud' Nouvelle-Calédonie la 1ère (1 February 2021)
'VAWA Special Domestic Violence Jurisdiction for Alaska Indian Tribes Is Essential' NIWRC (1 June 2020)
'Voto Di Scambio in Sicilia, 96 Indagati. C'è Anche l'ex Governatore Cuffaro – La Repubblica' (14 March 2014)
'Wounds Persist in Spain, Ten Years after ETA Lays down Arms' (France 24, 20 October 2021)

## BLOGS AND REPORTS

Fog in Belfast: A Hundred Years of Uneasiness, and No End in Sight (Directed by Duncan Morrow, 2020) accessed 19 December 2021
'Italy's Latest Legislation on Accounting Fraud Highlights the Country's Difficulty in Pursuing Real Economic and Political Reform' (EUROPP, 13 July 2015) (accessed 6 September 2020)
Rice C, 'A Road to Nowhere? The UK's Approach to Implementing the NI Protocol'. *A Road to Nowhere? The UK's Approach to Implementing the NI Protocol* (blog), 23 May 2020 <https://ukandeu.ac.uk/a-road-to-nowhere-the-uks-approach-to-implementing-the-ni-protocol/>.

Young SN, 'The Legal Limits on Beijing's Powers to Interpret Hong Kong's Basic Law' (accessed 20 October 2021)

Youngspiration's Sixtus 'Baggio Leung' Takes His Oath at the Hong Kong Legislature (Directed by Hong Kong Free Press, 2016) <www.youtube.com/watch?v=abkdv2X3RcE> (accessed 22 November 2021)

# Index

Aboriginal Peoples and Torres Strait Islanders *see* Australia
Alaska
    colonialism, legacy of 111–15
    dependent nation, as 105–7
    Federal institutions, systemic barriers created by 112
    population trends 103–4
Alaskan Native Peoples
    Alaska Native Claims Settlement Act 1971 89, 107
    Alaska Native Corporation Villages 107–9
    colonialist legacy 111–15
    consultative policy formation 103
    criminal investigatory powers 108–10, 113–14
    dehumanisation of 105–7, 111–14
    'doctrine of discovery' 106
    drivers of change 88, 105
        colonial legacy and racial stereotypes 110–14
        Native American–Alaskan institutional frameworks 104, 107–9
    genocide 102–5
    Indian tribes
        Indian Reorganization Act 1934 105–7
        variation in treatment from 106–7
    jurisdictional powers 108–10
    land ownership 105–7
    population trends 103–4
    Russian fur traders, exploitation by 112–13
    sovereignty 105–6
    status, colonial perceptions of 105–7, 111–14
    tribal powers 105–6
    US law
        Constitutional provisions 105
        dependence, judicial interpretation 106–7
    violence against women
        influences on 102–5, 111–15
        National Inquiry into Missing and Murdered Indigenous Women and Girls 103
        Violence Against Women Reauthorization Act 2022 103–5, 109–10, 114
Anderson, Benedict 158
Australia
    Aboriginal Peoples and Torres Strait Islanders
        Aboriginal children, abuse of 175–8
        Aboriginal Land Rights (Northern Territory) Act 1976 89, 173, 179
        constitutional recognition, lack of 182–4, 186
        corruption in leadership, claims of 184
        crime/criminal supervision rates 188–9
        cultural gap 190
        education and unemployment 188
        Federal government consultation, lack of 175–6, 178
        Federal policy-making, racialised assumptions in 176–8
        identity-formation, influences on 190–93, 195

*Kartinyeri v Commonwealth*,
    influences of 185–6
land ownership and community
    leasing, legislative
    restrictions 179–80, 194
life expectancy 188
*Little Children Are Sacred*
    Report 2007 175–6, 178
Native Title Act 1993 173
population, scope of 174
poverty in 187–90, 194–5
Racial Discrimination Act
    1975, suspension and
    reinstatement 173, 180,
    186
racist stereotyping 176–8,
    190–93, 195
rights, legislative restrictions on
    173–4, 179, 184–5
social justice gap 187–8
social justice targets 188–9
Stronger Futrures Policy,
    implications of 173–4
colonisation/decolonisation
    racism policies, generally
        185–6, 192
    recognition of native rights 183
Constitution
    Commonwealth of Australia
        Constitution Act 1990
        172
    communal land ownership 179
    Federal Constitution 172
    federal prerogative to pass any
        statute 7, 173, 179–80,
        185–6
    *Kartinyeri v Commonwealth*
        185–6
    parliamentary sovereignty 172
    recognition of Aboriginal
        peoples and their rights,
        lack of 182–4, 186
    territorial powers 172–3
drivers of change
    Aboriginal vs non-indigenous
        values and perspectives
        190–93, 195
    constitutional powers to
        legislate without
        consultation 182–6, 194

discriminatory legislation
    182–6, 194
poverty and geographical
    remoteness of
    Aboriginal communities
    187–90, 194–5
federalism
    land ownership 179–80, 184–5
    'race power' prerogative 7, 173,
        179–80, 185–6
    self-government powers,
        limitations on 172–3
generally
    population overview 174
    racism and stereotype
        perceptions 190–93, 195
    territorial administration 172
identity-formation
    Aboriginal vs non-indigenous
        values and perspectives
        190–93, 195
    constitutional failure to
        recognise diversity
        182–3
Northern Territory
    abuse of Aboriginal children
        175–8
    distributive justice policies
        187–8
    geography 187
    land ownership and leasing
        policies 179–80, 184–5,
        194
    Northern Territory Intervention
        173–81, 184–5, 194
    Northern Territory National
        Emergency Response
        Act 2007 173
    Northern Territory
        Self-Government Act
        1978 173
    poverty 187–90, 194–5
    pre-policy consultation, lack of
        175–6, 178, 184
    racial targeting of polices
        177–8
    Social Security and Other
        Legislation Amendment
        (Welfare Payment
        Reform) 2007 173

Stronger Futures policies 173–5
Northern Territory Intervention
   amendments under Stronger
      Futures Policy 181
   child abuse evidence,
      limitations of 177–9
   communal land leases transfer
      powers 179–80, 184–5,
      194
   consultation with Aboriginal
      Peoples, lack of 175–6,
      178, 184
   implementation, military role in
      184–5, 193
   Northern Territory Elders
      and Community
      Representatives
      responses to 181
   Northern Territory Emergency
      Response Board
      consultations 180
   overview 173–6, 194
   racial discrimination in 179–80
poverty
   child abuse in Aboriginal
      children, and 177
   domestic violence, link with
      176–7, 189
   geographical remoteness of
      Aboriginal Peoples, and
      187–90, 194–5
   racialised perceptions 176–7
autonomous communities *see also* New
   Caledonia; Northern Ireland;
   Sicily
Basque Country *see* Spain
Bougainville *see* Papua New Guinea

banal nationalism 137–8
Belfast Agreement 1998 16–17, 21–2,
   30–31, 226
*A Belfast Child* 19–20
Bell, David Avrom 158
Billing, Michaeli 137–8
Bougainville *see* Papua New Guinea
Brexit
   background 37
   Northern Ireland, and
      border controls 40, 41
      debate, limitations of 38–9
      democratic gap 38–9
      driver for change, as 19, 37–42,
         227
      EU economic support 40–41,
         43
      impacts, generally 19, 37–8,
         41–2
      Ireland, relations with 38–40
      political supporters 40–41
      Protocol 2020 38–9, 41, 43–4
      regional identity-making, and
         43–4
Brown, Kerry 144

Canada
   Constitution
      Aboriginal peoples, recognition
         of 93–4
      Constitution Act 1867 92, 94–6
      Constitution Act 1982 92–5
      driver for change, as 90, 93–6
      federal competences 95–6
      historical background 92–3
      multinational political basis
         90–91
      national identities or languages,
         references to 92–4
      Quebec legitimacy, lack of 90,
         93–6, 101
      War Measures provisions 95–6,
         100
   drivers of change
      constitutional recognition, lack
         of 90, 93–6, 101–2
      generally 88, 99–100
      October Crisis 101–2, 225
      Québécois identity 90, 93–4
      'steady-as-she-goes' scenario
         101–2
   identity-formation
      Catholic Church, role of 98–9
      constitutional references to
         national identities 92
      French influences 99–100
      French-speakers, attitudes of
         97–8
      magazines and newspapers 98
      *Maîtres chez nous* (slogan) 99
      October Crisis 96, 101–2, 225

Québécois identity 90, 93–4,
  96–100
radio and television
  broadcasting 97–8
Quebec
  Catholic Church, political
    influences of 98–9
  constitutional history 91–4, 101
  drivers of change 88, 90, 96
  emergency powers, application
    of 95–6, 100
  French support for regional
    government 99–101
  Front de la Liberation du
    Quebec 90
  independence referendum 93–4,
    101
  magazines and newspapers 98
  October Crisis 89–90, 93–6,
    101–2, 225
  Official Languages Act 1969 94
  Parti Québécois representation
    in National Assembly
    94–5, 101
  Québécois identity 90, 93–4,
    96–100
  Quiet Revolution 96, 99–101
  radio and television
    broadcasting 97–8
  rebellions (1838/1848) 92
  recognition of sovereignty/
    distinct nation 101
  terrorism/political violence
    88–93, 100–101
  Treaty of Paris 1763 92
Chambers, John 19
Chan, Elaine 137–8
Chan, Joseph 137–8
Chappell, David 163
China
  constitutional law
    Communist Party controls
      132–4
    history 116
    ideological basis 115, 117,
      132–3
    opposition to socialism,
      prohibition of 116
    pragmatic reasoning 132–4
  general overview
    Communist Party, influences of
      120, 133–4, 141–5
    Confucianism 142
    cultural homogeneity 145–6
    ethnic minorities, regional
      distribution 118–19
  governance system, generally
    administrative basis 119–20
    Chongfanpinan administrative
      reform 119
    civil service–Communist Party
      relationships 120
    conformity and compliance
      expectations 118
    elections 120, 134
    influences on 118–19
    regional governance and
      autonomy 116
    'Three Supremes' 134, 142,
      224
  Hong Kong, reforms in see Hong
    Kong
  identity-formation
    Chinese Communist Party,
      influences on 141–5
    Chongfanpinan administrative
      reform 119
    collective consciousness 142
    Hong Kong role in 143–6
    national language, promotion
      of 119
    sacred unity concept 143
    'Sons of the Dragon' 141–5
  legal principles
    Communist Party relationship
      with 133–4
    influences on 118
    rule of law 117, 133–4, 142–3
  see also Hong Kong
colonisation
  Australia, native rights 183, 185–6
  Hong Kong 120–21, 123–4
  New Caledonia, influences on
    Kanak People 150–53
  perceptions of constitutional
    legitimacy, influences on 8

US, Alsakan legacy 111–15
comparative law, generally
   future studies methodology 3–4,
      88–9, 129
constitutional crises, generally
   causes 220–21
   constitutional ability to adapt 225
   constitutional neutrality 222–3
   transgenerational trauma 221–2
constitutional futures methodology 3–5,
   88–9, 129
*Constitutional Futures: The History of
   the Next Ten Years* 4–5
constitutional interpretation, generally
   constitutional rules compared with
      administrative rules 50
   dispositive principle 53–4
   general approaches 49
   pragmatic reasoning 49, 132–4, 224
*Constitutional Law and Regionalism* 7–8
constitutional law, generally
   constitutional aspirations, role of
      222–4
   constitutional attachment, optimal
      conditions for 229
   driver for change, as 9
   perceptions of neutrality 2–3
   role of constitutions in modern
      society 224
corruption
   administrative effectiveness, and
      75–80
   neo-patrimonialist administrative
      systems, and 75–8, 86–7
   Northern Ireland 23, 35–6
   Papua New Guinea 200–203
   *see also* Mafia; organised crime
Covid-19 pandemic, effects of
   Hong Kong 128–9, 131, 145
   New Caledonia 12–13, 167–8
   Northern Ireland 18–19
   Papua New Guinea 197
   Spain 62
culture
   indigenous culture and customs
      cultural customs and liberal
         values, balance of
         209–10, 213
      cultural gap 190
      promotion of 166
   multi-cultural societies
      cultural distinctiveness 162–3
      cultural homogeneity 145–6
      deliberative democratic
         practices 209–10,
         217–18

D'Attona, John 79
Davies, Gregory 38
Davis, Megan 184
De Gaulle, Charles 99–100
decolonisation
   Hong Kong 131–2
   New Caledonia 150–52, 155, 164
   UNGA Resolution 164
deliberative democracy *see* Papua New
   Guinea
drivers of change, generally
   comparability 88–9
   constitutional futures methodology
      3–5, 88–9, 129
   sub-state nationalism 222

ethnic similitudes, negative impacts of
   138–9
Evershed, Jonathan 17, 24, 38–9, 41

federalism
   Alaska, systemic barriers 112
   Australia, overview 172
   Canada, competences 95–6
   Spain, fiscal federalism 51
First Nations people, Quebec *see* Canada
Fisher, Denise 165
France
   Constitution
      administrative decentralisation
         158–9
      extraordinary measures,
         restrictions on 159
      official language 157–8, 161–2
      position of New Caledonia
         under *see* New
         Caledonia
      recognition of sub-state national
         identities 156–7, 159

reforms 153, 156–7, 159–60,
    165–6
  unity of the republic concept
    155–9, 161–3
 identity-formation
  national languages, recognition
    of 157–8, 161–2
  superiority of French identity
    158–9
  unity of the republic concept
    155–9, 161–3
 regionalism
  administrative transfer of
    powers 165–6
  conflicts with unity of the
    republic concept 155–9,
    161–3
  immigration policies 150–53,
    163–4
  recognition of sub-state national
    identities 156–7, 159
 secession referenda
  New Caledonia 148, 151,
    154–5, 159–60

gender
 Aalaskan Native Peoples
  violence against women 102–5,
    109–15
 Bougainville, Papua New Guinea
  role of women in constitutional
    reform 211–13
  role of women in peace process
    204, 212

Habibis, Daphne 190
Haljan, David 17, 69
Hayward, Katy 39–40
Hazell, Robert 4–5
Hill, Liz 112
Hong Kong
 Chinese reforms
  electoral reforms 125–6
  Hong Kong Security Law
    128–9
  illegitimate interference,
    perceptions as 115
  inclusion in Chinese five-year
    plan 130–31

  mass protests 115, 125–6,
    128–9, 145
  mutual legal assistance 128–9
  stock market/investments
    131–2
 constitutional law
  Basic Law provisions 121,
    134–6
  Chinese Constitutionalism,
    attitudes towards
    115–17, 132–7, 224
  identity, British influences on
    115–16, 134–5
  ideological differences from
    Chinese law 115–17,
    132–7
  interference in autonomy,
    judicial interpretation
    135–6
  regional institutions, powers of
    128–9
  rule of law 117, 134–5, 142–3
  Standing Committee
    interpretation powers
    134–6, 145
 drivers of change
  Basic Law interpretation 134–6,
    145
  British constitutionalism
    vs Chinese
    Leninism-Marxism
    132–7
  constitutional law, China–Hong
    Kong ideological
    differences 115
  generally 115
  localism vs Chinese hegemony
    116–17, 137–45
 historical events
  autocratic legal system, creation
    of 124–5
  British colonialism 120–21,
    123–4
  Chinese immigration trends 122
  decolonisation 131–2
  First of July March 128
  LegCo oath ceremony
    controversy 139–40
  Letters of Patent 1843 124–5

mass protests 115, 125–6,
    128–9, 145
Opium Wars 122
post-handover developments
    131–2
Umbrella Movement protest
    136
UNGA Resolution 2908 124
identity-formation
    anti-gentrification movements
        127–8
    Chinese Communist Party
        influences on 141–5
    Chinese immigrants, attitudes
        towards 126–7, 138–9,
        141
    Chinese nationalism, opposition
        to 143–4
    Chinese 'Sons of the Dragon'
        national identity 141–5
    constitutional influences on
        116, 122
    ethnic similitudes, role of
        137–8
    HK SAR 121–2
    Lion on the Rock 122–3
    localism 116, 117, 121–2,
        127–8, 137–41
    multiplicity of ideologies
        140–41
    racist labelling 139–40
Special Administrative Region
    background 120–21, 125
    contribution to Chinese
        economy 130–32
    electoral reform 125–6
    financial sector, global position
        131–2
    fiscal and economic autonomy
        130–31
    lapse of, likely implications
        129–30
    legal basis (Basic Law) 116–17,
        121, 134–6
    powers under 116–17, 121,
        127–9
    rule of law and judicial
        precedent, role of 117
    status as 116, 124–5

Horowitz, Donald 7, 220
Hunter, Sally 176–7
Husa, Jaako 4, 142
hybrid institutions, Bougainville PNG
    development 206–11, 218
    role of women in 211–13

identity-formation, generally
    administrative efficiency, and 225–6
    dual national identities 61
    historical nationalities, recognition
        of 52–4, 61
    indigenous values and perspectives,
        receptivity to 190–93, 195
    influences on 190–93, 195, 225–6
    multiplicity of ideologies 140–41
    national languages
        promotion of 97–100, 119
        recognition of 157–8, 161–2
    perceptions of inferiority 61–2
    perceptions of violence 57–9
    racist labelling 139–40
    self-identification 225–6
    symbols of identity 61, 65
    transgenerational trauma, and
        60–61, 222
    unity concepts 143, 155–9, 161–3
Ignatieff, Michael 138
independence movements
    Bougainville see Papua New Guinea
    France, from see New Caledonia
    Papua New Guinea, from Australia
        203
    Quebec see Canada
*Interdisciplinary Comparative Law* 5
Italy
    autonomous regions
        fiscal powers 67, 78–9
    constitutional law
        competences of central/regional
            institutions 66–7
        constitutional disorder 66, 69
        Republican Constitution 1948
            70
        territorial governance 66–7
    corruption/organised crime
        administrative effectiveness,
            and 75–81

driver for change, as 66, 82–6, 227–8
history 69–74
legislative opposition (Law no.646) 72–4
Mafia families and hierarchical structures 83–5
Mafia wars 71–2
national identity, and 70
public perceptions of Mafia 78–81
public sector, perceptions of 78–81
scope of involvement in public sector 75–8, 86–7
state–Mafia relationship 74–8, 86–7
tax evasion, attitudes to 79
territorial governance system 66, 82–6
drivers of change
Mafia-controlled territorial governance 66, 82–6, 227–8
neo-patrimonialism of Italian public institutions 66, 74–82
neo-patrimonial political system
corruption and incompetence in 75–8, 86–7
driver for change, as 66, 74–82
fiscal management 67, 78–9
judicial independence, and 81
simulated efficiency 78–9, 226
*see also* Sicily

Kanak People *see* New Caledonia
Kelsen, Hans 75, 226

languages
minority/regional languages, recognition of
Canada 92–4
New Caledonia 157–8, 161–2
national/official languages, superiority
China 119
France 157–8, 161–2
Le Meur, Pierre-Yves 152
legitimacy, generally
elements, balancing 5–6
lexical construction focus of public law, and 2–3
social dynamics, relevance of 222
Levacher, Claire 152

Mafia *see* Sicily
Mallonee, Megan 112–13
Marrani, David 157, 161–2
matriarchal societies *see* Papua New Guinea
Mees, Ludger 56
#MeToo Movement 178
multinationalism
consequences of 7–8
constitutional effectiveness, and 225–6
constitutional limits to 8
Murphy, Mary 17, 24, 38–9, 41

nationalism, generally
recognition of national groups as peers 61
native peoples
Aboriginal Peoples and Torres Strait Islanders *see* Australia
Alaskan Natives *see* Alaska
First Nations people, Quebec *see* Canada
Kanak People *see* New Caledonia
neo-patrimonial political systems
corruption/organised crime relationship with 75–8, 86–7
driver for change, as 66, 74–82
fiscal management 67, 78–9
judicial independence, and 81
simulated efficiency 78–9, 226
New Caledonia
colonisation
decolonisation process 155, 164
immigration policies 150–53, 163–4
independence referenda 147–8, 151, 154, 159–60, 166–8

native Kanaks, influences on
    150–52
UNGA Resolution on
    decolonisation 164
constitutional system
    constitutional reforms, impacts
        of 153, 156–7, 159–60,
        162–3
    Customary Senate, role of
        159–61, 166
    electoral rolls 154–5, 163,
        166–7
    independence negotiations,
        legitimacy of 147–8, 151
    legislative and administrative
        autonomy 149, 153–4,
        156
    Matignon and Noumea Accords
        153, 156–7, 159–60,
        164–6
    place in French regime 147
    reallocation of administrative
        powers 159
    recognition of regional
        languages 157–8, 161–2
    recognition of sub-state national
        identity 156–7, 159
drivers of change
    constitutional negotiations and
        paradigm of French
        unity 155–62
    Covid-19 pandemic 167–8
    Kanak identity 162–9
generally
    archipelago overview 149
    civil war 147
    Covid-19 pandemic, influences
        of 13, 167–8
    economic support from EU 155
    economic support from France
        150
    immigration trends 152–3
    independence referenda 147–8,
        151, 154, 159–60
    Matignon and Noumea Accords
        153, 156–7, 159–60,
        164–6
    natural resources 149–50, 152
    status, international recognition
        148–9
    trade and revenue 149–50,
        152–3
identity-formation
    French unity of the Republic
        concept 155–6, 159,
        161–3
    Kanak culture and customs,
        promotion of 166
    Matignon and Noumea Accords
        164–6
    political organisations 163
    political violence 163
Kanak People
    Caledonian Union 162–3
    colonisation influences on
        150–53
    constitutional negotiations 153,
        159–60, 162–3
    cultural distinctiveness 162–3
    Customary Senate, role of
        159–61, 166
    electoral franchise status 153–4,
        159–60, 163, 166–7
    Gossanah Cave Crisis 164–5
    independence referenda,
        participation in 148, 151,
        154–5, 159–60, 162–3,
        166–8
    language, recognition of 166
    political role, policy impacts on
        163–4
    political violence 153, 159–60,
        163–5, 167–9
    recognition of Kanak identity
        161, 166
    regional distribution 148, 150,
        152
territorial governance, generally
    legislative and administrative
        autonomy 149, 153–4,
        156
    limitations of 226
    reallocation of administrative
        powers 159
Northern Ireland
    Brexit, and
        border controls 40, 41
        debate, limitations of 38–9
        democratic gap 38–9
        driver for change, as 19, 37–42

EU economic support 40–41, 43
impacts, generally 19, 37–8, 41–2
Ireland, relations with 38–40
political supporters 40–41
Protocol 2020 38–9, 41, 43–4
regional identity-making, and 43–4
devolution/territorial decentralisation
Belfast Agreement 1998 16–17, 21–2, 26, 30–31, 226
challenges of 23–4
historical overview 16–17
institutional arrangements 15–26
institutional inefficiency 226
limitations of 31, 38, 227
minority protection provisions 26
North–South axis cooperation 30–31
power sharing mechanism 26–7
process 19–23
purpose 21–2
realist influences on 21
reserved matters 25
restrictions 25–6
St Andrews Agreement 27
sectarian politics, historical effects 27
drivers of change
Brexit 19, 37–42, 227
institutional influences 18, 24–31, 42
overview 14–15, 18–19
sectarian identities 18–19, 22–3, 31–7, 42–3
ethnic and religious divisions *see* sectarian conflicts
institutional influences
conflict avoidance mechanisms 29–30
constitutional norms, role of 24–5
corruption 23
democratic arrangements 25–6
democratic incentives 27–9

electoral system 26
executive and legislative restrictions 25–6
external aid, effects of 31
generally 18, 42
inefficiencies and limitations 23, 226
instability, causes of 24, 27–8
National Assembly 35–7
non-aligned/Neither groups, power of 36–7, 42–3
North–South axis collaboration 30–31
organised crime 35–6
PEACE III (Operational Programme UK–Ireland) 30, 40–41
political accountability 17, 35–6
power sharing mechanism 26–7
Ireland, and
Brexit implications 38–40
independence, Constitutional amendment for 16
relationship with 15–16, 38–9
paramilitary violence 22–3, 33–5
political status
corruption 35–6
democratic accountability 17, 35–6
Democratic Unionist Party 18, 22–3, 27, 35
devolution process 16–17, 19–23
dysfunctional nature 42
elected representatives, attendance in British House of Commons 17–18
EU influences on 37–8, 40–41, 43
historical background 19–20
incentives for democratic moderation 27–9
Ireland, relationship with 15–16, 38–9
legitimacy of UK Parliament, acceptance of 17–18
organised crime 35–6

re-activation of National
Assembly (2019) 35–6
Sinn Féin 17–18, 23, 27, 35
sectarian conflicts
anti-sectarian policies,
development 20–21
avoidance, challenges of 29
Brexit protocols 39–41
economic impacts of 23
ethnic/religious demographics
15–16
historical effects of sectarian
politics 27
identity-formation 19–20, 31–7
incentives for democratic
deliberation 27–9
institutional corruption, and 23
mixed Catholic–Protestant
relationships 19–20
overview 16–19
paramilitary violence 22–3,
33–5
systemic instability, influences
of 227
sectarian identities
Bloody Sunday 33
Brexit protocols 39–40
formation process,
self-sustaining nature 43
generally 18–19, 22–3, 31–2,
42–3
militarisation 33–4
non-aligned/Neither groups
36–7, 42–3
Northern Ireland Civil Rights
Association 33
organised crime 34–6
paramilitary violence/terrorism
33–5
patrimonialism 44
silence, political relevance of
36–7
socio-political influences 32–3

organised crime
administrative effectiveness, and
75–6
Mafia *see* Sicily

neo-patrimonial administrative
systems, and 75–8, 86–7
Northern Ireland 34–5
Papua New Guinea 200–203

Papua New Guinea
Bougainville
Arawa Peace Agreement 2001
205
autonomous status 198, 205
civil war 199, 203–4
Constitution 198
constitutional reform 206–8,
213–14
cultural customs and liberal
values, balance of
209–10, 213
deliberative democratic
practices 208–9, 217–18
drivers of change 206–7
Era Kone Covenant 2021 198
independence referendum 198,
205, 206, 208
Lincoln Agreement 1998 204
mining sector 214–17, 218–19
population 199
secession schedule 198, 205,
217
unanimity requirement 210–11
women, role of 204, 211–13
civil war
administration, impacts on 215
blockades, effects of 204
contributory factors 199, 203–4,
214, 216
overview 203–4
peace process 204–5, 208–9,
212
colonisation
history 199–200
Constitution 1975
constitutional reform 207–8
devolution process 207–8
double-lock mechanism 207
emergency suspension of rights
197–8
Joint Supervisory Body, role
of 207
overview 197–8

qualified and unqualified rights 197
deliberative democratic practices
   consultative participation 208–9
   limitations of 210–11
   multi-cultural societies, benefits for 209–10, 217–18
   normative spillover effects of 209
   unanimity requirement 210–11, 218
drivers of change
   deliberative democratic practices 208–11, 217–18
   hybrid institutions, role of 206–7, 211–13, 218
   mining sector development 213–17, 218–19
   women, role of 211–13
generally
   aid from neighbouring states, attitudes towards 202
   corruption 200–203
   fiscal administration 207
   geography 196–7
   independence from Australia 203
   languages, multiplicity 200
   natural resources 201–2, 208, 215
   patrimonialism 200, 202–3
   population diversity 199–200
   regional administration 205–6
   social context 199
hybrid governance model
   hybrid institutions 206–11, 218
   role of women in 211–13
matriarchal society
   land title transfers 211
   role of women in constitutional reform 211–13
   role of women in peace process 204, 212
mining sector
   administration 207–8
   allocation of resources and royalties 203–4

civil war, influences on 203–4, 214, 216
control, conflicts over 214–16
curse of resources 208, 214, 217, 218
driver for change, as 213–17, 218–19
environmental impacts 215
overview 201–3
Panguna Mine 203, 215–17
territorial governance system, generally
   accountability and transparency 201–2
   basis for 198
paramilitary violence
   Northern Ireland 22–3, 33–5
   Quebec 88–93, 100–101
poverty
   Aboriginal Peoples, and 176–7, 187–90, 194–5
   domestic violence, link with 176–7, 189
   education and employment, and 67–8, 188
   racialised perceptions 176–7
pragmatic reasoning 49, 132–4, 224

referenda
   independence from France *see* New Caledonia
   independence of Quebec *see* Canada
   UK leaving EU *see* Brexit
Regan, Anthony J 210
regional identities
   institutional loyalties, and 7
   Northern Ireland, influences of Brexit on 43–4, 227
   Sicily, Mafia influences on 70
   Spain, national vs regional identity conflicts 63–4
regionalism, generally
   constitutionalism, influences on 224–5
   democratic benefits of 6–7
   emergence, reasons for 3
religion
   Catholic Church, influences on identity-formation 98–9

Confucianism 142
   sectarian conflicts *see* Northern Ireland
Rutherford, Paul 97

secession
   Basque Country *see* Spain
   Bougainville *see* Papua New Guinea
   France, from *see* New Caledonia
   Quebec *see* Canada
sectarianism
   political conflicts *see* Spain
   religious conflicts *see* Northern Ireland
shared values
   benefits for central/regional cohesion 1–2
   propaganda, nationalist/criminal/paramilitary use as 6–7
Sicily
   administrative governance
      corruption, influence on administrative effectiveness 75–6
      feudal system 70
      'golden triangle' 75–6, 227-8
      historical development 70–71
      inefficiencies 75–6, 79–81, 226
      productivity and competitive advantage, influences on 80–81
      public perceptions of 79–80
      scope of Mafia involvement in 75–6, 86–7
   constitutional disorder, reasons for 66, 69
   drivers of change
      Mafia-controlled territorial governance 66, 82–6, 227–8
      neo-patrimonialism of public institutions 66, 74–82
   employment
      education and employment skills 68–9, 86
      poverty, implications of 67–8
      public sector employment trends 68–9
      unemployment 67–8

Mafia
   accountability 82–3, 87
   administrative 'golden triangle' 75–6, 227–8
   bosses and affiliates, isolation of 72–4
   *Cupola*, liaison role of 71, 83
   driver for change, as 66, 82–6, 227–8
   families and hierarchical structures 83–5
   fees and penalties 71–2, 82–4
   history 69–74
   identity-formation influences 70
   investigatory bodies 74
   judicial independence, and 80
   legislative opposition (Law no.646) 72–4
   Mafia wars 71–2
   public perceptions of 78–80, 228
   public sector, scope of involvement in 74–6, 86–7, 228
   state, relationship with 74–5, 77–8, 86–7, 228
   syndicate controls 69–72, 77–8, 85–6, 87, 228
   territorial governance system 66, 82–6
Spain
   Basque Country
      ceasefire and demilitarisation 45, 48, 59–60
      Constitutional reforms, relevance of 51–2, 63–5
      drivers of change 46, 65
      electoral patterns 62
      Euskadi Ta Askatasuna, role of 45, 48, 56–60, 62
      fiscal provisions 51
      Ibarretxe Plan 63–4
      identity-formation process 48, 55–60, 63–4
      *órgano foral* system 51
      overview 46–7
      political violence, symbolic legacy of 46, 55–9

secessionist dialogue, political restrictions on 59–60
social features of Basque nation 47
Spanish nationalism, attitudes regarding 61
Statute of Autonomy 2006 52, 63
victimhood narrative 48, 52, 57–8
Catalonia, legitimacy crisis 45–6
Constitution
    background 49
    Basque Country, references to 51–2
    devolution proposals 53–4, 63–4
    dispositive principle 53–4
    EU membership, and 52, 60, 65
    fiscal federalism 51
    harmonisation process (1981) 54
    historical nationalities, recognition of 52–4, 61
    legitimacy, recognition of 60–61
    limitations of 50–55, 64
    national unity preservation mechanisms 61
    normative priority to Spanish nation over other nationalities 7
    *órgano foral* 51
    past atrocities, relevance of 60–61
    precision, lack of 50–55
    regional powers vs sovereignty powers 53–4
    Spanish nation, definition 50–51, 54
    Statute of Autonomy 2006 52, 63
    territorial governance provisions 46, 49–54, 64
    Transitional Provisions 51
drivers of change
    constitutional limitations regarding territorial governance 46, 49–54, 64
    devolution proposals 63–4
    electoral performance 62
    generally 46, 65
    political violence, symbolic legacy of 46, 55–9
identity-formation
    constitutional definition of Spanish nation 50–52, 54
    dual national identity 61
    effects of ETA activities on 55–9, 62
    free association proposals 63–4
    historical nationalities, recognition of 52–4, 61
    martyrdom idolatry 56–7
    national vs regional identity conflicts 63–4
    past atrocities, relevance of 60–61
    perceptions of inferiority 61–2
    perceptions of violence 57–9
    Spanish nationalism trends 60
    symbols of Spanish identity 61, 65
    victimhood narratives 48, 52, 57–8
political violence
    ceasefire and demilitarisation 45, 48, 59–60
    legacy of 46, 55–9
    perceptions of 57–9
    victimhood narratives 48, 52, 57–8

terrorism
    Northern Ireland 22–3, 33–5
    Quebec 88–93, 100–101
    US 9/11 attacks, influences on perceptions of violence 58
*Together: Building a United Community* 18
transgenerational trauma
    cultural genocide 102–5
    effects of, generally 221–2
    identity-formation, and 60–61, 222
    martyrdom idolatry, and 56–7
    paramilitary violence 22–3, 33–5
    racially discriminatory laws 173, 179–80, 182–6, 194

violence against native women
102–5, 111–15
Trudeau, Pierre Elliott 98
Tuner, Pat 180

UK
  Brexit
    background 37
    Northern Ireland, effects on
      37–42, 227
  constitutional system
    literary studies 4–5
    overview 14–15
    radical transformation 4
    regional institutions, powers
      of 15
  regional devolution
    administrative and legislative
      powers 20–21
    political influences on 21–2
    purpose 20–22

  *see also* Northern Ireland
US
  Alaskan Natives *see* Alaskan Native
    Peoples
  Constitution
    Native peoples, references to
      105–6
  terrorism
    9/11 attacks, influences on
      perceptions of violence
      58
  violence against women
    Alaskan Natives as victims
      102–5, 111–15
    racial and interracial trends
      111–12

Wang, Chang 142
*Warrior Honour* 138
Watson, Nicole 180
Wilford, Rick 27, 102